NELSON BLACKIE

MATHS IN ACTION PLUS

AUTHORS

R. Howat	Adviser, Ayr
G. Marra	Linlathen High School, Dundee
E. Mullan	Galashiels Academy
R. Murray	Hawick High School
J. Thomson	Galashiels Academy

TEACHER'S RESOURCE BOOK

3

Thomas Nelson and Sons Ltd
Nelson House Mayfield Road
Walton-on-Thames Surrey
KT12 5PL UK

Thomas Nelson Australia
102 Dodds Street
South Melbourne
Victoria 3205 Australia

Nelson Canada
1120 Birchmount Road
Scarborough Ontario
MIK 5G4 Canada

Cover photograph courtesy of Rolls Royce

First published by Thomas Nelson and Sons Ltd 1996
I(T)P Thomas Nelson is an International Thomson Publishing Company
I(T)P is used under licence

ISBN 0-17-431457-4
NPN 9 8 7 6 5 4 3 2 1

Printed in China

CONTENTS

INTRODUCTION

Maths in Action 3 Plus and *4 Plus* provide a comprehensive course in mathematics for students following a Foundation course at Standard Grade in Scotland and the National Curriculum in the rest of the UK.

The course is dependant upon the criteria set out in the various guidelines of the examining boards in the UK. Since these courses differ slightly, some material in the books may not be relevant to a particular course.

There is, of course, a broad spectrum of ability and this series is aimed at the lower end. Certain aspects of algebra and geometry highlighted for the less able in the English syllabus are well beyond the reach of most of the pupils in our target population. Adequate coverage of these aspects can be found in *Book 3A* of the series.

Some material in the books is starred thus:

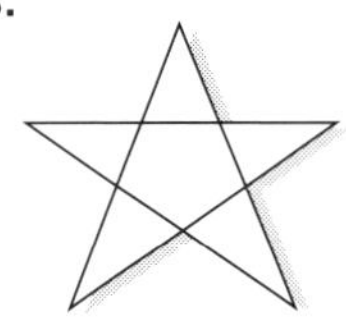

This material is seen as being on the interface between Foundation and the next higher level. (In Scotland, for example, this material is non-italicised in the *Conditions and Arrangements*.) When such work is starred in the Students' Book the authors feel that it is well within the better pupil's grasp; when it is found in the Teacher's Book, it has been accented in the *Conditions and Arrangements* but the teacher should use his or her discretion before exposing the pupil to this level of difficulty.

Maths in Action 3 Plus and *4 Plus* follow the format of *1 Plus* and *2 Plus* where the Students' Book is supported by the Teacher's Book which:

- maps content to curriculum coverage
- gives guidance on how material should be used
- provides necessary worksheets, optional more practice sheets and ancillary enrichment materials
- supplies answers to all the questions in both the Students' and Teacher's Books.

Teacher's Book 4 also contains mock exam papers.

The books follow closely the aims and objectives and teaching approaches set out by the various exam boards. They assume approximately 200 hours allotted to a two-year course.

Much consideration has been given to the style and presentation of these books.

- The language is simple. The sentences are kept short.
- Traditional problems with spacing of lines, lack of white space, size of text, visual clutter and readability have all been addressed.
- All material has been scrutinised with respect to reading ages.
- The material is almost entirely in familiar real-life contexts to stimulate and maintain interest.
- Looking Back and Check-up sections provide welcome milestones for these students to help them identify progress.

1 WHOLE NUMBERS AND DECIMALS

CURRICULUM COVERAGE

Standard Grade Guidelines

Foundation Level:
Addition, subtraction, multiplication and division of whole numbers and decimals.
Rounding decimals to the nearest unit.
Odd, even, prime and square numbers.

National Curriculum

AT 2 Levels 3, 4 and 5. (Work covering the rounding of numbers to 1 and 2 decimal places is included on two photocopiable sheets in this Teacher's Book.)

NI Curriculum

AT Number Levels 3, 4, 5 and 6.

AIMS AND OBJECTIVES

The chief aim of this chapter is to boost the student's confidence with regard to handling number. An objective of the chapter, therefore, is to give the student further practice with number, first of all free of context and then with contexts which are familiar and interesting.

NOTES

1 Regarding the use of calculators, teachers know best which of their students will have their interest best served by having access to a calculator on any particular occasion. The calculator can clearly help, but we should never lose sight of the importance of trying to improve a student's basic understanding of number.
2 It is expected that the habit of estimating the answer during calculator use will be exercised throughout the course. It was felt that to focus on it for one exercise only in this chapter would have the adverse effect of giving students the notion that it was only relevant here.
3 Some of the work in this chapter will not be new, but it is more important than a simple revision chapter. The content is fundamental to most of the work in any Foundation course.
4 The rounding numbers strand from the 5–14 Guidelines is also exercised for the sake of continuity.
5 Extension work covering rounding to 1 and 2 decimal places (part of the General syllabus) is included in the Teacher's Book.

TEACHER'S RESOURCES

As practice at mental work is important, a sheet containing four mental tests is supplied.
A worksheet is provided to facilitate the 'copy and complete' questions in the Looking Back exercise and Exercises 1, 5 and 7.
More Practice sheets 1–2 provide work on 'Paper Round' and 'Milk Round' themes, while More Practice 3 contains mixed examples. These can be fitted in when it is felt appropriate.
Worksheets on rounding to 1 and 2 decimal places provide an extension to General Level, if required.
The 'Fast Going Mental' game consists of 50 cards to be photocopied and cut up to provide additional practice at mental work.
The 'BODMAS Maze' game, consisting of 25 cards, has been adapted from Book 2 of the main series to provide practice in carrying out operations in the correct order.

PROGRESS ROUTE

Success at the check-up could allow students to be directed to *Students' Book 3A*, pages 1–8, 26 and 27.

MENTAL TEST A

1 One carton of juice costs 99p. What is the cost of two cartons?
2 A bottle of milk costs 39p. What change is given from £1?
3 How many 5p coins are needed to make £1?
4 What is 88 + 33?
5 Write the following number in figures: eight hundred and seven thousand, three hundred and ten.
6 What is 2100 ÷ 100?
7 What is 36.23 × 10?
8 Write down the tenth odd number.
9 Write down the fifth prime number.
10 Calculate 3 plus 6 plus 9 plus 12.

MENTAL TEST B

1 Which number is not a square number: 25, 50 or 81?
2 What is £6.53 to the nearest pound (£)?
3 Zero is the first even number. What is the eighth even number?
4 What is the next square number after 100?
5 The attendance at a pop concert was 27 846. Round this to the nearest thousand.
6 What is 3.49 metres rounded to the nearest metre?
7 Mary's change is 38p. What is the least number of coins she could be given?
8 Which number is not a prime: 7, 17 or 27?
9 How many 26p scones can I buy for £1?
10 Take 3.1 away from 10.

MENTAL TEST C

1 A golf ball costs £1.99. What is the cost of two golf balls?
2 A box of tissues costs 63p. What change is given from £1?
3 How many 10p coins make £1?
4 What is 105 minus 17?
5 Write the following number in figures: three million two hundred and fifty thousand, six hundred and ten.
6 Divide 12.34 by 10.
7 What is 96.54 multiplied by 10?
8 Write down the twelfth odd number.
9 Write down the seventh prime number.
10 Calculate 2 × 4 × 6.

MENTAL TEST D

1 If 1 is the first square number, write down the sixth square number.
2 What is £12.48 to the nearest pound (£)?
3 Which number is not a prime number: 23, 29 or 39?
4 What is the next square number after 64?
5 The population of Bradon is 43 398. Round this to the nearest thousand.
6 What is 7.62 kilograms to the nearest kilogram?
7 What is the next prime number after 31?
8 Tom gets 69p change. What is the least number of coins he could be given?
9 How many 34p bars of chocolate could I buy for £1?
10 Laura played a round of golf. She had 16 fives and two fours. What was her total score?

Worksheet

Looking Back question 7

	H	T	U	t	h
	2	6	5	3	4
(i)					
(ii)					
(iii)					
(iv)					
(v)					
(vi)					

Exercise 1 question 2

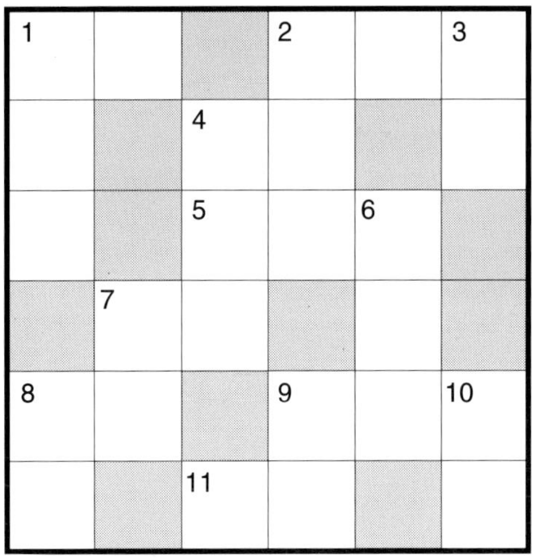

Exercise 5 question 6b

Name *Adam*

Throw	Score
(1, 3)	4
(2, 5)	3
(4, 1)	3
(4, 4)	16
(3, 5)	
(1, 1)	
(4, 2)	
Total	

Name *Bill*

Throw	Score
(6, 2)	12
(4, 3)	
(3, 1)	
(5, 2)	
(1, 3)	
(6, 2)	
(2, 2)	
Total	

Exercise 7 question 5

The Kitchen Cupboard

10 The High Street,
New Town.

	£	p
5 soups at £1.45		
2 haddock at £4.85		
3 pizzas at £3.75		
4 apple pies at £2.85		
1 ice-cream at £2.15		
Total		

Exercise 7 question 7

Type	Number	Amount (p)
1p	18	18
2p	13	26
5p		
10p		
20p		
50p		
£1		
Total		£

Maths in Action Plus Book 3 Published by Thomas Nelson and Sons Ltd © R. Howat, G. Marra, E. Mullan, R. Murray and J. Thomson 1996

More Practice 1: Paper Round

Sara delivers morning papers to some houses in Crocus Avenue. Daily papers are delivered from Monday to Saturday. The *Report*, *Gazette* and *Chat* are delivered only on a Sunday.

Prices

Daily Bulletin	44p
Daily News	45p
Daily Echo	42p
Daily Gossip	38p
Daily Update	50p
Sunday Report	55p
Sunday Gazette	62p
Sunday Chat	54p

Sara keeps a record of her deliveries as follows:

House number	Papers delivered	Charge	
1	*Echo, Gazette*	6 × 42p + 62p =	314p
2	*News*		
5	*Update, Report*		
6	*Gossip, Gazette*		
8	*Bulletin, Report, Chat*		
10	*Update, Report, Gazette*		
11	*Gazette, Chat*		
14	*Bulletin*		
15	*News, Echo*		
16	*News, Update, Report*		
20	*Echo, Gossip, Chat*		
24	*Update, Report, Chat*		
29	*Gossip*		
30	*Bulletin, Echo, Gazette*		
	Total		

1 Calculate the weekly paper bill for each of these houses.

2 Calculate the total money Sara collects.

3 Sara is paid 3p for each paper she delivers.
How much is she paid each week for delivering the papers?

More Practice 2: Milk Round

Sam delivers milk and other dairy products every morning.

The prices are shown below.

Monty's Dairy Milk (1 pint)	39p
Yoghurt	35p
Cream	64p
Eggs (half dozen)	79p
Rolls (each)	10p

Sam keeps a record of his weekly deliveries in Crocus Avenue.

House number	Weekly delivery	Charge	£
1	7 pints milk, 3 cream	$7 \times 39p + 3 \times 64p =$	
3	9 pints milk, 4 yoghurts		
4	14 pints milk, half dozen eggs		
5	7 pints milk, 1 dozen eggs		
7	10 pints milk, 6 yoghurts		
10	11 pints milk, 1 dozen rolls		
11	14 pints milk, 1 dozen eggs, 10 rolls		
12	12 pints milk, 2 dozen eggs, 2 cream		
15	7 pints milk,1 dozen rolls		
16	5 pints milk, 5 yoghurts, 1 cream		
24	12 pints milk, 2 dozen eggs, 14 rolls		
30	8 pints milk, 20 rolls		
	Total		

1 Calculate the weekly bill for each of these houses in Crocus Avenue.

2 Calculate the total money to be collected.

More Practice 3

1 It cost Tony £3.36 to have 24 photographs developed.
How much is that per photograph?

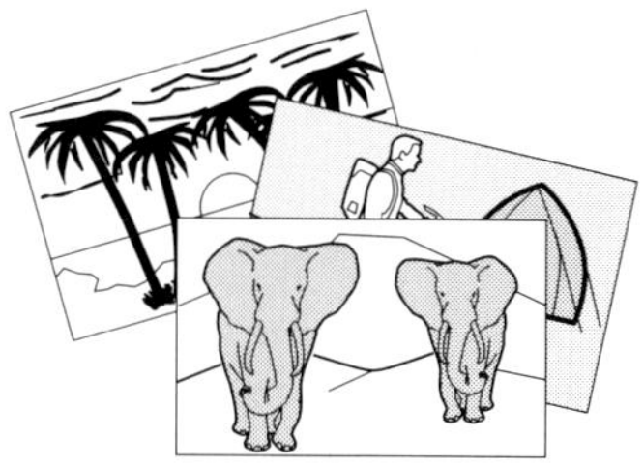

2 A plumber charges £29.34 for 3 hours' work.
How much is that per hour?

3

Bryan and Taj organised a disco.
They had to pay £10 to get the tickets printed and £25 to hire the hall.
Juice and crisps cost them £29.10.
They sold 78 tickets at £2 each.
At the disco they sold 45 packets of crisps at 15 pence each and 62 cartons of juice at 40 pence each.

a What were the total takings for the disco?
b What did it cost to organise the disco?
c What profit did they make?

4 Ahmed, Bob, Chris and Dave are four finalists in the shot-putt.
The lengths, in metres, of their attempts are:
Ahmed 15.36, 15.4, 15.22
Bob 14.98, 15.86, 14
Chris 15.72, 16, 15.01
Dave 14.39, 14.87, 15.16.

a Rewrite each competitor's list in order, longest first.
b The person with the longest throw is the winner. Who wins?

5

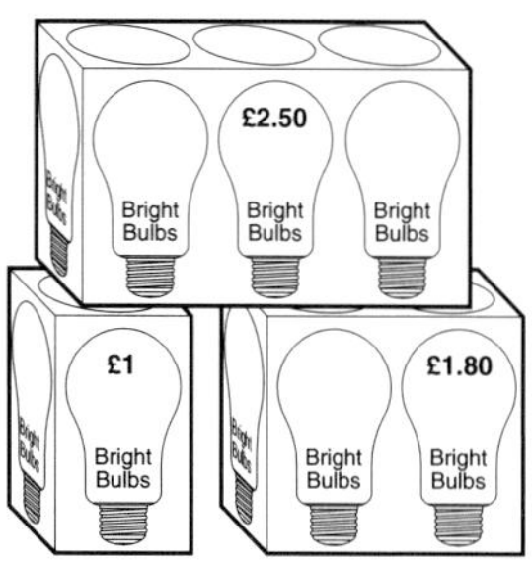

Mrs Watt wants to buy six light bulbs.

a How much will it cost her to buy:

(i) six single bulbs (ii) three two-packs
(iii) two three-packs?

b What is the difference between the dearest and cheapest way?

6 Kevin knows that to change kilometres to miles you need to divide by 8 and then multiply by 5.

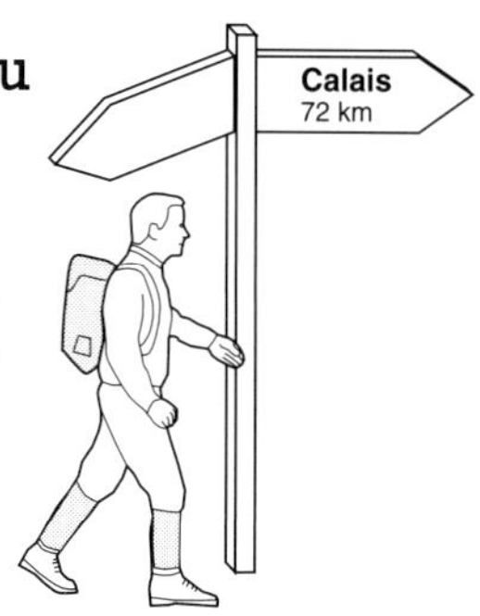

km → ÷ 8 → × 5 → miles

a What is the distance to Calais in miles?
b Change these distances to miles.

(i) 80 km (ii) 32 km (iii) 88 km (iv) 96 km (v) 112 km

Rounding to 2 Decimal Places

Example 1 How would you split £4 into 3 equal portions?
On a calculator 4 ÷ 3 = 1.3333333.
Because this is money we want to say £1.33 or £1.34.
We want two figures after the point.

Bracket the third figure.	1.33(3)3333
Ignore the figures after the bracket.	1.33(3)~~3333~~
The bracketed number is less than 5 so drop it.	1.33
The answer is **£1.33** to 2 decimal places.	

Example 2 What about £10 ÷ 7? The calculator gives 1.4285714.

The steps above give:	1.42(8)~~5714~~
The bracketed number is not less than 5, so as we drop it we add 1 to the last figure we want to keep.	1.43
£10 ÷ 7 = **£1.43** to 2 decimal places.	

1 Round the following numbers to 2 decimal places.

a 3.24361 **b** 12.23671 **c** 23.5151515 **d** 34.246 **e** 294.112 **f** 4.355
g 5.329 **h** 1.507 **i** 14.673 **j** 40.381 **k** 19.555 **l** 24.7352

2 Example: 4.236 is between 4.23 and 4.24. It is nearer 4.24.
Complete this table in a similar way.

	Number	is between	It is nearer
a	4.236	4.23 and 4.24	4.24
b	7.319	7.31 and 7.32	
c	6.463	6.46 and 6.47	
d	8.079	8.07 and 8.08	
e	0.965	0.96 and 0.97	
f	12.728	12.72 and 12.73	

3 Calculate the following, giving your answers to 2 decimal places.

a 4.876 + 8.934 + 7.218 **b** 19.938 + 21.247 **c** 101.453 – 59.877
d 2.7 × 3.1 × 5.2 **e** 3.1 × 4.25 **f** 3.876 ÷ 2

4 George and Nat went fishing. They caught four fish which weighed:
3.421 kg, 2.457 kg, 3.299 kg and 5.114 kg.
What is the total weight of the catch to 2 decimal places?

Rounding to 1 Decimal Place

Examples

Round these numbers to 1 decimal place.

1 7.346 = 7.3(4)~~6~~ = 7.3 as (4) is less than 5

2 12.2784 = 12.2(7)~~84~~ = 12.3 as (7) is not less than 5

3 3.751 = 3.7(5)~~1~~ = 3.8 as (5) is not less than 5

1 Round each of these numbers to 1 decimal place.

a 8.482 **b** 3.63 **c** 12.751 **d** 19.08 **e** 80.26
f 15.3724 **g** 26.060 **h** 85.5555 **i** 52.3297 **j** 50.99

2 Example: 8.73 is between 8.7 and 8.8. It is nearer 8.7.
Complete this table in a similar way.

	Number	is between	It is nearer
a	8.73	8.7 and 8.8	8.7
b	1.66	1.6 and 1.7	
c	36.39	36.3 and 36.4	
d	15.25	15.2 and 15.3	
e	96.07	96.0 and 96.1	
f	3.7214	3.7 and 3.8	
g	11.6924	11.6 and 11.7	
h	36.7508	36.7 and 36.8	
i	47.065	47.0 and 47.1	
j	26.009	26.0 and 26.1	

3 Calculate the following, giving your answers to 1 decimal place.

a $7.93 + 8.18$ **b** $18.625 + 31.407$ **c** $53.875 - 29.78$ **d** $14 - 2.015$
e $4.8 \times 5.1 \times 2.3$ **f** $1.9 \times 3.3 \div 2.1$ **g** $(9.62 - 5.19) \div 5.26$ **h** $0.45 \div 0.031$

4 Four vehicles queue for a ferry. Their lengths are:
3.91 m, 2.24 m, 3.31 m and 4.18 m.
What is the total length of the queue of traffic?
(Give your answer to 1 decimal place.)

INSTRUCTIONS FOR GAMES

Game 1: Fast Going Mental

(A game for the whole class)

Preparation

Photocopy the 50 playing cards onto card, enlarging them to a suitable size, and cut them out.

Rules

The cards are shuffled by the teacher and dealt out to each member of the class. It does not matter if some students get more cards than others. The teacher decides who starts. The first student reads out one of his/her cards, e.g. '20 subtract 12'. The student with the number 8 card calls out '8 multiply by 6' and so on ... until all 50 cards have been read out.
Any student failing to call out the correct number (after an agreed time delay) gives that card to the person who asked the question, who then shouts out the information on the received card. To be effective the time delay should be quite short.
The winners are the students with the most cards at the end.

Game 2: The BODMAS Maze

(A game for individual students)

This is a variation of the Count's Castle game in Chapter 1 of *Teacher's Resource Book 2.* It is included here with changed data as many of the students using this book will have come from *Book 2 Plus* and hence missed this game.

Preparation

Photocopy the two sheets of cards back-to-back onto card and cut out the 25 cards. The 1 of hearts should back up with the card saying 'Enter the castle'.

Rules

Place the cards face down in the order shown.

1❦	2❦	3❦	4❦	5❦
1♠	2♠	3♠	4♠	5♠
1♦	2♦	3♦	4♦	5♦
1♣	2♣	3♣	4♣	5♣
1♥	2♥	3♥	4♥	5♥

Starting at the 1 of hearts, the player turns the cards over one at a time, answering the questions and going in the direction indicated by the answer they choose.
Once the player has picked his/her next direction he/she should replace the old card back in the grid face down.
The object of the game is for the player to discover the password BODMAS, then to get the card which tells him/her to ask for direction. The teacher then knows the player has succeeded and tells him/her to go east, i.e. out of the maze.

'FAST GOING MENTAL' CARDS

(33) take away 5	(28) divide by 7	(4) times 8	(32) divide by 2	(16) add 8
(24) divide by 8	(3) times 9	(27) multiply by 2	(54) decrease by 9	(45) divide by 5
(9) plus 8	(17) times 2	(34) subtract 8	(26) take away 7	(19) add 11
(30) add 14	(44) take away 8	(36) divide by 2	(18) divide by 9	(2) divide by 2
(1) times 11	(11) multiply by 5	(55) subtract 8	(47) take away 22	(25) minus 5
(20) subtract 12	(8) multiply by 6	(48) add 12	(60) divide by 10	(6) multiply by 7
(42) divide by 3	(14) add 26	(40) divide by 8	(5) multiply by 2	(10) add 28
(38) subtract 9	(29) multiply by 2	(58) subtract 21	(37) take away 14	(23) multiply by 3
(69) subtract 20	(49) divide by 7	(7) multiply by 5	(35) add 15	(50) subtract 11
(39) divide by 3	(13) add 9	(22) subtract 7	(15) add 6	(21) add 12

THE BODMAS MAZE – CARD BACKS

1 *The BODMAS Maze* ❦	2 *The BODMAS Maze* ❦	3 *The BODMAS Maze* ❦	4 *The BODMAS Maze* ❦	5 *The BODMAS Maze* ❦
1 *The BODMAS Maze* ♠	2 *The BODMAS Maze* ♠	3 *The BODMAS Maze* ♠	4 *The BODMAS Maze* ♠	5 *The BODMAS Maze* ♠
1 *The BODMAS Maze* ♦	2 *The BODMAS Maze* ♦	3 *The BODMAS Maze* ♦	4 *The BODMAS Maze* ♦	5 *The BODMAS Maze* ♦
1 *The BODMAS Maze* ♣	2 *The BODMAS Maze* ♣	3 *The BODMAS Maze* ♣	4 *The BODMAS Maze* ♣	5 *The BODMAS Maze* ♣
1 *The BODMAS Maze* ♥	2 *The BODMAS Maze* ♥	3 *The BODMAS Maze* ♥	4 *The BODMAS Maze* ♥	5 *The BODMAS Maze* ♥

THE BODMAS MAZE – CARD FRONTS

There might be danger here!

Go back now or go South

Which way now?

$\frac{1}{2}$ *of* $2 + 6$

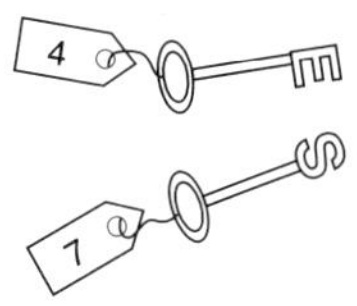

Pick a key!

$\frac{1}{2}$ *of* $(2 + 6)$

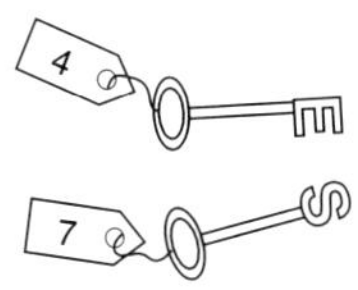

Choose wisely!

$\frac{1}{2}$ *of* $(8 + 4)$

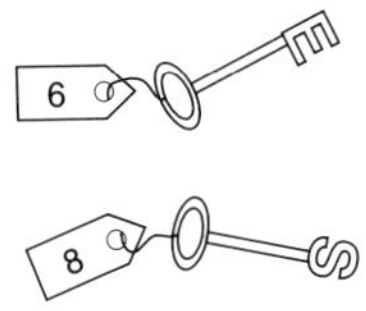

BO stands for ***'brackets' then 'of'.***

Go East.

Aarghhhhh!

You are dead.

DM stands for ***'divide and multiply'.***

Go South.

The writing is on the wall!

Go West.

B stands for ***'brackets'.***

Go West.

O stands for ***'of'.***

$\frac{1}{2}$ *of* $6 = 3$

Go North.

There might be danger here!

?

Go back or go South.

Watch your step!

$8 + 8 \div 2$

Pick a key.

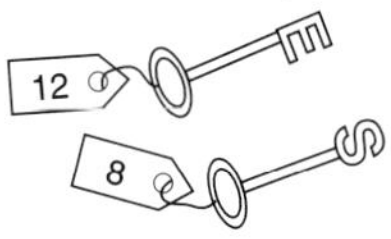

Phew!

That was close.

Go West. Quickly now!

The password is ***BODMAS.***

$8 + 2 \times 6$

The choice is yours.

Tough luck!

Give the Dungeon Master the password and ask for direction.

Well done.

A grave error.

Divide before you add.

Go South.

Great danger! Ask for help.

$12 - 5 \times 2$

You're alive, but not out of danger. Be careful!

$12 - 3 \times 3$

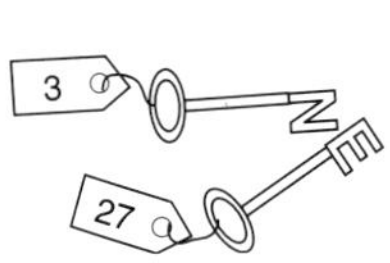

Well done! Now a life and death decision!

$5 + 3 \times 4$

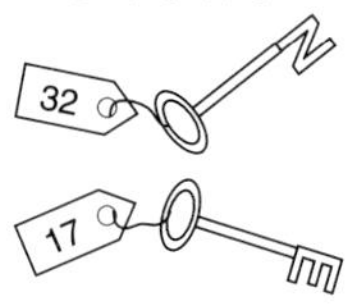

Teleport.

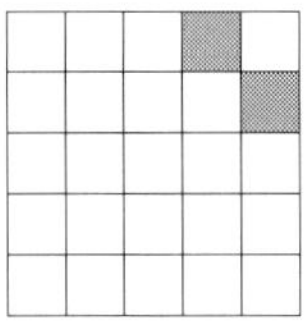

Go to one of the shaded squares.

Go East for a last chance.

Goodbye.

That was quick.

Wrong choice. You are in danger. Try again.

$3 \times 5 + 4$

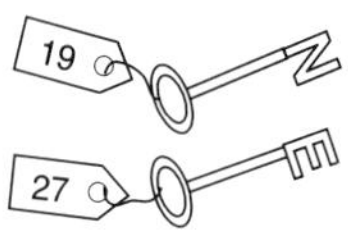

Enter the castle. Which door? Follow the clues.

$7 \times 2 + 1$

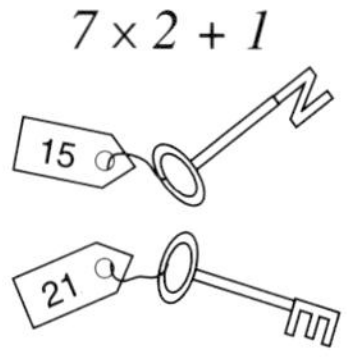

2 SYMMETRY

CURRICULUM COVERAGE

Standard Grade Guidelines
Foundation Level:
Line symmetry.
Repeat patterns.
General level:
Rotation.

National Curriculum
AT 3 Levels 3, 4 and 5.

NI Curriculum
AT Shape and Space Levels 3, 4, 5 and 6.

AIMS AND OBJECTIVES

To familiarise students with the language associated with symmetry (mirror, glide and turn).
To give students an understanding of:
(i) mirror symmetry (how to find an axis of symmetry, shapes that exist with more than one axis, how diagrams can be completed)
(ii) the meaning of turn symmetry (recognise centres, order, half-turn, and be able to complete related diagrams)
(iii) glide symmetry (recognise examples and continue them).

NOTES

1 Some previous knowledge of symmetry is expected but is not a prerequisite to starting this chapter.
2 Enlargement will be dealt with in Book 4, Chapter 8.
3 Coordinates used in the context of symmetry will also be dealt with in Book 4.
4 Some basic geometry related to glide symmetry has been included as a possible simple bridge to General work.
5 The 3-D aspects of symmetry have not been covered here as it is felt that for students at this level such activity must, by its nature, be practical.
6 Centimetre squared paper or squared dotted paper is best used for completing diagrams and finding axes of symmetry in this chapter.

TEACHER'S RESOURCES

Worksheets 1-5 assist in Exercises 1, 2, 4 and 5.
More Practice sheets 1-2 provide harder examples of drawing in axes of symmetry and drawing mirror images.
The 'Driving Using the Mirror' sheet provides a practical, fun exercise on reflections.

PROGRESS ROUTE

Success at the check-up should allow students who wish to cover the General interface to attempt *Book 3A* Chapter 2, Exercise 3, questions 1, 2, 3, 7, 8 and 9.

Worksheet 1

No lines of symmetry

One line of symmetry

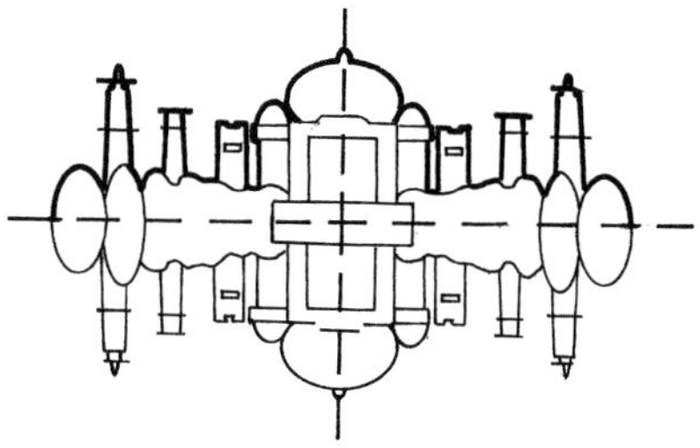

Two lines of symmetry

Mark in all the lines of symmetry you can find below.

1

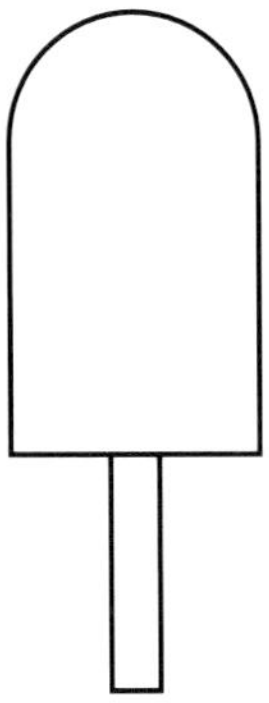

2

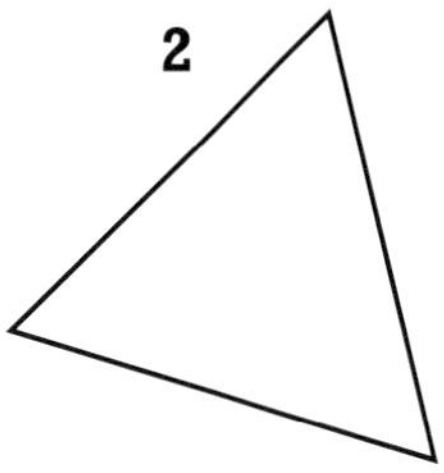

3

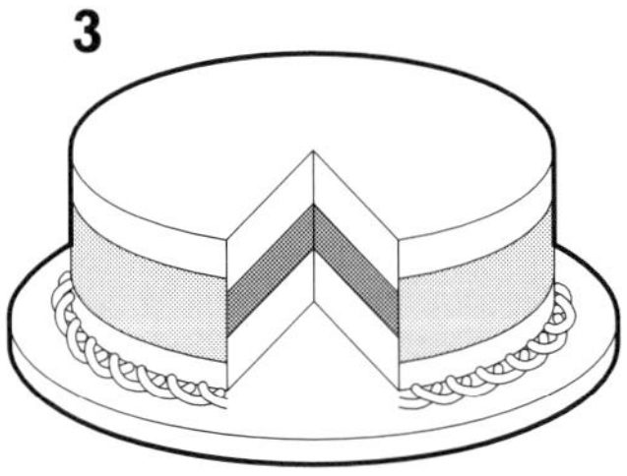

4

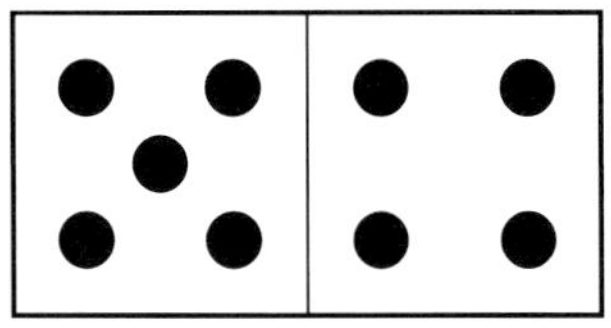

5

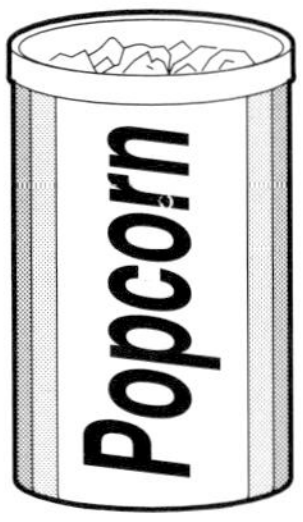

6

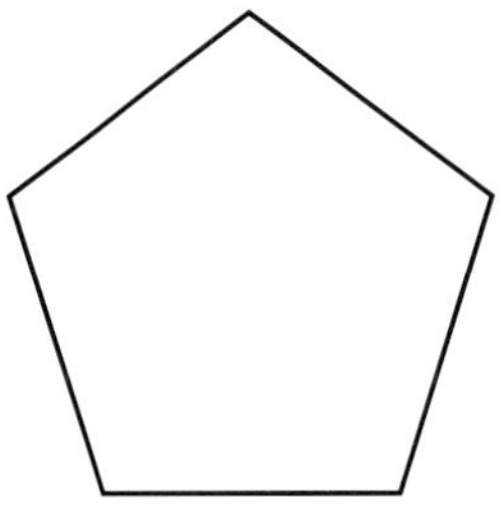

7

8

9

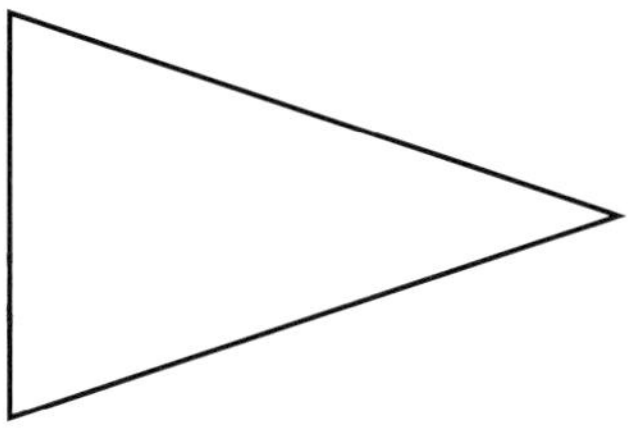

10

11

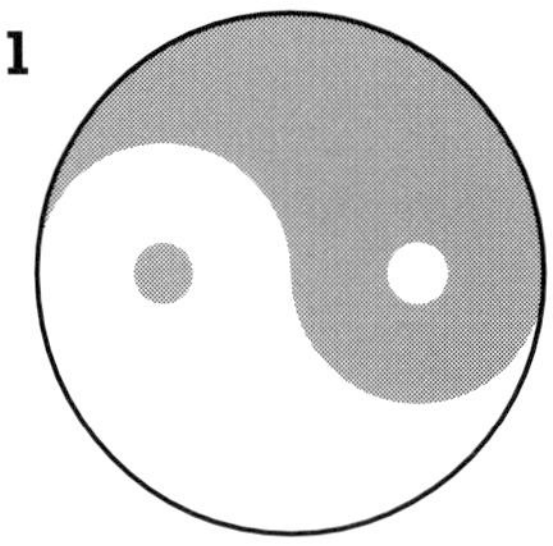

12

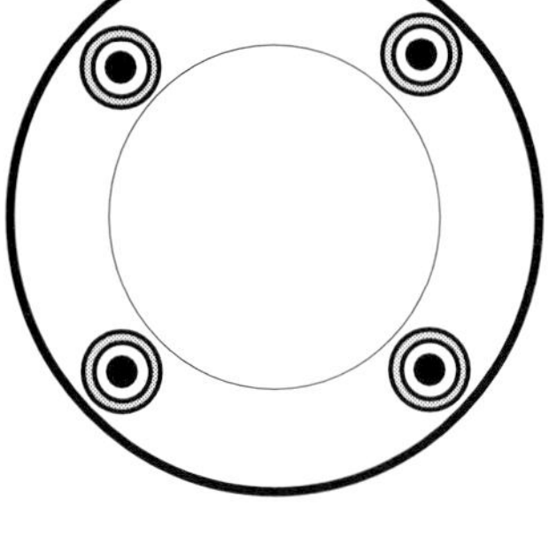

13

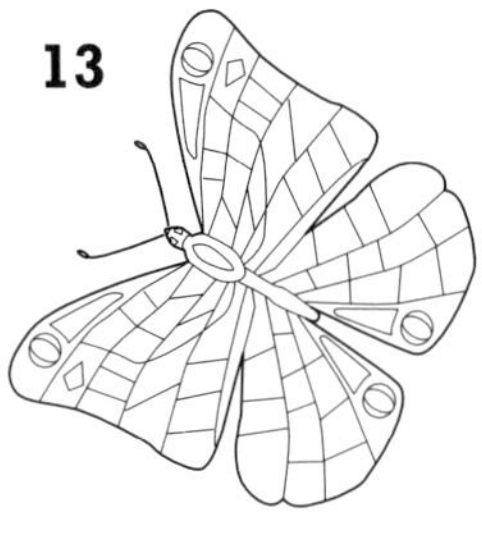

14

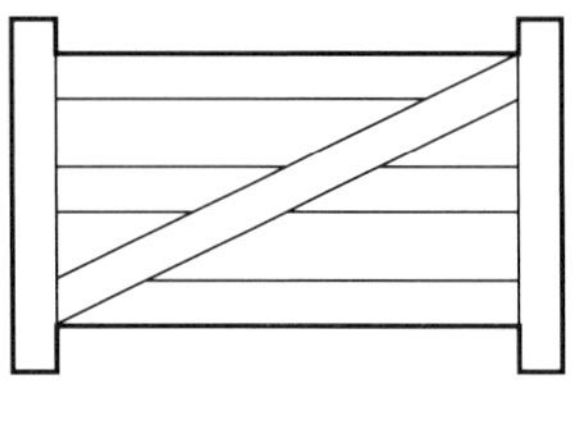

15

Worksheet 2

1 Complete these drawings so that the dotted line is an axis of symmetry.

a

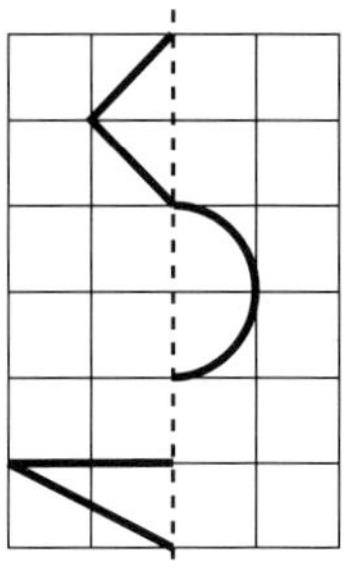

b

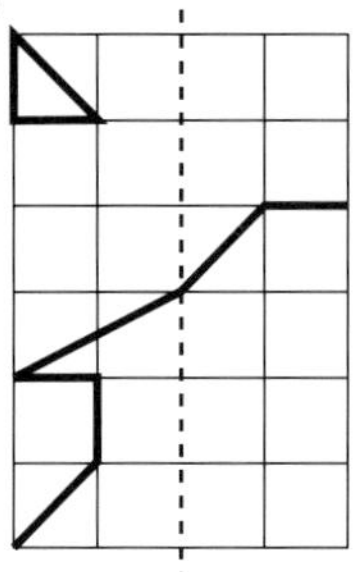

c

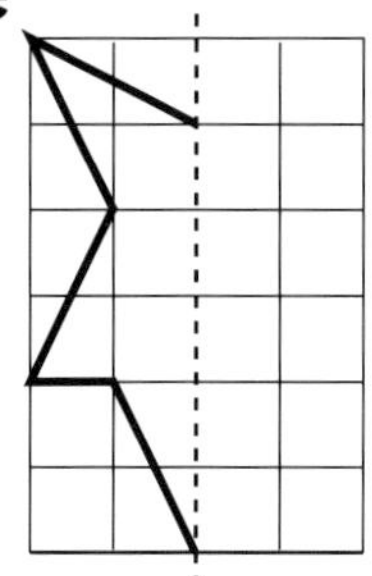

d

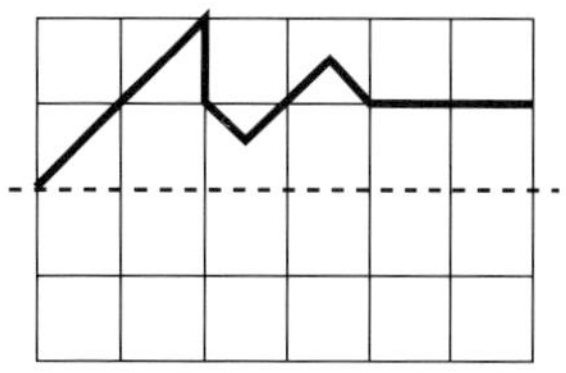

e

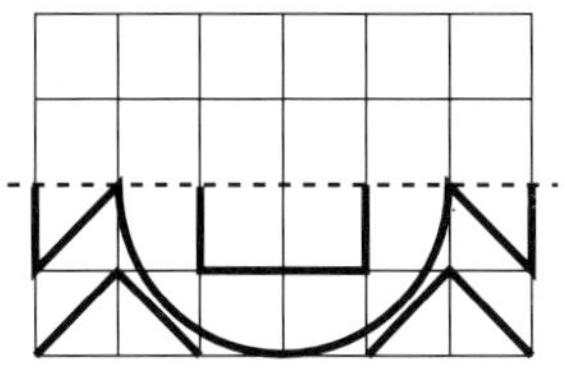

f

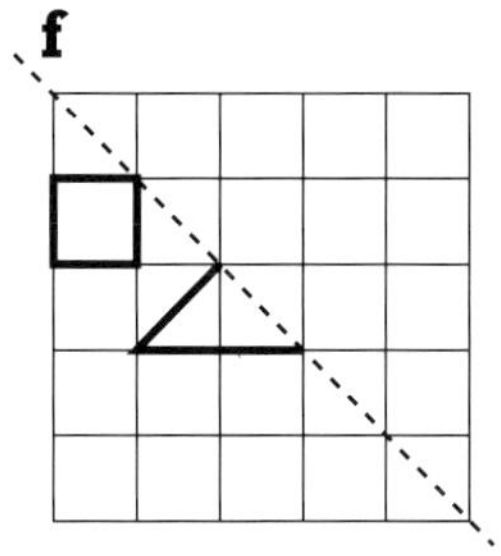

g

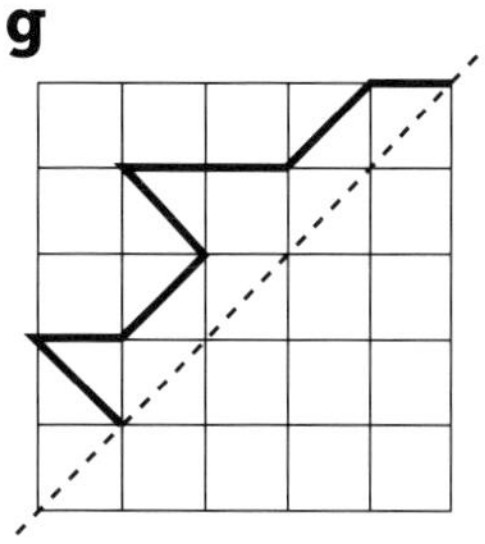

2 To complete a drawing with two axes of symmetry:

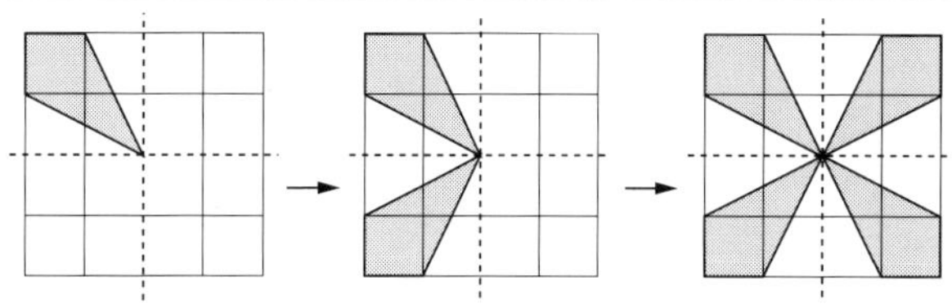

first reflect in the horizontal axis

then reflect in the vertical axis.

a

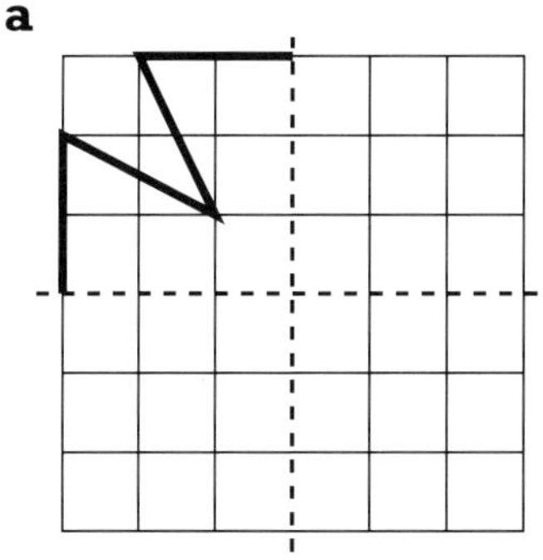

b

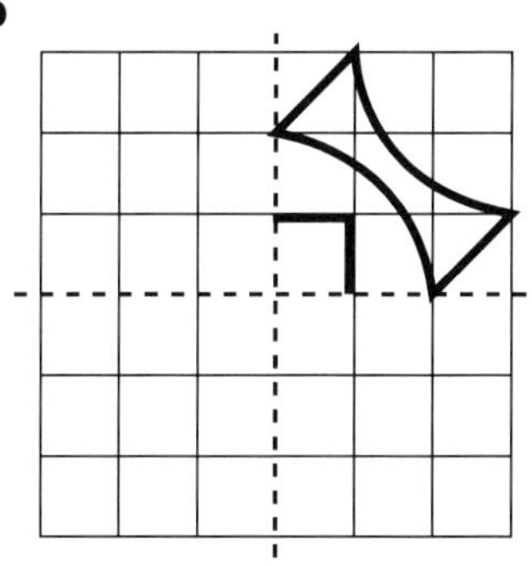

c

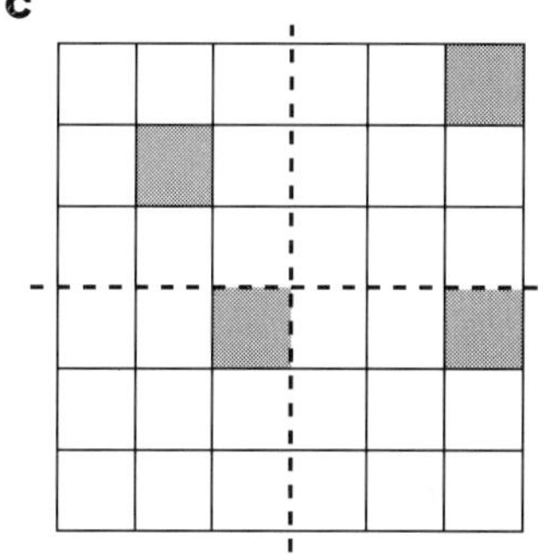

3 Now try these. Reflect in axis A first.

a

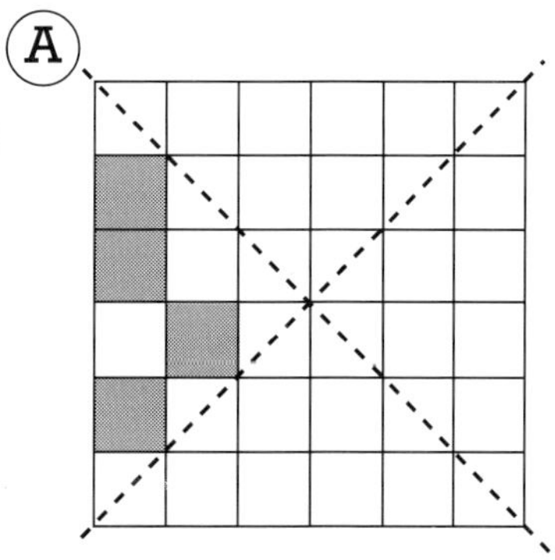

b

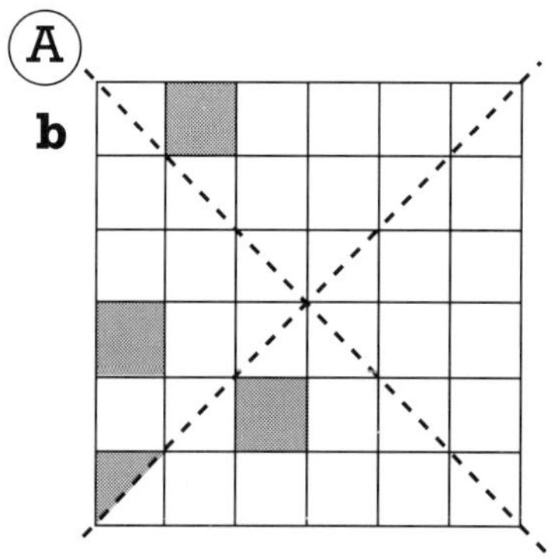

Worksheet 3

1 Draw in the axes of symmetry where they exist.

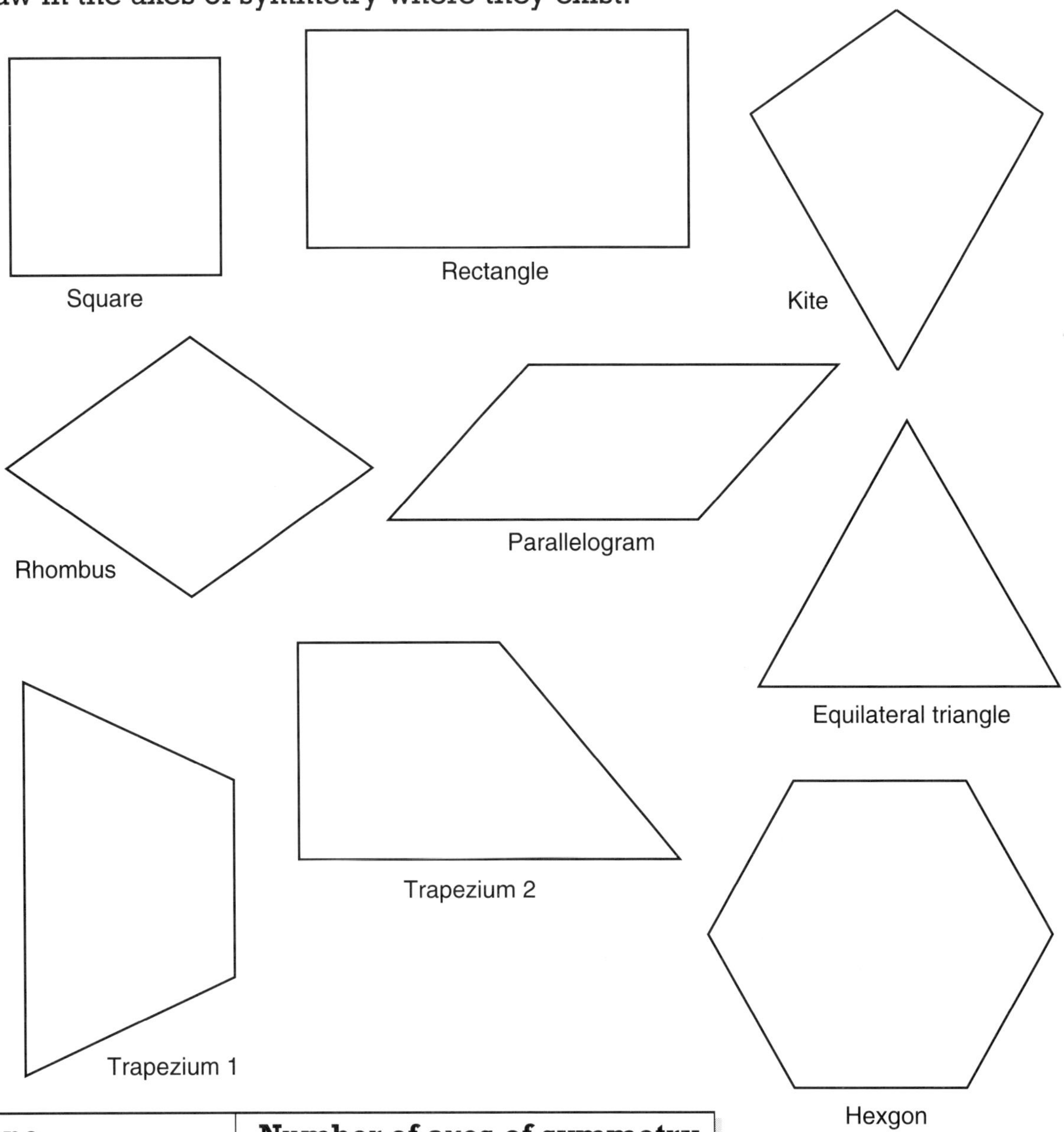

Shape	**Number of axes of symmetry**
Square	
Rectangle	
Kite	
Rhombus	
Parallelogram	
Trapezium 1	
Trapezium 2	
Equilateral triangle	
Regular hexagon	

2 Complete this table for the above shapes.

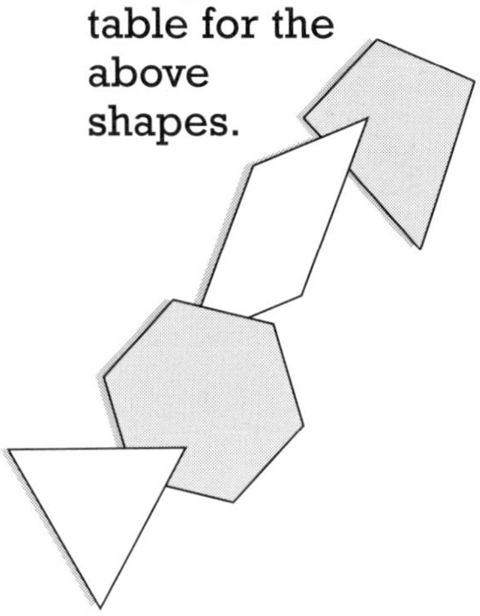

Worksheet 4

Continue each of these patterns.

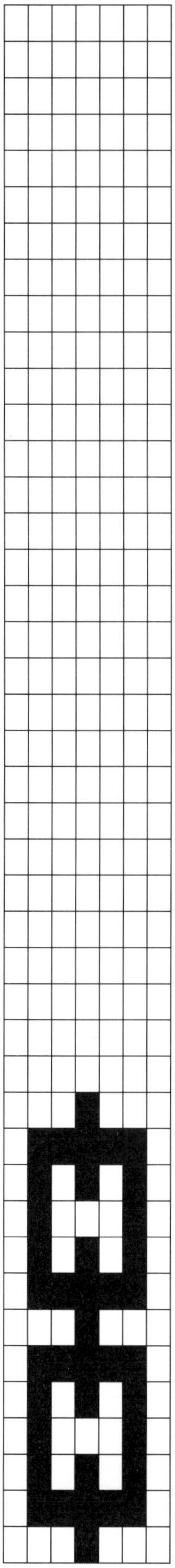

1

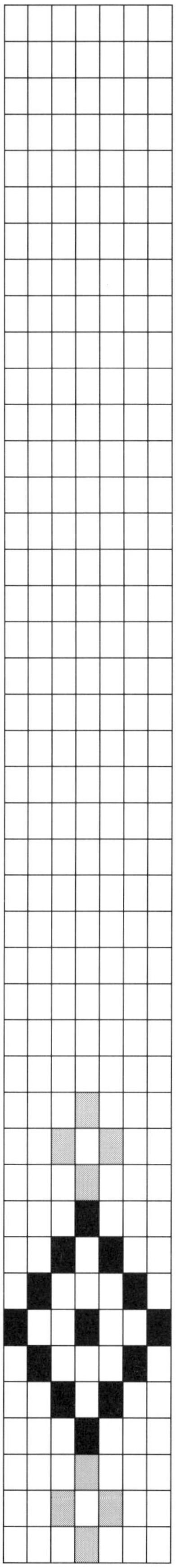

2

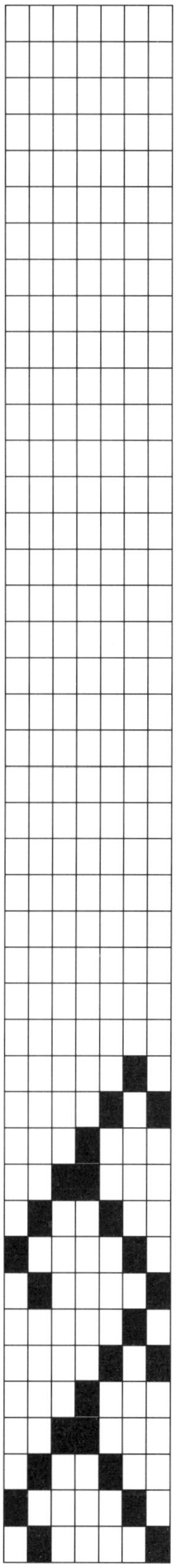

3

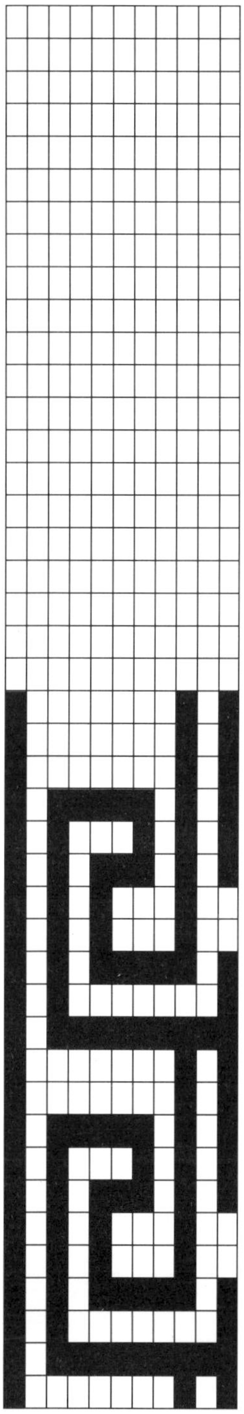

4

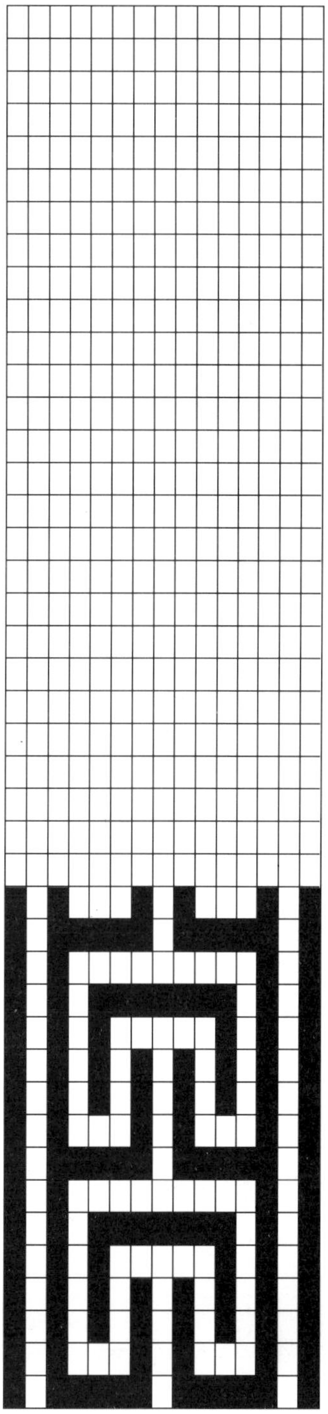

5

Worksheet 5

This picture has half-turn symmetry.
How do you find the centre?

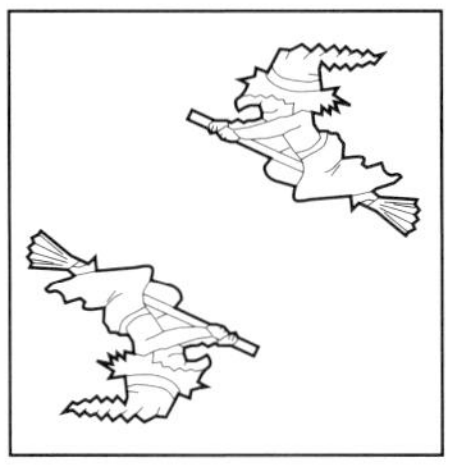

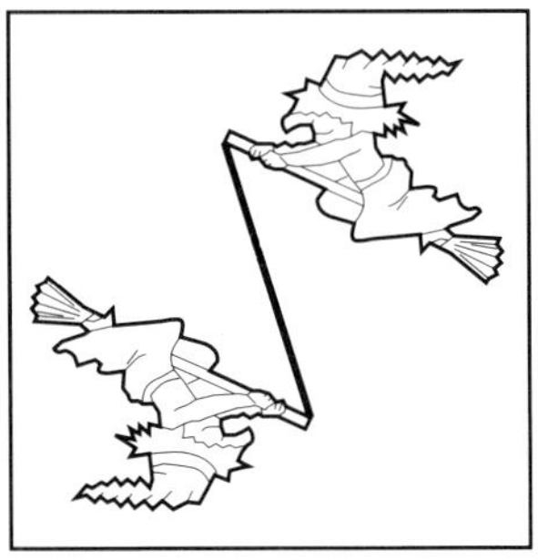

Join any point and its partner.

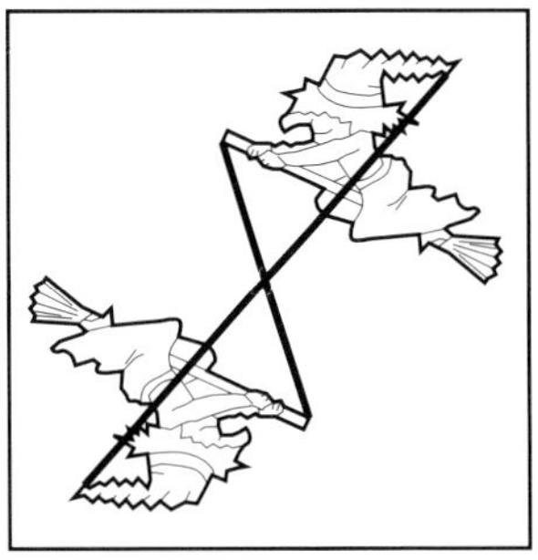

Join another point and its partner.

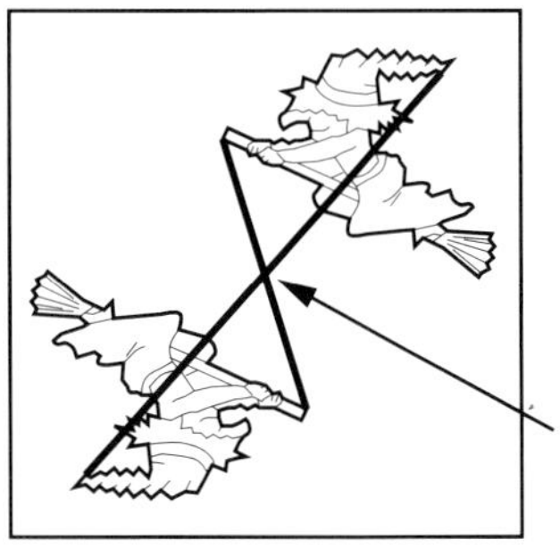

These two lines will cross at the centre.

1 Now try these.

a

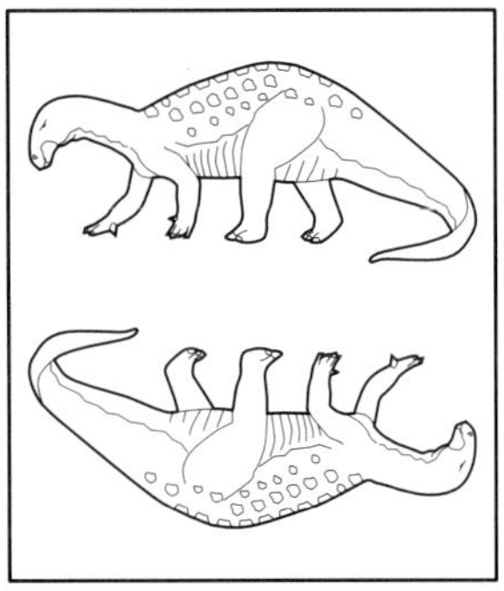

b

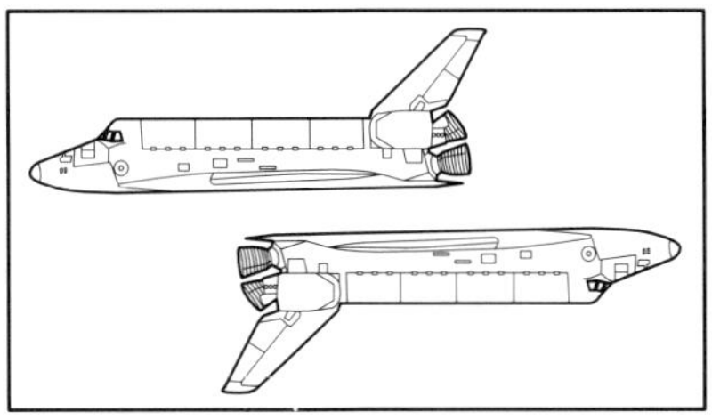

c

d

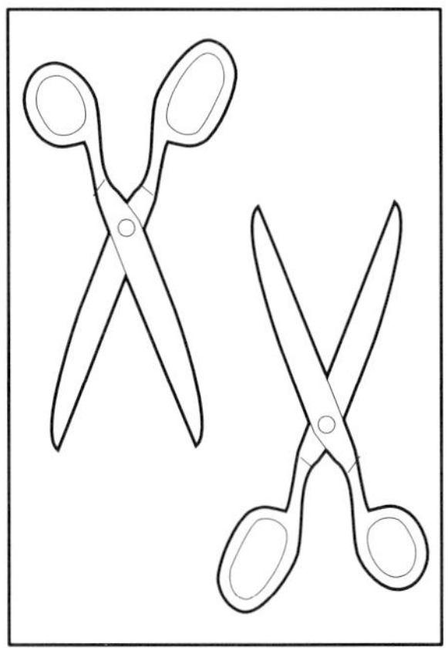

2 Here are some plain ones to try.

a

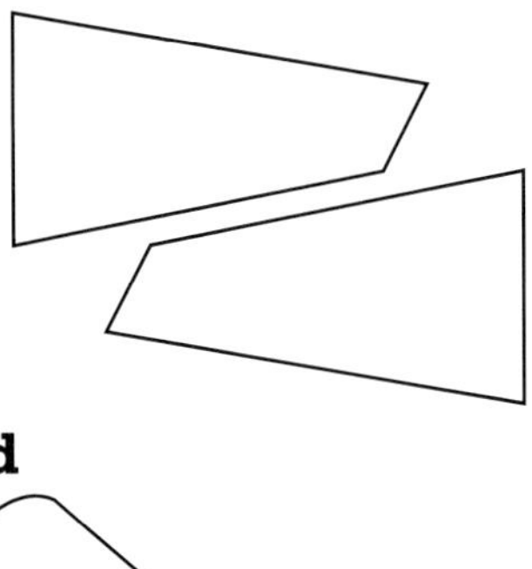

b

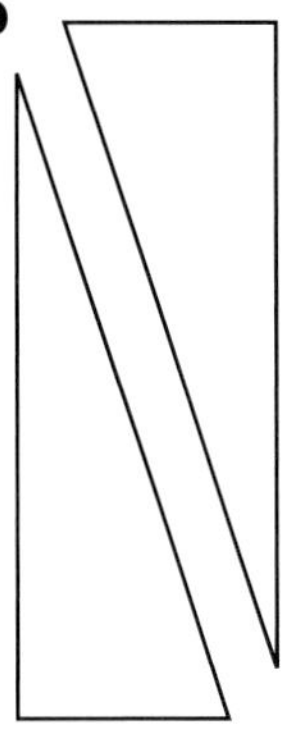

c

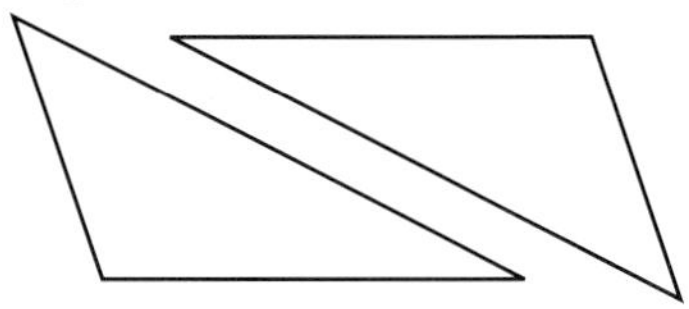

d

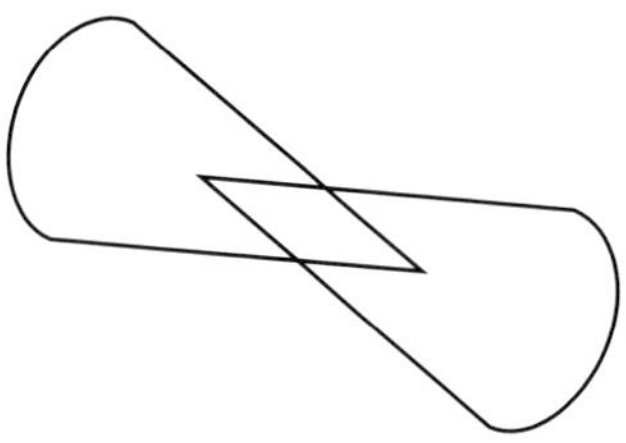

e

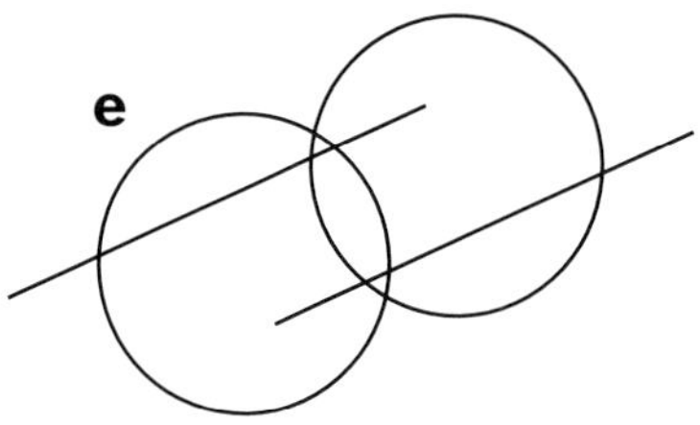

f

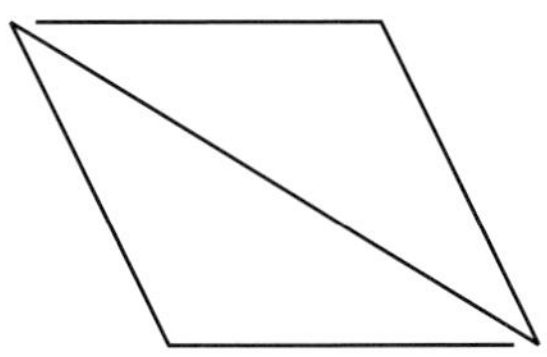

More Practice 1

1 Draw in an axis of symmetry for each pair of shapes.

a

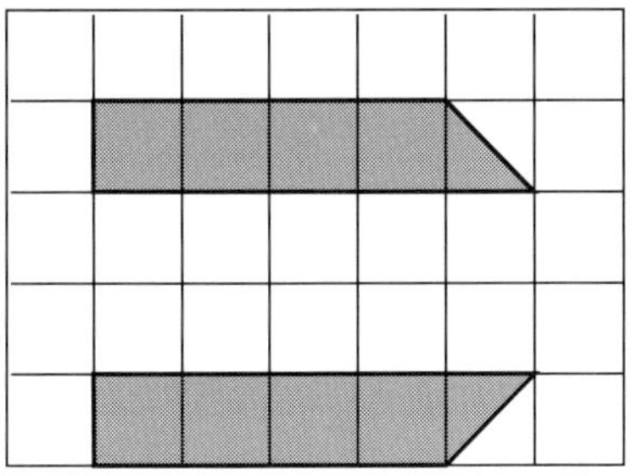

b

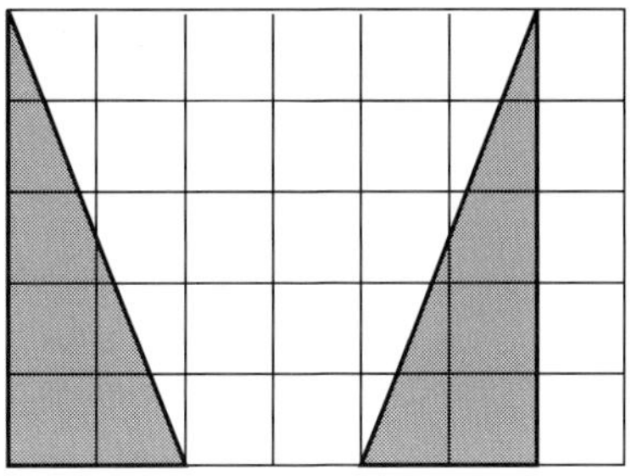

c

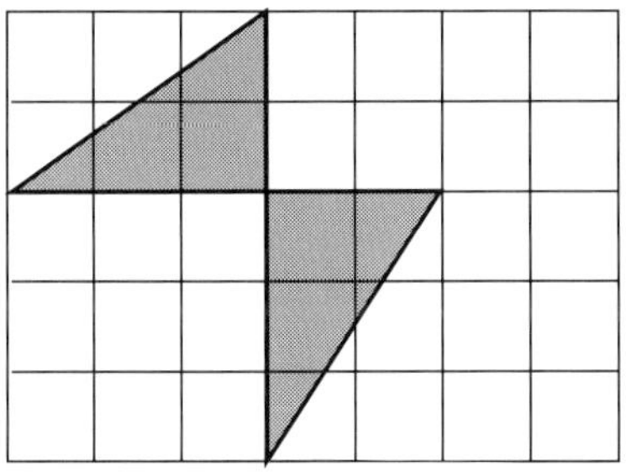

d

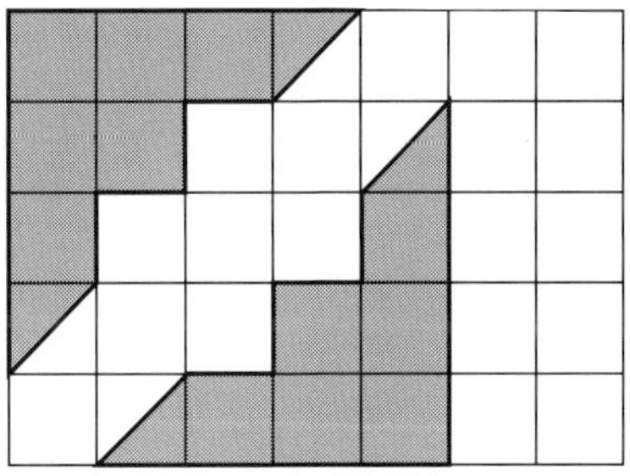

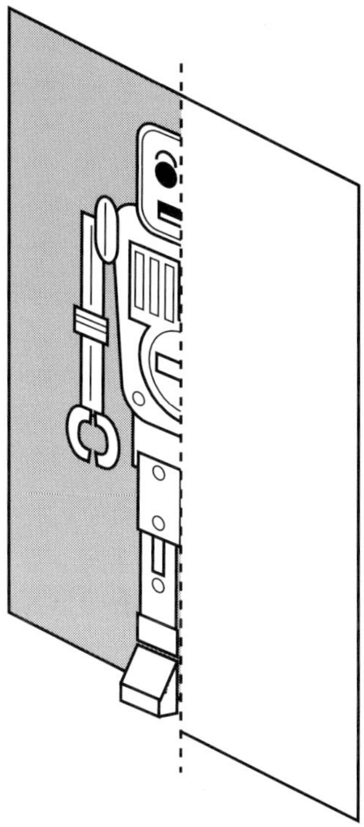

2 Draw the mirror image of each shape.
The dotted line is the axis of symmetry.

a

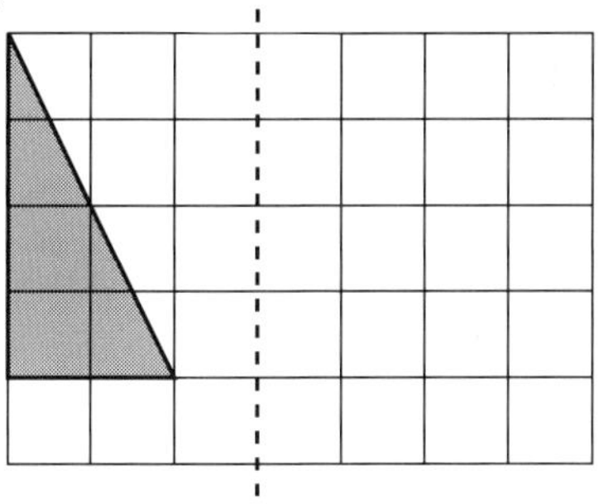

b

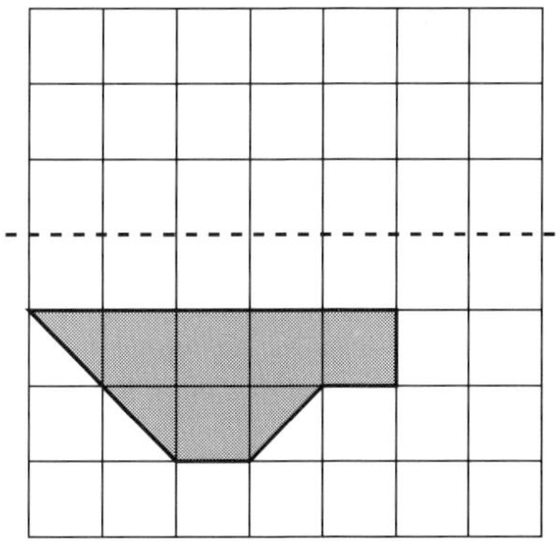

c

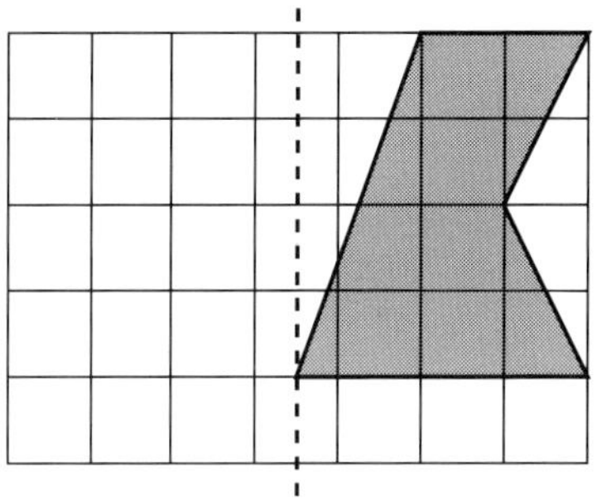

d

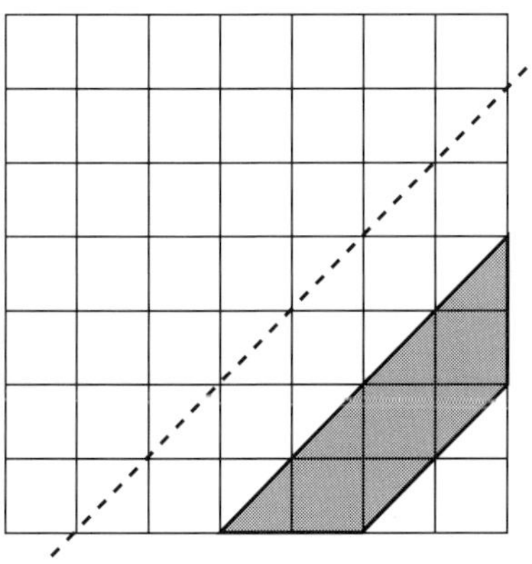

e

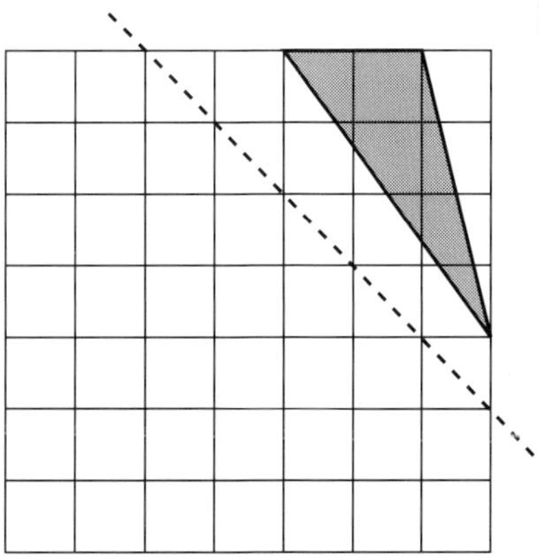

f

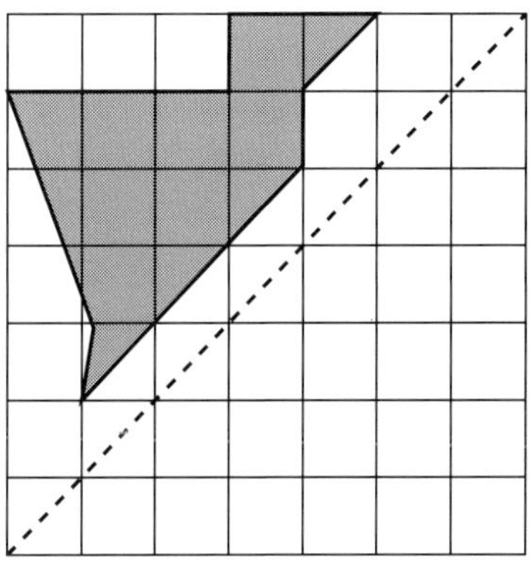

More Practice 2

1 A six-pointed star

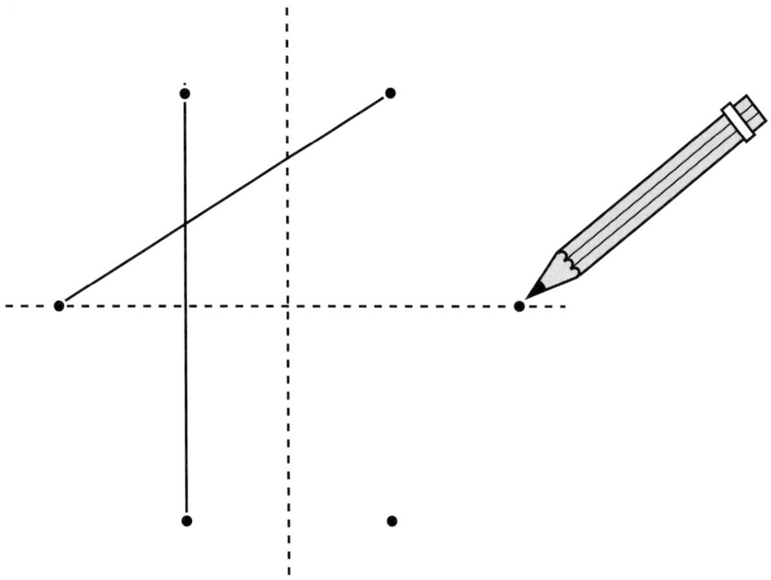

a Complete this diagram so that the dotted lines are axes of symmetry.
(Reflect in the horizontal axis first.)
b Draw a circle passing through all six points.
c Colour your design in a symmetrical way.

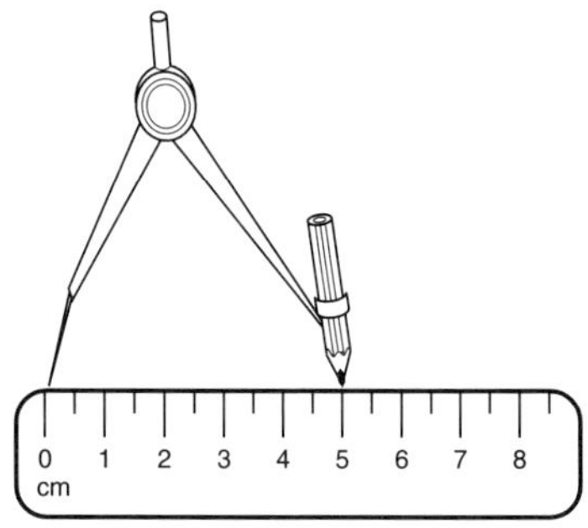

2 A twelve-pointed star
Repeat the above steps to make a twelve-pointed star.

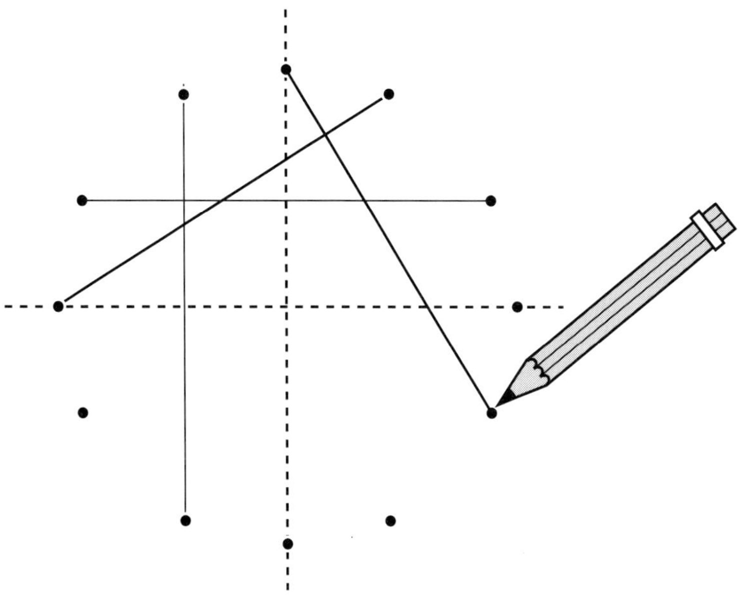

Driving Using the Mirror

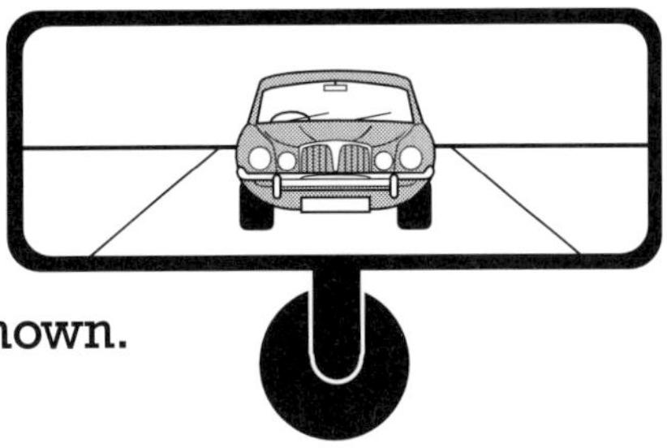

Make a box like the one shown.

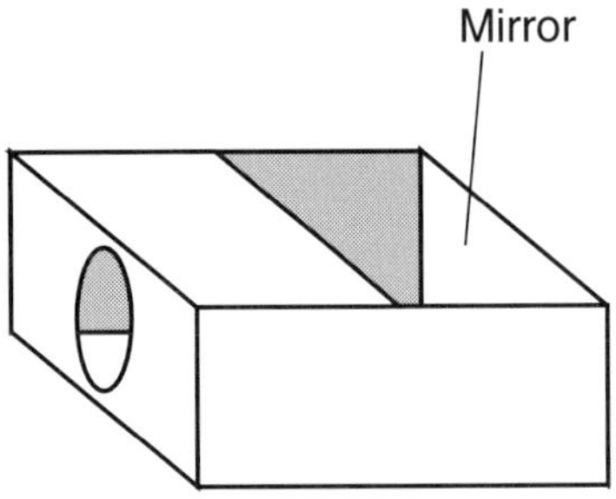

The hole should be big enough to let your hand through.

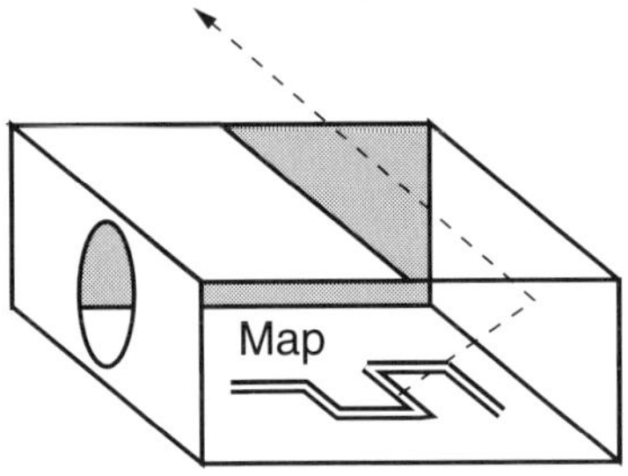

Cut out one of the maps below and place it in the box. You should be able to see the road in the mirror by looking through the top.

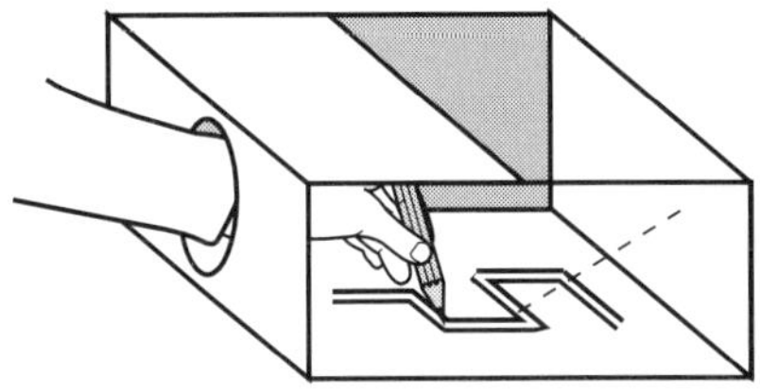

Put a pencil through the hole and hold it on 'start'. Can you steer your pencil along the road without crashing?

Specimen Map 1

Specimen Map 2

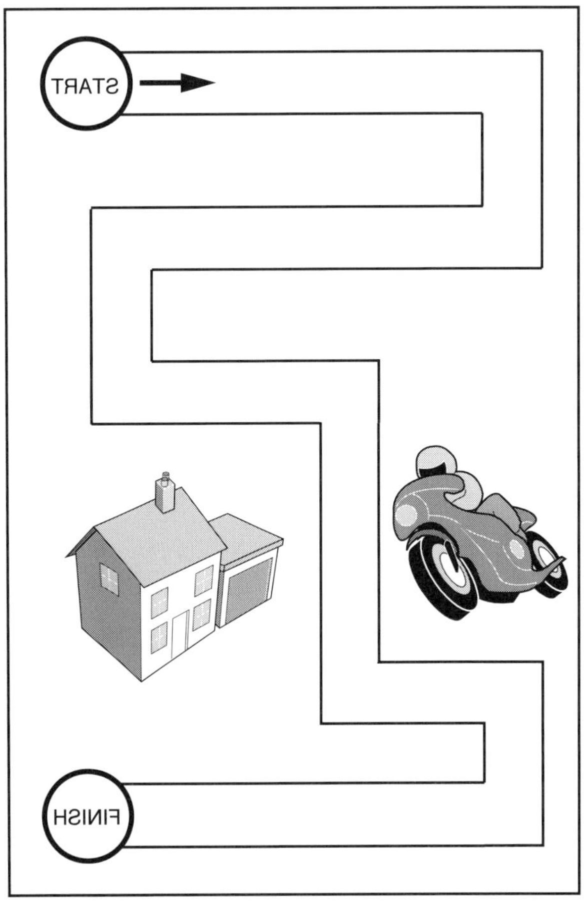

3 STRUCTURED DIAGRAMS

CURRICULUM COVERAGE

Standard Grade Guidelines

Demonstrate the ability to interpret and communicate mathematical information in the form of straightforward tables.
Follow instructions presented in the form of a structured diagram (K1).
Extract information from tables and mathematical diagrams (K2).
Communicate information in tabular and diagrammatic form (K6).
Select a form in which to communicate information, given guidance with structure (R4).
Enumerate possibilities (R15).
Reason (R16).
Take an organised approach (R17).

National Curriculum

AT 1 Levels 2, 3, 4 and 5.
AT 4 Levels 2 and 3.

NI Curriculum

AT Processes Levels 3, 4 and 5.

AIMS AND OBJECTIVES

The main aim of the chapter is to give students some useful means of organising their thoughts, data and strategy plans. It should also provide practice in interpretational skills.

NOTES

This chapter and Chapter 4 appear at this point in the book because the skills and techniques introduced are perceived as being useful for the whole course.

TEACHER'S RESOURCES

Worksheets 1-4 are provided to ease the 'copy and complete' nature of Exercises 1 and 3.
More Practice on Tree Diagrams provides additional work on this topic.
'Go with the Flow' is a game to strengthen awareness of the conventions of flowcharts and Carroll diagrams.

PROGRESS ROUTE

This chapter has no particular equivalence in *Book 3A*.

Worksheet 1

1

2

3

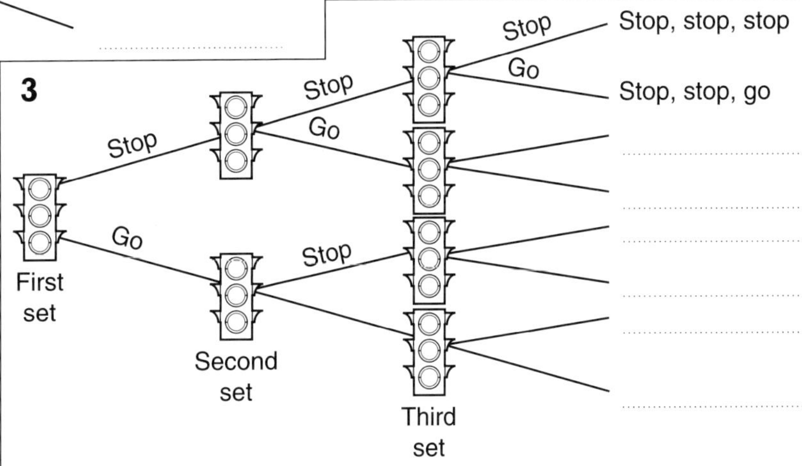

4

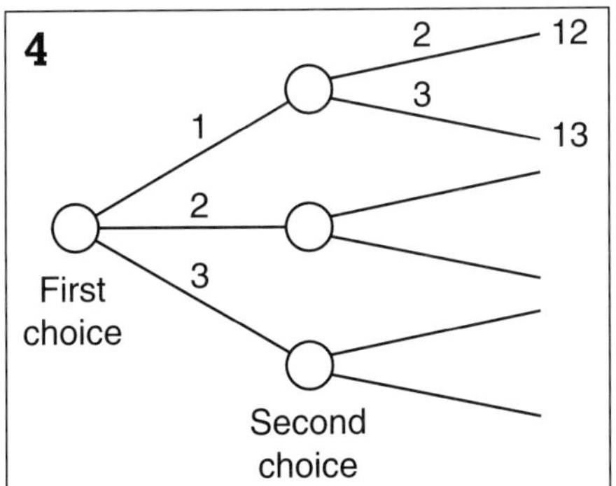

5

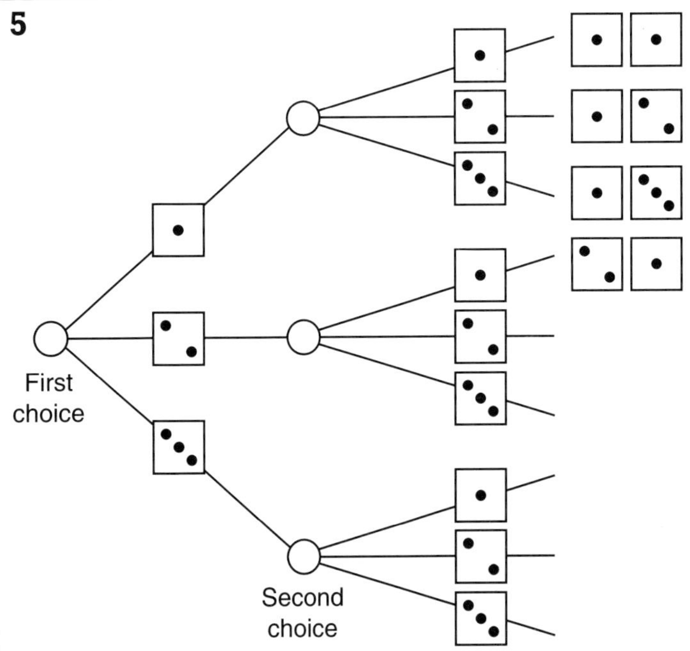

Worksheet 2

1 Jamie is playing a spelling game.

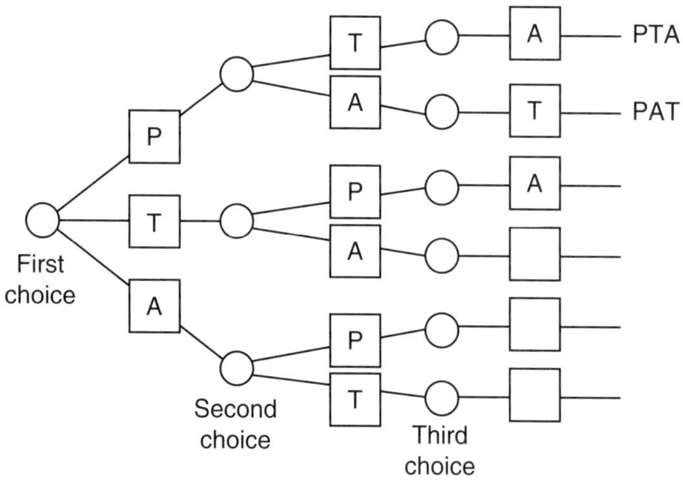

He has to make a three-letter word with these tiles.

a Complete the tree diagram to find how many ways the three letters can be arranged. (Notice that at the second choice you only have two options.)

b How many arrangements are actually words?

2 Mae's small sister is colouring in a picture of a frog like the one shown.

She only has red, green and blue crayons.

She will colour the hat, the jacket and the trousers.

Complete the tree diagram to find out how many different pictures are possible.

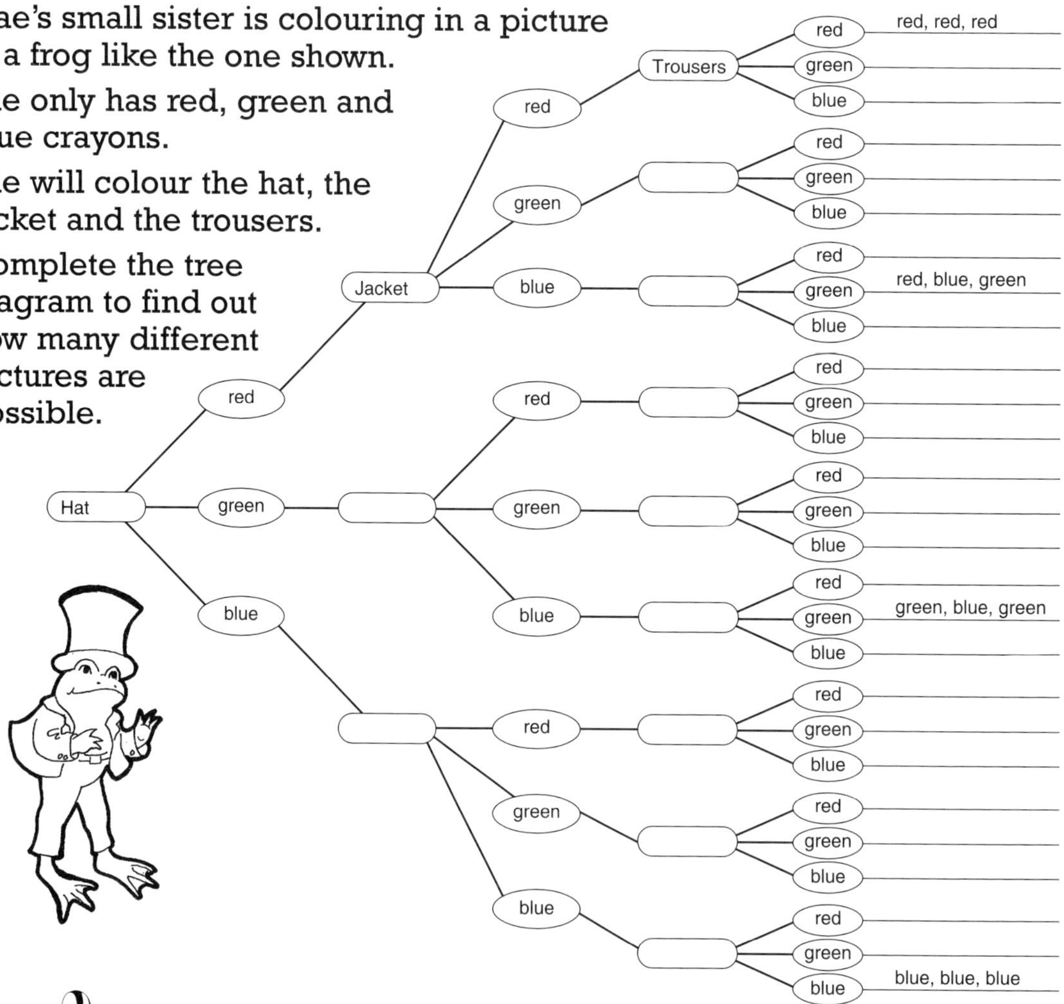

3 Four motorcyclists cross the finishing line at different times.
The picture shows a finishing order of 3, 2, 4, 1.
How many other ways could they have finished?

Worksheet 3

1

	Thrush	Not thrush
Gull	6	1
Not gull		

2

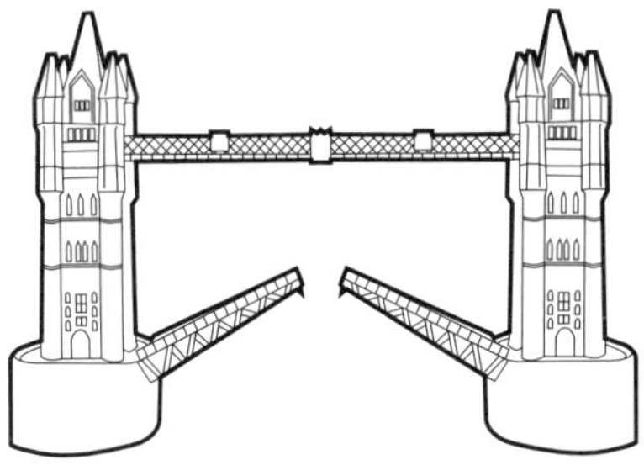

	Abroad	Not abroad
London	2	
Not London	1	

3

	After 10	Not after 10
Boys	7	
Not boys	4	

4

	Watched	Not watched
Played	6	
Not played	3	

5

	Sister	Not sister
Brother	4	
Not brother		

Worksheet 4

Complete the Carroll diagrams to help you answer the questions.

1 There were 26 in the class. They were all taken to the dinosaur exhibition. When questioned later,

21 remembered seeing the stegosaurus,
23 remembered seeing the triceratops and
19 remembered both.

How many could remember neither?

	Triceratops	Not triceratops
Stegosaurus	19	
Not stegosaurus		

2

	Hotdog	Not hotdog
Popcorn	4	
Not popcorn		

Not everyone took advantage of the free food.
Of the 10 pupils who went into the café,

7 took popcorn,
6 took a hotdog and
4 took both.

How many took neither?

3 Seven pupils were given the choice of lollipops or ice-creams.

4 wanted ice-cream.
5 wanted something lemon flavoured.
3 asked for a lemon flavoured ice-cream.

How many wanted a lollipop that wasn't lemon flavoured?

	Lemon	Not lemon
Ice-cream		
Not ice-cream		

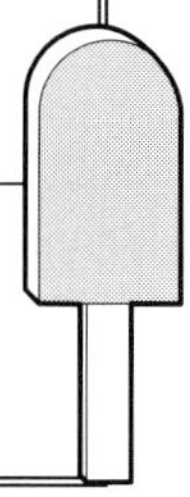

4

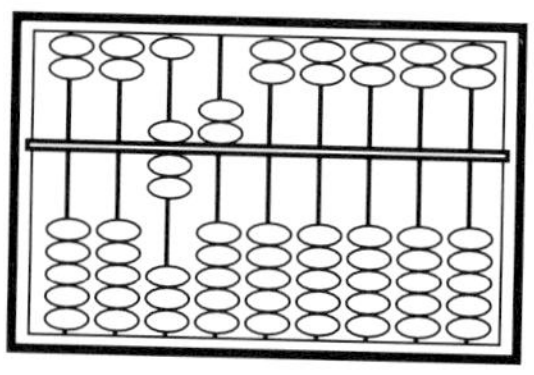

	Head	Not head
Abacus		
Not abacus		

A teacher asked 17 pupils how many could work out $27 \div 9$:

a on an abacus (13 put their hands up.)
b in their head (13 put their hands up.)
c both on an abacus and in their head. (8 claimed they could.)

Show that someone is not being honest.

More Practice on Tree Diagrams

1 In a competition, Niall had to put three films in order of popularity. He chose this order: *The Indians, Greek Heroes, The Vikings.*

Complete the tree diagram to find all the possible lists he could have made.

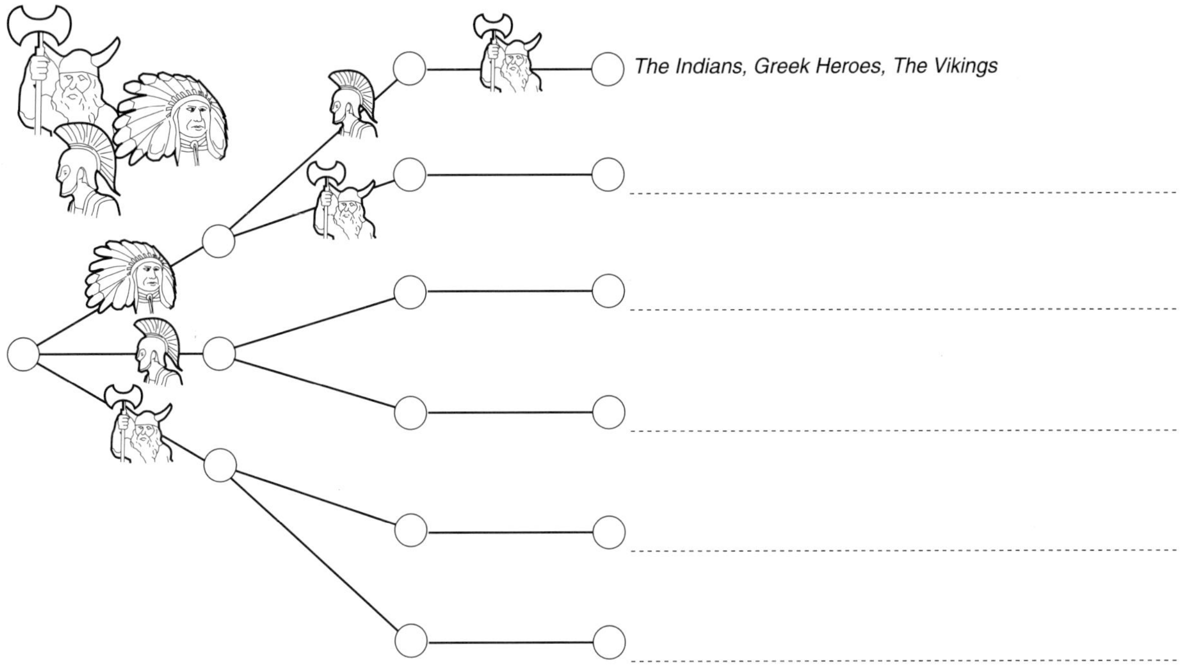

2 Make a tree diagram to find all the ways of putting these three items in order.

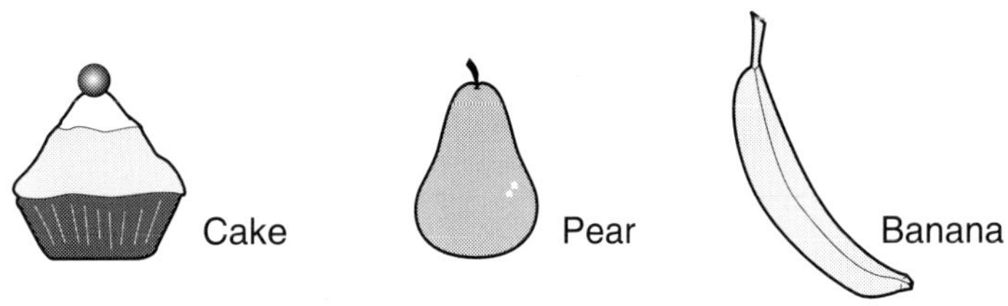

3 Using only the digits 1, 2 and 3, how many three-digit numbers can you make? You may repeat a digit (so 222 is allowed).

4

You need at least two of these ingredients mixed with water to make a soup: leeks, onions, tomatoes and mushrooms.

Use a tree diagram to help you find how many varieties of soup are possible.

5 There are four channels on Tina's TV. Tina watches for three hours. Every hour she decides which channel to watch.

Complete the tree diagram to find all of Tina's possible viewing patterns.

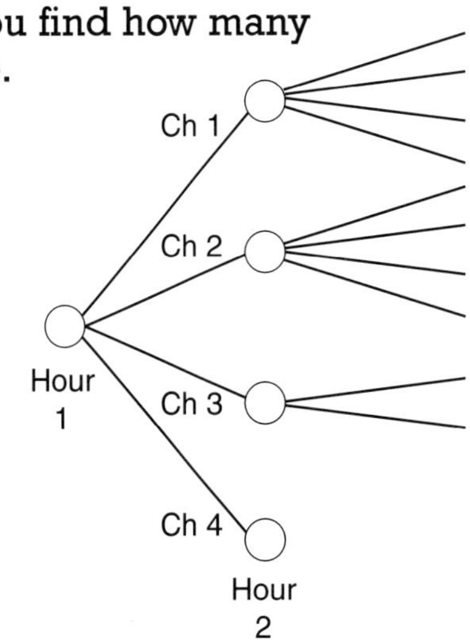

Go with the Flow
(A game for 2-4 players)

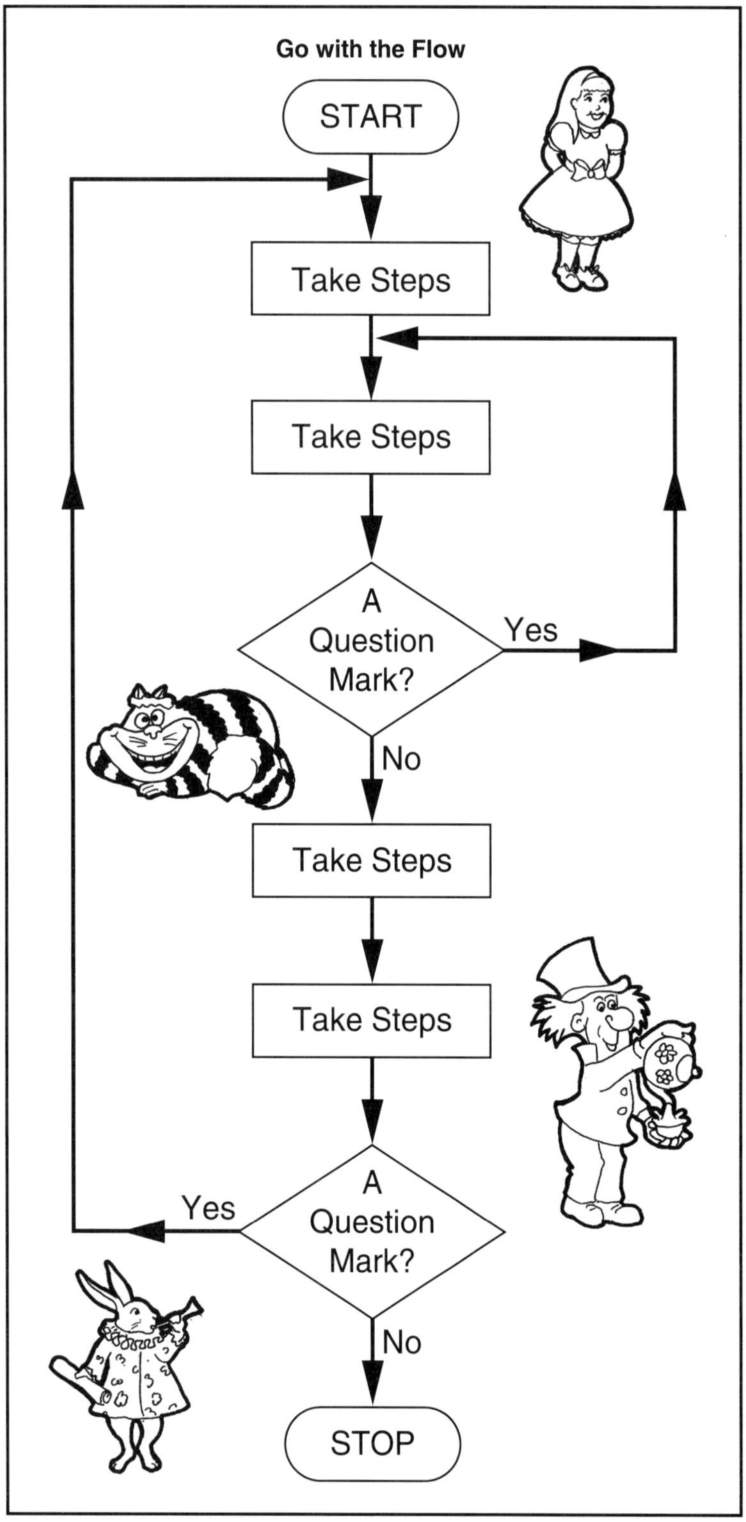

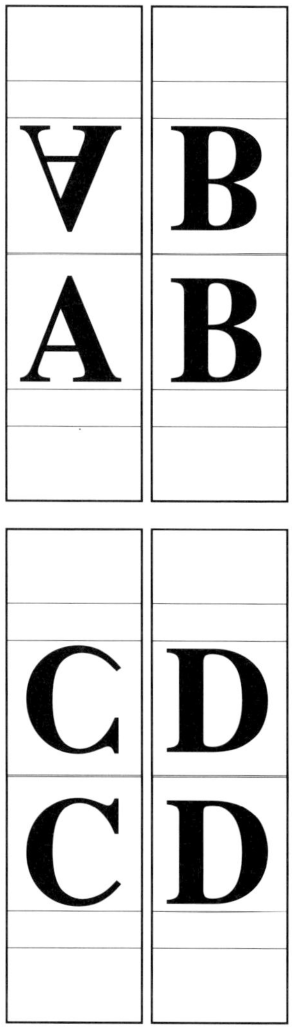

Cut and fold to make stands.

Preparation
Photocopy the two sheets of process cards back-to-back onto card and cut them out to make a pack of 25 cards. Do the same with the question cards. Shuffle both packs of cards and place them face down in two separate piles.
Photocopy the game chart and stands onto card and cut them out. Fold and glue the stands and give one to each player.

Rules
1 Each player starts at START with a score of 10.
2 On his/her turn a player follows the arrows to the next box.
3 When a player lands in a process box, he/she takes a process card from the top of the pile. This card will tell the player what to do with his/her score.
4 When a player lands in a question box, he/she takes a question card. On each card is a Carroll diagram and a statement. The player should follow the appropriate route: **yes** if the statement is true or **no** if it is not. If a player makes a mistake, he/she loses 10 points and his/her turn.
5 The winner is the player who reaches STOP with the highest score.

GO WITH THE FLOW – PROCESS CARD BACKS

Take Steps	Take Steps	Take Steps	Take Steps	Take Steps
Take Steps	Take Steps	Take Steps	Take Steps	Take Steps
Take Steps	Take Steps	Take Steps	Take Steps	Take Steps
Take Steps	Take Steps	Take Steps	Take Steps	Take Steps
Take Steps	Take Steps	Take Steps	Take Steps	Take Steps

GO WITH THE FLOW – PROCESS CARD FRONTS

+ 1 + 1 + 1	+ 2 + 2 + 2	+ 3 + 3 + 3	+ 4 + 4 + 4	+ 5 + 5 + 5
– 1 – 1 – 1	– 2 – 2 – 2	– 3 – 3 – 3	– 4 – 4 – 4	– 5 – 5 – 5
× 1 × 1 × 1	× 2 × 2 × 2	× 3 × 3 × 3	× 4 × 4 × 4	× 5 × 5 × 5
÷ 1 ÷ 1 Ignore remainder ÷ 1	÷ 2 ÷ 2 Ignore remainder ÷ 2	÷ 3 ÷ 3 Ignore remainder ÷ 3	÷ 4 ÷ 4 Ignore remainder ÷ 4	÷ 5 ÷ 5 Ignore remainder ÷ 5
+ 0 + 0 + 0	– 0 – 0 – 0	× 0 × 0 × 0	Double Double Double	Treble Treble Treble

GO WITH THE FLOW – QUESTION CARD BACKS

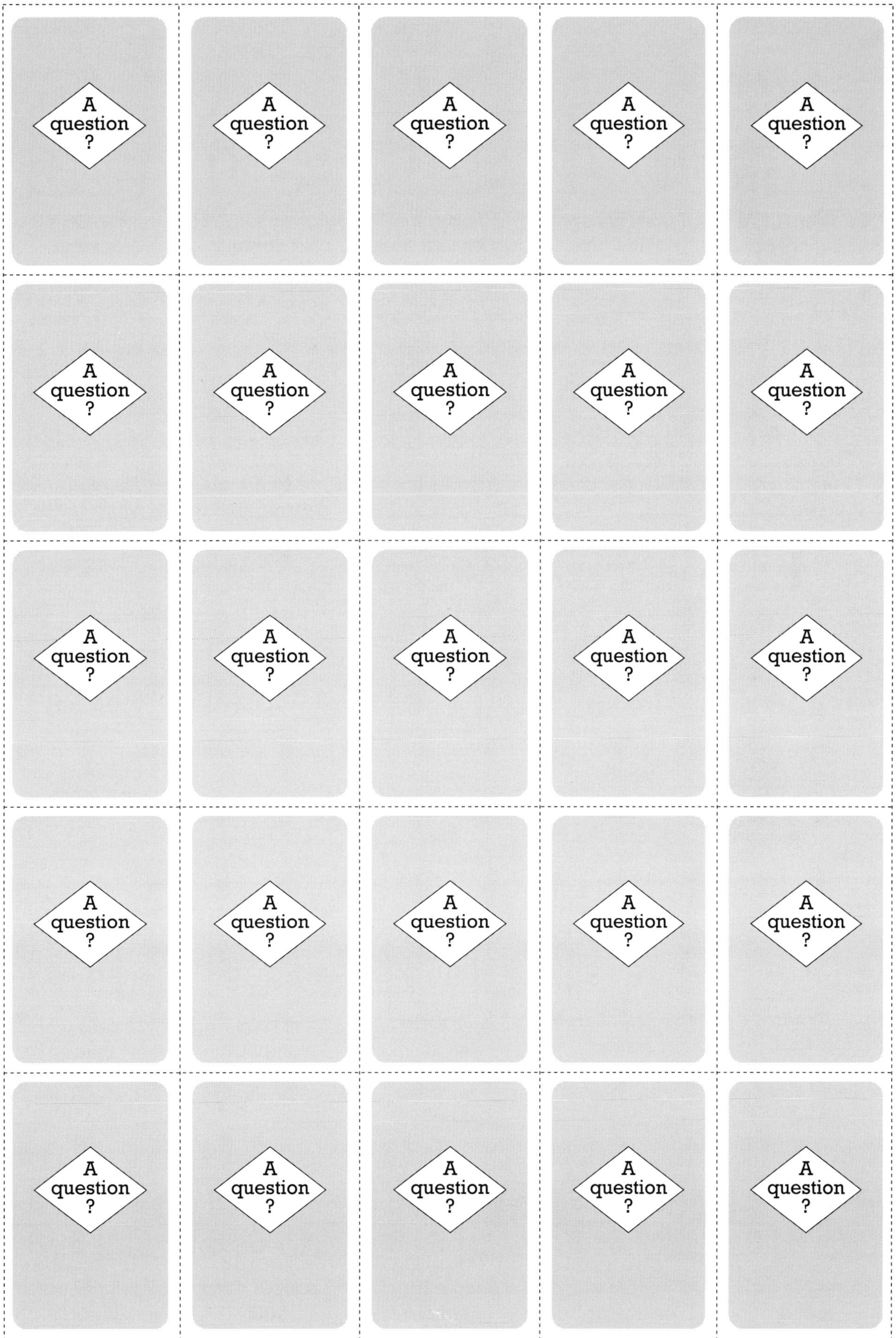

GO WITH THE FLOW – QUESTION CARD FRONTS

Colours in flowers

	Blue	Not blue
Red	3	2
Not red	1	4

2 flowers have red but not blue.

Colours in flowers

	Blue	Not blue
Red	3	2
Not red	1	4

3 flowers have red and blue.

Colours in flowers

	Blue	Not blue
Red	3	2
Not red	1	4

1 flower has red but not blue.

Colours in flowers

	Blue	Not blue
Red	3	2
Not red	1	4

1 flower has blue but not red.

Colours in flowers

	Blue	Not blue
Red	3	2
Not red	1	4

There are 9 flowers.

A look at lambs

	Black	Not black
Male	1	4
Not male	2	8

10 lambs are female.

A look at lambs

	Black	Not black
Male	1	4
Not male	2	8

3 lambs are black.

A look at lambs

	Black	Not black
Male	1	4
Not male	2	8

2 lambs are black and male.

A look at lambs

	Black	Not black
Male	1	4
Not male	2	8

8 lambs are male but not black.

A look at lambs

	Black	Not black
Male	1	4
Not male	2	8

There are 11 white lambs.

Chessmen on the board

	Pawn	Not pawn
White	5	3
Not white	4	6

18 men are on the board.

Chessmen on the board

	Pawn	Not pawn
White	5	3
Not white	4	6

10 men are not white.

Chessmen on the board

	Pawn	Not pawn
White	5	3
Not white	4	6

Half the men are pawns.

Chessmen on the board

	Pawn	Not pawn
White	5	3
Not white	4	6

4 pawns are white.

Chessmen on the board

	Pawn	Not pawn
White	5	3
Not white	4	6

Only 3 men are not pawns and not white.

Phonecalls

	Local	Not local
Quick	8	4
Not quick	9	9

8 quick calls were not local.

Phonecalls

	Local	Not local
Quick	8	4
Not quick	9	9

32 calls were made.

Phonecalls

	Local	Not local
Quick	8	4
Not quick	9	9

12 calls were not local.

Phonecalls

	Local	Not local
Quick	8	4
Not quick	9	9

9 local calls were not quick.

Phonecalls

	Local	Not local
Quick	8	4
Not quick	9	9

12 calls were quick.

Viewing habits

	Sport	Not sport
Westerns	7	9
Not westerns	6	8

30 people were asked.

Viewing habits

	Sport	Not sport
Westerns	7	9
Not westerns	6	8

15 people watch westerns.

Viewing habits

	Sport	Not sport
Westerns	7	9
Not westerns	6	8

8 people watch neither.

Viewing habits

	Sport	Not sport
Westerns	7	9
Not westerns	6	8

7 people watch both.

Viewing habits

	Sport	Not sport
Westerns	7	9
Not westerns	6	8

7 people watch westerns.

4 A PROBLEM SOLVING TOOLKIT

CURRICULUM COVERAGE

Standard Grade Guidelines
Select steps required to solve routine problems (K8).
Experiment (R13).
Recognise patterns (R14).
Enumerate possibilities (R15).
Reason (R16).
Take an organised approach (R17).

National Curriculum
AT 1 Levels 3, 4 and 5.

NI Curriculum
AT Processes Levels 3, 4, 5 and 6.

AIMS AND OBJECTIVES
To provide appropriate activities and practice of different problem-solving strategies.
To consolidate earlier work.
To prepare students for internal assessment work.
To provide a challenge for students in problem-solving skills.

NOTES

1 One would expect this chapter to be visited and revisited over an extended period, and the suitable strategies to be mentioned as and when they are encountered in other chapters.

2 Although provided as one chapter, this work is designed to provide a range of problems which can be selected by the teacher throughout the session in preparation for internal assessment of problem solving.

3 The first five exercises provide problems with a directed strategy for solving them.

4 Many of the problems involve practical work and the worksheets may benefit from being enlarged onto A3 paper in order to make the puzzle pieces a more appropriate size.

TEACHER'S RESOURCES
Worksheet 1 contains six identical tangrams, which should be photocopied onto card, for use in trial and improvement problems in Exercise 1.
Worksheet 2 provides extra practice in trial and improvement problems.
Worksheet 3 on pentominoes should be photocopied onto card and the pentominoes cut out to provide practice in fitting them into the shapes supplied.
Worksheet 4 provides practical materials to make a model of the frog problem which precedes Exercise 2.
Worksheet 5 provides extra practice in using a model.
Worksheet 6 contains nets of cubes which should be photocopied onto card, cut out and assembled into a calendar, providing more practice in using a model.
Worksheet 7 has more work on looking for patterns.

Worksheet 1: Tangrams

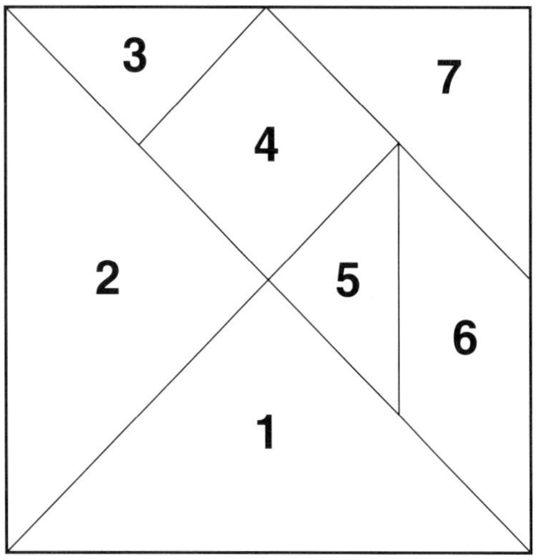

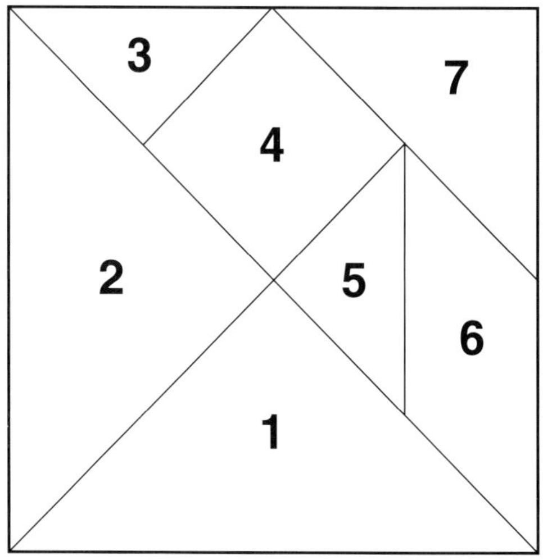

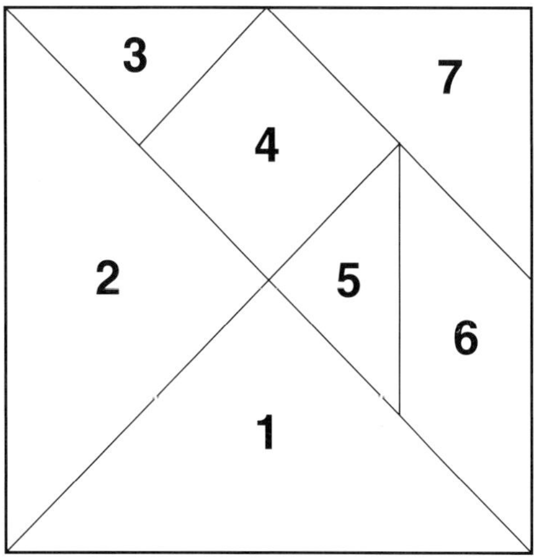

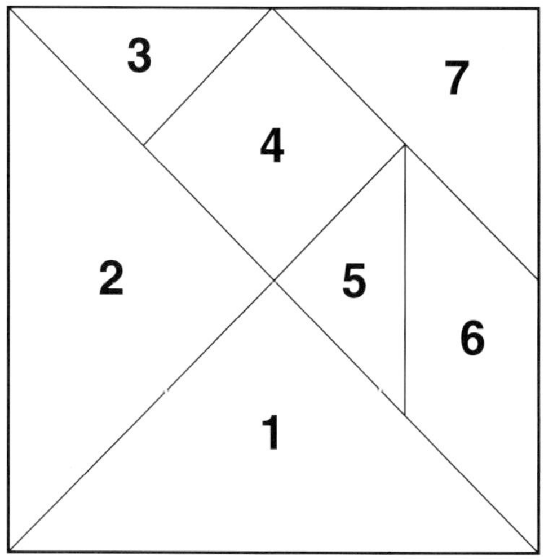

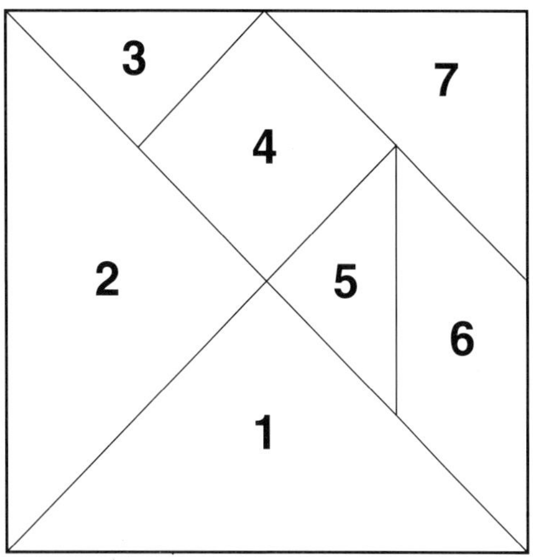

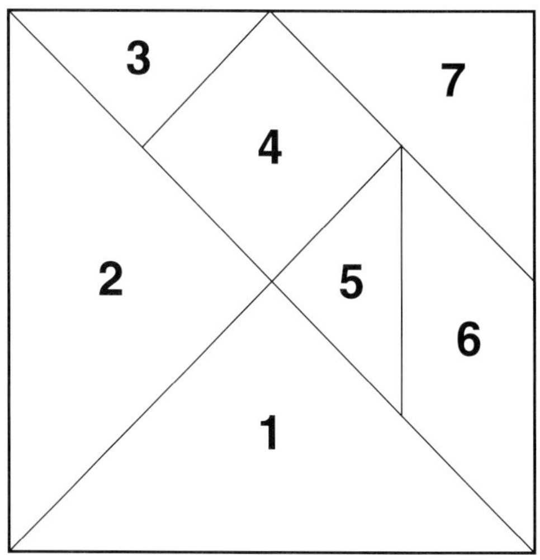

Worksheet 2

1

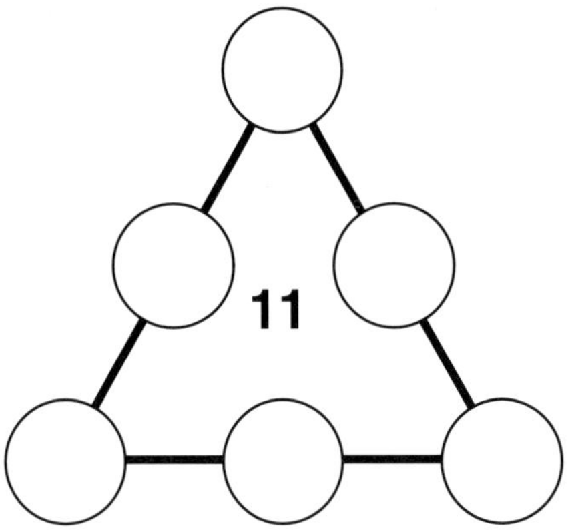

Cut out these counters. They may help you in your trials.

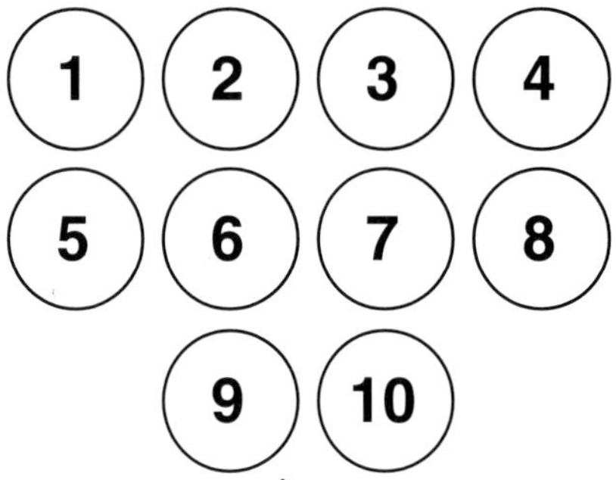

Place the numbers 1, 2, 3, 4, 5 and 6 in the circles so that each side of the triangle adds up to the number in the centre of the triangle.
Use each number only once.

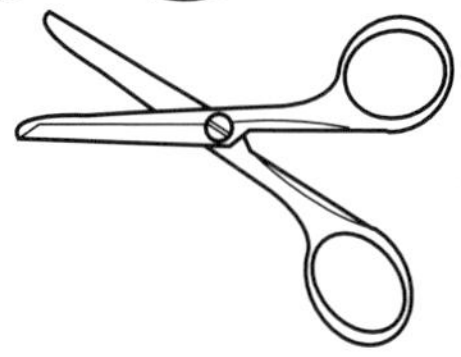

2

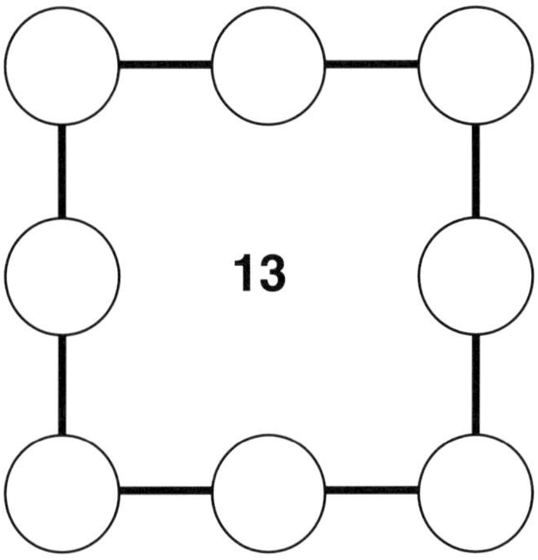

Place the numbers 1, 2, 3, 4, 5, 6 , 7 and 8 in the circles so that each side of the square adds up to the number in the centre of the square.
Use each number only once.

3

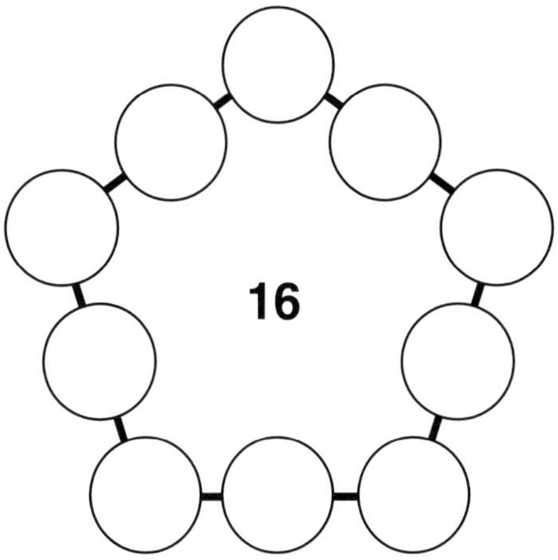

Place the numbers 1, 2, 3, 4, 5, 6, 7, 8, 9 and 10 in the circles so that each side of the pentagon adds up to the number in the centre of the pentagon.
Use each number only once.

4 Find a way for the nightwatchman to visit every checkpoint in the exhibition centre and return to the security office without visiting any checkpoint twice.

Draw the route on the diagram.

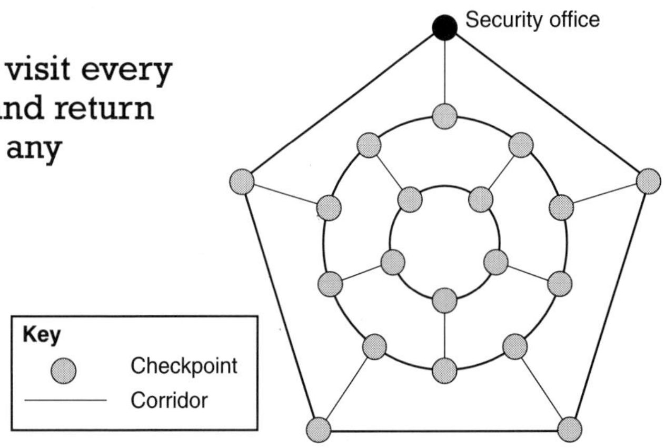

Worksheet 3

Cut out the pentominoes and use them to complete the shapes below. Record your results by drawing the pentominoes inside the shapes.

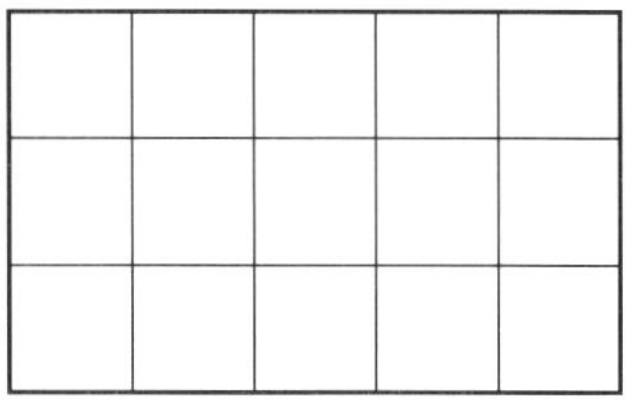

1 Find three pentominoes which will fill this rectangle.

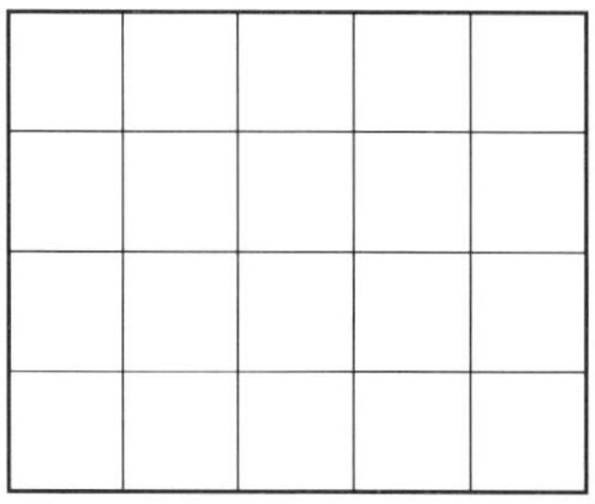

2 Find four pentominoes which will fill this rectangle.

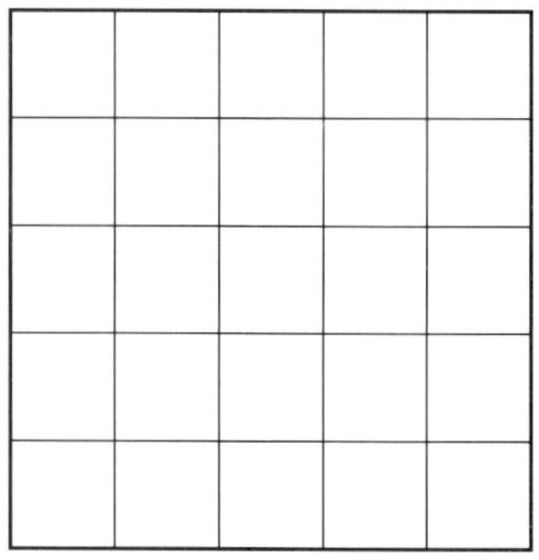

3 Find five pentominoes which will fill this square.

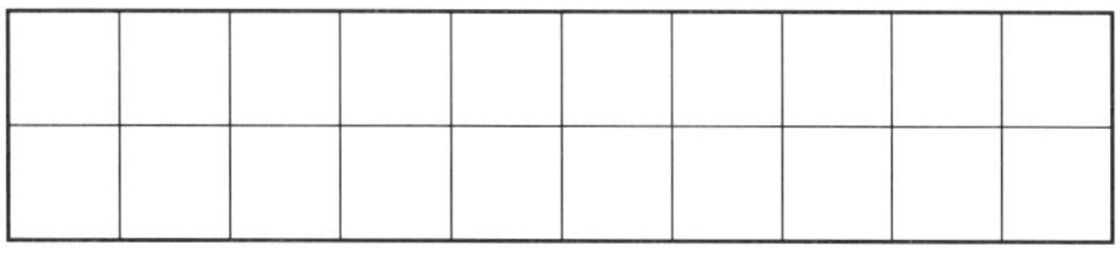

4 Find four pentominoes which will fill this rectangle.

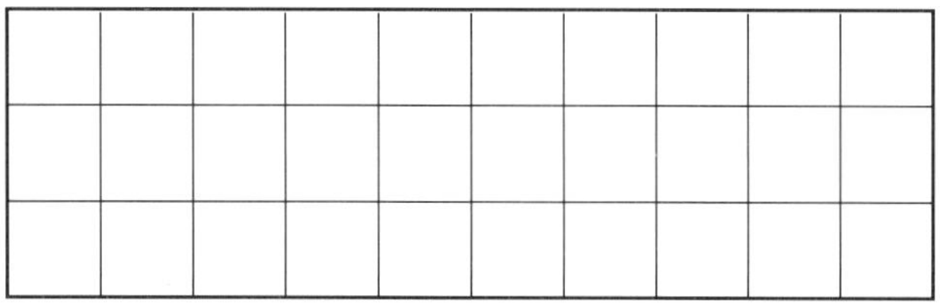

5 Find six pentominoes which will fill this rectangle.

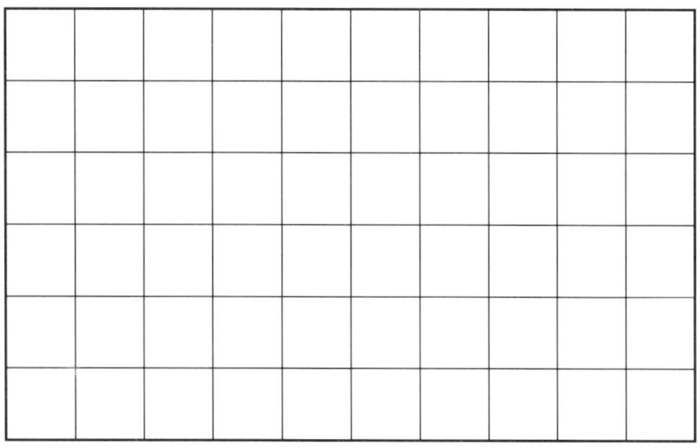

6 Fill this rectangle using all twelve pentominoes.

7 Explain why it is impossible to form a 2×5 rectangle.

Pentominoes

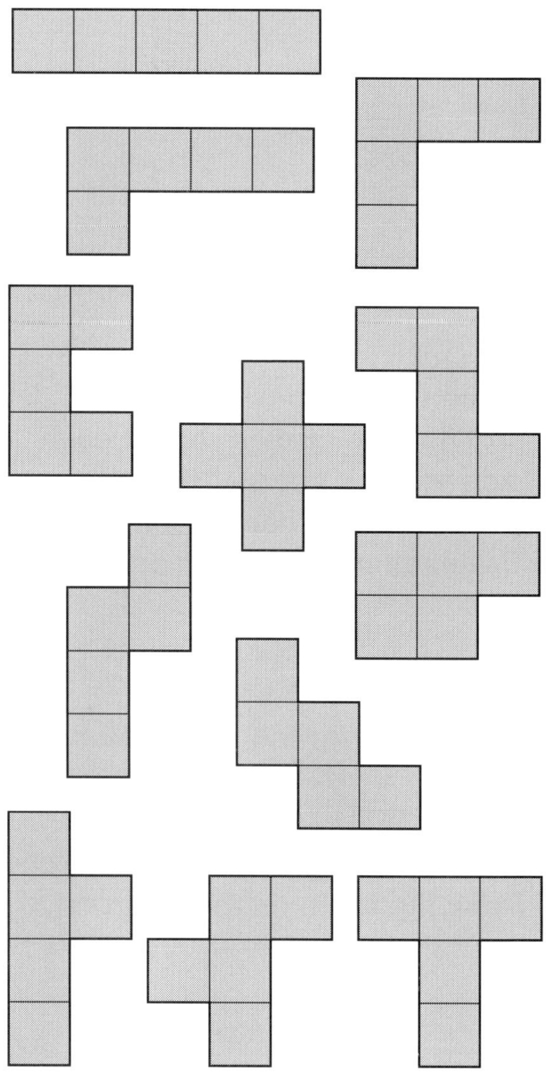

Worksheet 4

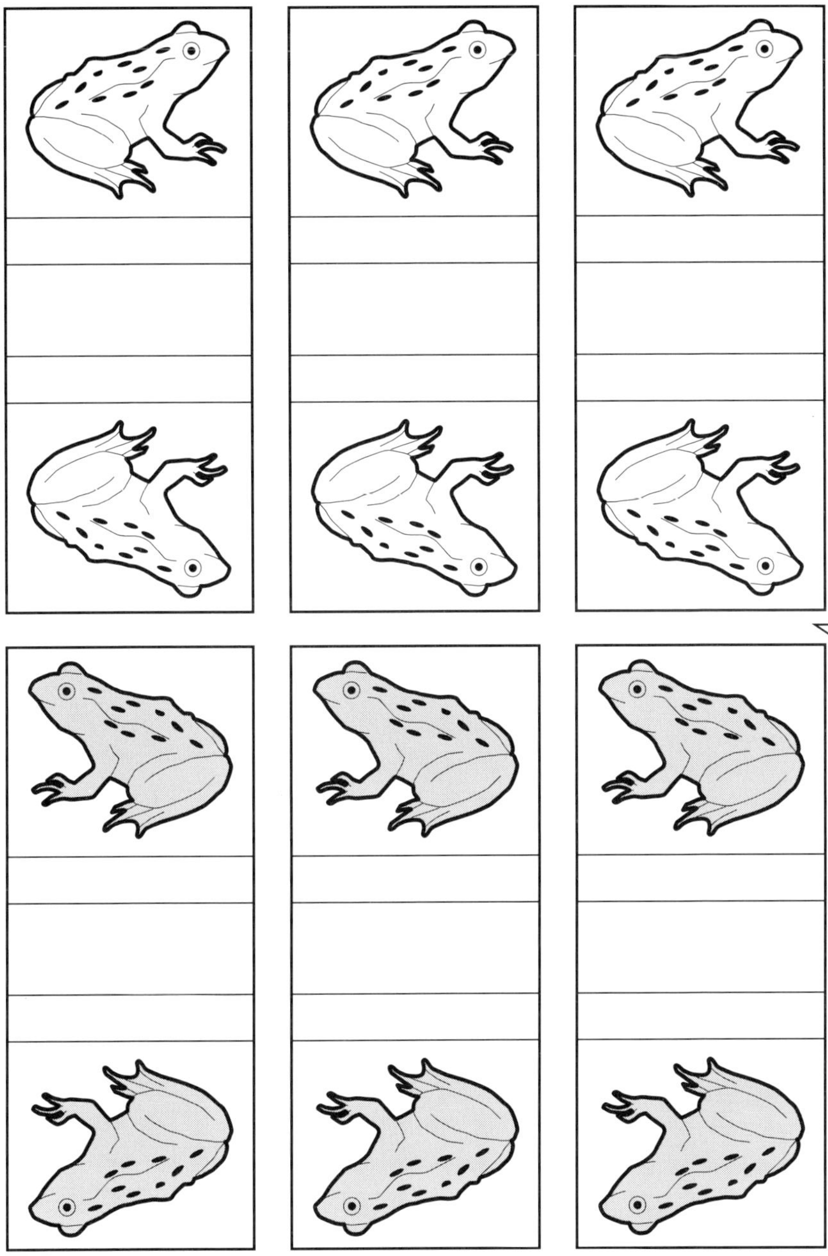

Cut out all six frogs.
Fold carefully and glue to make six upright frogs.
Cut out the seven lilypads.
Glue them onto a piece of card in a straight line.

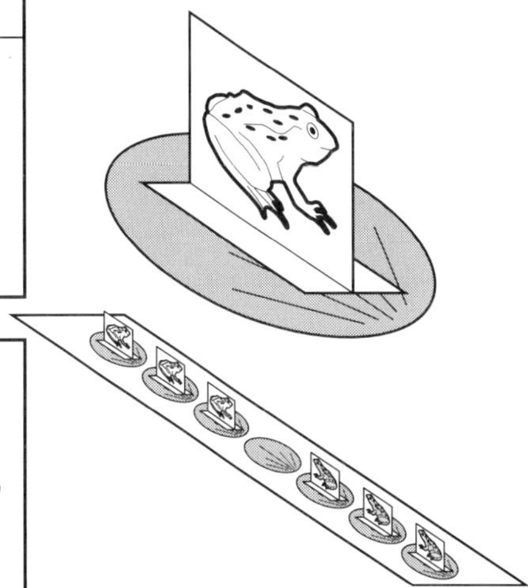

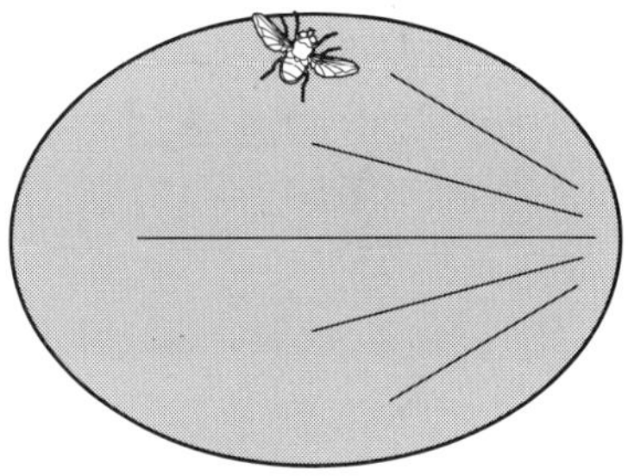

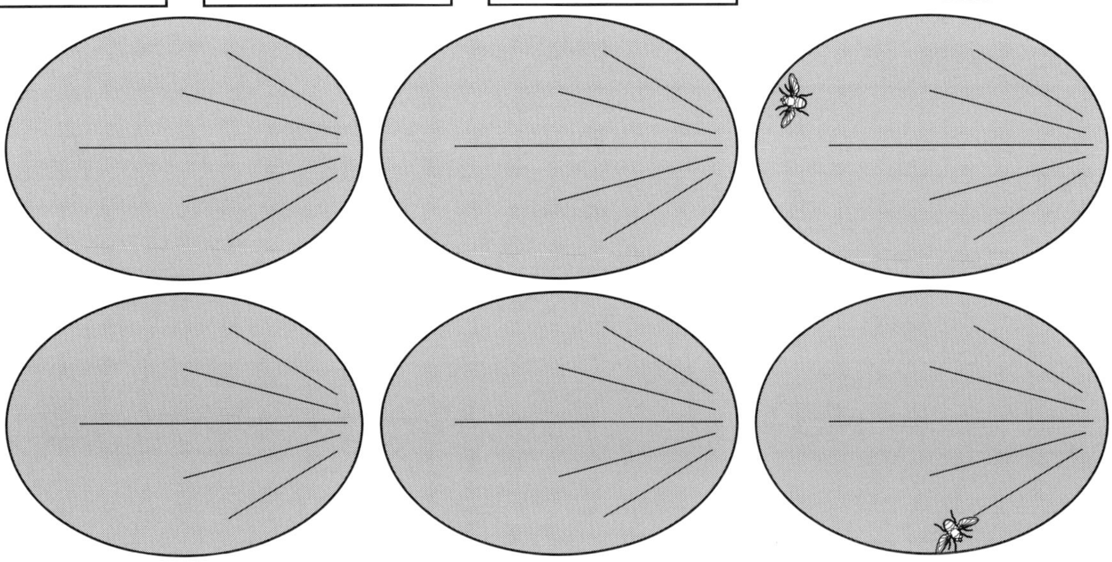

Worksheet 5

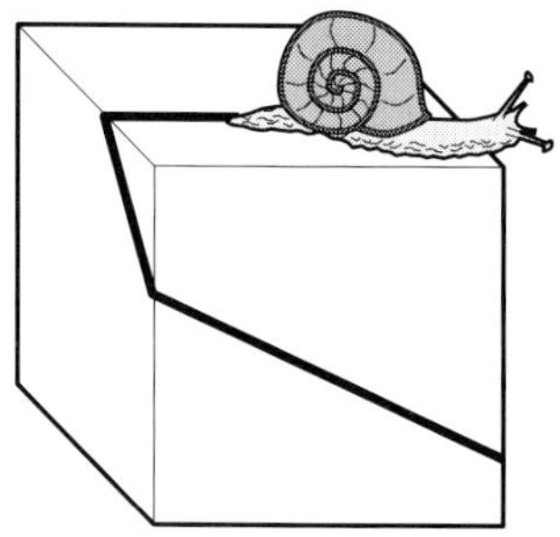

A snail crawled round a cube.

It ended up back where it started.

It left an unbroken trail on the cube.

Which of the nets below will make an unbroken trail when the cube is made?

Check your answers by cutting out the nets and building the cubes.

1

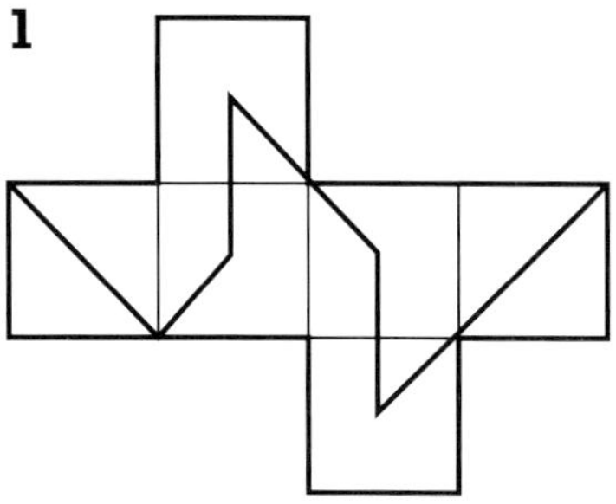

2

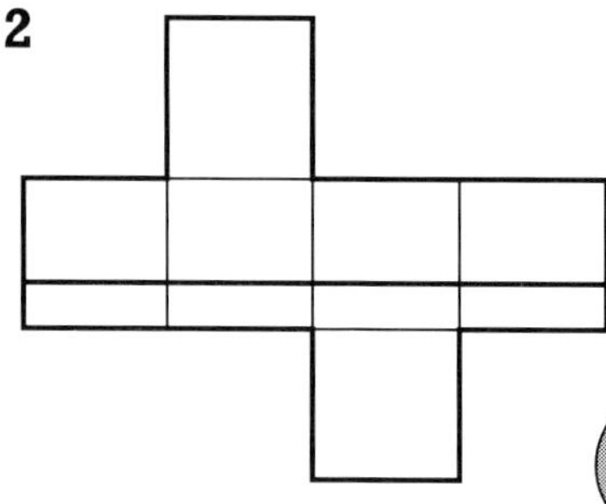

3

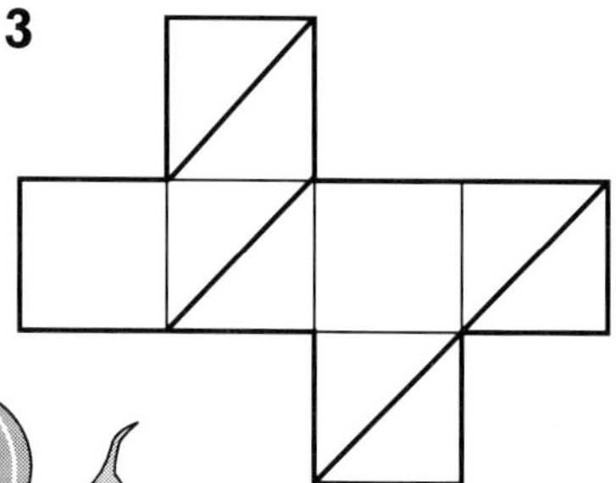

4

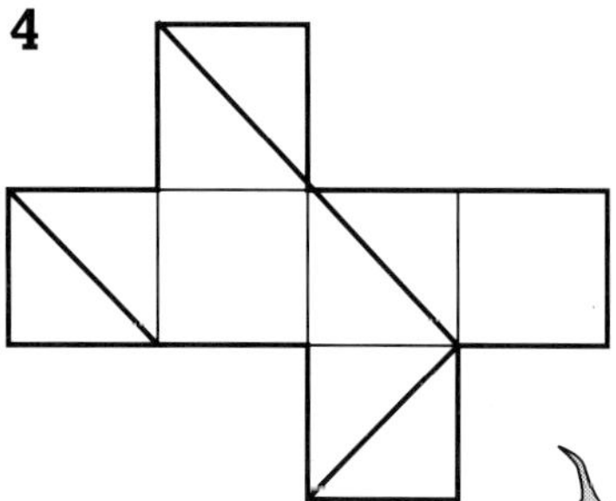

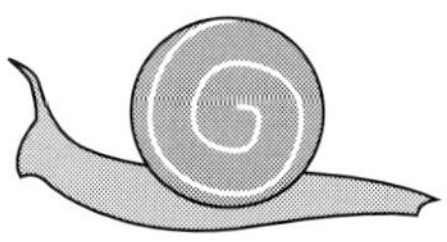

5

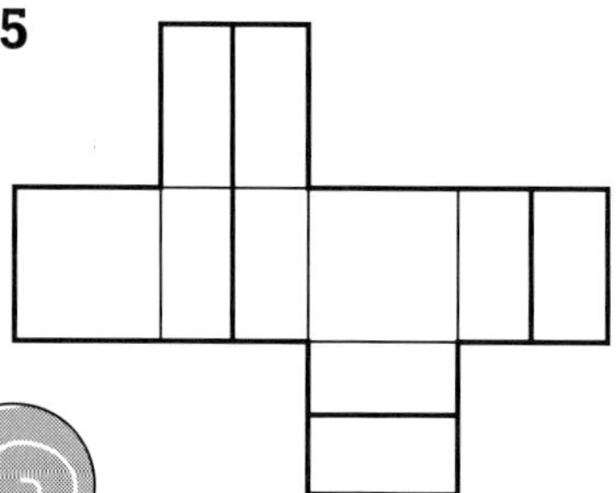

6

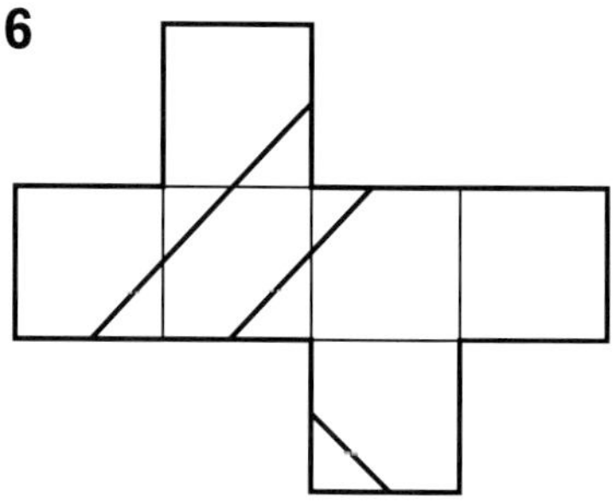

7

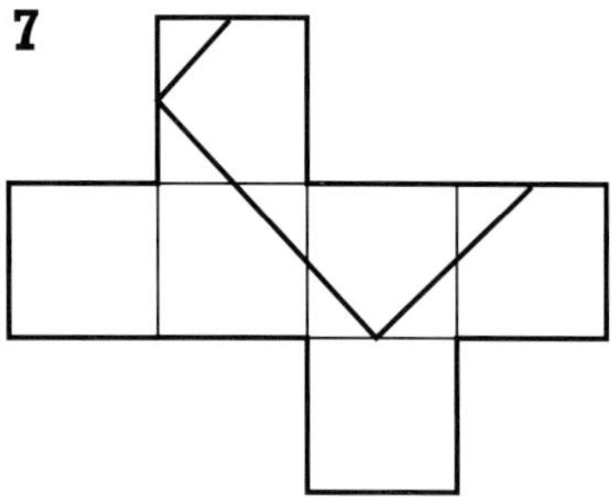

8

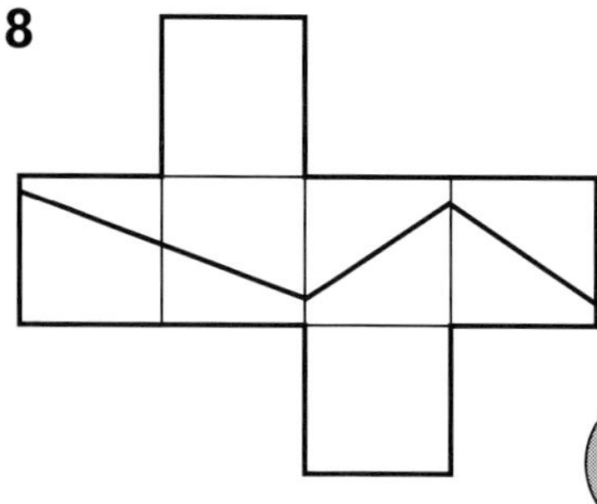

9

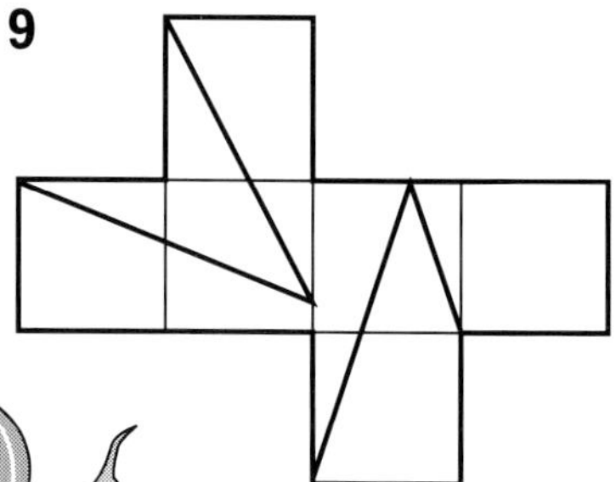

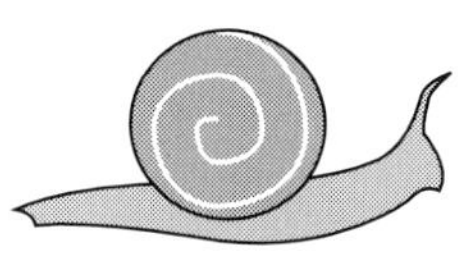

10

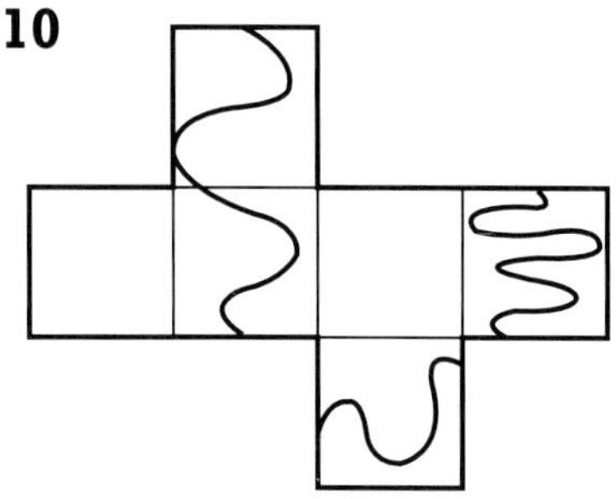

11

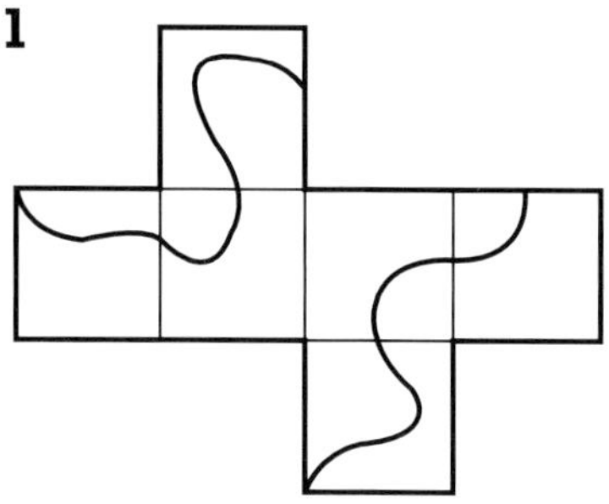

12

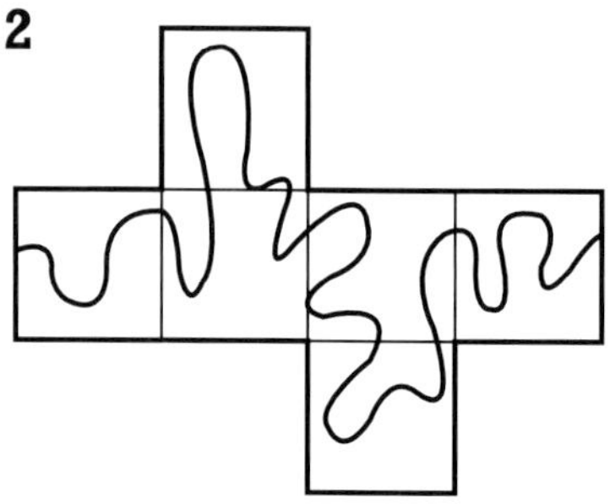

Worksheet 6

The shapes below are nets of a cube.

Cut out the nets to make your own calendar.

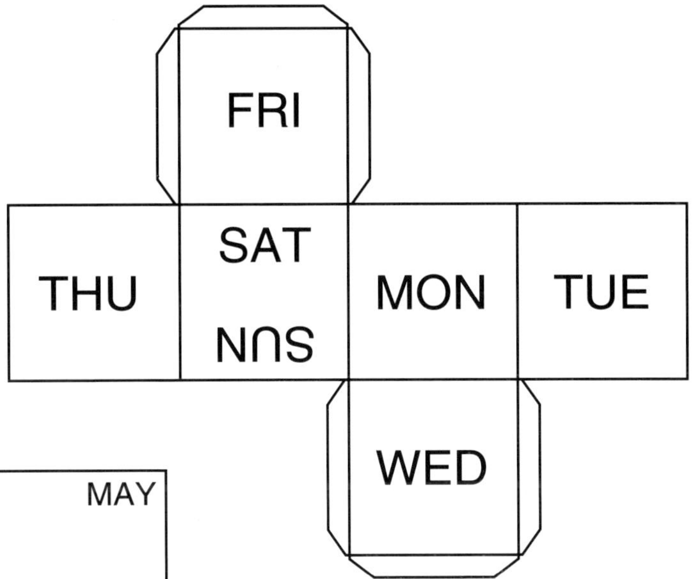

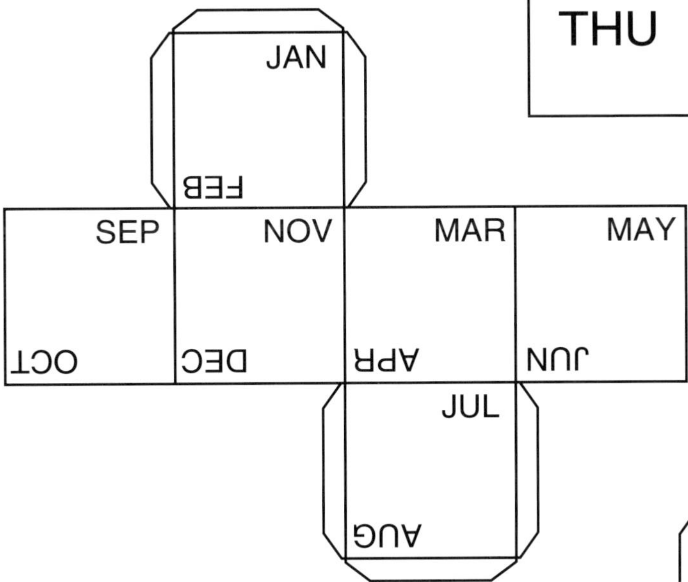

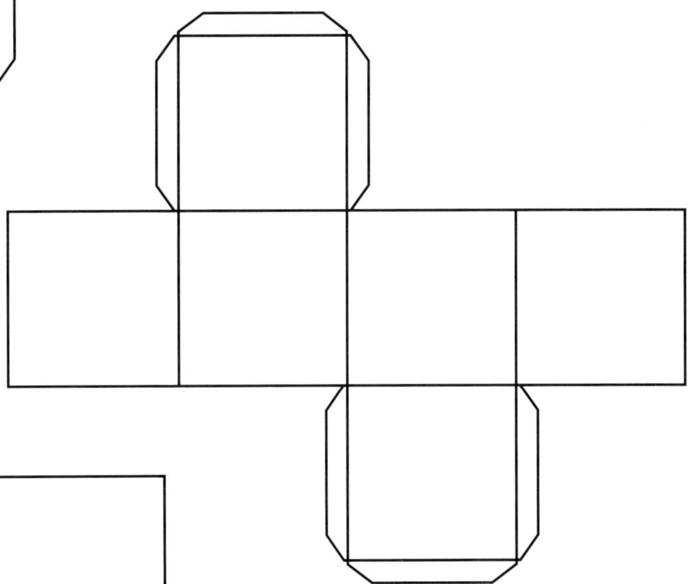

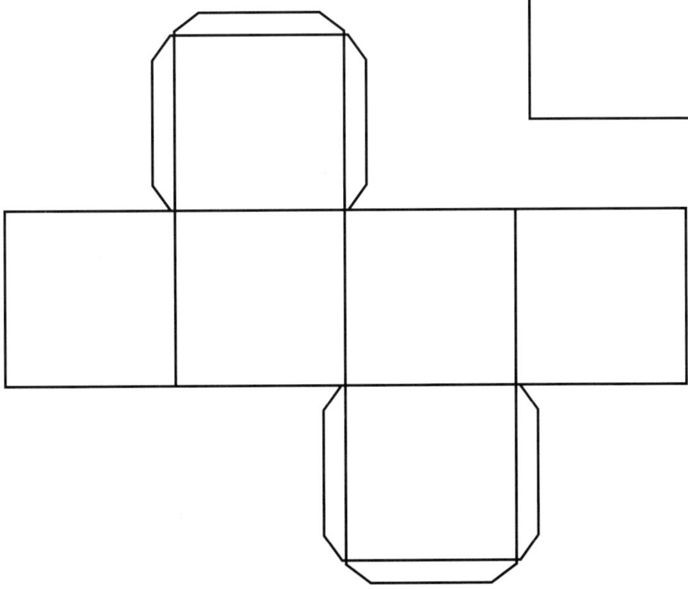

Use the blank nets to complete the calendar.

Each face will carry one number.

You must be able to make every number from 1 to 31.

Worksheet 7

1 Peter designs tiles. He is trying out odd shapes for borders. The perimeter of the finished border interests him.

For each border below:

(i) describe what to do to the number of tiles to get the perimeter
(ii) find the perimeter of a border which uses 20 tiles.

a Triangles

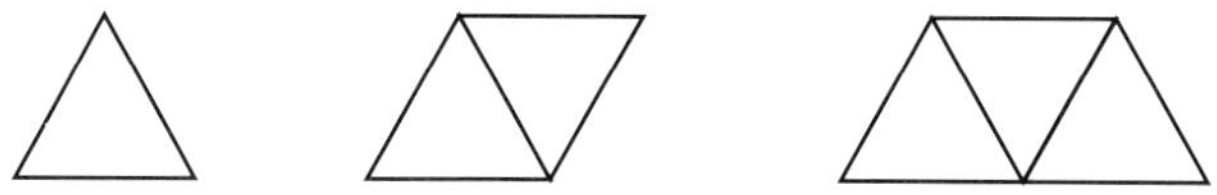

Perimeter 3 4 5

b Pentagons

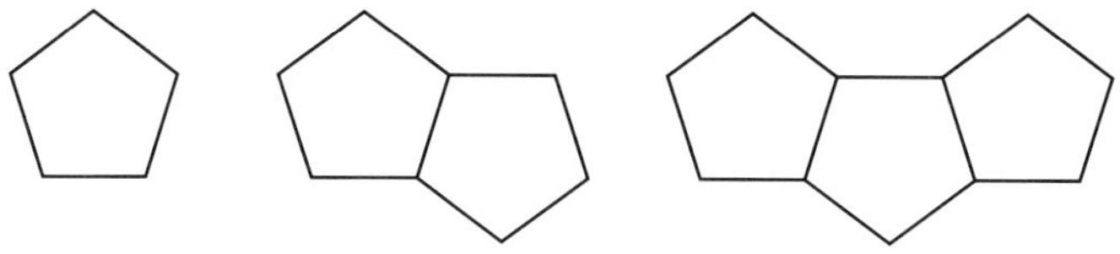

Perimeter 5 8 11

c Hexagons

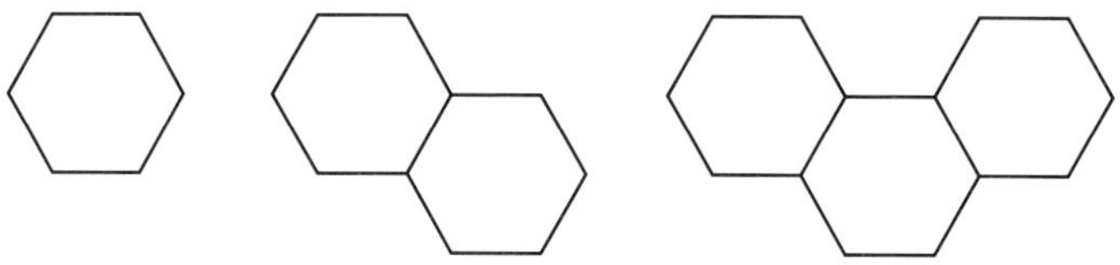

Perimeter 6 10 14

d Octagons

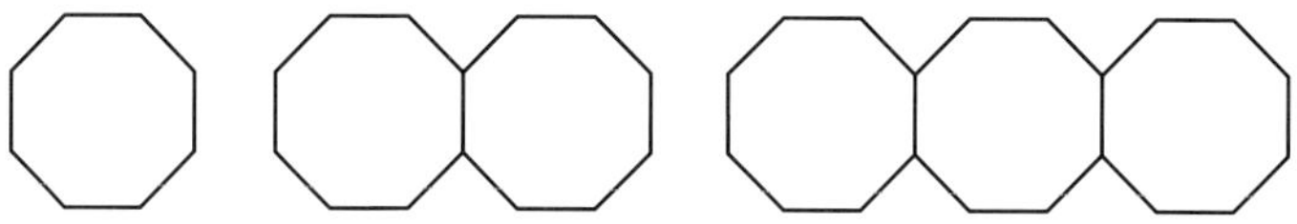

Perimeter 8 14 20

2 Sometimes a pattern cannot be spotted straight away. You may have to look for the pattern in the steps.

Jane is building a house of cards. She has built one with four storeys.

a How many **more** cards will she need to build a five-storey house?

b How many cards will she need to build a six-storey house?

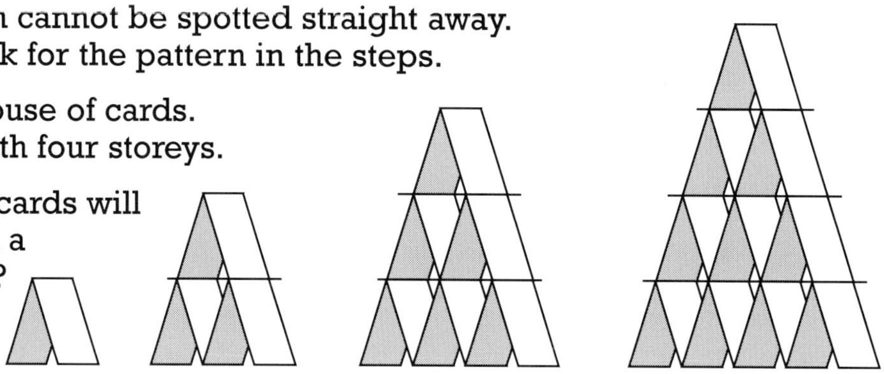

1 storey 2 cards

2 storey 7 cards (5 more than 1 storey)

3 storey 15 cards (8 more than 2 storeys)

4 storey 26 cards (11 more than 3 storeys)

3 Here is a pattern of squares.

How many squares will be needed for a tenth diagram?

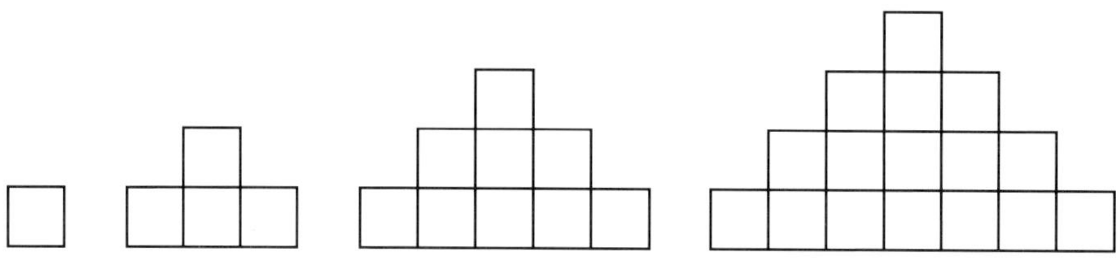

1 2 3 4

5 SCALES

CURRICULUM COVERAGE

Standard Grade Guidelines
Foundation Level:
Decimal graduated scales; directed numbers on scales (temperature only).
General Level:
Contexts, + and – directed numbers.

National Curriculum
AT 2 Levels 3, 4 and 5.
AT 3 Level 4.

NI Curriculum
AT Number Levels 3 and 4.
AT Measure Levels 3 and 4.

AIMS AND OBJECTIVES

The main objective of the chapter is to exercise the following skills:

(i) ordering numbers
(ii) calculating intermediate values
(iii) reading values from a scale, up to two decimal places
(iv) using negative temperatures
(v) finding equivalences in measures, using scales when two different units are used.

A secondary aim is to familiarise the students with the everyday contexts in which scales appear.

NOTES

Much of this work can be enhanced and reinforced by practical work.

TEACHER'S RESOURCES

Worksheets 1 to 4 provide students with ready-made scales to avoid too many time-consuming 'copy and complete' exercises.
More Practice 1: Temperatures Below Zero is designed to provide extra practice in reading negative temperatures and as an introduction to 'adding' and 'subtracting' on a numberline, without formalising it as such.
More Practice 2: Special Agent 003 provides extra work involving above and below sea-level, and should be accessable to the majority of Foundation students, whilst going beyond the usual contexts used in Foundation.
More Practice 3: Comparing Scales is designed as a bridge to General Level and will be beyond the capability of many of the students.

PROGRESS ROUTE

Success at the check-up should allow students to attempt *Book 3A* Review: Numbers 1, page 26 question 10, page 27 question 1, and page 29 questions 11 to 16.

Worksheet 1

Early Flight

1 Use the time-scale to complete the sentences below.

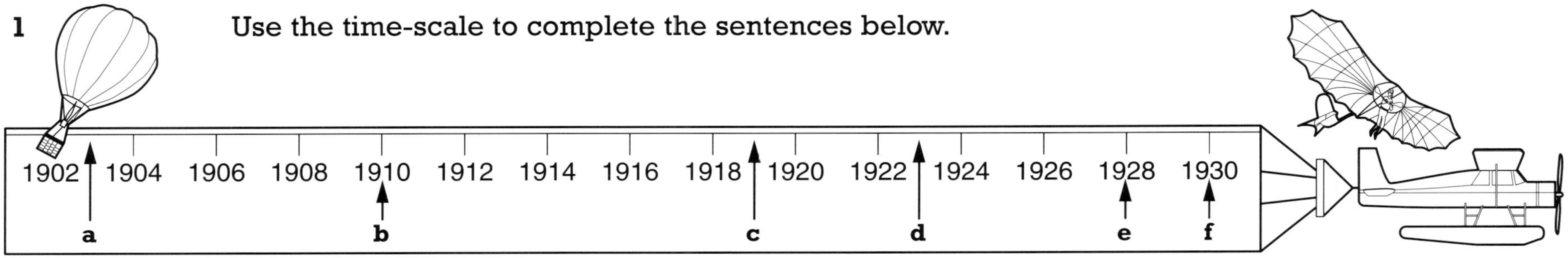

a The first flight by Wilbur and Orville Wright was in ....
b The first commercial airline (an airship) was established by Count Zeppelin in ....
c The first non-stop transatlantic aeroplane flight was in ....
d The first autogyro flight was in ....
e The first transatlantic passenger flight was in ....
f Amy Johnson became the first woman to fly solo from England to Australia in ....

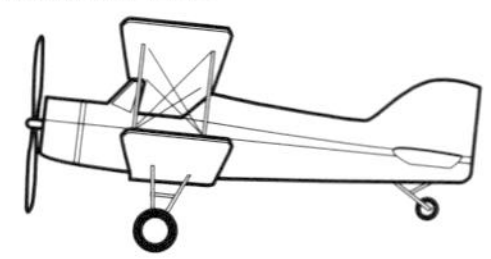

Animal Speed Records

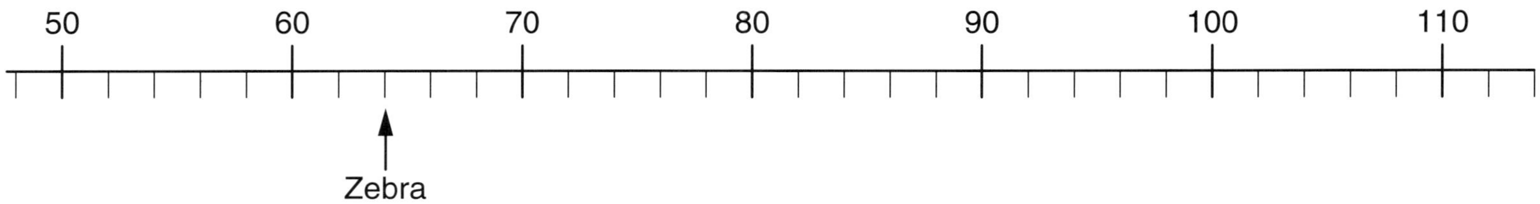

2 The speed records for some animals are given below.

Put an arrow and the animal's name on the scale to show how fast each can travel.

The first one has been done for you.

a zebra 64 km/h
b lion 80 km/h
c rabbit 55 km/h
d cheetah 105 km/h
e giraffe 51 km/h
f sailfish 109 km/h
g antelope 97 km/h
h grizzly bear 48 km/h

Worksheet 2

Sometimes only part of a scale is shown.
You must work out what each small step is worth, as you did before.

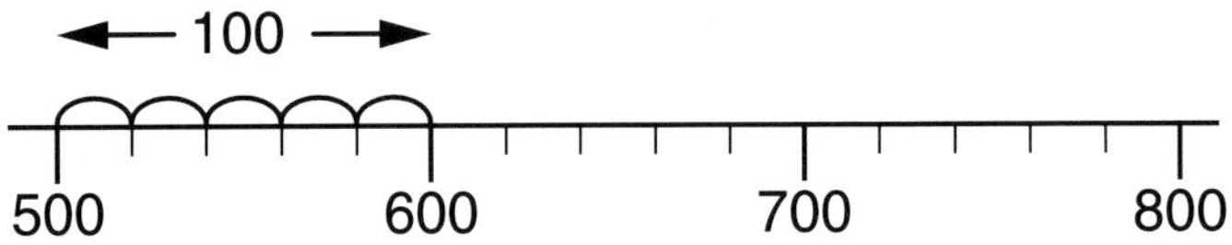

To get from 500 to 600 takes five steps.
Each 100 is divided into five parts.
100 ÷ 5 = 20
Each small step is worth 20.

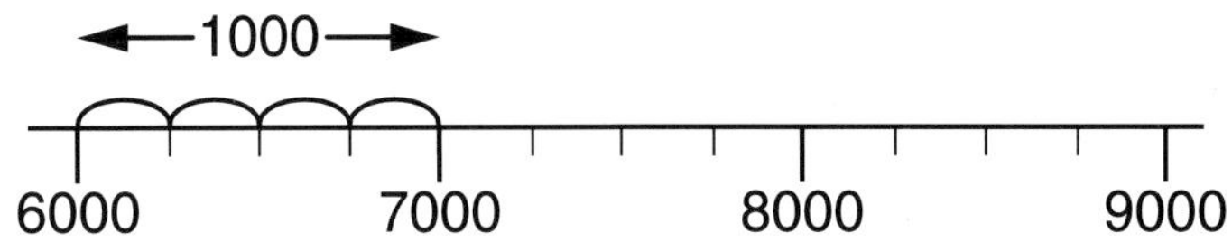

Each 1000 is divided into four parts.
1000 ÷ 4 = 250
Each small step is worth 250.

Write down the number to which each arrow points.

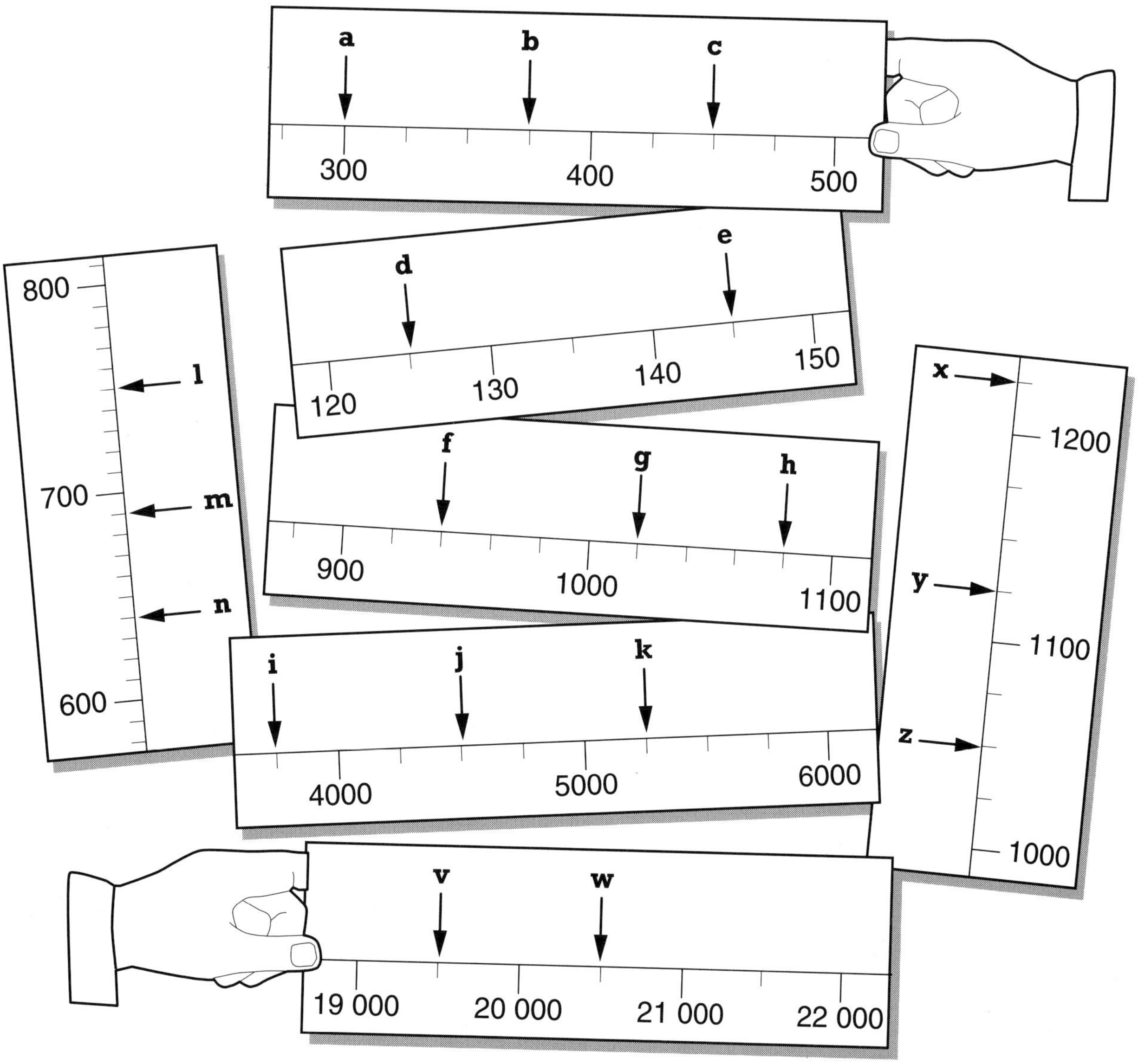

Worksheet 3

Put an arrow and the letter beside it to represent each number.

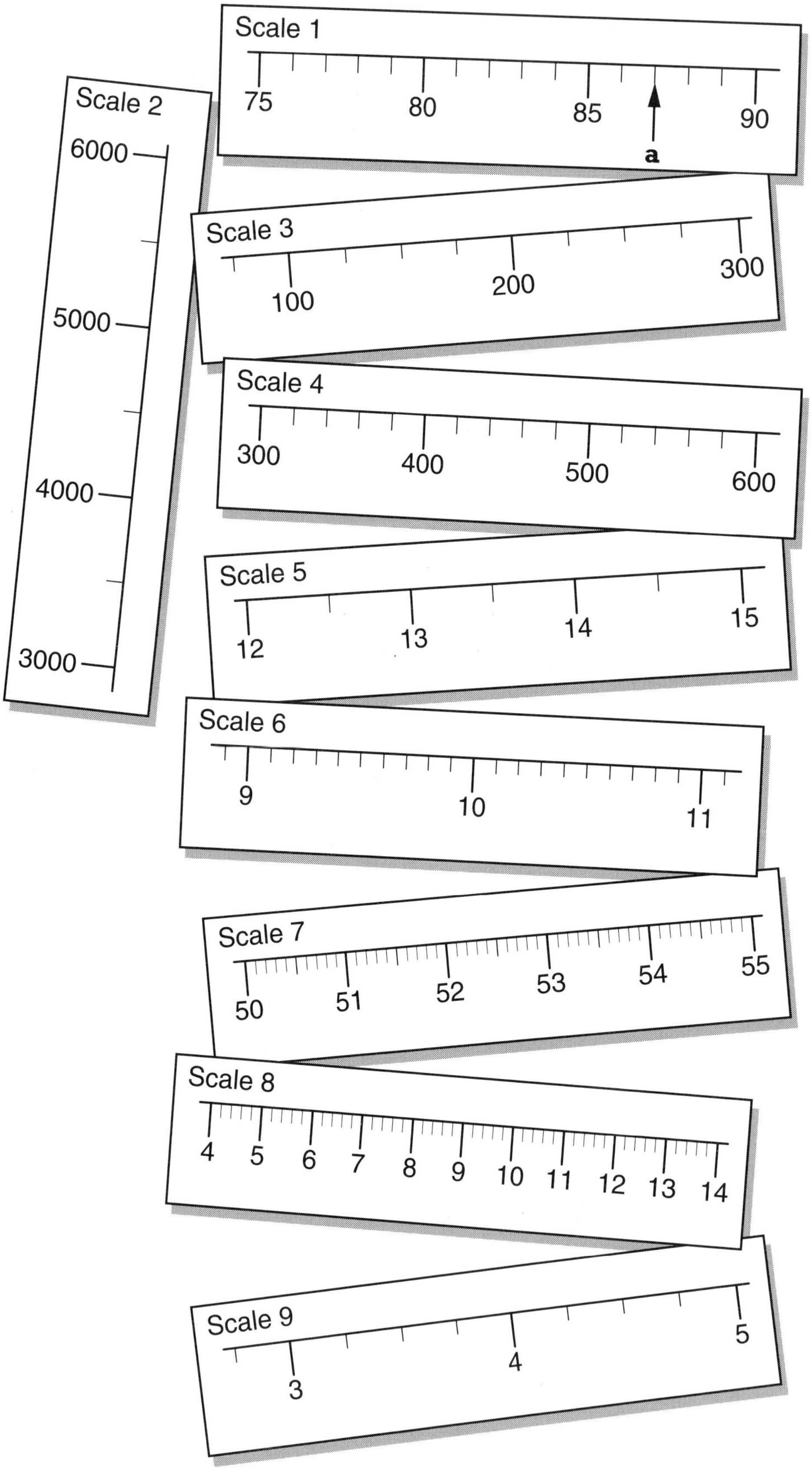

On Scale 1, show:
- **a** 87
- **b** 76
- **c** 89.

On Scale 2, show:
- **d** 4000
- **e** 5500
- **f** 3250.

On Scale 3, show:
- **g** 250
- **h** 125
- **i** 75.

On Scale 4, show:
- **j** 440
- **k** 320
- **l** 550.

On Scale 5, show:
- **m** 14.5.

On Scale 6, show:
- **n** 9.6
- **o** 10.5
- **p** 8.9.

On Scale 7, show:
- **q** 53.5
- **r** 51.1
- **s** 50.4.

On Scale 8, show:
- **t** 12.4
- **u** 13.6
- **v** 4.2
- **w** 8.5.

On Scale 9, show:
- **x** 4.5
- **y** 3.25
- **z** 4.75.

Worksheet 4

1

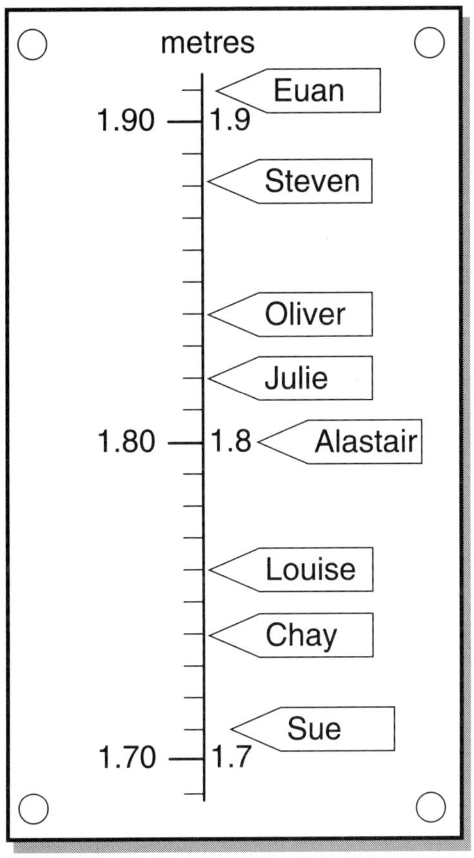

A group of friends measured their heights. They recorded them on a wall chart.

Complete the table listing their heights.

Name	**Height**
Chay	1.74 metres
Oliver	
Alastair	
Julie	
Euan	
Louise	
Steven	
Sue	

2 Rachel and her friends measured their heights.

Show their heights on the wall chart. Ailidh's height has been put on already.

Name	**Height**
Rachel	1.62 metres
Alan	1.54 metres
Miranda	1.46 metres
Claire	1.38 metres
Fiona	1.40 metres
Marian	1.55 metres
Ailidh	1.48 metres
Sarah	1.51 metres

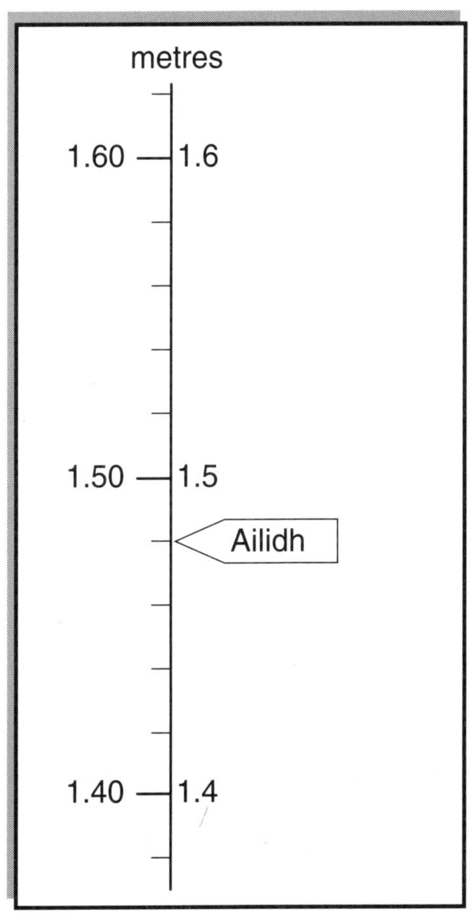

More Practice 1: Temperatures Below Zero

1 This chart shows the temperature in degrees Celsius in Newbury during a 24-hour period.

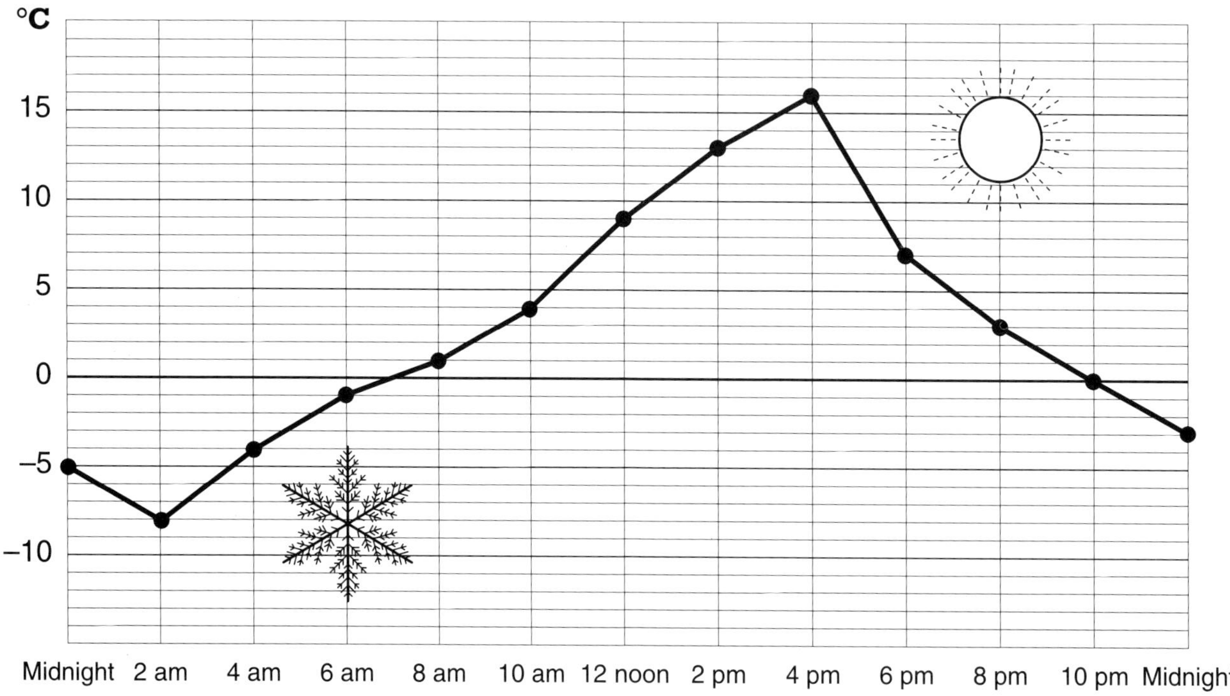

a What was the temperature in Newbury when the first reading was taken?
b What was the temperature at 4 am?
c What was the **maximum** temperature recorded that day?
d What was the **minimum** temperature recorded?
e At what **two** times during the day was the temperature **0 °C**?

2

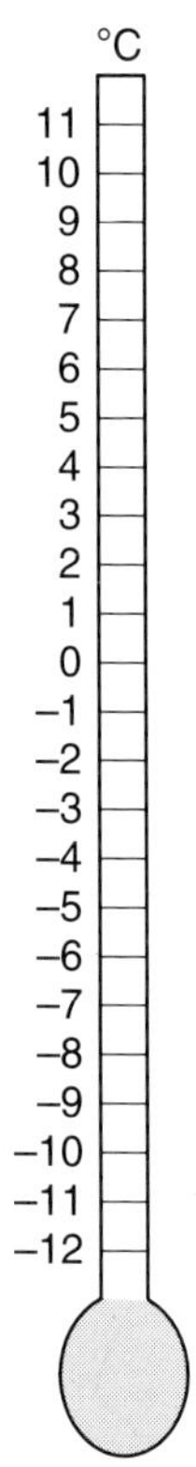

Use the thermometer to help you answer these questions.

a Which is warmer, –2 °C or –5 °C?
b Which is colder, 4 °C or –1 °C?
c Put these temperatures in order, starting with the coldest:
5 °C, –3 °C, –5 °C, 0 °C, 3 °C, –1°C.
d It is 2 °C. The temperature drops 3°. What is the new temperature?
e It is –3°C. The temperature rises 2°. What is the new temperature?
f It is 0 °C. The temperature drops 4°. What is the new temperature?
g Here are some more examples. Copy and complete the table.

Starting temperature	What happens	New temperature
5 °C	drops 4°	
1 °C	drops 3°	
–1 °C	rises 4°	
–6 °C	rises 3°	
0 °C	drops 10°	

More Practice 2: Special Agent 003

Special Agent 003 has a machine which can fly through the air and can operate under water. She starts her journey at point A.

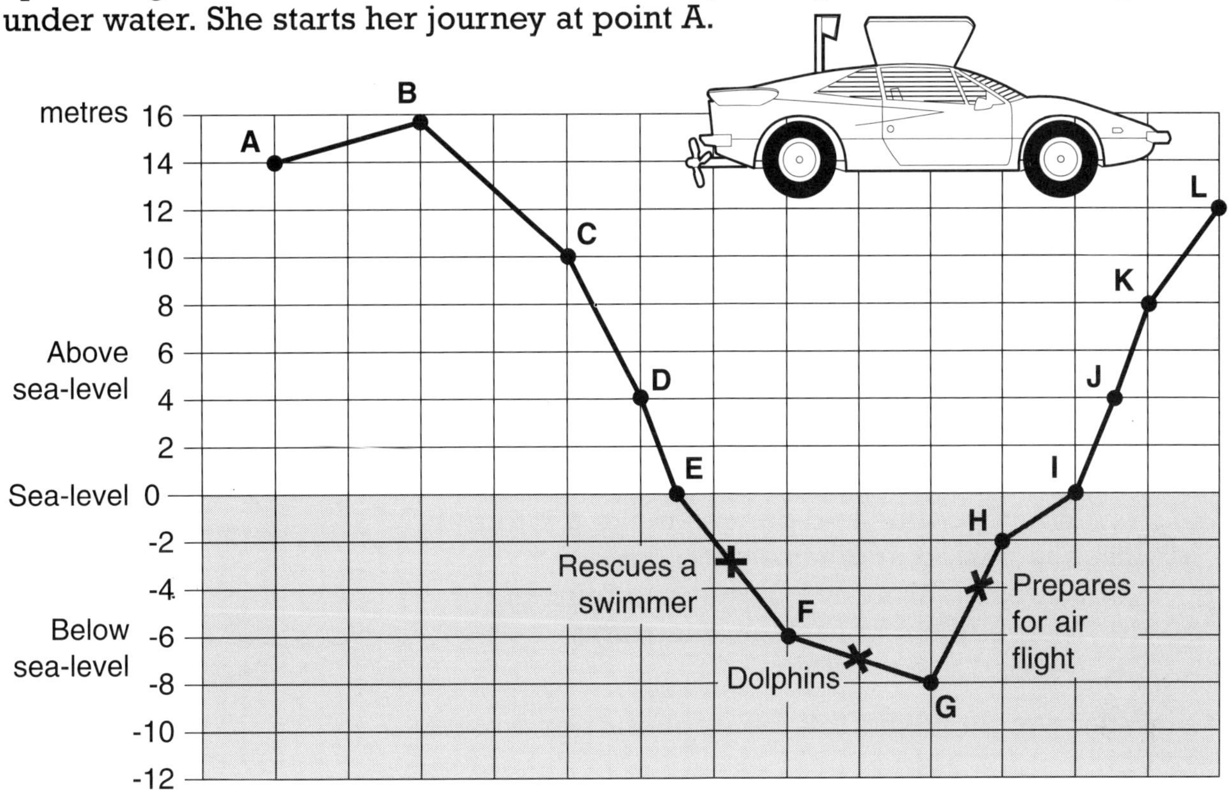

1 How high is Special Agent 003 at point A?

2 How many metres does she climb through to point B?

3 How many metres does she fall through from point C to point D?

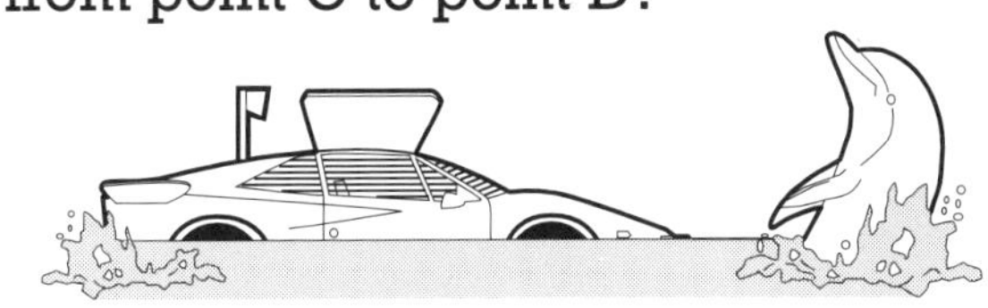

4 At what point does she enter the sea?

5 How deep does Special Agent 003 go?

6 At what depth are the dolphins swimming?

7 At what depth does she rescue the swimmer?

8 At what point is Special Agent 003 6 metres below sea-level?

9 At what depth does she prepare for air flight?

10 Name a point which is at 0 metres above sea-level.

11 How many metres lower is point F than point B?

12 How many metres does Special Agent 003 climb through between H and L?

More Practice 3: Comparing Scales

1 Weight can be measured in pounds or kilograms.

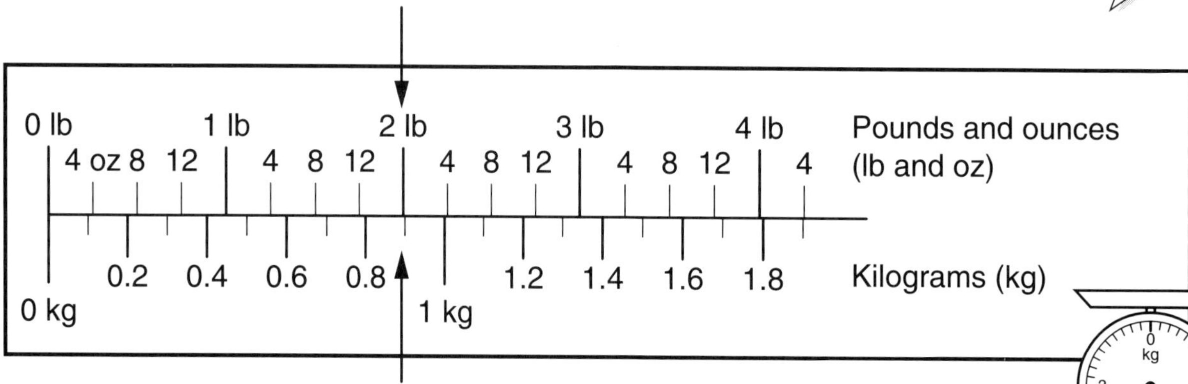

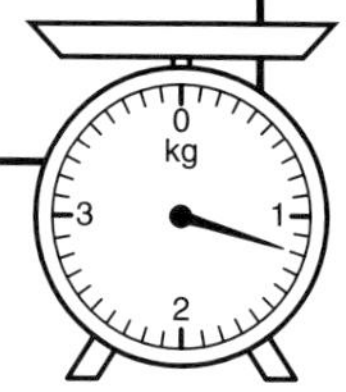

2 lb is almost the same weight as 0.9 kg.

a Convert 4 lb to kilograms.

b How many pounds and ounces make a kilogram?

c Susan is baking and has a problem.
Her scales measure in pounds and ounces.
Her recipe gives weights in kilograms.
She needs 1.1 kg of flour.

What weight would that be in pounds and ounces?

d 

Kenneth has the opposite problem.
He has scales that measure in kilograms,
but his recipe uses pounds and ounces.
How much of a kilogram of rice should he
measure out if the recipe says 4 ounces?

2 Temperature can be measured in degrees Celsius or degrees Fahrenheit.
The scale below compares the two.

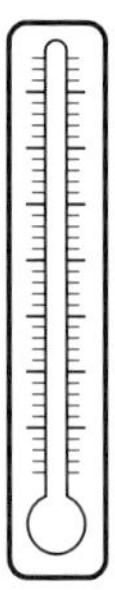

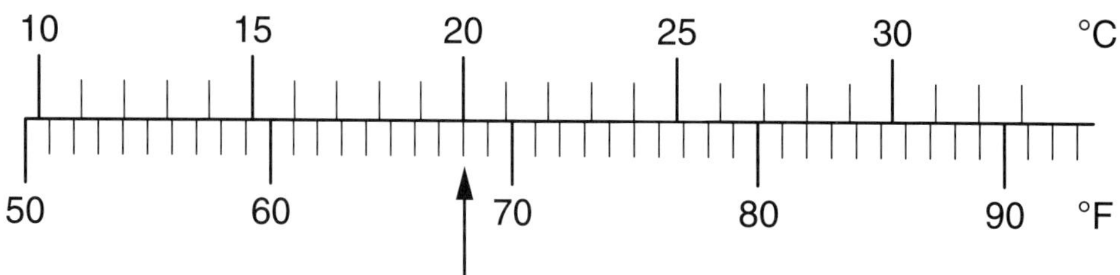

Here we can see that 20 °C is the same temperature as 68 °F.

Use these scales to answer the following questions.

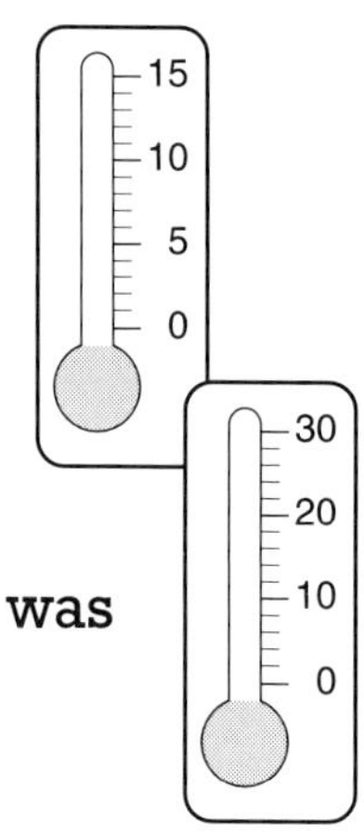

a What is 80 °F in Celsius temperature?

b 16 °C is the same as which Fahrenheit temperature?

c The weather girl said that it would be 28 °C tomorrow.
What is that temperature in degrees Fahrenheit?

d The travel agent said that in Malta in July the temperature was expected to be somewhere between 75 °F and 89 °F.
What Celsius temperatures are these the same as?

6 FRACTIONS AND PERCENTAGES

CURRICULUM COVERAGE

Standard Grade Guidelines
Foundation Level:
Fractions as an operator, normally unit numerators.
Percentage of a quantity.
Equivalence of percentage and fraction.
Profit, loss, discount and VAT.
General Level:
Converting fractions to decimals; equivalence.
Addition and subtraction.
Expressing one quantity as a percentage of another.

National Curriculum
AT 2 Levels 4 and 5.

NI Curriculum
AT Number Levels 5 and 6.

AIMS AND OBJECTIVES
To strengthen the students' awareness of fractions in some simple contexts.
To enable students to see the relationship between fractions in vulgar, decimal and percentage forms.

NOTES

1 Most of the fractions have unit numerators but there are some simple exceptions.

2 Algorithms for using a calculator to evaluate a fraction of a quantity depend on using a calculator programmed with the priorities, for example:
   - $1 \div 3 \times 6$ yields 1.9999999 on a simple arithmetic calculator but gives the answer 2 on a scientific one;
   - $6 \times 1 \div 3$ will always give the correct answer, but the first method follows more naturally from the expression 'a third of six'.

3 The rules of the game are for the teacher who should supervise early attempts. Students should recognise the equivalences before they are allowed to move on them.

TEACHER'S RESOURCES
More Practice 1-3 can be used to strengthen basic skills.
The 'Fractions on the Calculator' sheet will extend the work into General Level.
The 'Extension Work' sheet also includes General Level material.
The 'Diving Dice' game is intended to strengthen some simple well known equivalences.

PROGRESS ROUTE
The extension work on the calculator should enable some students to attempt Chapter 1 in *Book 3A.*

More Practice 1

1 Work out the following:

a $\frac{1}{2}$ of 64 **b** $\frac{1}{3}$ of 93 **c** $\frac{1}{4}$ of 52 **d** $\frac{1}{5}$ of 85
e $\frac{1}{6}$ of 102 **f** $\frac{1}{7}$ of 91 **g** $\frac{1}{8}$ of 96 **h** $\frac{1}{9}$ of 117
i $\frac{1}{10}$ of 320 **j** $\frac{1}{11}$ of 132 **k** $\frac{1}{12}$ of 156 **l** $\frac{1}{13}$ of 130

2 James had collected only silver coins in his piggy bank.

There were no 50p pieces.

He counted 114 coins.

a $\frac{1}{2}$ were 5p coins. What is $\frac{1}{2}$ of 114?
b $\frac{1}{6}$ were 10p coins. How many 10p coins did he have?
c $\frac{1}{3}$ were 20p coins. How many is that?
d Add up all your answers to check all the coins are counted.

3

On a trip to the seaside 60 pupils were given a choice of ice lollies.

a $\frac{1}{2}$ chose lemon flavour. What is $\frac{1}{2}$ of 60?
b $\frac{1}{15}$ chose cola flavour. What is $\frac{1}{15}$ of 60?
c $\frac{1}{10}$ chose strawberry. How many is this?
d $\frac{1}{3}$ chose orange. How many pupils chose orange?
e Add up all your answers to check they all got a lolly.

4 In a survey about bed-times, all 600 pupils in a school said when they went to bed.

a $\frac{1}{20}$ went before 9 pm. What is $\frac{1}{20}$ of 600?
b $\frac{1}{5}$ went between 9 pm and 10 pm. What is $\frac{1}{5}$ of 600?
c $\frac{1}{2}$ went between 10 pm and 11 pm. How many is this?
d $\frac{1}{6}$ went between 11 pm and 12 midnight. How many is this?
e $\frac{1}{12}$ went after midnight. How many pupils went to bed after midnight?
f Add up all your answers to check that no-one has been missed.

More Practice 2

1

Nial had £1.20 pocket money.

The diagram shows how he spent it.

a How much money did he spend on:

(i) the comic (ii) the juice
(iii) sweets (iv) the bus?

b How much did he give to charity?
c Add all the answers together to check that he spent all his money.

2 Express each percentage as a fraction.

a 30% **b** 3% **c** 27% **d** 61% **e** 36% **f** 70%
g 83% **h** 4% **i** 8% **j** 50% **k** 72% **l** 96%

3 Write each percentage as a decimal fraction.

a 5% **b** 7% **c** 9% **d** 11% **e** 38% **f** 45%
g 74% **h** 64% **i** 88% **j** 41% **k** 1% **l** 86%

4 Work out:

a 5% of 90 **b** 18% of 150 **c** 96% of 100 **d** 11% of 1000
e 28% of 200 **f** 60% of 500 **g** 16% of 80 **h** 66% of 700
i 8% of 50 **j** 52% of 25 **k** 25% of 20 **l** 80% of 5

5 The school office took 50 phonecalls today.

a 20% were complaints. How many is that?
b 50% were about pupils who were ill. How many were ill?
c 6% were from teachers who were ill. How many teachers were ill?

6

A farmer collected his free-range eggs.

40% were size 3.
25% were size 2.
15% were size 1.
The rest were size 4.

If he collected 20 eggs how many of each size did he get?

7 At a café 150 people took tea.

18% added milk only. 38% added sugar only.
26% added milk and sugar. The rest took it black.

Work out how many of each type there were.

More Practice 3

1

Work out:

a the discount on each item
b the new price of each item.

2 A supermarket advertised its prices as shown.

Prices went up by 4%.

Work out:

a the increase on each price
b the new price of each item.

3

Some of your wages are taxed.

The taxman takes 25% of this money.

How much tax will the taxman take from:

a £10 000 **b** £2000 **c** £1200 **d** £800 **e** £4000?

4 VAT is added to many prices.

17.5% is added to each price.

How much VAT do you pay on the following prices?

a £500 **b** £22 **c** £86 **d** £124

5 Copy and complete these bills:

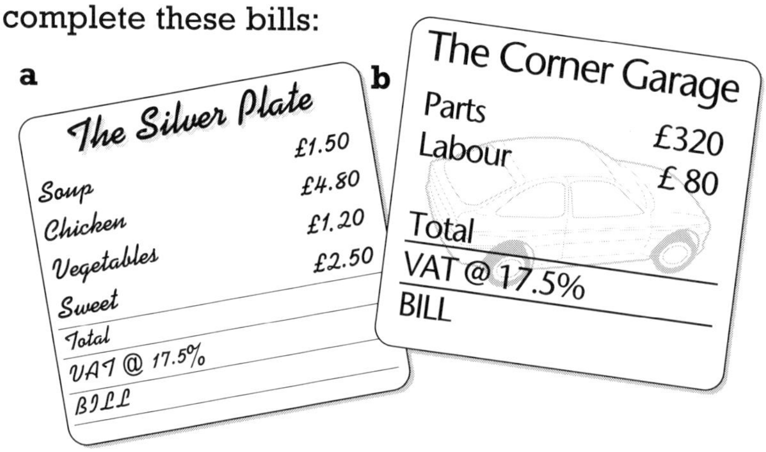

Fractions on the Calculator

[a b/c] If your calculator has this button, then you can use it to do fractions.

Simplest Form

Example

To find the simplest form of $\frac{27}{81}$

27 [a b/c] 81 [=] gives 1⌐3 — so $\frac{27}{81} = \frac{1}{3}$

1 Use your calculator to find the simplest form of:

a $\frac{7}{77}$ **b** $\frac{9}{90}$ **c** $\frac{5}{45}$ **d** $\frac{9}{54}$ **e** $\frac{7}{56}$

f $\frac{15}{20}$ **g** $\frac{18}{30}$ **h** $\frac{15}{50}$ **i** $\frac{25}{100}$ **j** $\frac{20}{100}$

Adding

Example

To calculate $\frac{1}{12} + \frac{1}{6}$

1 [a b/c] 12 [+] 1 [a b/c] 6 gives 1⌐4 — so $\frac{1}{12} + \frac{1}{6} = \frac{1}{4}$

2 Add the following:

a $\frac{1}{6} + \frac{1}{30}$ **b** $\frac{1}{12} + \frac{1}{24}$ **c** $\frac{1}{12} + \frac{1}{36}$ **d** $\frac{1}{20} + \frac{1}{30}$

e $\frac{1}{2} + \frac{1}{6}$ **f** $\frac{1}{3} + \frac{1}{15}$ **g** $\frac{2}{3} + \frac{1}{6}$ **h** $\frac{3}{4} + \frac{2}{3}$

3 

Akim ate $\frac{1}{4}$ of the pie. Bev ate $\frac{1}{12}$ of the pie.
Colin ate $\frac{1}{9}$ of the pie. Diane ate $\frac{1}{18}$ of the pie.
Calculate: $\frac{1}{4} + \frac{1}{12} + \frac{1}{9} + \frac{1}{18}$ to find what fraction of the pie was eaten.

Subtracting

4 Subtract the following:

a $\frac{1}{2} - \frac{1}{6}$ **b** $\frac{1}{3} - \frac{1}{12}$ **c** $\frac{1}{4} - \frac{1}{12}$ **d** $\frac{1}{6} - \frac{1}{18}$

e $\frac{1}{3} - \frac{1}{9}$ **f** $\frac{1}{3} - \frac{1}{21}$ **g** $\frac{3}{4} - \frac{1}{8}$ **h** $\frac{4}{5} - \frac{2}{3}$

5 A TV programme lasted for $\frac{3}{4}$ of an hour.
$\frac{1}{3}$ of an hour was spent on adverts.
$\frac{3}{4} - \frac{1}{3}$ = the time spent on the actual show.
How long was the show?

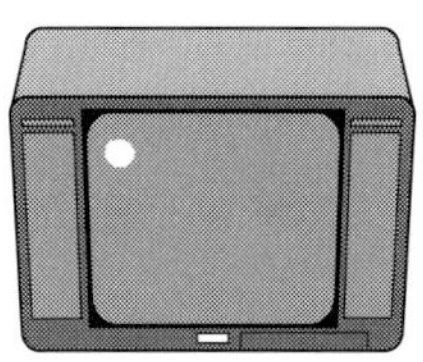

Extension Work

Example

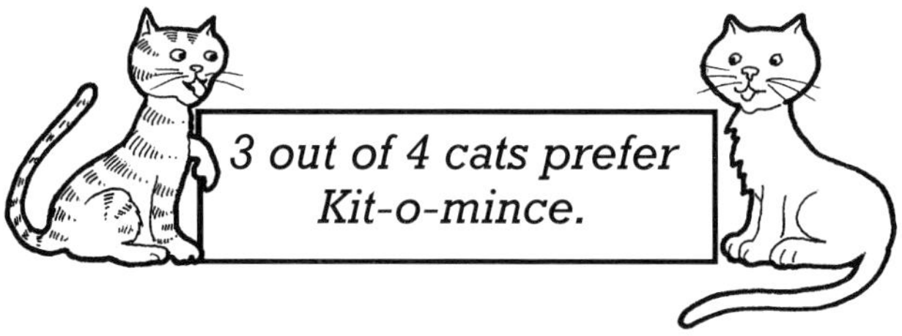

What percentage likes Kit-o-mince?
$3 \div 4 \times 100 = 75\%$

1 20 out of 50 pupils take the bus.

What percentage take the bus?

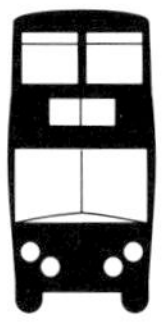

2 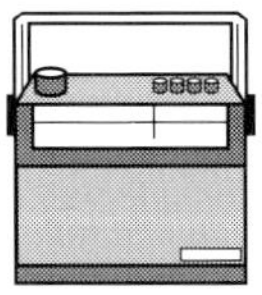

4 out of 12 listeners tune in to Radio 7.

What percentage of listeners tune in to Radio 7?

3 60 of the 80 motorists asked said they used unleaded petrol.

What percentage of motorists used unleaded petrol?

4 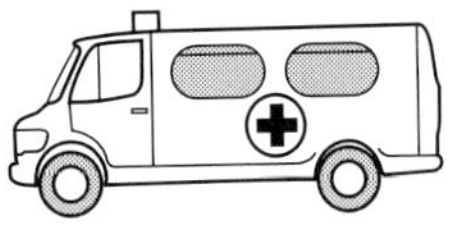

14 out of 20 accidents happen at home.

What percentage of accidents happen at home?

5 **a** 3 motorists out of 15 asked said they had a car phone.
Give this as a percentage.

b 6 of the 15 had a new car.
What percentage is this?

6 

a Graham sat a test in October. He scored 56 out of 80.
Calculate $56 \div 80 \times 100$ to turn his mark into a percentage.

b He sat another test in December.
He scored 48 out of 64.

(i) Turn this into a percentage mark.
(ii) Did he do better or worse?

7 Turn the following exam marks into percentages.

a 12 out of 48 **b** 28 out of 35 **c** 35 out of 56 **d** 86 out of 200

DIVING DICE

Preparation
Photocopy the game board, dice nets, counters and dice cup onto card. Cut out and assemble the dice and dice cup.

Dice nets

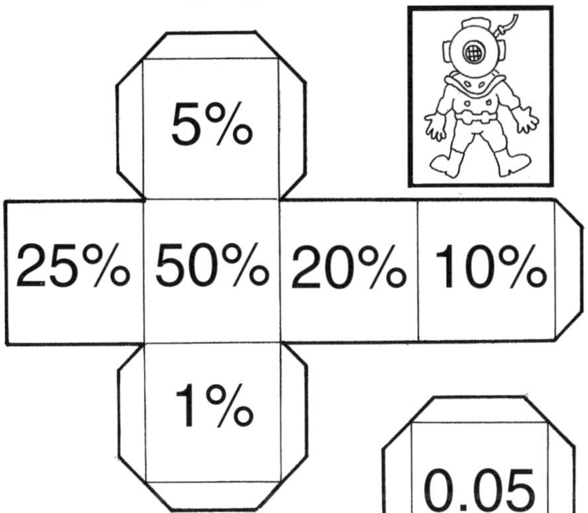

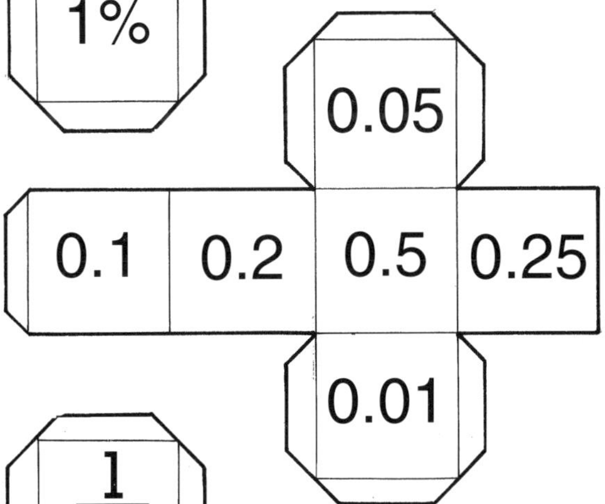

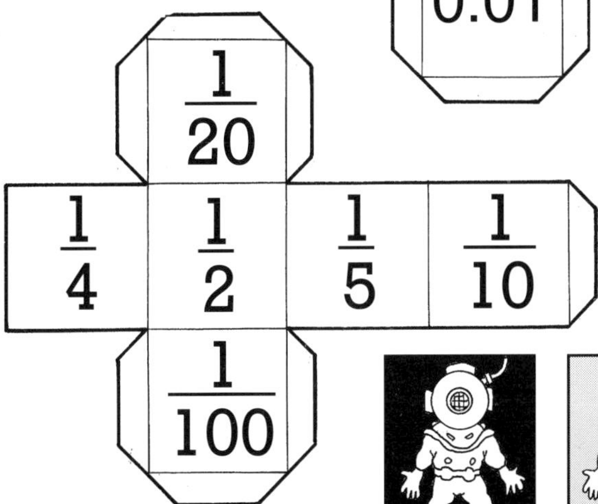

Counters

Game board

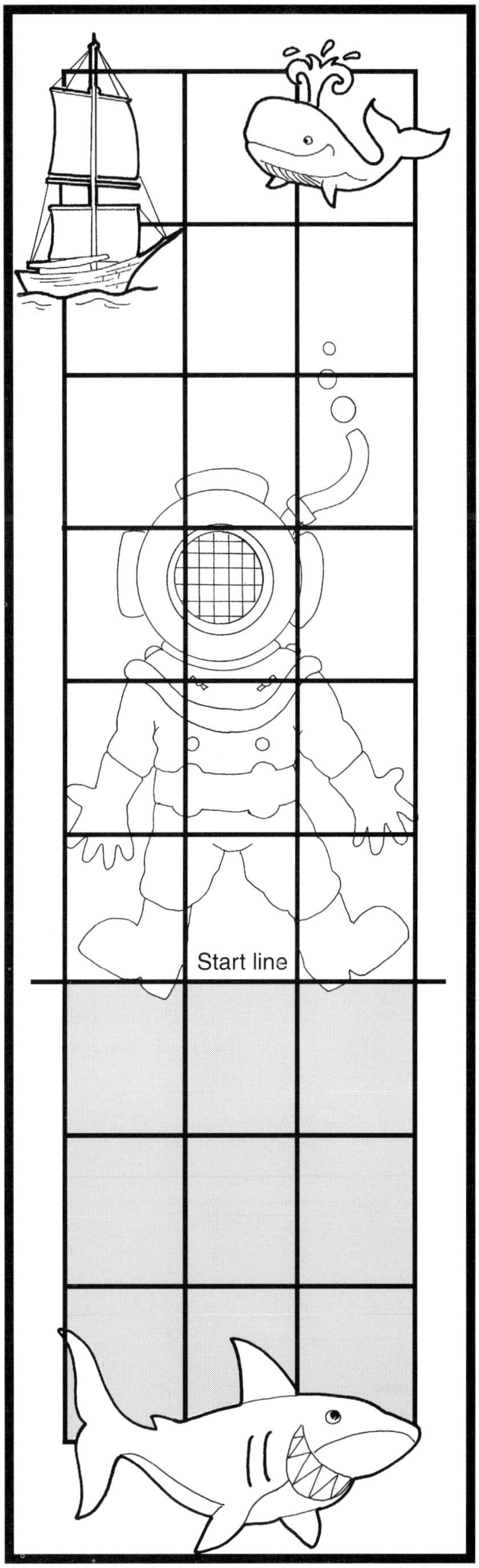

Rules
Each player puts his/her counter on the start line.
The first player throws all three dice.
If the player scores two equivalences (e.g. 50% and 0.5), then he/she moves up 2 squares.
If the player scores 3 equivalences, he/she moves up 3 squares.
If the player scores no equivalences, he/she moves down 1 square.
The dice are then passed to the next player.
If a player hits the bottom square he/she is eaten by the shark and is out.
The winner is the first to reach the top of the board or the last survivor.

Dice cup

7 ANGLE

CURRICULUM COVERAGE

Standard Grade Guidelines

Foundation Level:
Measure and draw angles.
Number of degrees in a right angle, straight angle and a full turn.
Angle sum of a triangle. Using these to calculate angles.

National Curriculum

AT 3 Levels 2, 3 and 5.

NI Curriculum

AT Shape and Space Levels 4 and 5.
At Measure Level 5.

AIMS AND OBJECTIVES

To provide appropriate activities and practice on measuring and calculating angles.
To consolidate earlier work.

NOTES

1 The More Practice sheets can be photo-enlarged for students who are experiencing difficulty with measurement.
2 A 360° protractor will help when measuring reflex angles.

TEACHER'S RESOURCES

More Practice 1 provides extra practice in measuring angles.
More Practice 2 gives additional work on measuring reflex angles. Students may use circular protractors or discuss strategies for measuring reflex angles using ordinary protractors after work with complete turn, i.e. reflex angle = 360 – measurable angle.
More Practice 3 contains extra practice on finding the missing angle (complementary and supplementary).
More Practice 4 also has extra practice on finding the missing angle, this time in complete turns.
'Vertically Opposites' and 'Angles and Parallels' provide extension work on vertically opposite and corresponding angles.
360° protractor templates (single scale) are supplied for copying onto acetate.

PROGRESS ROUTE

Success at the check-up would allow students to attempt the extension material provided and pages 12 and 13 in *Book 3A*.

More Practice 1

1 Use a protractor to measure each angle.

Record your results in the table.

Angle	Size
a	
b	
c	
d	
e	
f	

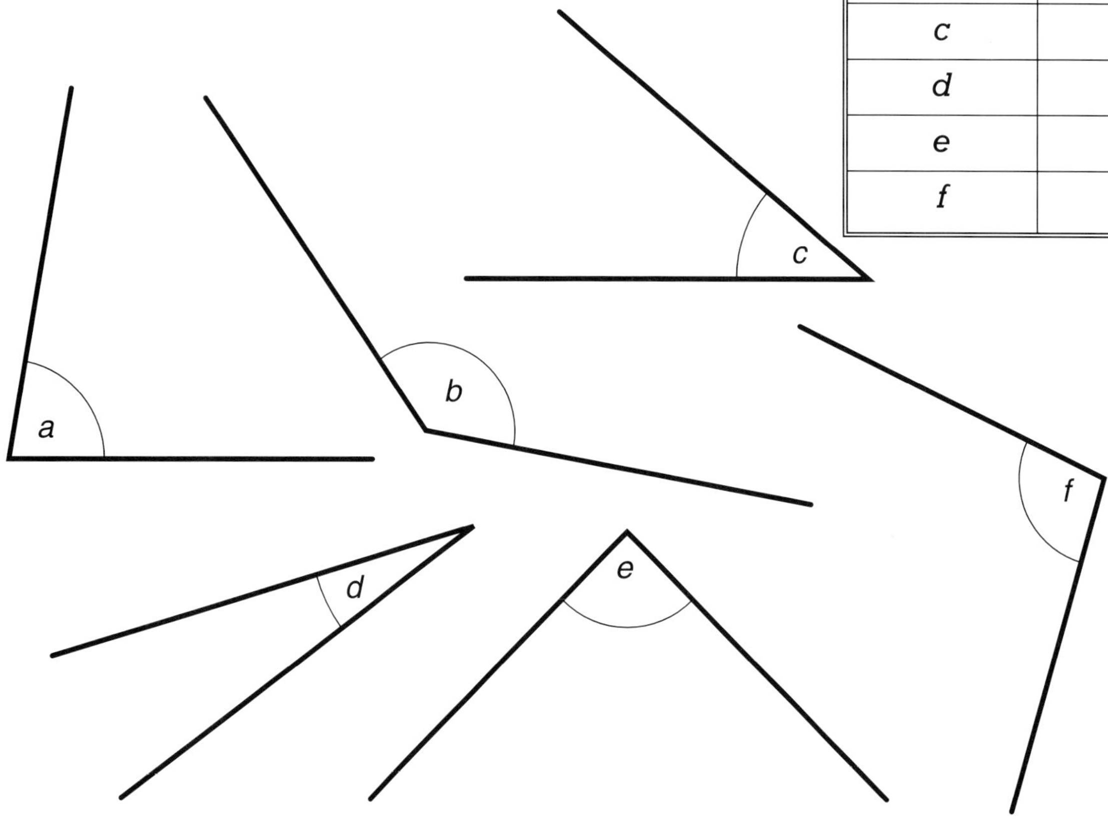

2 To avoid obstacles a robot needs to know the angles it must go round.

Measure each angle and complete the table.

Angle	Size
p	
q	
r	
s	
t	

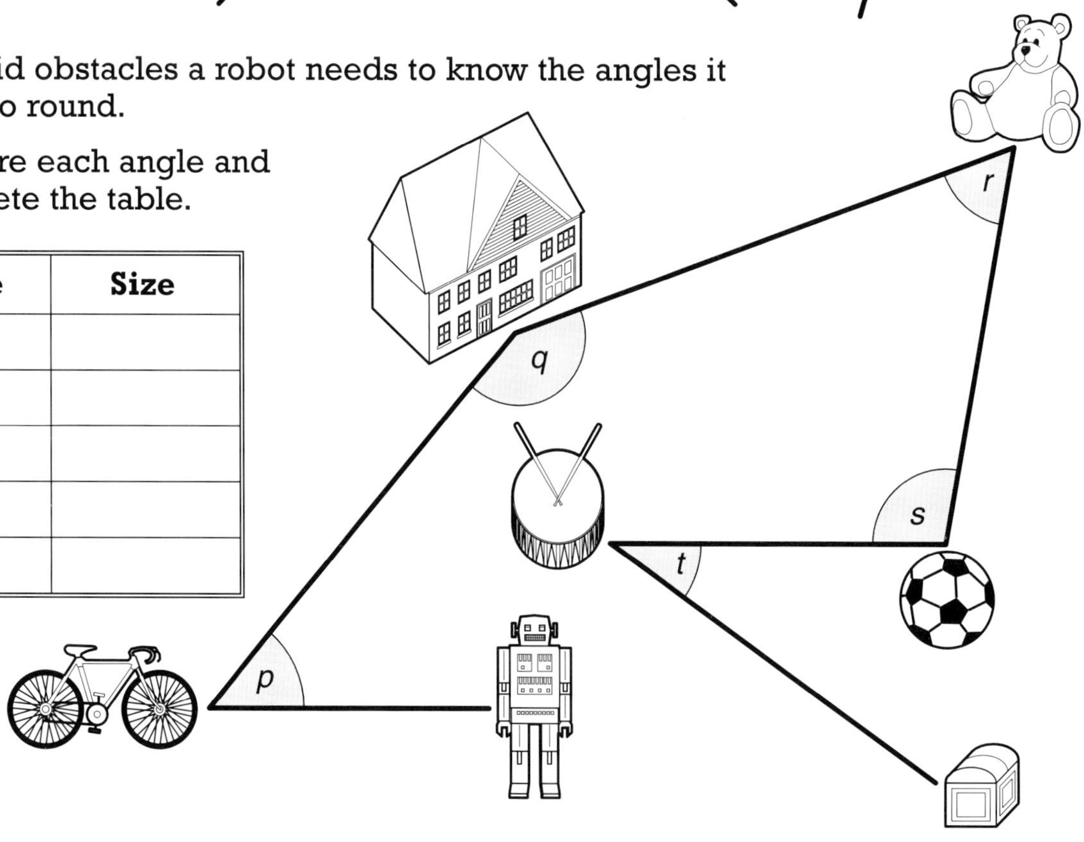

More Practice 2

1 Measure these reflex angles.

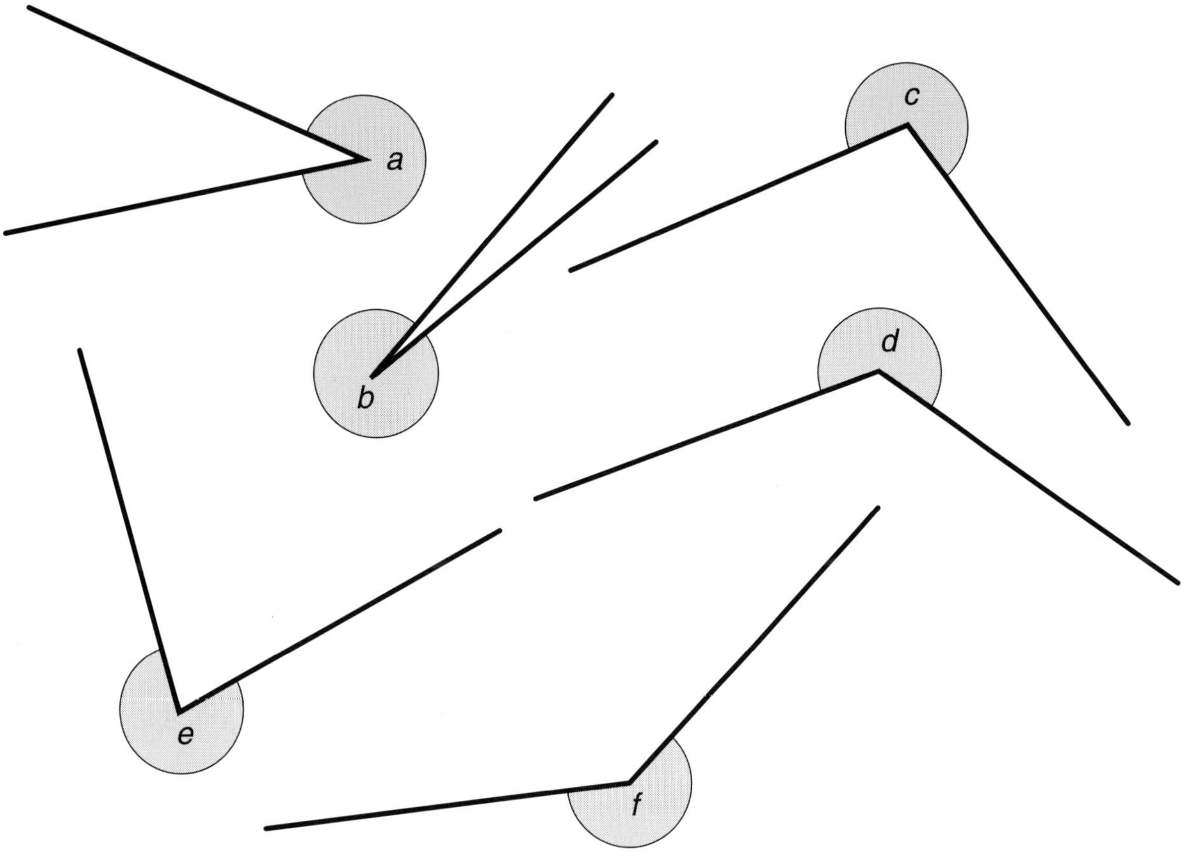

2 Making Christmas star decorations.

Measure the marked angles inside each star.

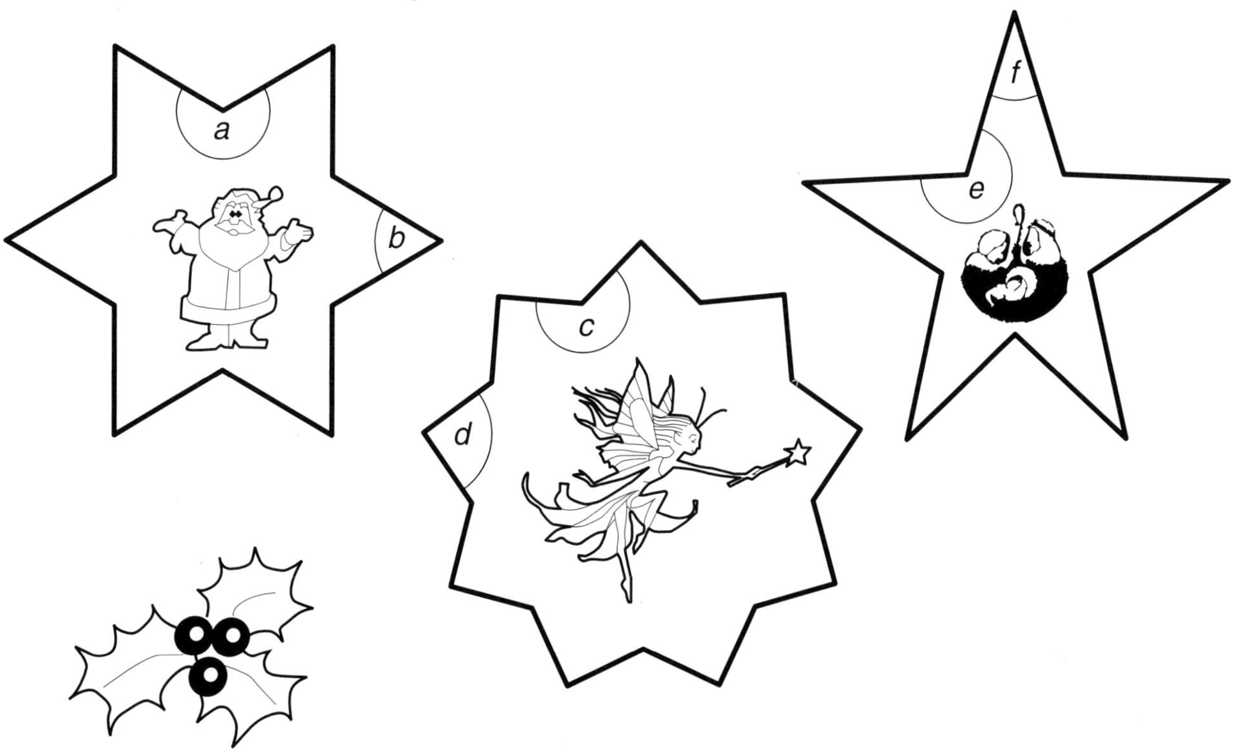

More Practice 3

Mike and his friends are camping.
Mike's camping knife has many uses.

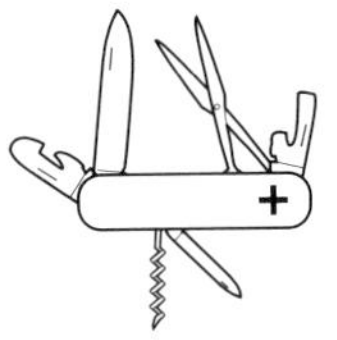

1 The peeler opens 180°.

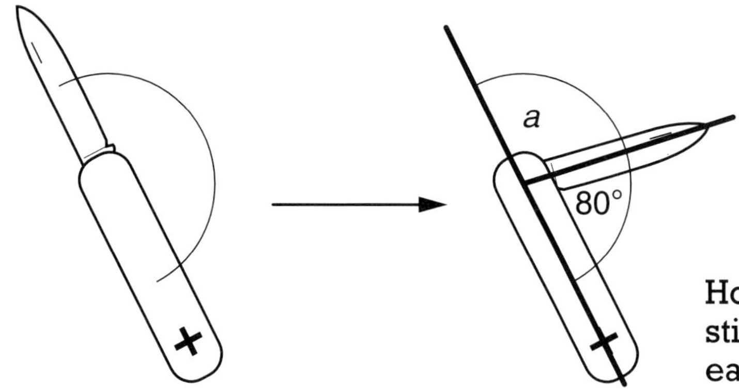

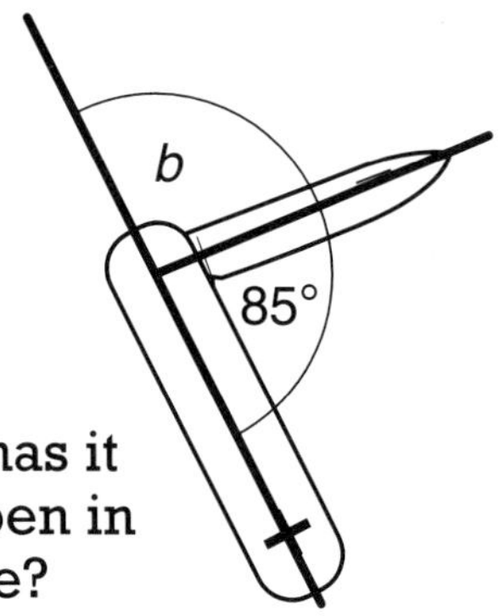

How far has it still to open in each case?

2 The nail-clippers also open out 180°.

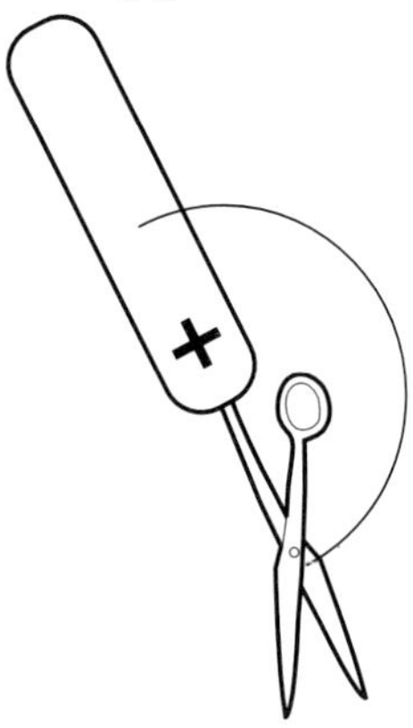

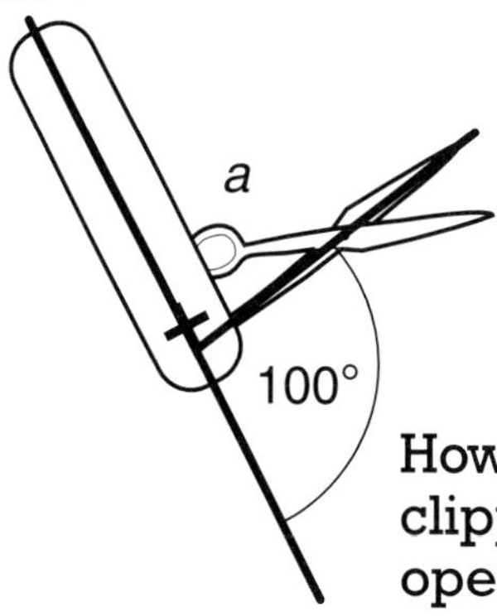

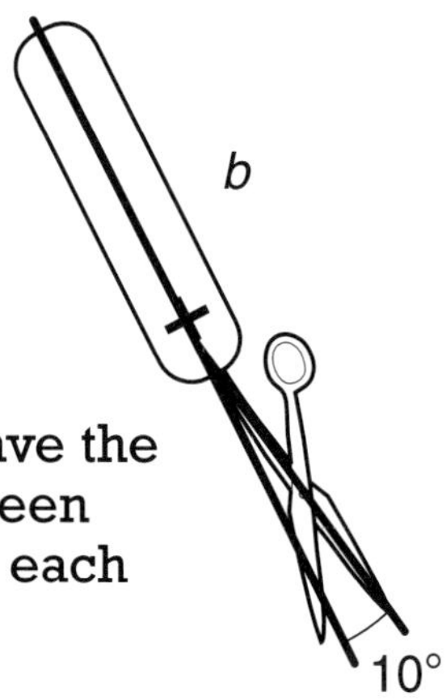

How far have the clippers been opened in each case?

3 The corkscrew only opens 90°.

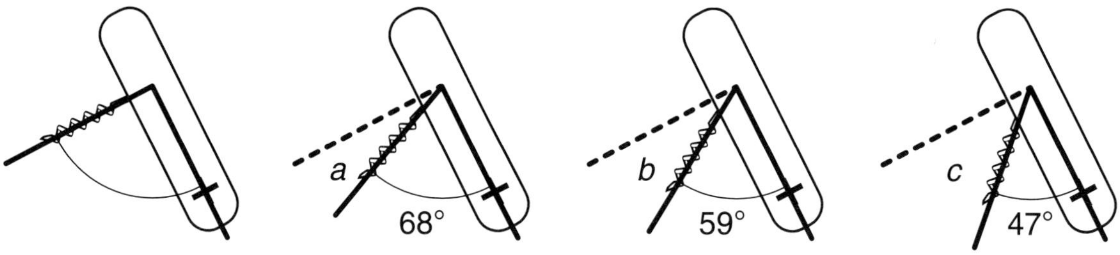

How far has it still to go in each case?

4

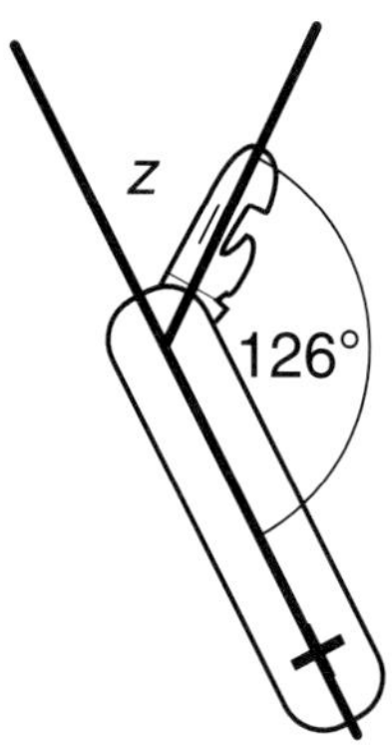

The bottle-opener should open through 180°.

How far has it still to go?

5

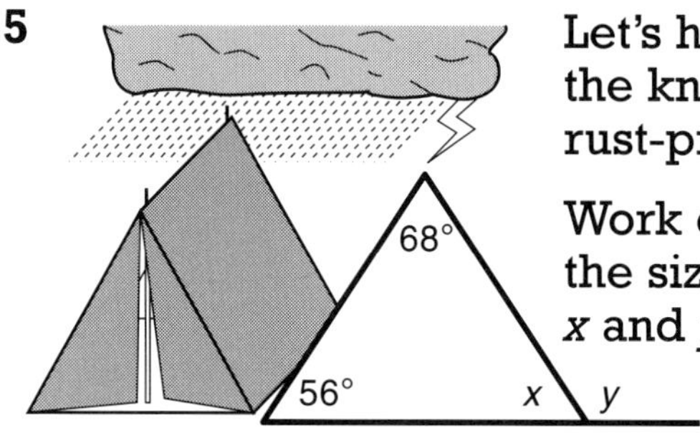

Let's hope the knife is rust-proof!

Work out the size of x and y.

More Practice 4

1 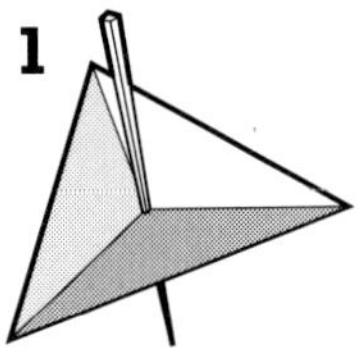

Tracey is making spinners.
Each segment has to be the same size if the spinners are to be fair.

Work out the size of the angles at the centre of each spinner.

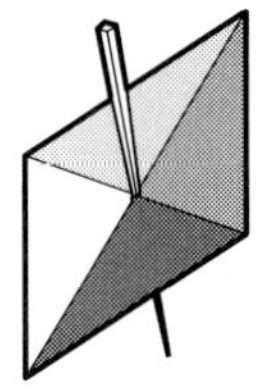

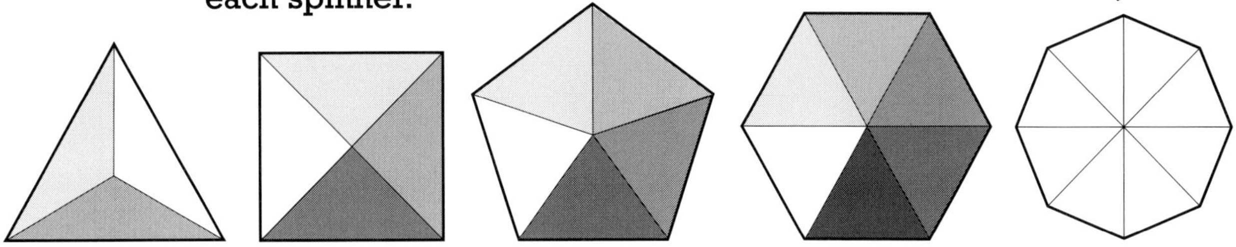

a Triangle **b** Square **c** Pentagon **d** Hexagon **e** Octagon

2 The heptagon is the basic shape of the 20p and 50p piece.

Work out the size of the angles at the centre to the nearest degree.

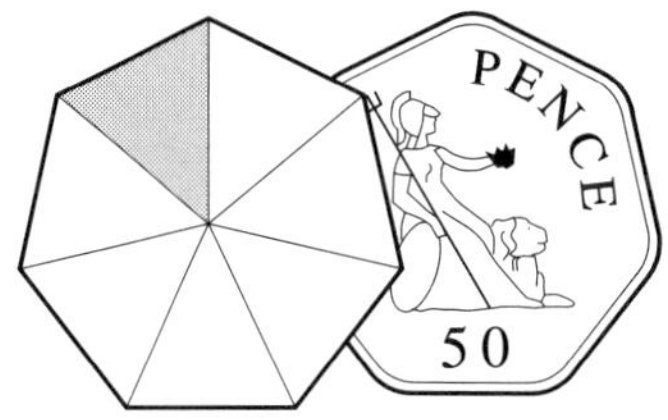

3 Find the size of the missing angle in each diagram.

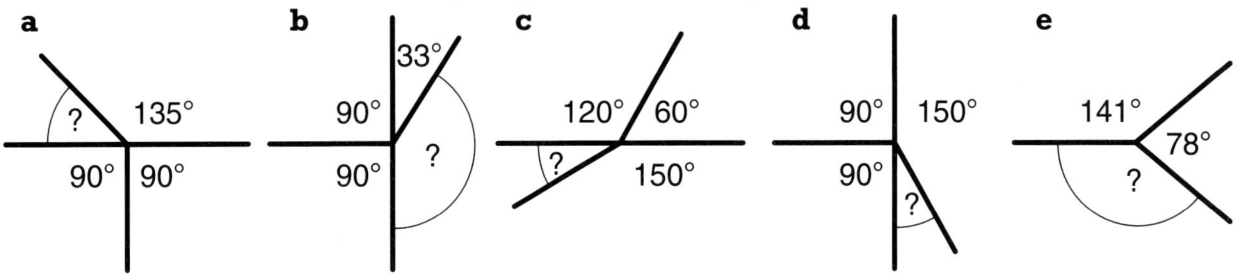

4 The wind makes the balloon pull at its mooring.

What is the size of the missing angle in the diagram?

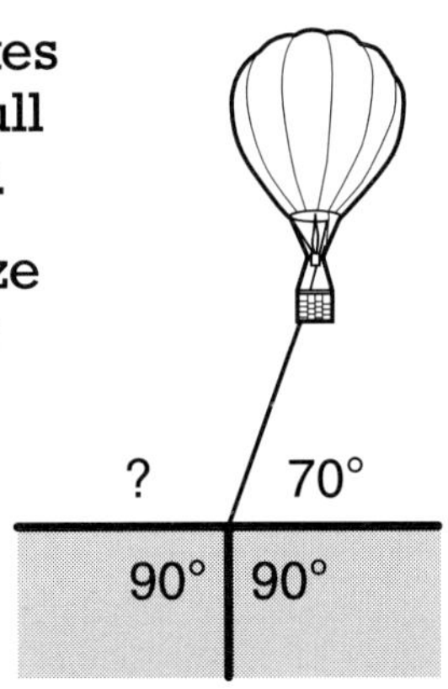

5 The spoon is being used to stir some soup.

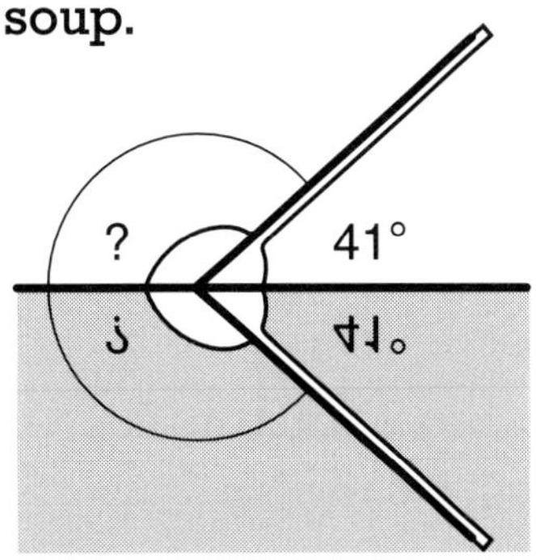

Its reflection shows in the soup.

What is the size of each marked angle?

6 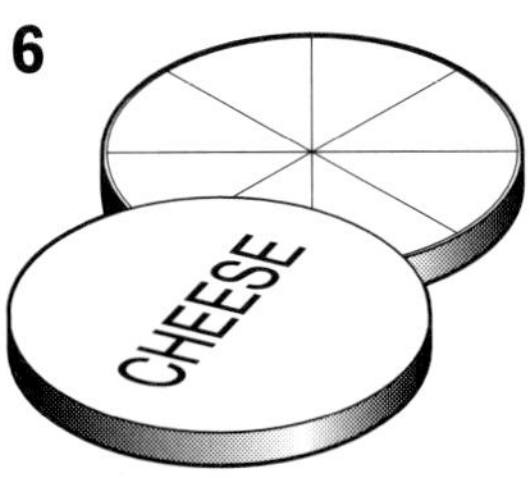

George buys a box of cheeses.

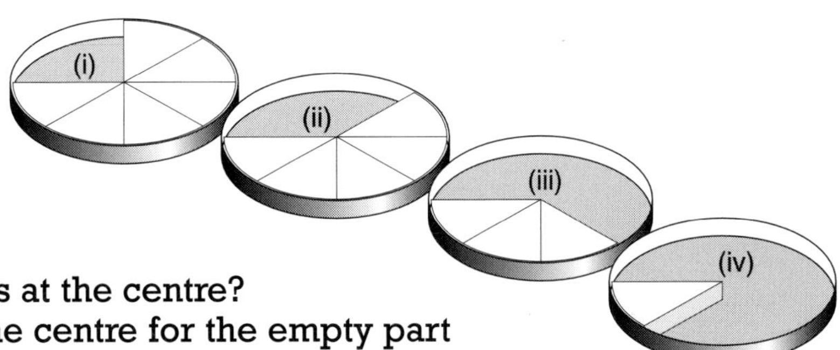

a What size are the angles at the centre?
b Work out the angle at the centre for the empty part of the box in each picture.

Vertically Opposites

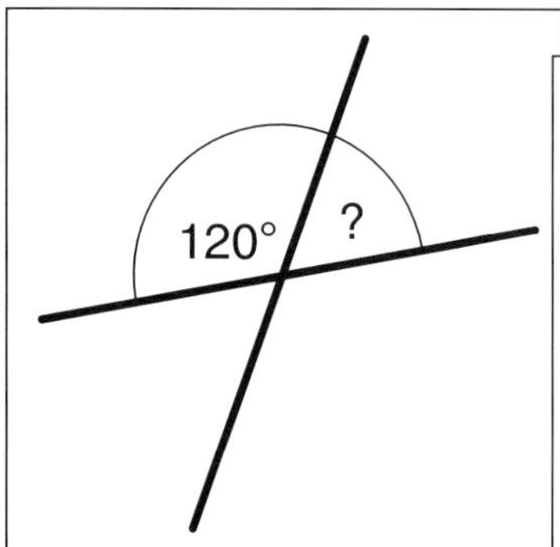

The missing angle is $180^\circ - 120^\circ = 60^\circ$.

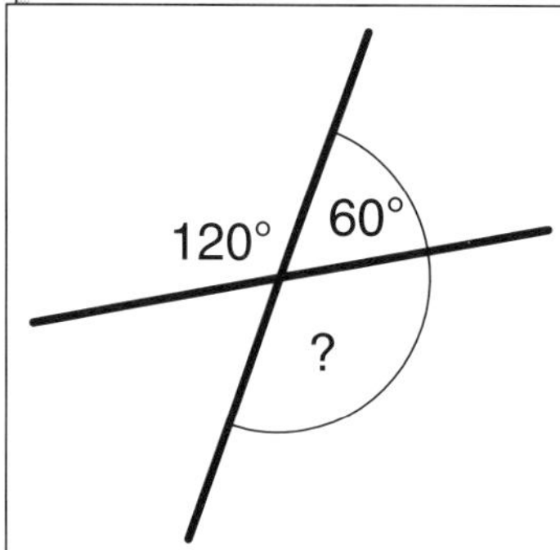

The missing angle is $180^\circ - 60^\circ = 120^\circ$.

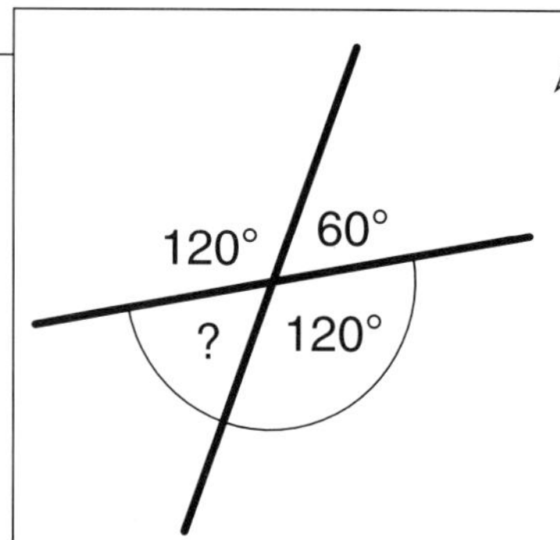

The missing angle is $180^\circ - 120^\circ = 60^\circ$.

1 Copy the diagrams and work out the size of each angle.

a

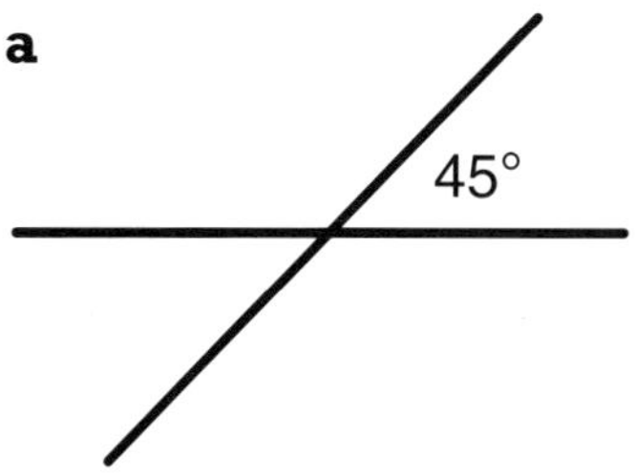

b

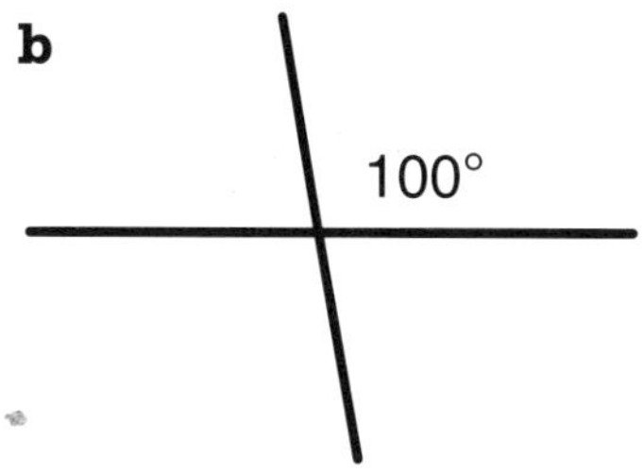

c

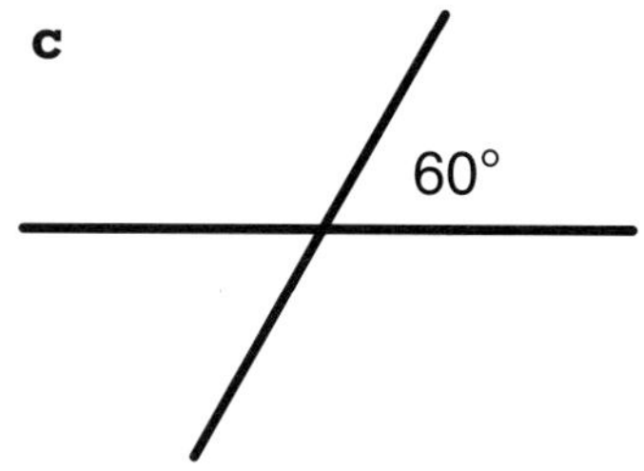

When lines form an X the angles opposite each other are equal.

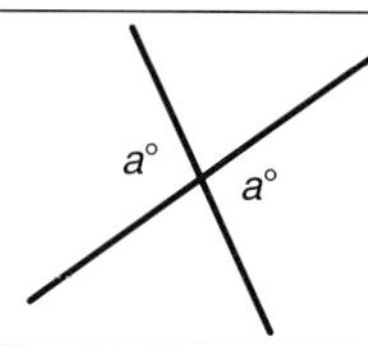

2 Copy each diagram.
Mark in the angle which is equal to the one given.

a

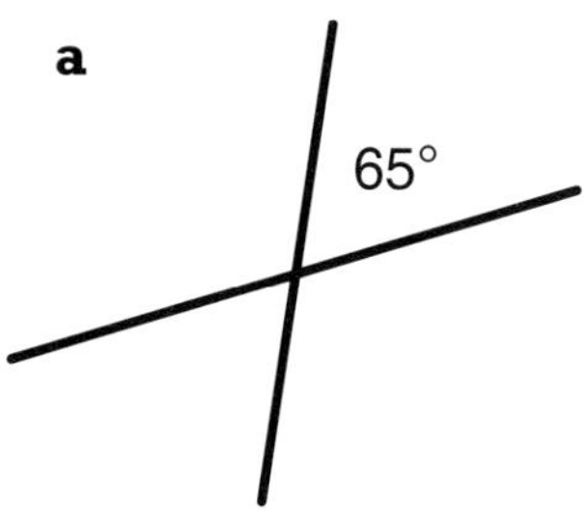

b

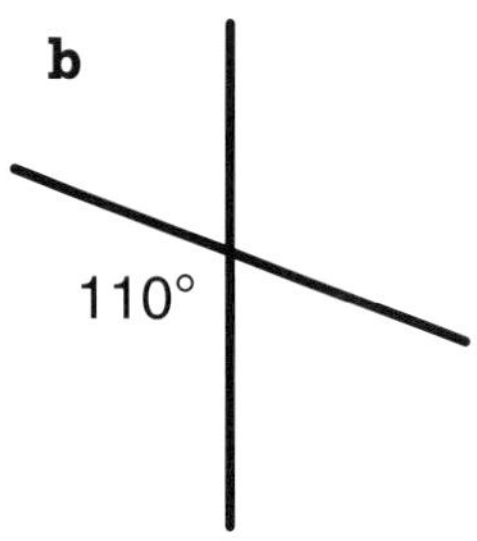

c

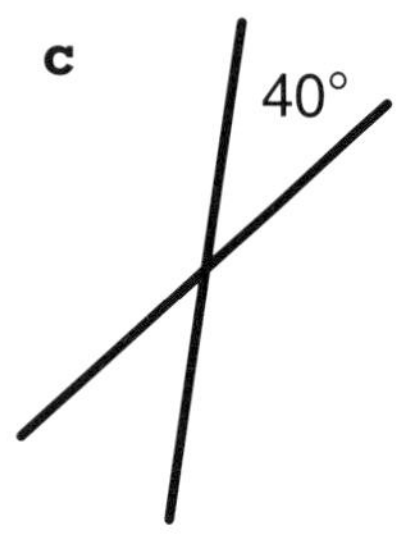

d

3 Calculate the labelled angles.

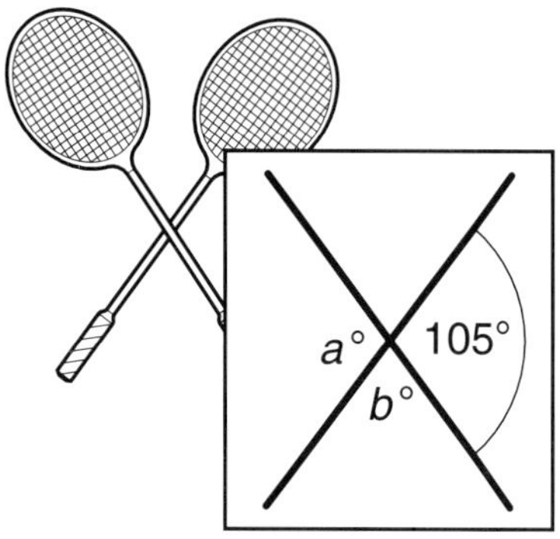

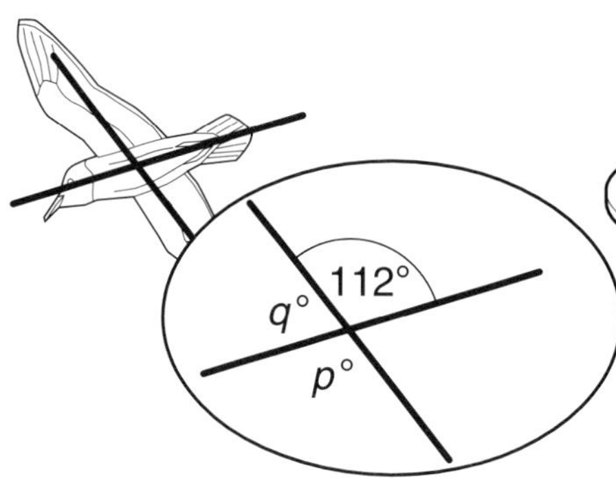

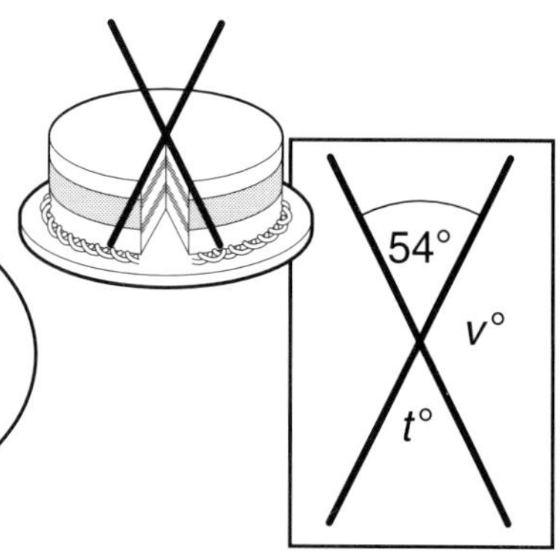

Angles and Parallels

When a line crosses a pair of parallel lines,

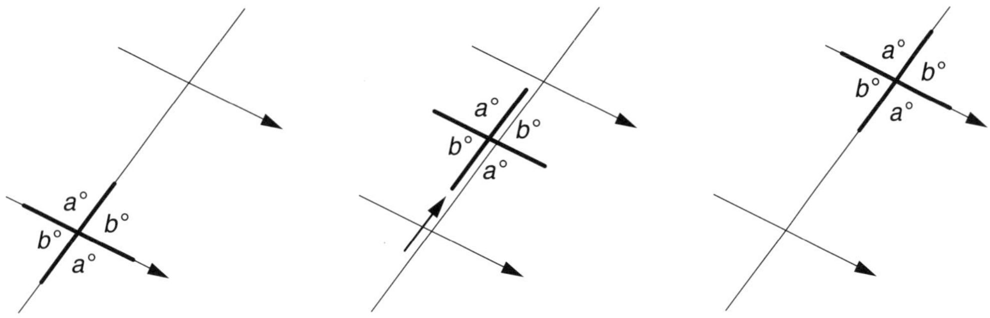

the angle pattern at one crossing ... ... is the same as at the other crossing.

Example

If we see this ... ... then we can do this ... or even this

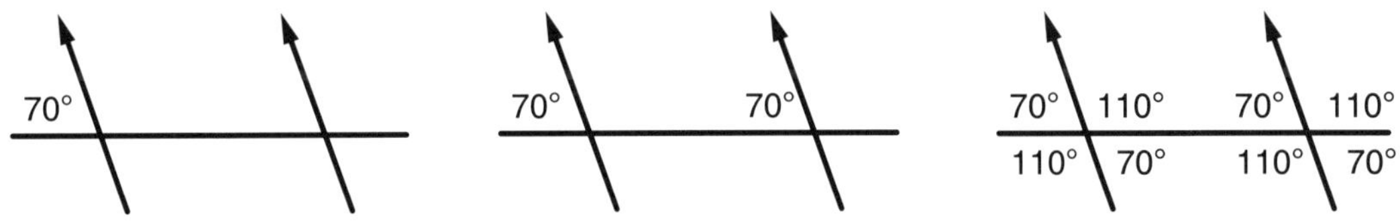

1 For each of the following:
(i) copy the diagram (ii) work out the size of each angle round A
(iii) work out the size of each angle round the point B.

a

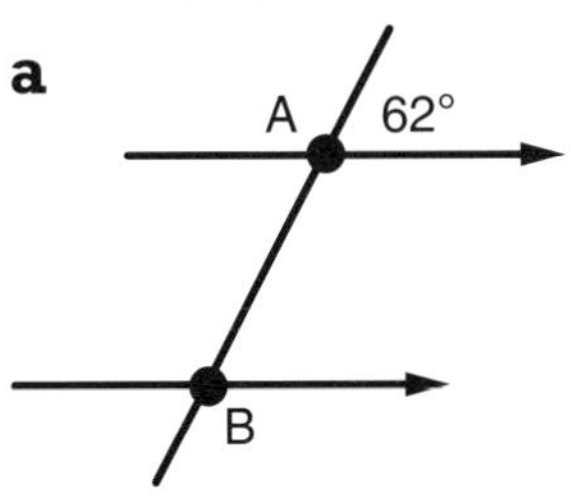

b

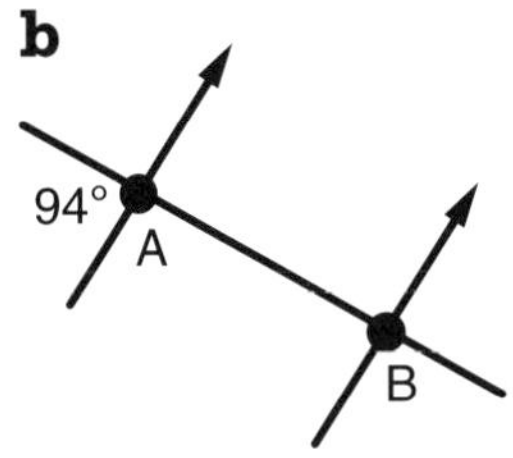

c

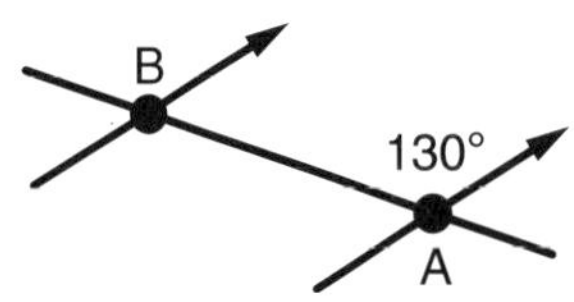

2 Find all the missing angles.

a

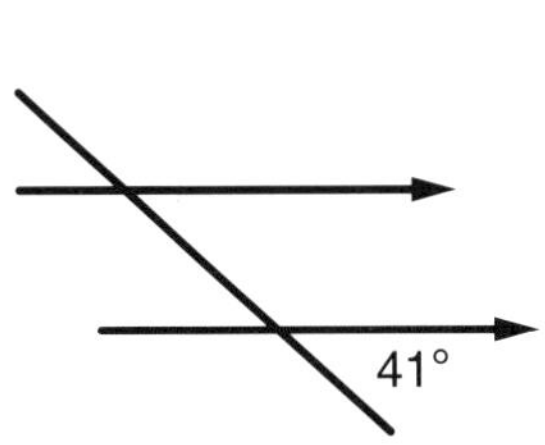

b

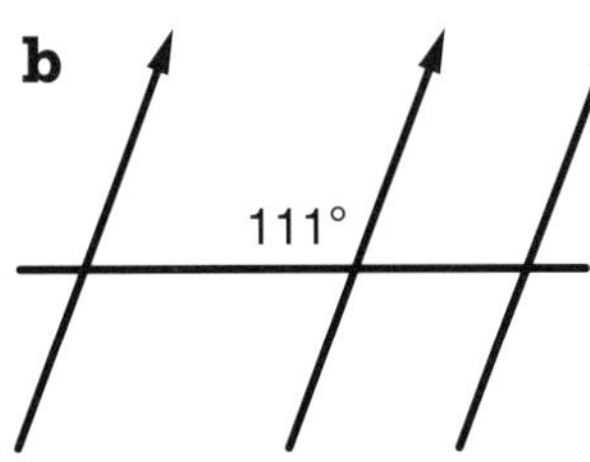

c

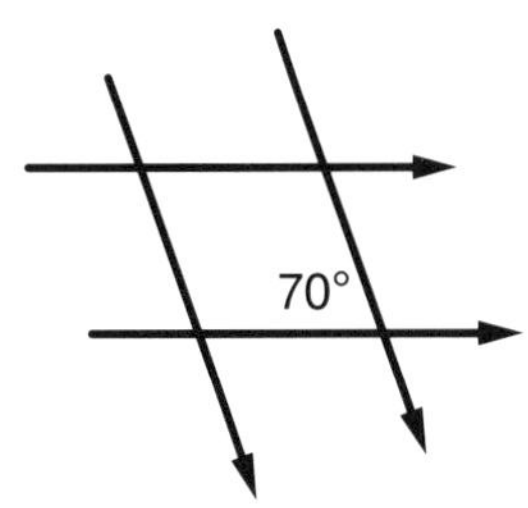

3 Work out the size of angles x and y.

4 Careful! Can you work out all the angles in the railway logo?

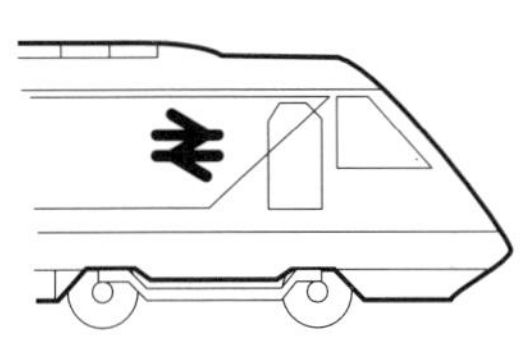

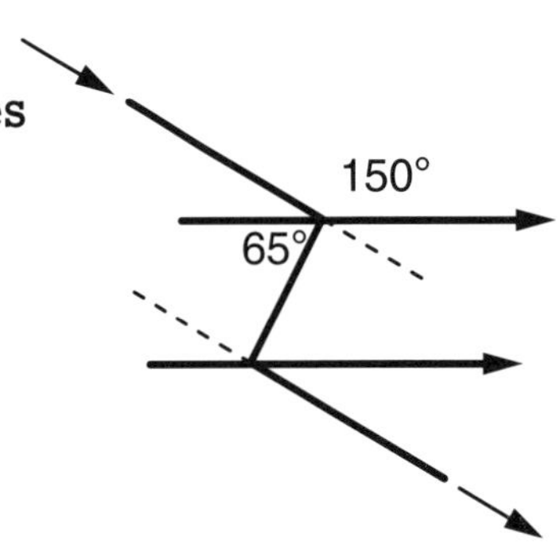

360° Protractors

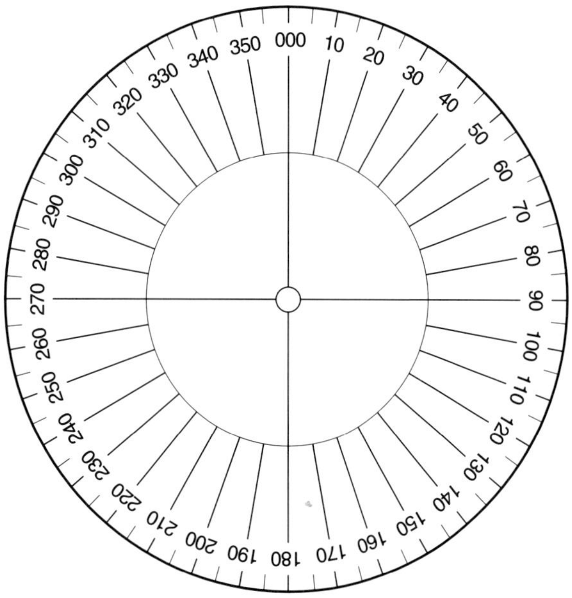

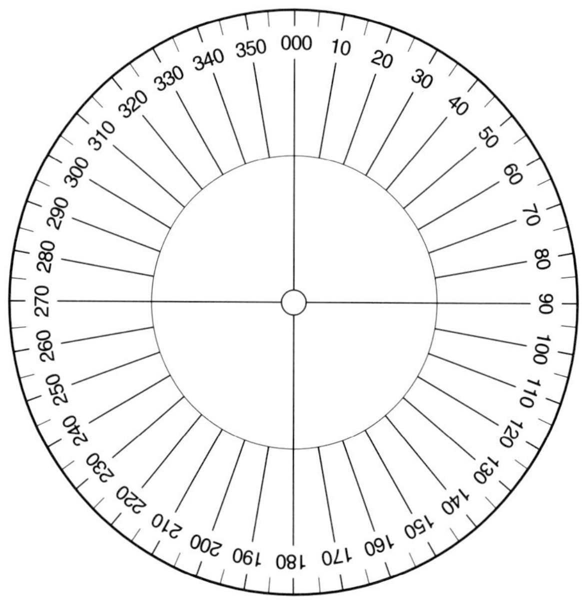

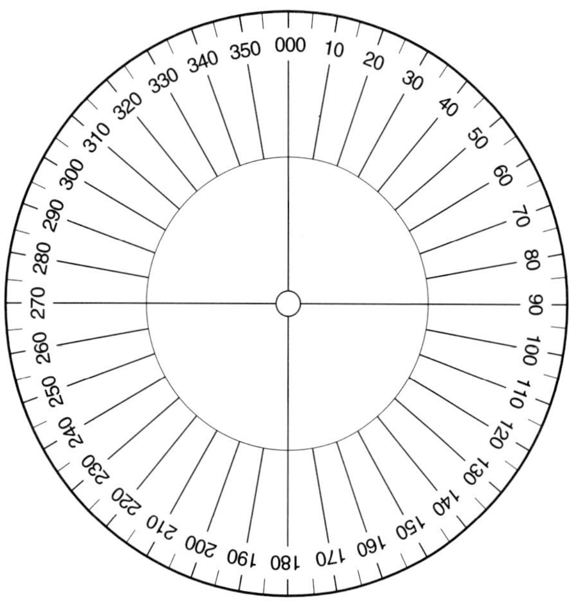

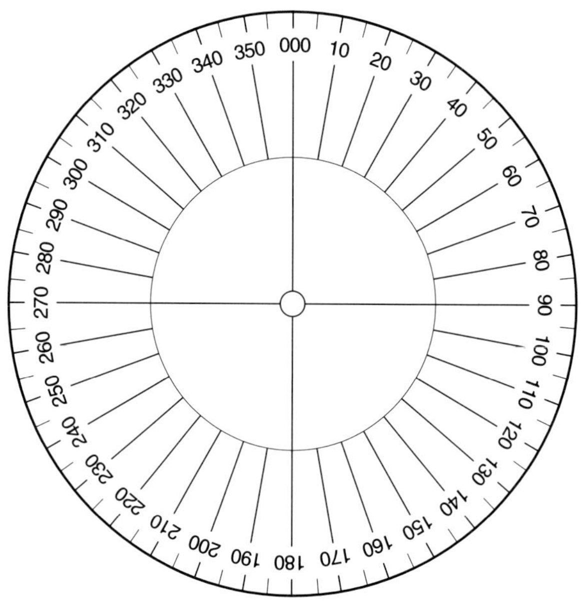

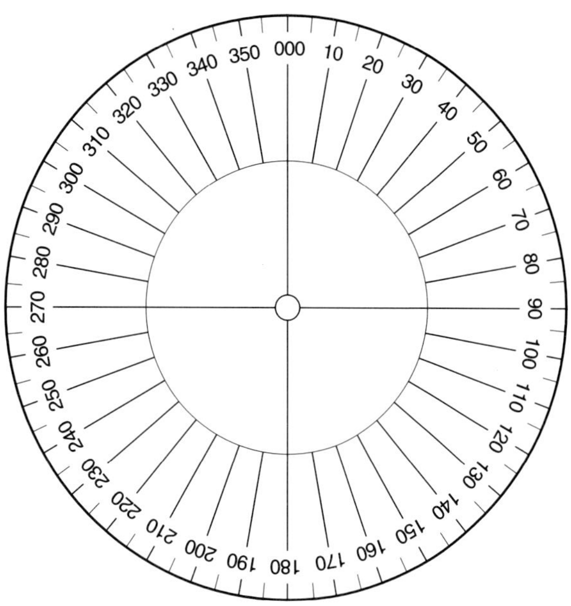

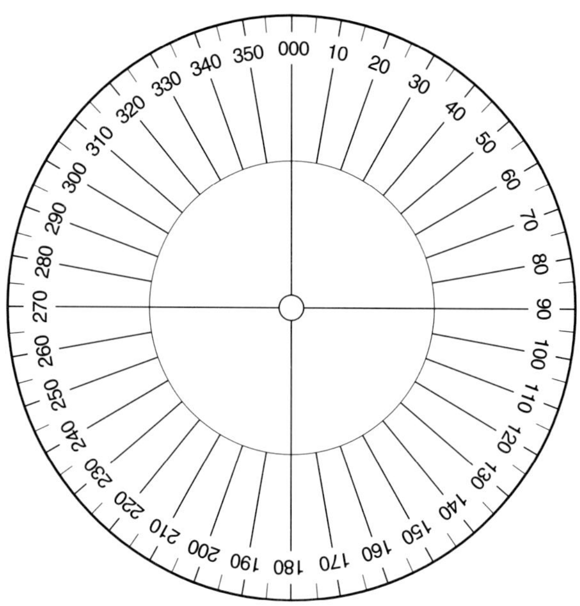

8 TIME

CURRICULUM COVERAGE

Standard Grade Guidelines

Foundation Level:
Tell and record the time using the 12-hour and 24-hour clock.
The units second, minute, hour, day, week, month, year and leap year, and their inter-relationship.
Calculate time intervals within a given half day on the 12-hour clock or within the same day on the 24-hour clock.
General Level:
Calculate time intervals over midnight or midday on the 12-hour clock. (This is included on photocopiable sheets in this Teacher's Book.)

National Curriculum

AT 3 Levels 3 and 4.
AT 1 Levels 3 and 4.

NI Curriculum

AT Measures Levels 3 and 4.

AIMS AND OBJECTIVES

Many students have particular difficulties with this topic, probably because time is the one measure they meet which is not decimalised. Therefore, the aim is to consolidate, and develop at an appropriate pace, the student's understanding of time, and to extend his/her practice with units of time and time intervals in a variety of relevant, meaningful contexts (with both the 12-hour clock and the 24-hour clock).

NOTES

1 Extension work covering time intervals over midnight and midday on the 12-hour clock and over midnight on the 24-hour clock is included on pages 69 and 70 in this Teacher's Book.
2 A simplified rule to calculate leap years has been used. Within a familiar, real-life context it is the only rule needed. The only century year in the student's life is 2000, which is a leap year. It is left to the teacher's discretion whether he/she wishes to adapt the rule to meet the needs of other century years.

TEACHER'S RESOURCES

Mental exercises.
Cross-number puzzles on time, to be tackled when it is felt appropriate.
A More Practice sheet on the scheduling of television programmes.
Three worksheets, on intervals over midnight on the 24-hour clock, and over noon and midnight on the 12-hour clock, provide an extension into the General Level of Standard Grade.

MENTAL TEST A

1 Add together the days in June and the days in July.

2 Queen Elizabeth's coronation was in 1953.
How many years ago was this?

3 How many months have 30 days?

4 How many weeks are there in 63 days?

5 How many minutes are in three-quarters of an hour?

6 Add 90 minutes and 90 minutes and give your answer in hours.

7 A 50-minute programme is recorded on a 2-hour video tape.
What time is left on the tape?

8 Write 16 30 as an am or pm time.

9 The bus leaves at 10.20 am and arrives $1\frac{1}{2}$ hours later.
What time is this?

10 Jill goes to bed at 10.30 pm and has eight hours' sleep.
When does she waken up in the morning?

MENTAL TEST B

1 Write 7 am as a 24-hour time.

2 George leaves home at 7.30 am. He takes 45 minutes to travel to work.
When does he arrive at work?

3 Mary starts work at ten minutes to nine. Her travel time is half an hour.
When does she need to leave home?

4 At ten past eleven Andrew has a fifteen minute tea-break.
When does he start work again?

5 Lunch-time starts at 12.30 pm and lasts for 50 minutes.
When does it finish?

6 Write 2 pm as a 24-hour time.

7 Darren plays football from 16 00 until 17 30. How long is this?

8 Laura's round of golf started at 6.30 pm and finished 2 hours and 15 minutes later.
When did she finish?

9 Monica's tennis match started at 6.45 pm and finished at 8.30 pm.
How long did it last?

10 Tim watches television from 7.20 pm until 11 o'clock.
How long is this?

Time for Cross-number Puzzles

1

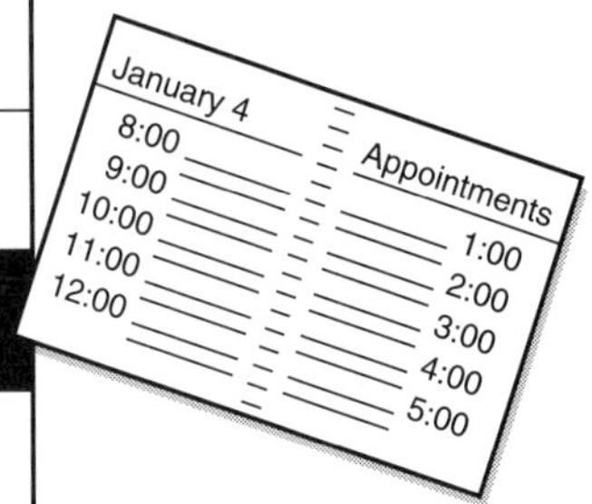

Across

1 Days in January
2 Days in a year (not a leap year)
4 Weeks in six months
5 Days in 43 weeks
9 Hours in a day
10 Seconds in five minutes
11 Minutes in quarter of an hour

Down

1 Days in a leap year
2 Minutes in six hours
3 Weeks in a year
4 20 minutes after 2.10 pm
6 Months in ten years
7 Days in a fortnight
8 Years in a century

2

Across

1 11 am
3 10.30 pm
6 7.12 pm
7 2 pm
8 1.15 pm
10 11 pm
11 5.15 am
12 midnight
14 1.52 pm
16 five minutes to midnight
17 8 pm
18 15 minutes after midnight

Down

1 10.12 am
2 1 am
3 9.10 pm
4 10.35 pm
5 five minutes to seven in the morning
9 twenty-five to twelve in the morning
12 2.20 am
13 ten minutes to one in the morning
14 7.25 pm
15 midnight

More Practice: Television Programmes

Today's programmes on Channel X of Telstar TV are set out below.

CHANNEL X

TELSTAR TV

6.00 Breakfast News
8.30 Pop Video
9.00 Health and Fitness
9.20 FILM: Moby Dick
11.30 Golf International
12.45 Lunchtime News
1.00 The Holiday Show
1.50 FILM: The Great Escape
4.05 Big Buster Cartoons
4.30 Master Quiz
5.00 The Holly Lane Show
5.50 Evening News
6.15 Clever Cooking
7.00 Pop Hits
7.35 FILM: Mercy
9.25 News
9.50 Football – Goal!
11.45 Police File
1.00 Weather and Programme News
1.10 Close Down

1 

a What pop programmes are there?
b How long does each one last?
c What is the total time for pop?

2 a How many sports programmes are there?
b How much time is given to sport?

3 

a How many news programmes are there?
b How much time is devoted to news?

4 a How many films are there? Give their titles.
b What time is taken up by films?

5 How long is Channel X on the air?

6 a Obtain a list of TV programmes from a recent newspaper or magazine.
b Answer questions **1–5** for this list.
c Compare your answers with the ones you got above.

Intervals over Midnight (24-hour Clock)

From 21 00 until midnight (24 00) is **3 hours**.

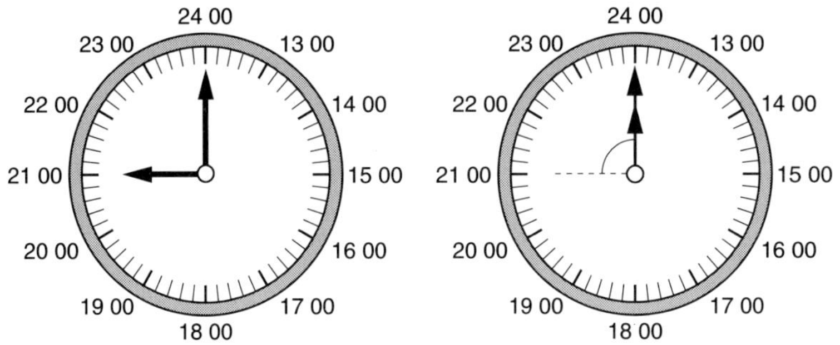

From 22 25 until midnight (24 00) is 1 hour and 35 minutes.

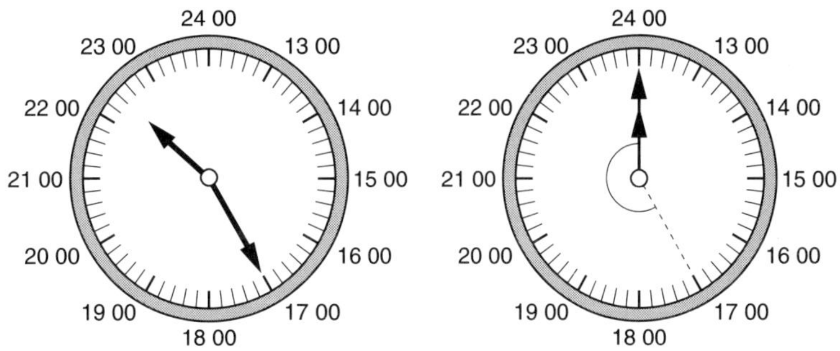

1 How many hours is it to midnight from:

a 23 00 **b** 22 00
c 20 00 **d** 18 00
e 14 00 **f** 12 00
g 10 00 **h** 07 00?

2 How many hours and minutes is it to midnight from:

a 22 30 **b** 21 30
c 18 30 **d** 16 30
e 22 40 **f** 20 50
g 14 20 **h** 15 10?

3 How long after midnight is:

a 03 00 **b** 06 00 **c** 11 00 **d** 14 00
e 05 30 **f** 08 20 **g** 07 45 **h** 04 05?

Midnight is 24 00 or **00 00**.
02 00 is 2 hours after midnight.

4 The 'Midnight Express' leaves Glasgow at 22 00 and arrives in London at 06 00. Copy and complete:

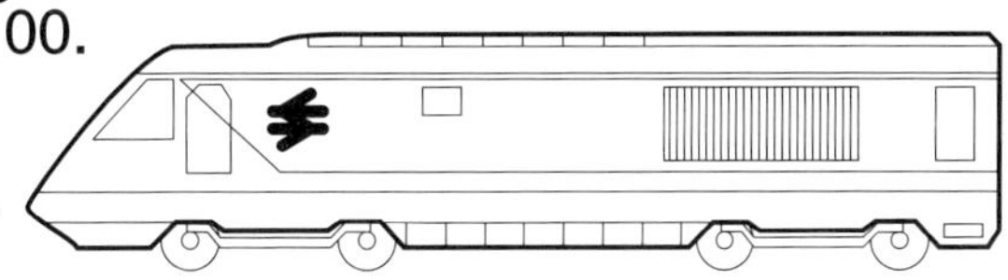

a 22 00 is ... hours before midnight.
b 06 00 is ... hours after midnight.
c The total time is ... hours.

5 The Thomsons leave Edinburgh at 20 20 and arrive in Brighton at 10 15 the next day. Copy and complete:

a 20 20 is ... hours ... minutes before midnight.
b 10 15 is ... hours ... minutes after midnight.
c The total time is ... hours ... minutes.

6 Calculate the total time of these journeys:

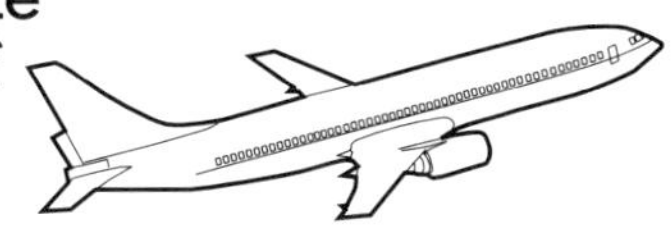

	Depart	Arrive
a	20 00	08 00
b	21 30	09 00
c	18 30	10 30
d	16 30	09 15
e	21 40	07 10
f	19 15	08 30

Intervals over Midnight and over Noon (12-hour Clock)

From 8 pm until midnight (12 pm) is 4 hours.

From 7.15 pm until midnight (12 pm) is 4 hours 45 minutes.

7.15 pm to 8 pm is 45 minutes.
8 pm to midnight is 4 hours.

1 How many hours is it to midnight from:

a 9 pm **b** 7 pm **c** 3 pm
d 6 pm **e** noon?

2 How many hours and minutes is it to midnight from:

a 9.30 pm **b** 6.30 pm **c** 4.30 pm
d 10.45 pm **e** 8.40 pm **f** 9.15 pm
g 2.50 pm **h** 7.20 pm?

3 How long is it to noon from:

a 7 am **b** 3 am **c** 5.30 am **d** 10.45 am
e 6.40 am **f** 4.55 am **g** 8.15 am **h** 6.20 am?

4

Charity Marathon Dance

Begins 9.30 pm

Dawn and her friends danced until 3.15 am.

How long did they dance?

5 The street lights came on at 8.35 pm and went off at 5.45 am.

How long were the lights on?

6 Parveen posted a letter at 5.15 pm.

It arrived at her friend's house at 7.30 am the next morning.

How long did it take to deliver the letter?

7 A plane left Glasgow at 10.40 am.

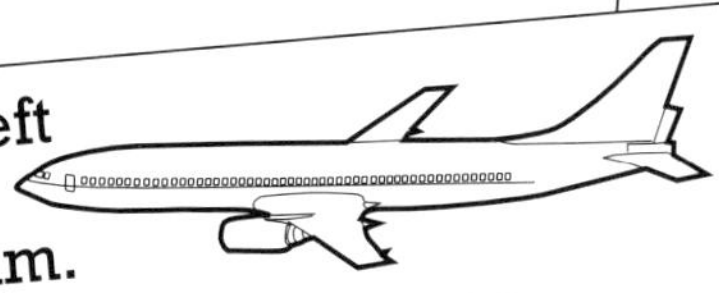

It arrived in Athens at 2.30 pm.

How long did the flight take?

8 A normal working day for Tom is from 8.45 am until 5.10 pm.
When he works nightshift, he works from 9.30 pm until 7.15 am.

a How long is a normal working day?
b How long is a nightshift?

Time Intervals

1 Megan works part-time as an office supervisor.

She needs to 'clock-in' and 'clock-out'.

Her timecard for last week looked like this:

Complete Megan's timecard.

Megan Murphy Employee No. 21 Week 34			
	Time in	**Time out**	**Time worked**
Monday	8.30 am	2 pm	
Tuesday	9.40 am	3 pm	
Wednesday	8.15 am	2.30 pm	
Thursday	11.45 am	4.15 pm	
Friday	10.20 am	3.15 pm	
	Total time		

2 Fraser works nightshift at Spencer's Sports Factory.

His timecard for last week looked like this:

Complete Fraser's timecard.

Fraser Forbes 00248 Week 34			
	Time in	**Time out**	**Time worked**
Monday	21 00	07 00	
Tuesday	21 15	07 00	
Wednesday	20 45	07 15	
Thursday	21 30	07 10	
Friday	22 40	08 20	
	Total time		

3 The Barassie Lifeboat was launched at 22 17 in answer to a distress flare. Two boys were sighted on an overturned dinghy at 00 15.
They were admitted to Ayr Hospital at 03 40 after a 20-minute helicopter journey.

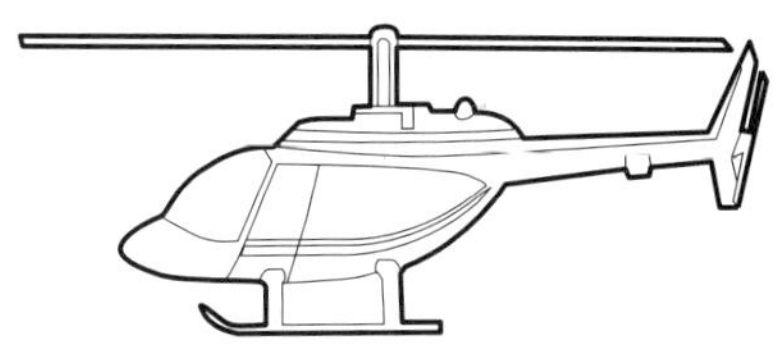

a How long after the launch were the boys sighted?
b How long after the launch were the boys admitted to hospital?
c When did the helicopter pick up the boys?

4 The information board at Gatwick Airport gives news of flight delays.

Complete the final column.

Flight no.	**From**	**Due at**	**Delayed**	**New arrival time**
10036	Paris	23 05	1 hour 15 minutes	
2601	Madrid	21 45	3 hours 30 minutes	
7004	Rome	22 50	2 hours 15 minutes	
3605	Oslo	23 40	1 hour 20 minutes	
11132	Athens	22 46	1 hour 40 minutes	

9 CHARTS AND TABLES

CURRICULUM COVERAGE

Standard Grade Guidelines
Foundation Level:
Demonstrate the ability to interpret and communicate mathematical information in the form of straightforward tables.
Extract information from tables.
Communicate information in tabular form.
General Level:
Extend the above to handle up to five categories.

National Curriculum
AT 1 Level 4.
AT 4 Levels 4 and 5.

NI Curriculum
AT Processes Levels 4 and 5.
AT Handling Data Level 4.

AIMS AND OBJECTIVES

The main aim of the chapter is to give students practice in extracting data from tables, in everyday contexts. They should be able to build up their own tables and ready reckoners with help.

TEACHER'S RESOURCES

Worksheet 1 provides work on using and making 'distance charts'.
Worksheet 2 contains a ready reckoner with more categories.
Worksheet 3 has a ready reckoner involving currency conversion.
Worksheet 4 provides work on making and using ready reckoners.
More Practice 1 has additional work on extracting information from more complicated tables (three categories).
More Practice 2 is also concerned with extracting information from tables but this time more reasoning is involved.
More Practice 3 provides further examples similar to those in Exercise 3.

PROGRESS ROUTE

Success with this chapter should give students more confidence when extracting information from tables. Whilst there is no equivalent chapter to this in *Book 3A*, tables appear throughout the book.

Worksheet 1: Distance Charts

1

Edinburgh			
44	Glasgow		
121	145	Aberdeen	
126	86	232	Stranraer

This mileage chart shows the distances between towns and cities in Scotland.

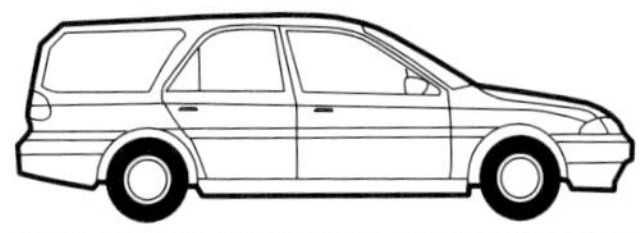

Example

Edinburgh			
44	Glasgow		
121	145	Aberdeen	
126	86	232	Stranraer

How far is it from Edinburgh to Aberdeen?

Find the Edinburgh column.
Look along the Aberdeen row.
See where they cross over.

121 miles

a How far is it from Glasgow to Stranraer?
b How far is it from Aberdeen to Glasgow?
c Which two towns are the furthest apart?
d Which two towns are closest?
e Which two towns are 126 miles apart?
f A salesman travels from Edinburgh to Glasgow, then from Glasgow to Stranraer and finally from Stranraer back to Edinburgh.
Calculate the total distance he travelled.

2 This chart shows the shortest distances, in kilometres, between four towns.
Use the map to help you fill in the distance chart.

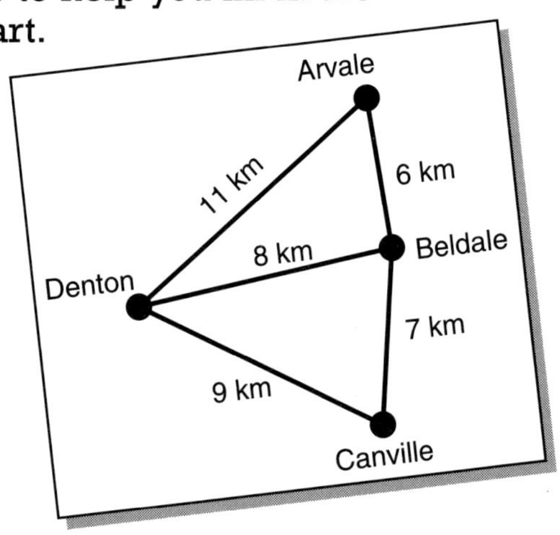

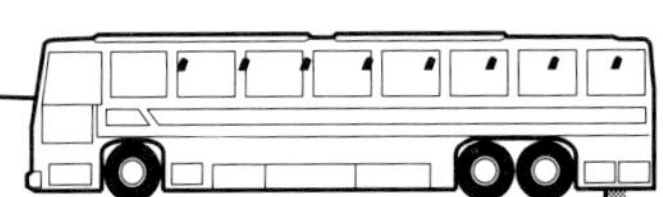

Arvale			
	Beldale		
13		Canville	
			Denton

Worksheet 2

Pick Your Own Fruit

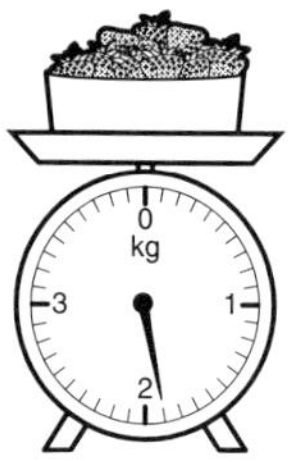

Raspberries 90p per pound
Strawberries 85p per pound
Blackcurrants 95p per pound

Heather works on the stall at the 'Pick Your Own Fruit' farm.
She has a ready reckoner to help her with the prices.

Weight of fruit (in pounds)	Raspberries	Strawberries	Blackcurrants
1	90p	85p	95p
2	£1.80	£1.70	£1.90
3	£2.70	£2.55	£2.85
4	£3.60	£3.40	£3.80
5	£4.50	£4.25	£4.75
6	£5.40	£5.10	£5.70
7	£6.30	£5.95	£6.65
8	£7.20	£6.80	£7.60
9	£8.10	£7.65	£8.55
10	£9.00	£8.50	£9.50
20	£18.00	£17.00	£19.00
30	£27.00	£25.50	£28.50
40	£36.00	£34.00	£38.00

1 Write down the cost of:

a 5 pounds of raspberries
b 8 pounds of blackcurrants
c 3 pounds of strawberries.

2 Work out the cost of:

a 16 pounds of strawberries
b 21 pounds of blackcurrants.

3 Mrs Turner paid £5.70 for blackcurrants.
How many pounds did she buy?

4 Work out how much each of these people should pay.

a Mrs Thom: 6 pounds of raspberries and 4 pounds of strawberries
b Alan Wylie: 5 pounds of strawberries and 12 pounds of blackcurrants
c The Jam-Makers Cooperative: 40 pounds of raspberries, 24 pounds of strawberries and 32 pounds of blackcurrants.

Worksheet 3

The Mackie family are going to Tenerife on holiday.
The ready reckoner shows how many Spanish pesetas they get for their pounds and pence.

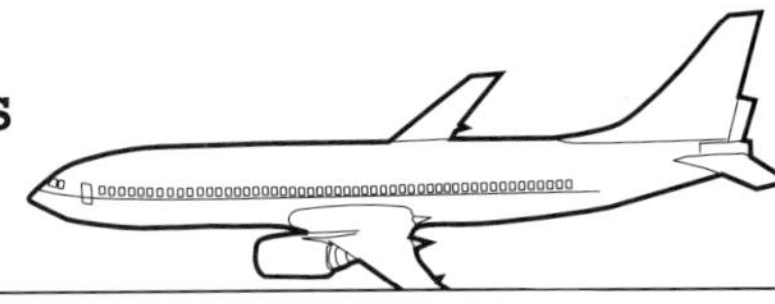

British money (pence)	5p	10p	20p	30p	40p	50p	60p	70p	80p	90p
Spanish money (pesetas)	10	20	40	60	80	100	120	140	160	180

Pounds	£1	£2	£3	£4	£5	£6	£7	£8	£9	£10
Pesetas	200	400	600	800	1000	1200	1400	1600	1800	2000

Richard exchanges £8 for pesetas. He gets 1600 pesetas.

1 How many pesetas would be worth:

a £2 **b** 70p **c** £13 **d** £7.30?

2 A snack cost the Mackies 1200 pesetas. How many pounds is that?

3 It cost the family 3000 pesetas to go on a boat trip.
How much is that in pounds?

4 Work out the cost in pounds and pence of:

a

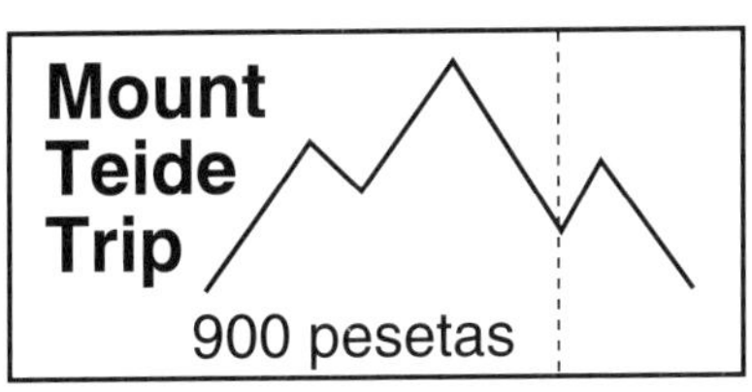

b

c

5 Matthew made friends with Carlos, who lived in Tenerife.
They decided to swop coins with each other.
Matthew gave Carlos £3.65 worth of British coins.
How many pesetas should Carlos give Matthew in exchange?

6 Anne was reading a novel on holiday. It cost her £6.99 at home.
She saw the same book in a shop in Tenerife. It cost 1420 pesetas.
Was the book cheaper in Tenerife or in Britain?

7

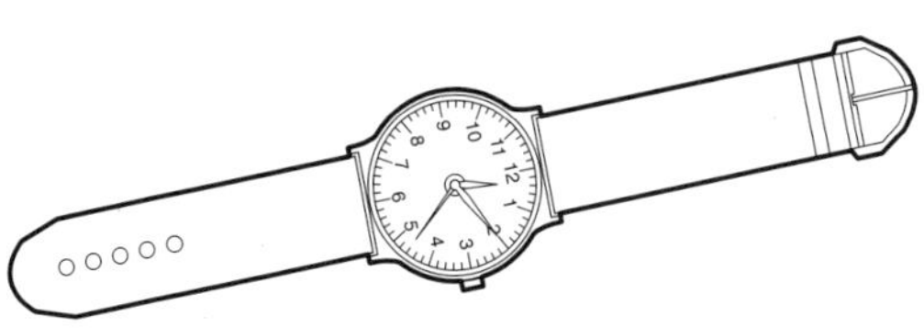

On the way home on the plane Sandy bought a watch.
The air hostess said the watch cost £25.
Sandy paid for it with Spanish money.
How many pesetas did she pay?

Worksheet 4: Making and Using Ready Reckoners

1 Material costs £2.45 per metre.

Use a calculator to help you make a ready reckoner.

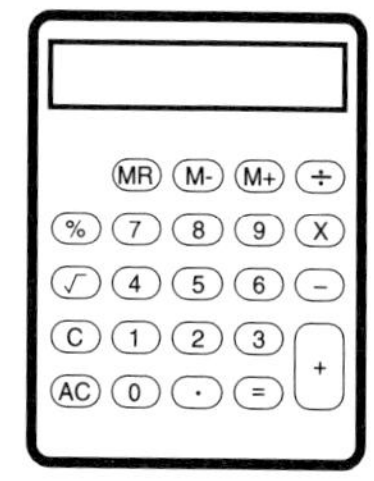

Length in metres	Cost
1	£2.45
2	£4.90
3	
4	
5	
6	
7	
8	
9	
10	
20	
30	
40	
50	

← $2 \times £2.45 = £4.90$

Use your ready reckoner to answer these questions.

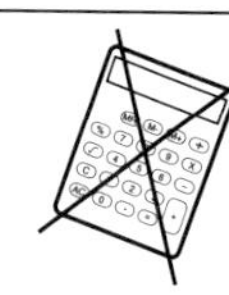

a How much would you pay for 5 metres of this material?
b How much would 8 metres of this material cost?
c Sarah paid £7.35 for some of this material. How much did she buy?
d Calculate the cost of:
(i) 12 metres
(ii) 26 metres of this material.
e The factory made 100 metres of this material.
How much is it all worth?

2 A petrol station has a ready reckoner for changing litres into gallons. 1 litre is the same as 0.22 gallon.

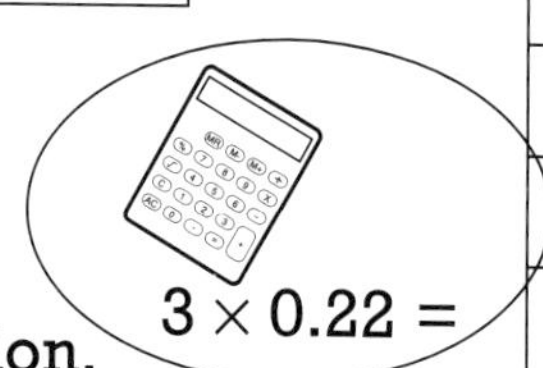

Use a calculator to help you fill in the rest of the ready reckoner.

Litres	Gallons
1	0.22
2	0.44
3	
4	
5	
6	
7	
8	
9	
10	
20	
30	
40	
50	

Use your ready reckoner to answer these questions.

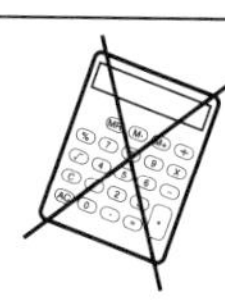

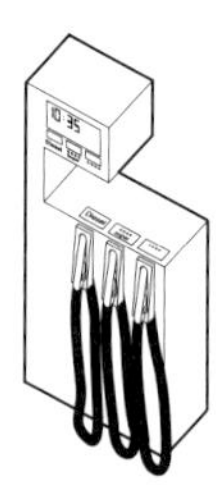

a How many gallons are the same as:
(i) 4 litres (ii) 9 litres (iii) 30 litres?
b Work out how many gallons are the same as:
(i) 17 litres (ii) 22 litres (iii) 70 litres.
c George fills a 25 litre can with petrol for his farm bike.
How many gallons is this?
d A tank holds 500 litres of diesel.
How many gallons is this?

More Practice 1

1 Alex has five dairy cows.
She milks them in the morning and at night.
She records how many litres of milk they produce.

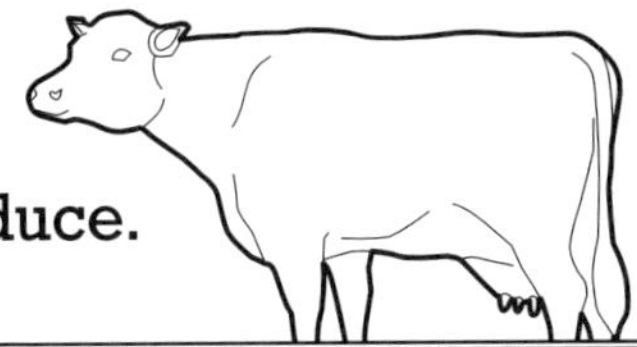

Name of cow	Monday		Tuesday		Wednesday	
	am	pm	am	pm	am	pm
Pooh	13.5	9	14	9	15	8.5
Beatrice	9.5	6	10	5.5	10	6
Lightning	11	8	12	8.5	11.5	8
Biscuit	10	7.5	10.5	7	10.5	7
Silver	12.5	8.5	12.5	9	12	8.5

a How many litres of milk did Pooh give on Tuesday morning? (Hint: look for Pooh, then Tuesday and am.)
b When did Lightning give 11.5 litres of milk?
c How much milk did Silver give on Monday evening?
d (i) Which cow gave the least milk at one milking?
(ii) How much was it?
(iii) When was it?
e How much milk did Silver give altogether on Wednesday?
f Alex poured all of Monday's milk into the tub for making cheese. How many litres of milk was it?

2

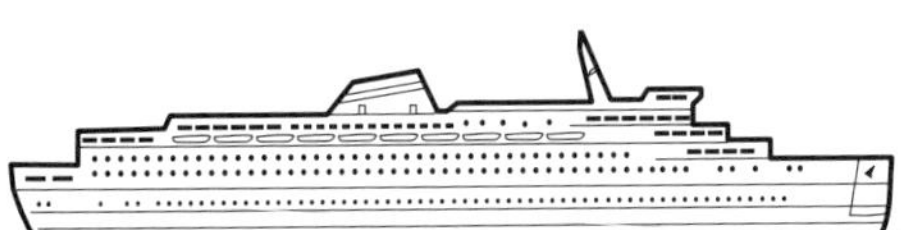

A newspaper advert showed these prices for Channel ferry crossings.

	July		August	
	Day sailing	Night sailing	Day sailing	Night sailing
P & Q Ferries	£280	£252	£325	£295
Anglo-French Ferries	£310	£276	£364	£330

a The McTaggart family want an overnight ferry to France. They are going during August. They choose P & Q Ferries. How much do they pay?
b Mr and Mrs Viera and their family want to travel to France in July. They prefer a day sailing. They choose to travel with Anglo-French Ferries. How much does it cost them?
c Terri and her family pay £364 to travel to France.
(i) Which ferry company did they choose?
(ii) Did they travel during the day or at night?

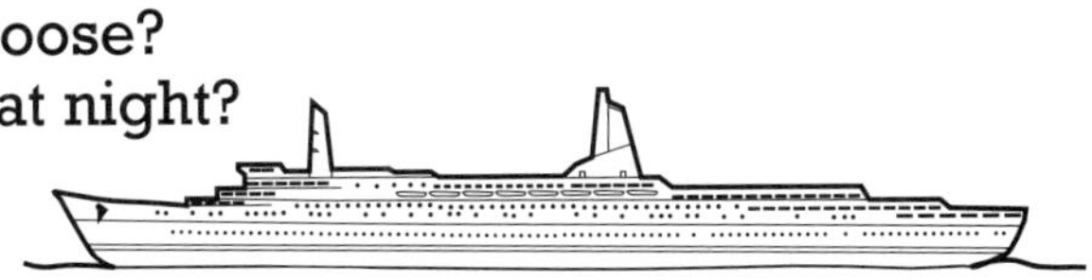

More Practice 2

1

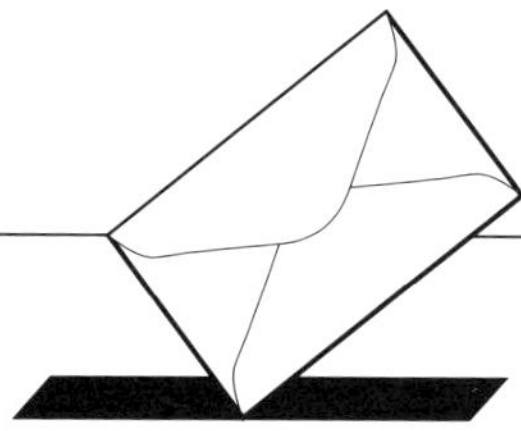

The cost of posting letters and small packages to people in the armed forces is shown below.

	Not over 60 g	**Not over 100 g**	**Not over 150 g**	**Not over 200 g**	**Not over 250 g**	**Not over 300 g**	**Not over 350 g**
BFPO addresses **in Europe**	25p	38p	47p	57p	67p	77p	88p
BFPO addresses **outside Europe**	19p	29p	36p	43p	52p	61p	70p

a How much would it cost to send a 60 g letter to a BFPO address in Europe?
b How much would it cost to send a 250 g package to a BFPO address outside Europe?
c Jim sends a 200 g package to a BFPO address. It costs him 43p. Did he send it to someone in Europe or outside Europe?
d How much would it cost to send a 90 g letter to Europe?
e Alana's package weighs 330 g. She is sending it to her husband who is a major in the army, stationed in Germany.
How much will it cost to post it?
f Tony's RAF base is in Canada. His mum sends him a letter that weighs 125 g. How much did it cost to post?

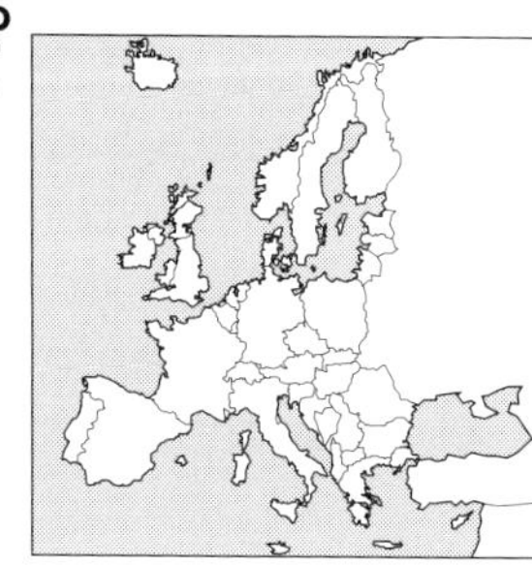

2

This table was in the 'Summersun' travel brochure. It compares the temperatures and hours of sunshine in Crete and London.
For example, in May, the average daily temperature in Crete was 74 °F and there were nine hours of sunshine.

Temperature (°F) and sunshine (hours)

Crete	London	
74° **9**	**62°** **6**	May
81° **12**	**69°** **7**	June
84° **13**	**71°** **6**	July
84° **12**	**70°** **6**	August
81° **10**	**65°** **5**	September

a What is the temperature in London in June?
b How many hours of sunshine would you expect in Crete in August?
c Which months are warmest in Crete?
d Which month is sunniest in London?
e How much warmer is Crete than London in September?
f How many more hours of sunshine each day has Crete than London in July?

More Practice 3

1 The same calculator is advertised in two different catalogues.

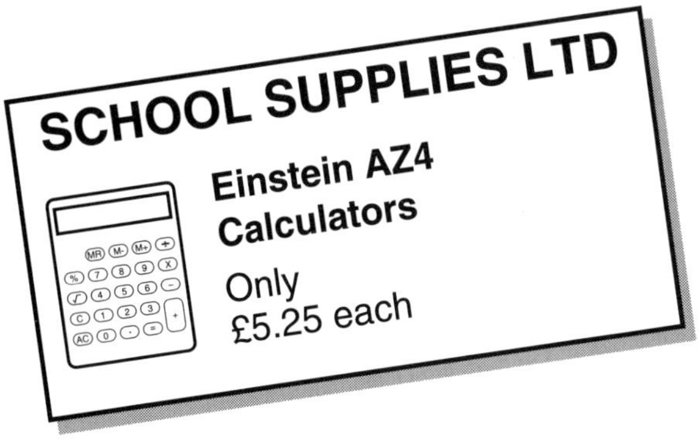

a How much would it cost to order six calculators from School Supplies Ltd?
b How much would eight calculators cost from Student Services Ltd?
c Mr Reed needs to buy 15 calculators.
  (i) How much would they cost from School Supplies?
  (ii) How much would they cost from Student Services?
  (iii) Which should he choose and why?
d Mrs Firth needs 21 new calculators for her class.
How much will she save if she buys them from Student Services rather than School Supplies?

2 'Angle measurers' were advertised in a catalogue.

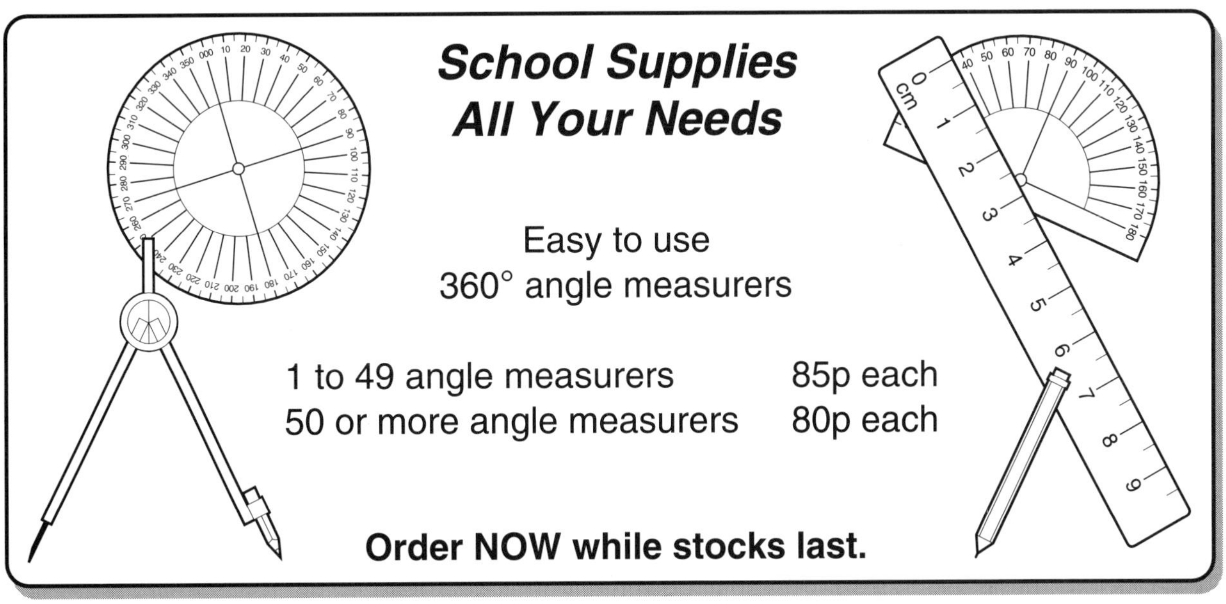

a Work out the cost of buying:
(i) 40 (ii) 65 (iii) 49 angle measurers.
b Miss Ramage needs 48 new angle measurers.
However, she decides to order 50.
Work out the cost and explain why she did this.

10 GRAPHS

CURRICULUM COVERAGE

Standard Grade Guidelines
Foundation Level:
Extract data from pictographs, bar and line graphs, and pie charts.
Construct these given scale and structure.
Trends and average (mean).
General Level:
Construct graphs as above, given no scale.
Read pie charts.

National Curriculum
AT 4 Levels 3, 4, 5 and 6.

NI Curriculum
AT Handling Data Levels 3, 4, 5 and 6.

AIMS AND OBJECTIVES
To extend the uses of pictorial representation of information in the form of bar and line graphs and pie charts.
To develop skills in:
(i) the interpretation of these graphs
(ii) using data to construct these graphs
(iii) drawing inferences from these graphs.
To introduce students to a first measure of central tendency, i.e. the mean.

NOTES

1 Some previous knowledge is expected of all the graphing methods used here.
2 Pictographs are only mentioned in the Looking Back exercise as students should be well acquainted with them from previous work.
3 Some NC handling of data will be covered in Chapter 13 on Probability and Statistics.
4 Trends and inferences are built into the exercises, often at the tail end of an exercise.

TEACHER'S RESOURCES
Worksheet 1 continues the work of Exercise 1 on bar graphs, giving students the opportunity to draw their own bar graphs.
Worksheet 2 provides similar opportunities for students to draw line graphs, to consolidate the work in Exercise 2.
More Practice 1 provides a more interpretive example of a line graph.
More Practice sheets 2–3 contain additional pie chart examples.
The survey sheet contains instructions on how to complete a statistical survey, to consolidate the skills learnt in this chapter.
Fraction and percentage pie chart templates are provided – these can also be copied onto acetate.

PROGRESS ROUTE
Success at the check-up should allow students who wish to cover the General interface to attempt the *Book 3A* Review: Statistics and Probability, Statistics 1 questions 1 to 7.

Worksheet 1

1 Here are some temperatures from one day in August.
Use the grid to draw a bar graph showing these figures.

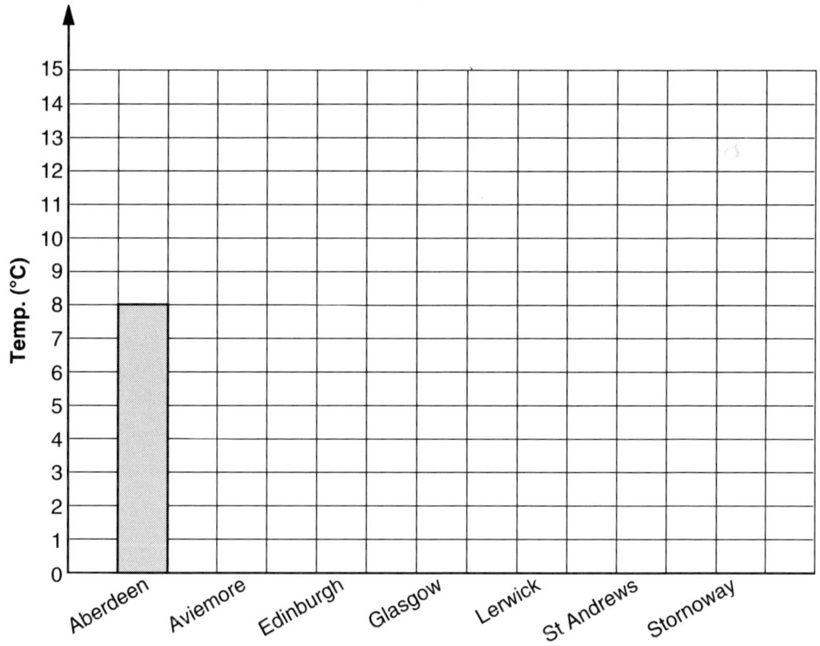

Aberdeen	8 °C
Aviemore	5 °C
Edinburgh	7 °C
Glasgow	5 °C
Lerwick	10 °C
St Andrews	8 °C
Stornoway	12 °C

2 Astronomers measure the distances between stars in light years.
The table gives the distances to some of the nearer stars.

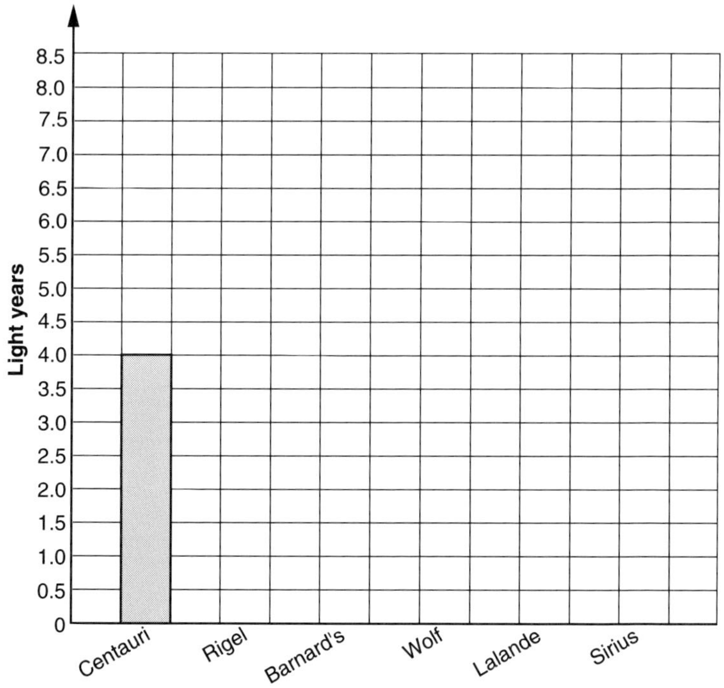

Star	Light years
Centauri	4.0
Rigel	4.5
Barnard's star	6.0
Wolf	7.5
Lalande	8.0
Sirius	8.5

Draw a bar graph for these stars.

a How far from Earth is Lalande?
b Which of these stars is furthest from Earth?
c How much closer to Earth is Barnard's star than Sirius?

Worksheet 1 (continued)

3 Flocks of geese are winter visitors to our islands every year. Their arrival is watched for and their numbers counted.

Greylag goose	5500
Pink-footed goose	2500
Barnacle goose	8500
Brent goose	8000
Bean goose	6500
White-fronted goose	3500

This table shows the numbers of some of these visitors.

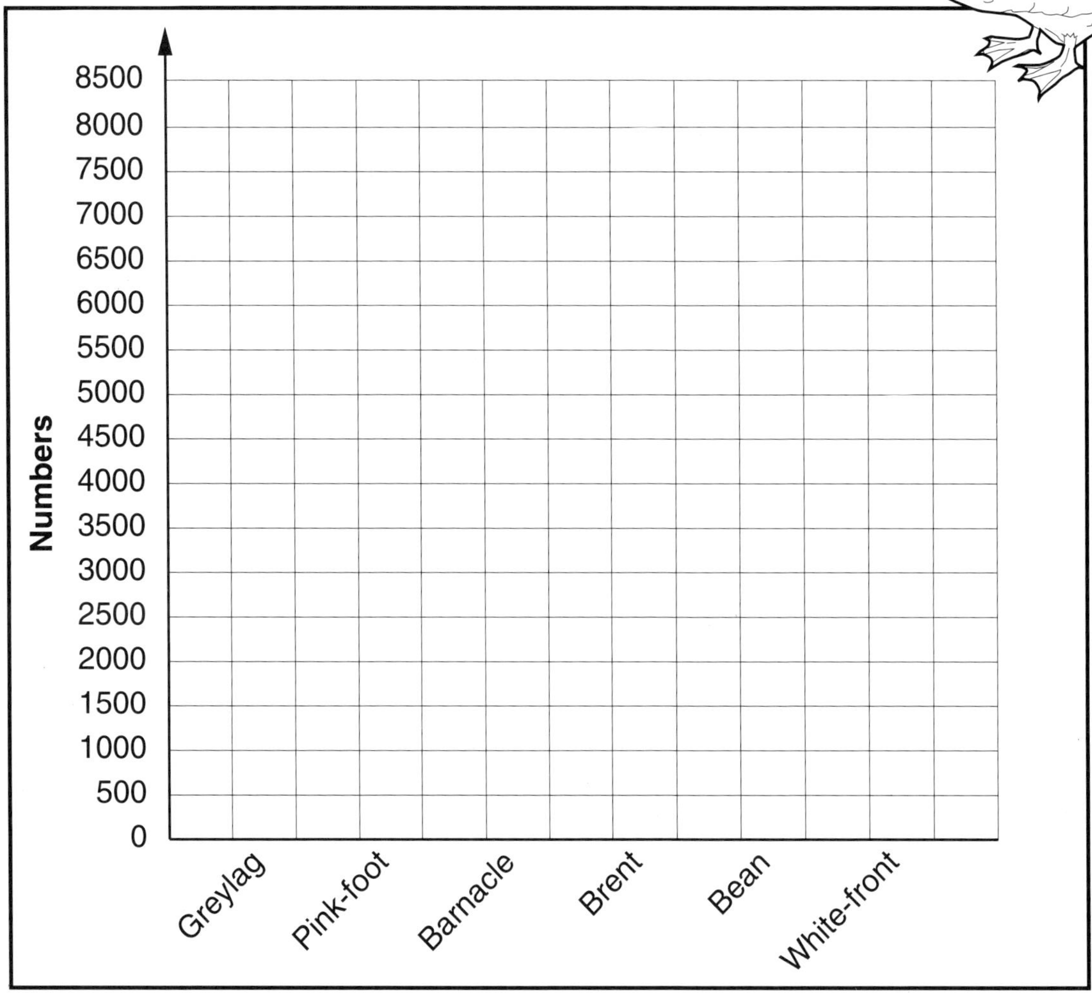

Draw a bar graph from the table.
Use your graph to answer the following questions.

a List the geese in order starting with the most common.

b Altogether how many of these geese were spotted?

c List the geese for which more than 7000 were spotted.

Worksheet 2

1

Month	1	2	3	4	5	6
Sales	100	150	180	220	260	290

A new brand of bottled water has come on the market.
Its sales over six months are noted.

a Use the grid to draw a line graph of sales.
b Describe the trend of the graph.

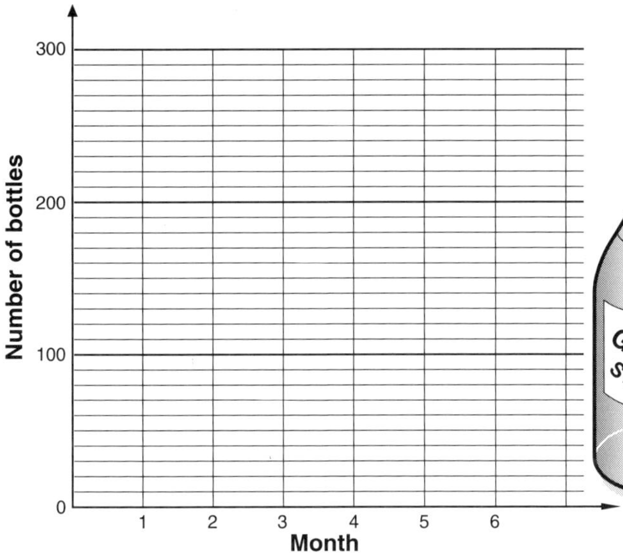

2 A motorbike is timed over an obstacle course. Its speed (in miles per hour) is recorded every two minutes.

a Use the grid to draw a line graph of speed against time.
b Describe the trend of the graph.

Time (minutes)	0	2	4	6	8	10
Speed (mph)	50	20	0	25	10	35

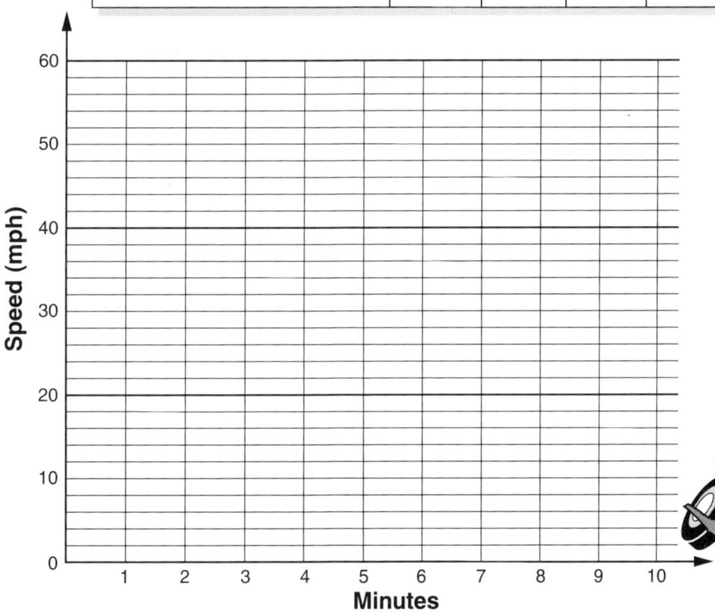

3

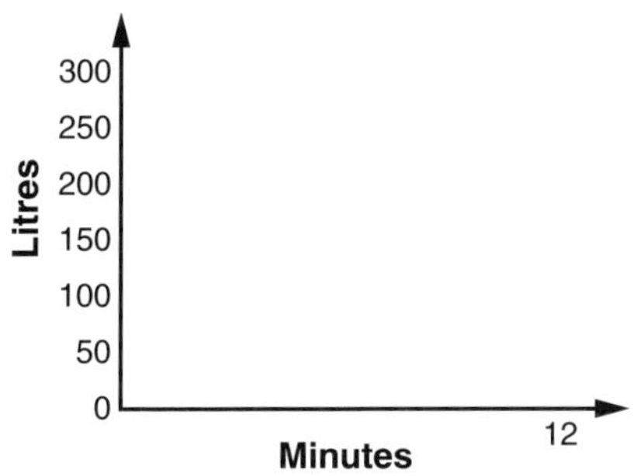

Minutes	2	4	6	8	10	12
Litres	50	100	150	200	250	300

A petrol tank at a garage is slowly filled up.
This table shows how it filled over 12 minutes.

a Using the axes as a guide, draw a line graph of the figures.
b Describe the trend.

More Practice 1

1 Iain set out on his motorbike at 7.30 pm to visit his girlfriend Jennie.

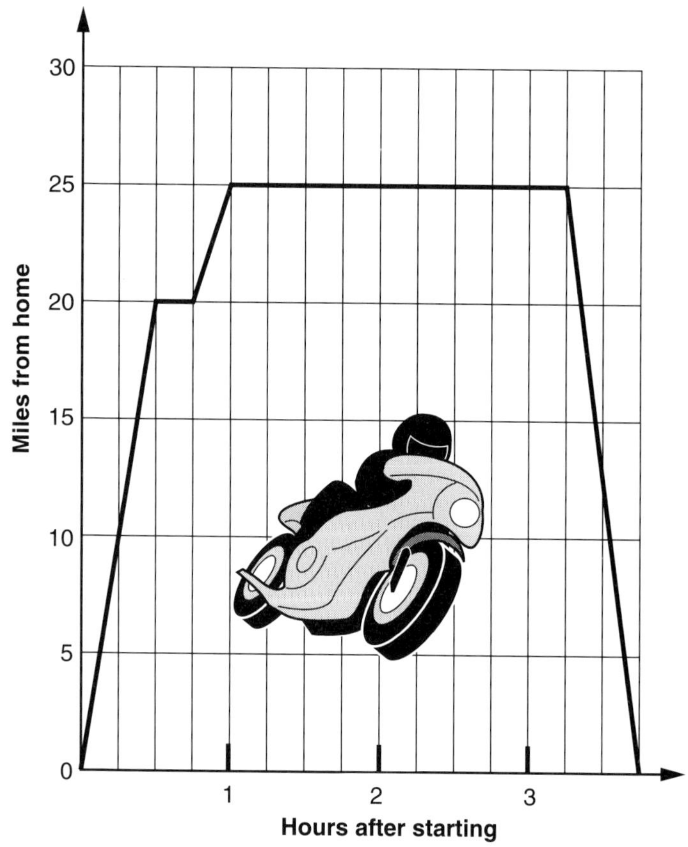

a On the way there, Iain stopped at a garage. How far from home was he?

b How long did he stop at the garage?

c What time was it when Iain stopped at the garage?

d Iain took half an hour to travel the 20 miles to the garage. Write down his speed in miles per hour.

e What time did Iain arrive at Jennie's home?

f How far from Iain's home did Jennie live?

g How long did Iain stay with Jennie?

h What was the time when Iain set off to return home?

i How long did it take Iain to return home?

2 Calum left home to visit Iain. He left at 7.30 pm.
The dotted line graph shows his journey.

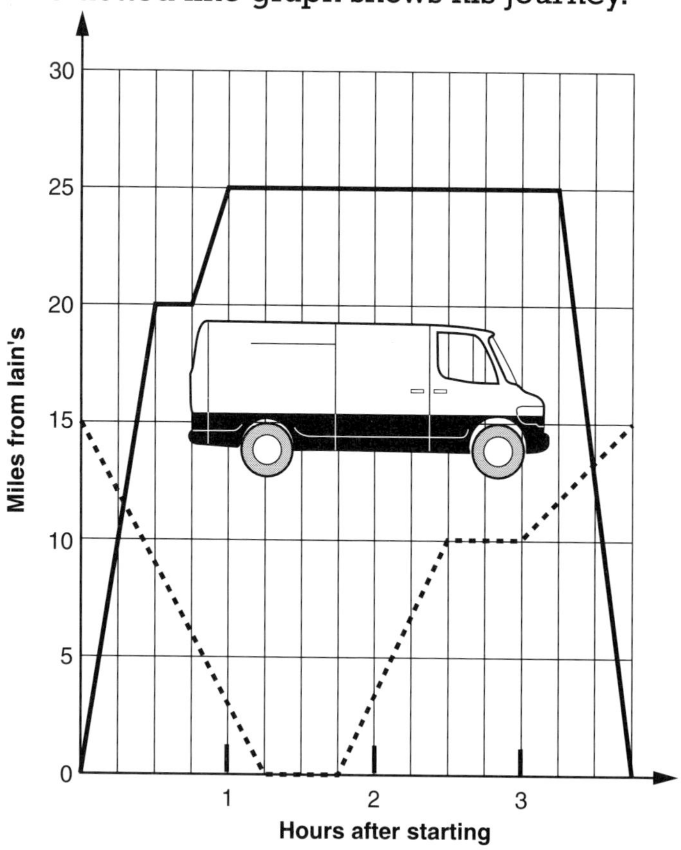

a How far does Calum live from Iain?

b How long did it take him to reach Iain's?

c How long did he wait at Iain's before giving up and going home?

d Going home he passed Iain on the road. At what time was this?

More Practice 2

1 A youth club has a variety of games and activities.
This table shows the favourite activities of 50 of its members.

	Bowls	Darts	Dominoes	Snooker	Cards
Number	10	10	5	20	5
Parts	2	2	1	4	1

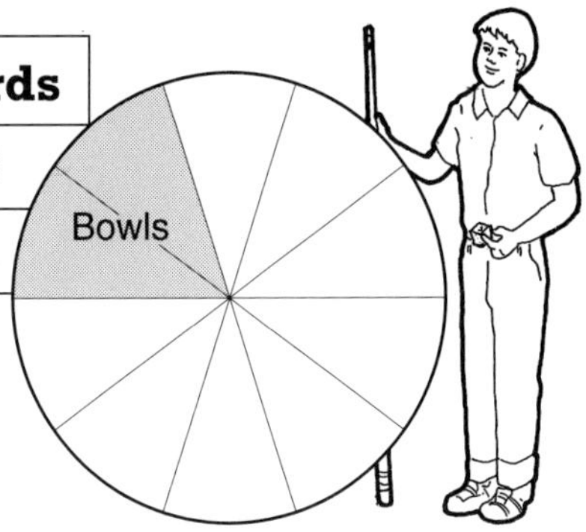

The blank pie chart has 10 parts.
$50 \div 10 = 5$, so each part represents 5 people.

Complete the pie chart to show this information.

2

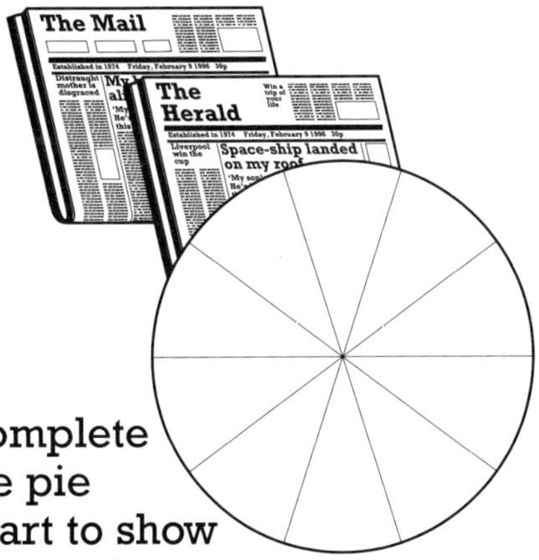

150 people are asked which newspaper they bought.
Complete the table.

	News	Herald	Post	Mail
Number	60	45	30	?
Parts	4			

The blank pie chart has 10 parts.
$150 \div 10 = 15$, so each part represents 15 people.

Complete the pie chart to show the results.

3 A school band has 120 players.
This table shows how many belong to each section of the band.

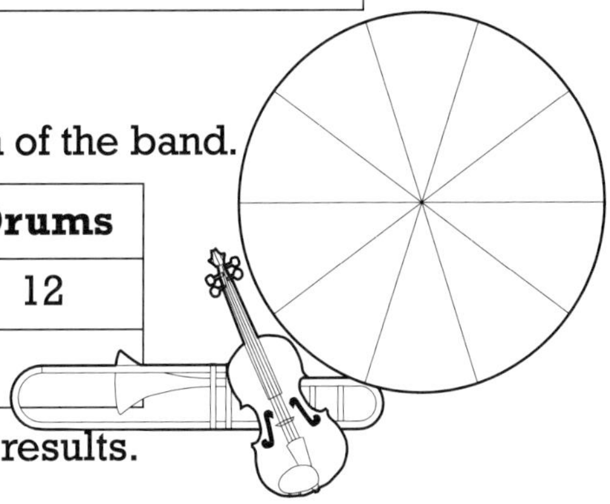

	String	Brass	Woodwind	Piano	Drums
Number	24	12	36	36	12
Parts					

Complete the table and draw a pie chart of your results.

4

A national survey on favourite take-away foods in Britain was reported in the newspapers.
This table shows the percentage (parts out of 100) vote for each kind.

The blank pie chart has 20 parts.
$100 \div 20 = 5$, so each part is 5%.

	Chips	Chow mein	Curry	Burger	Pizza
Number	25%	20%	15%	30%	10%
Parts					

Complete the table and draw a pie chart.

More Practice 3

1 300 people were asked to name their favourite holiday city.

City	Votes	Parts
Edinburgh	75	
Vienna	45	
Paris	60	
New York	30	
London	15	
Rome	75	

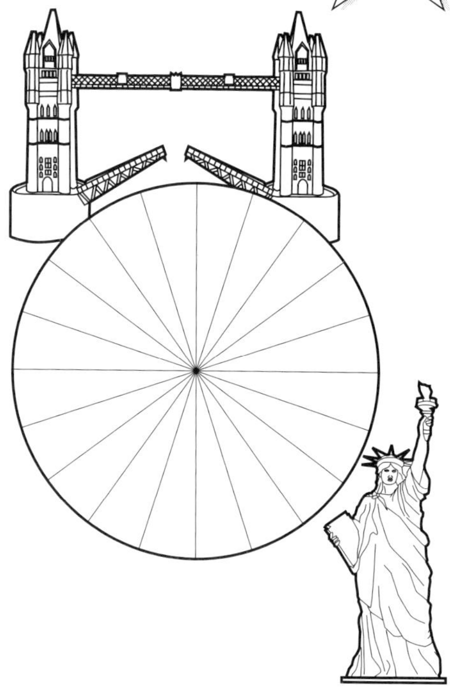

a A 20-part circle stands for 300 votes. What does one part of the circle stand for?
b Complete the pie chart using the figures in the table.

2

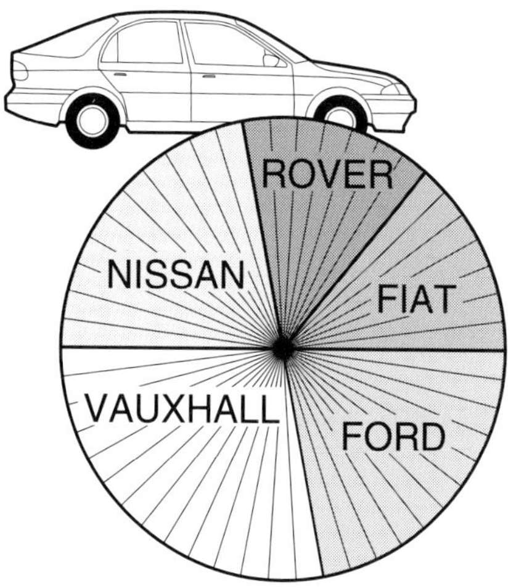

300 motorists were asked which kind of car they had bought.

a The circle has 50 parts to represent 300. How many motorists does each part represent?
b What fraction of the pie chart had bought a Nissan car?
c How many had a Nissan car?
d What fraction had bought a Ford?
e How many altogether bought a Rover, Fiat or Vauxhall?

3 This circle is divided into 100 parts. 25% means 25 parts out of 100.

This pie chart shows the popularity of some pets.

If 200 people were surveyed, how many said they liked:

a birds
b dogs
c ponies
d fish
e cats?

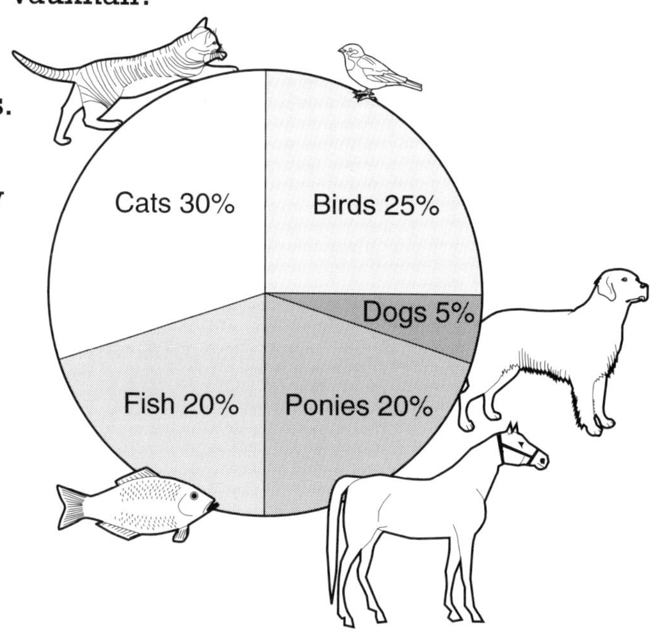

Survey

Work with a partner.

Prepare a table for collecting your information so that it is easy to enter data.

Organise a topic which will give the object under question five options.

You can collect lots of little categories under the title 'Others'.

Try to pick a fairly large sample.

Draw a graph. Decorate and display it in your classroom.

Possible Surveys

1 What do pupils eat for breakfast?

There is plenty of scope for categories here.

Don't forget that 'no breakfast' is a possible option.

Decorate the questionnaire with pictures of cereal packets which you are offering as options.

2 What kinds of cars do teachers drive?

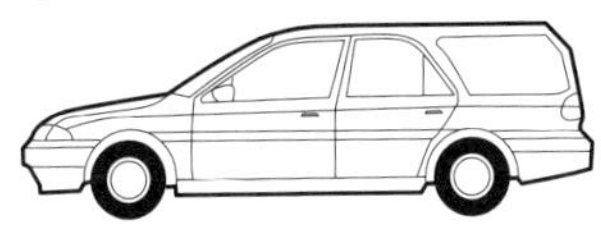

If the results are to be shown in a bar graph, the columns could be coloured to match the colour of the cars.

Offer examples of five basic colours on your questionnaire and ask the person questioned to select the nearest.

3 What are pupils favourite school subjects?

Prepare a list of subjects.

Allow each person two votes.

Pie charts would be appropriate for this survey.

4 Make a collage of statistical information by collecting tables or graphs from newspapers and magazines.

Add some of your own by looking up general knowledge books in your school library.

Use frieze paper for your collage.

Decorate and display your collage on your classroom wall.

Pie Chart Templates

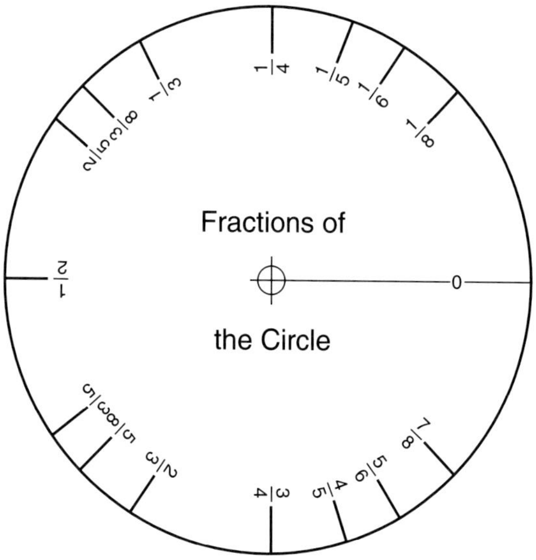

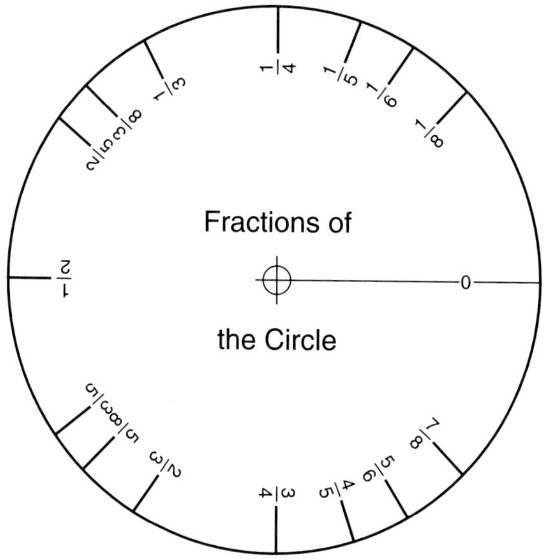

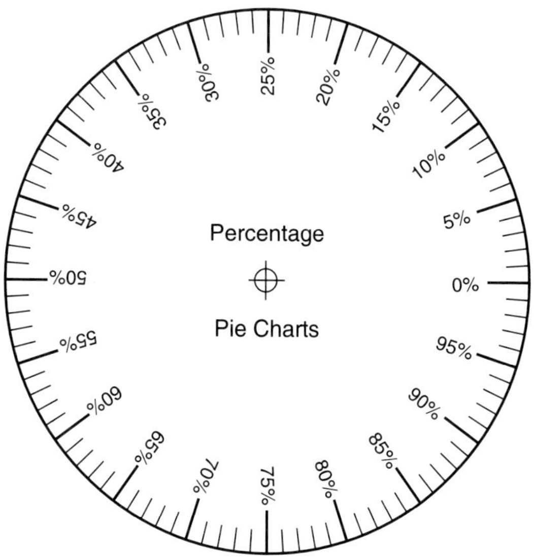

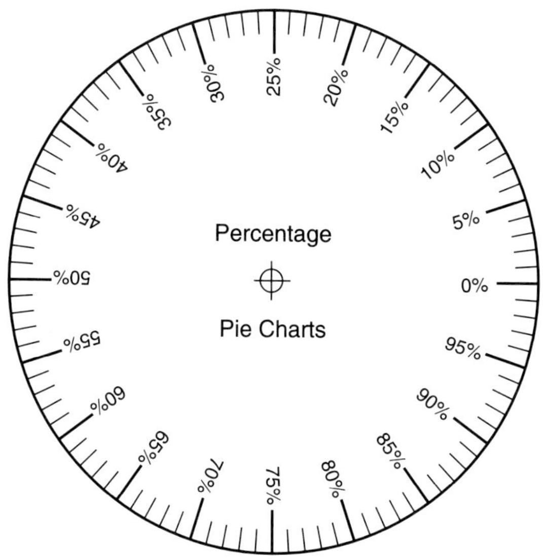

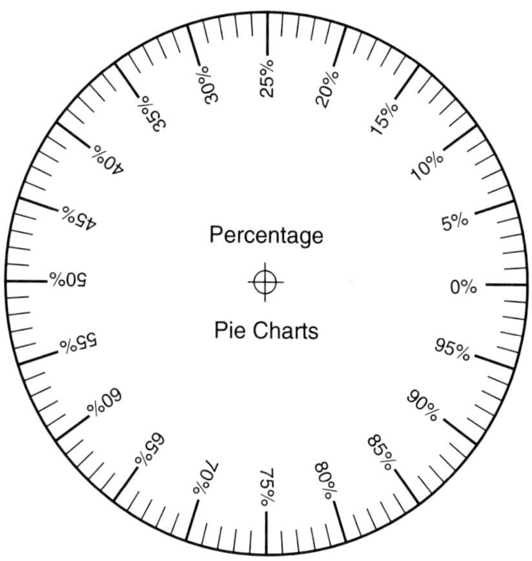

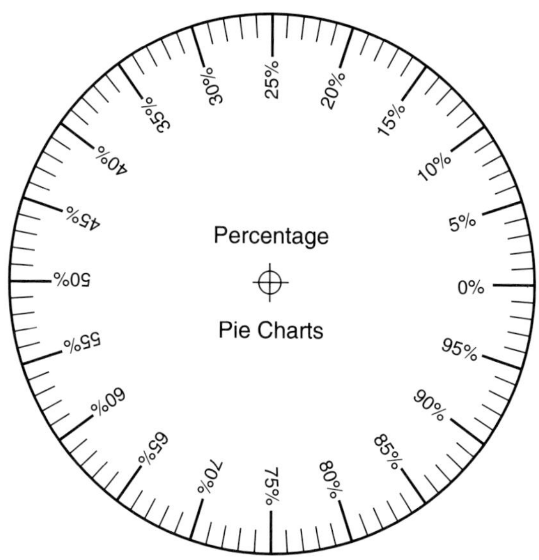

11 2-D SHAPES

CURRICULUM COVERAGE

Standard Grade Guidelines
Foundation Level:
Side, angle and diagonal properties of the square and rectangle.
Radius and diameter properties of a circle.
General Level:
Kite, parallelogram and rhombus.
Sum of angles of a triangle.
Isosceles and equilateral triangles.
Theorem of Pythagoras.

National Curriculum
AT 3 Levels 3, 4 and 5.

NI Curriculum
AT Shape and Space Levels 3 and 4.

AIMS AND OBJECTIVES
To consolidate and extend students' knowledge relating to 2-D shapes.

NOTES
1 Some previous knowledge is assumed.
2 No attempt is made in this chapter to deal with area and perimeter. Perimeter is covered in Chapter 12 and area will be dealt with in *Book 4*.
3 The word 'polygon' is never used here although mentioned in the National Curriculum. It is appropriate for students at this level to confine work to triangles and quadrilaterals.
4 It is impossible within the scope of this book to teach the theorem of Pythagoras. The topic is, however, un-italicised material in the *Arrangements*. For that reason a sheet of easy problems is included in the Teacher's notes. If a student is felt capable, then he/she may be taught the steps and given this sheet. If further development is required, then *Book 3A* will provide this.

TEACHER'S RESOURCES
Worksheets 1, 2 and 3 are to assist in Exercises 2, 4 and 5 respectively.
More Practice 1 provides enrichment material through the use of the tangram.
More Practice 2 provides a simple extension to General Level.
Further enrichment is provided with Jacob's Ladder, Magic Squares and a dissection puzzle sheet.
A General Level extension sheet is provided for work on Pythagoras. (See note 4 above.)

PROGRESS ROUTE
Success at the check-up should allow students who wish to cover the General interface to attempt *Book 3A,* Chapter 2, Exercise 1 up to question 9, all of Exercise 2, and pages 181-2 of the Review on Shape and Space.

Worksheet 1

1 The diagrams show some roof structures.
Work out the size of each labelled angle.

a

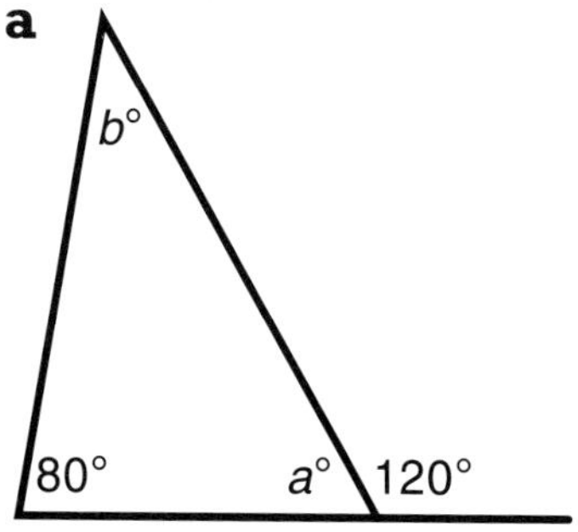

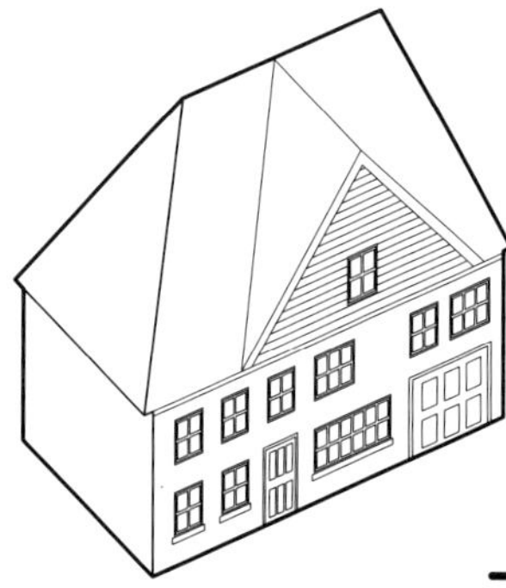

b

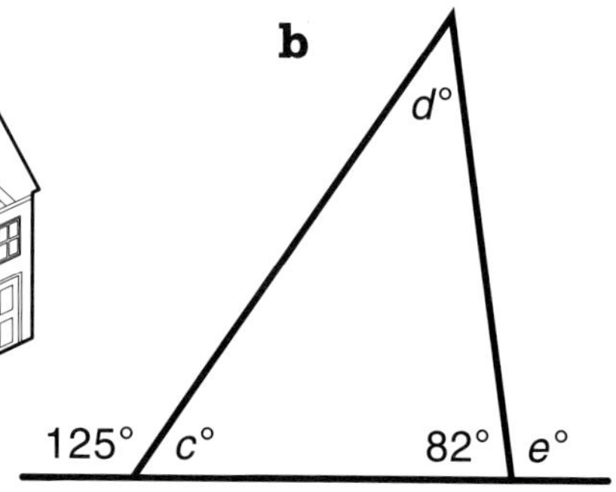

c

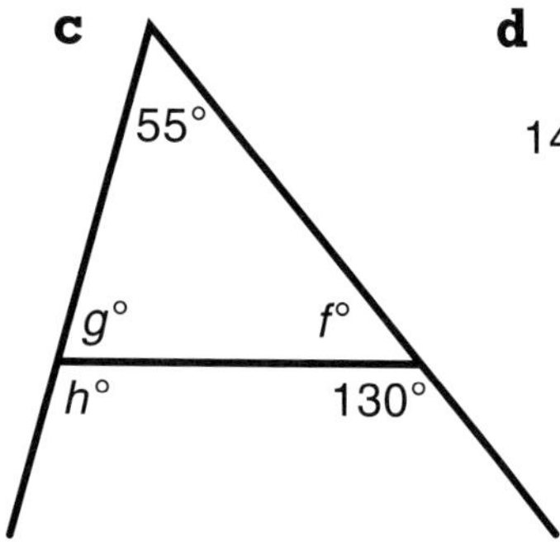

d

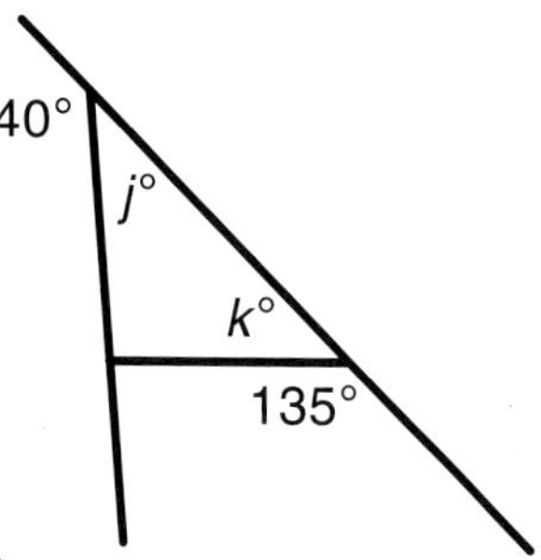

e

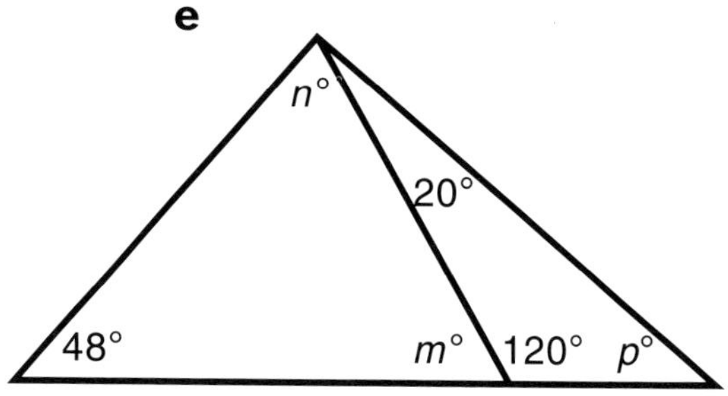

2 Each envelope has a line of symmetry.
Sketch each one and fill in the sizes of as many angles as you can.

a

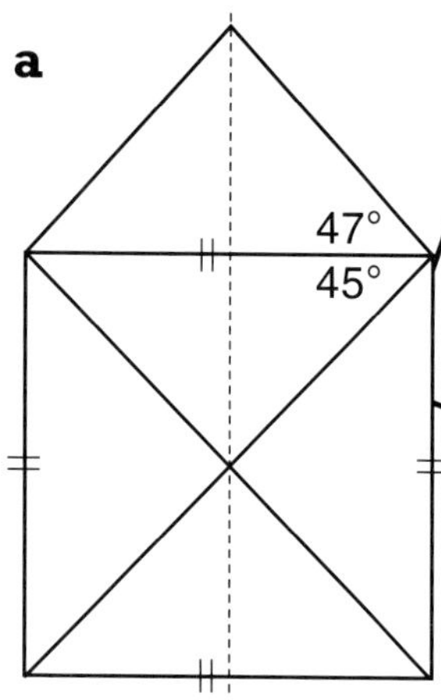

b

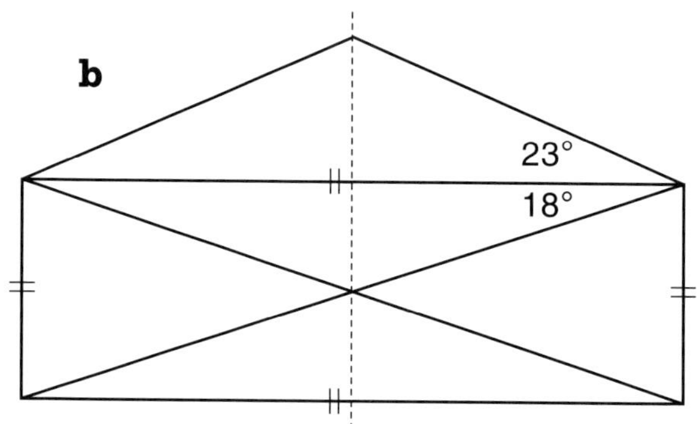

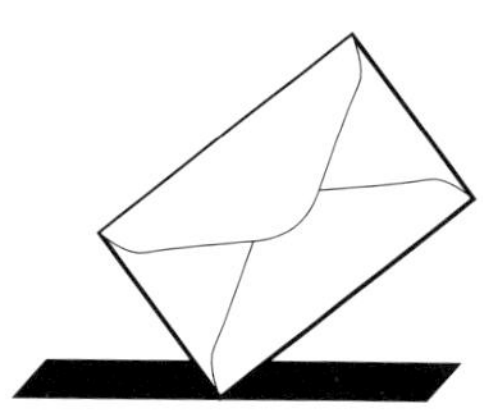

c

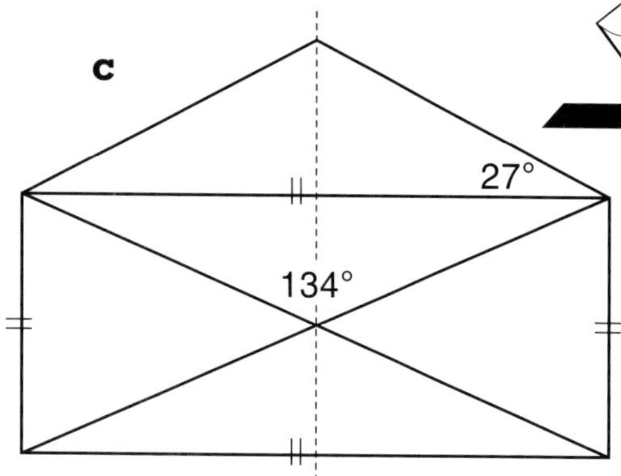

d

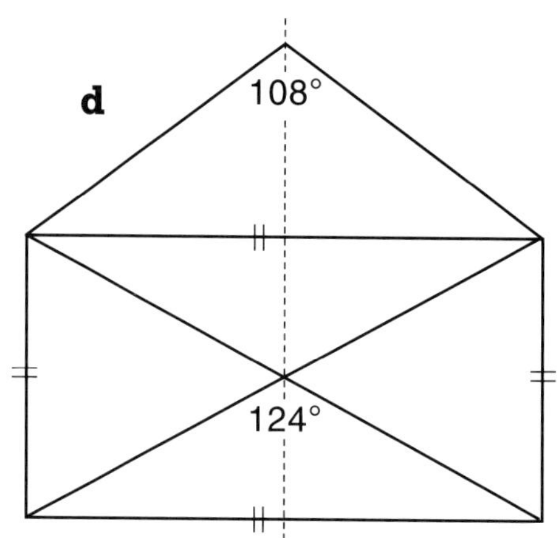

Worksheet 2

You will need scissors and glue.
Cut out the shapes and tile them.

Worksheet 3

1

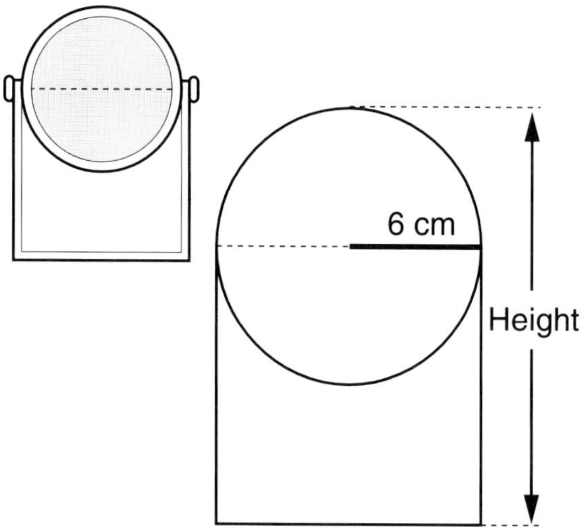

This circular mirror swivels on a square stand.

The radius of the mirror is 6 cm.

a What is the diameter of the mirror?
b What is the length of the square?
c How high is the mirror?

2 The bridge is symmetrical.

The half-circle arch has a radius of 10 m.

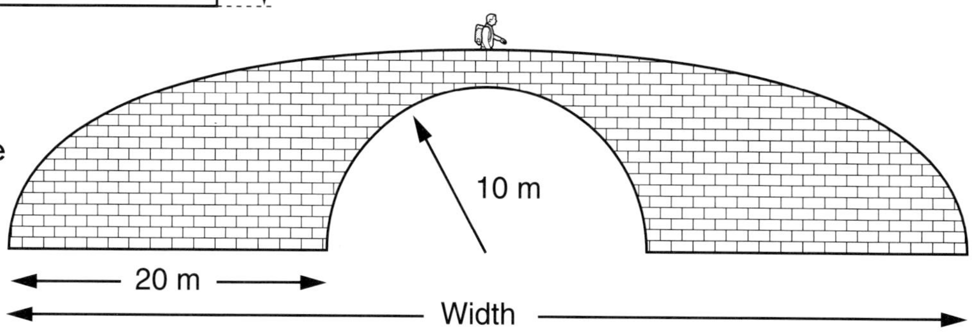

What is the overall width of the bridge?

3

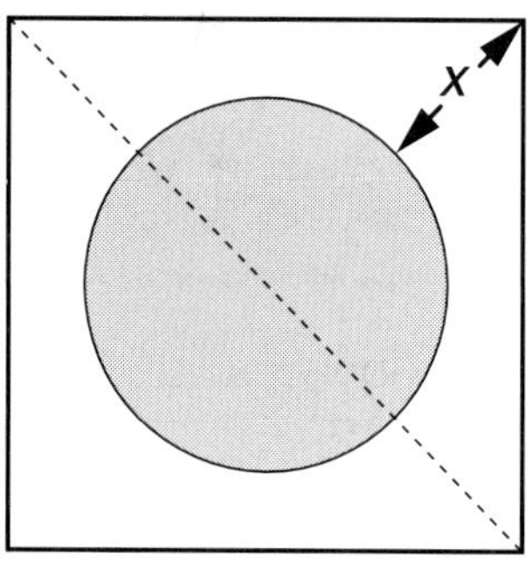

A square nut is as shown.

The diagonal of the square is 4 cm.
The radius of the hole in the middle is 1 cm.

Work out the length of x.

4 The diameter of each tin of peas is 6 cm.
How many tins of peas will fit in the box?

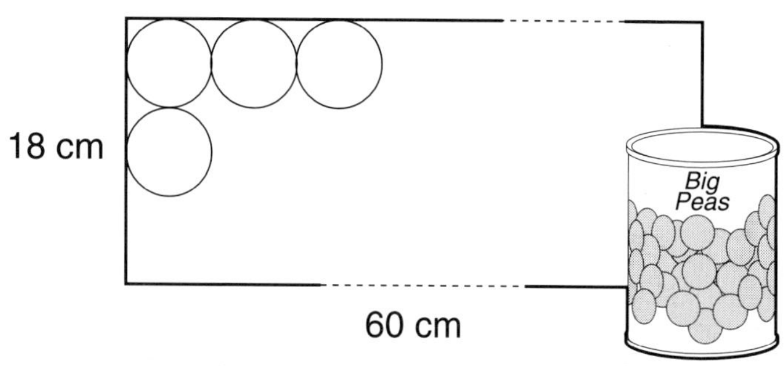

5

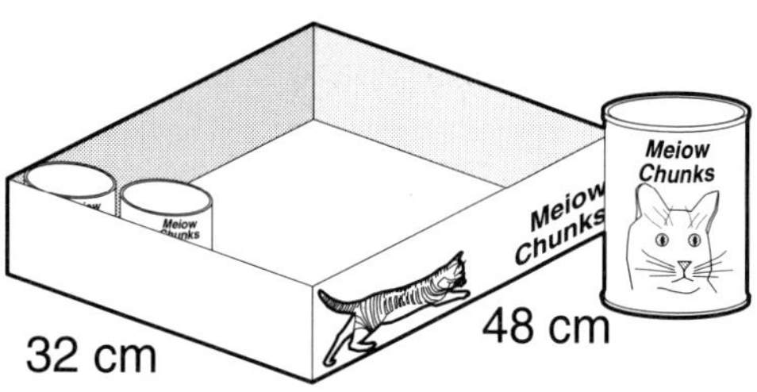

The radius of the cat-food tin is 4 cm.

How many will fit in the box?

(The tins are packed in the same way as in question 4.)

More Practice 1

The tangram

Make a copy of this square.

Cut it up as shown into seven pieces.

1 Make a square using only:

a two of the pieces
b three pieces
c four pieces
d five pieces.

2 Make each shape below. You need a set of all seven pieces for each.

a

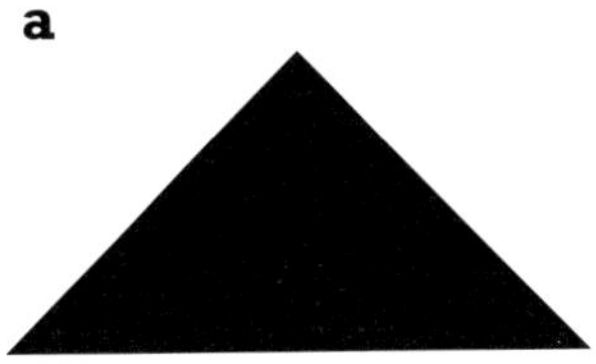

Triangle

b

Square

c

Parallelogram

d

Rectangle

3 Now make each of these shapes. Again you need a set of all seven pieces for each.

a

b

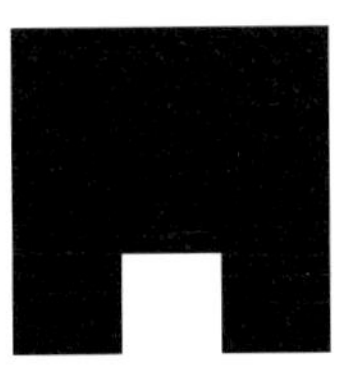

c

d

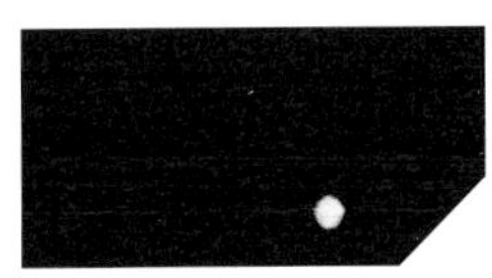

4 How do the seven pieces fit together to make each of these?

a

5 sides

b

6 sides

c

7 sides

More Practice 2

The diagonals of some four-sided shapes are shown below.

a Join the dots.
b Write the name of the shape beneath the drawing.

1

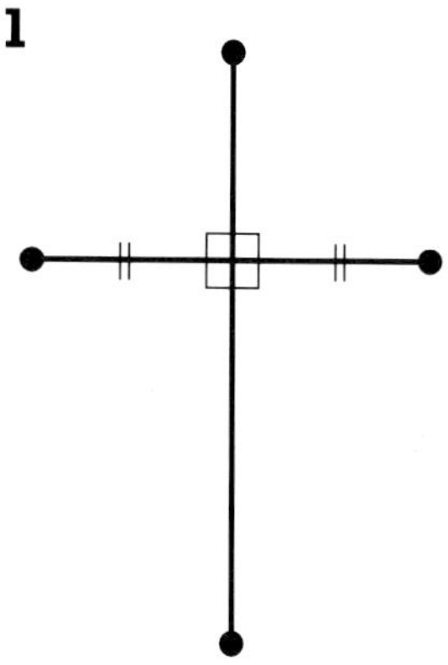

Name:

2

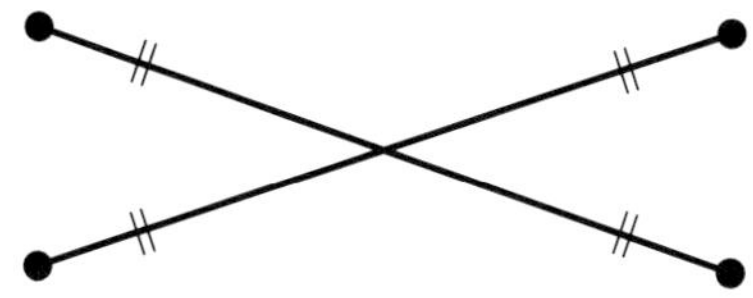

Name:

3

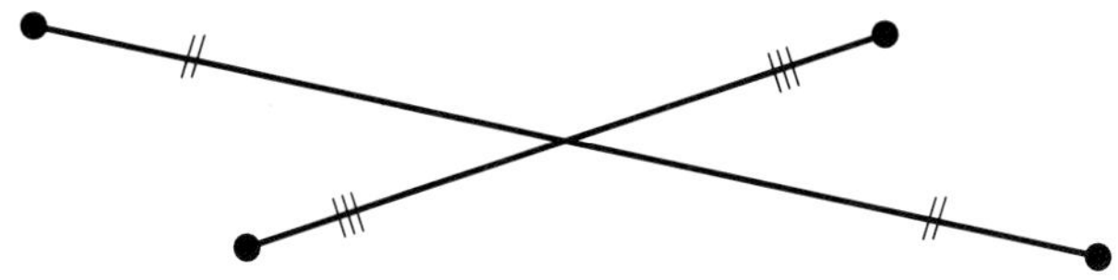

Name:

4

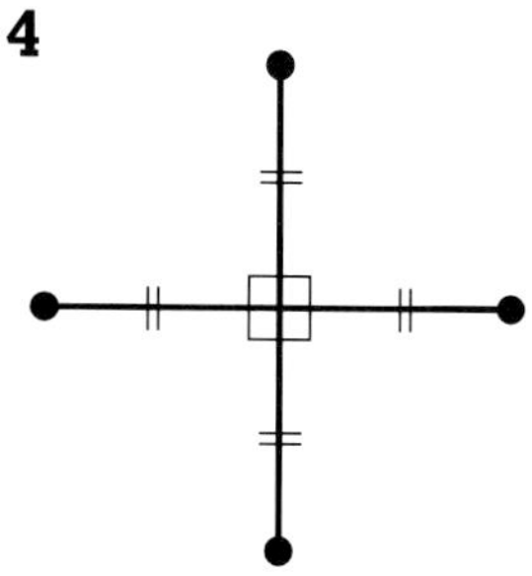

Name:

5

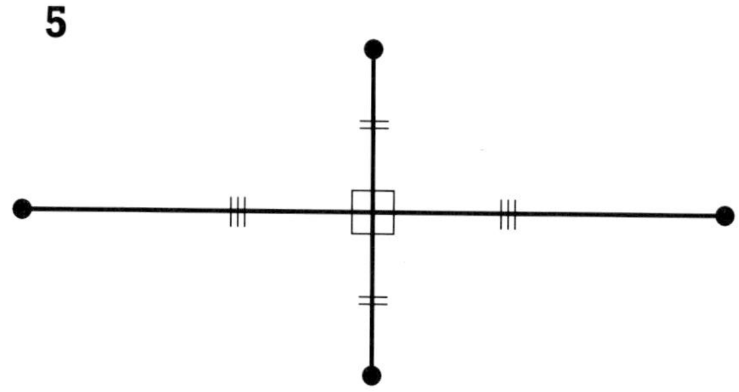

Name:

6

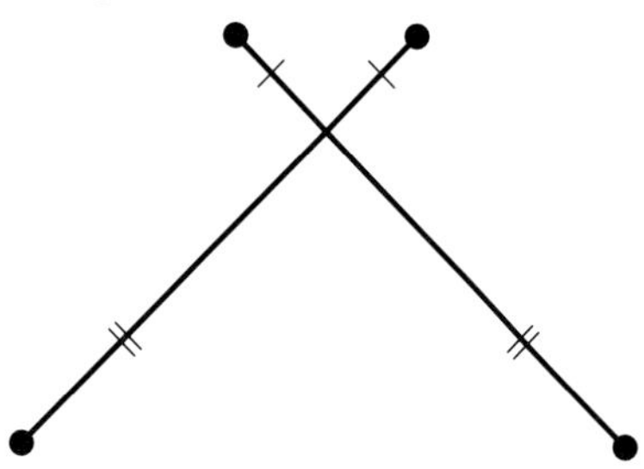

Name:

7

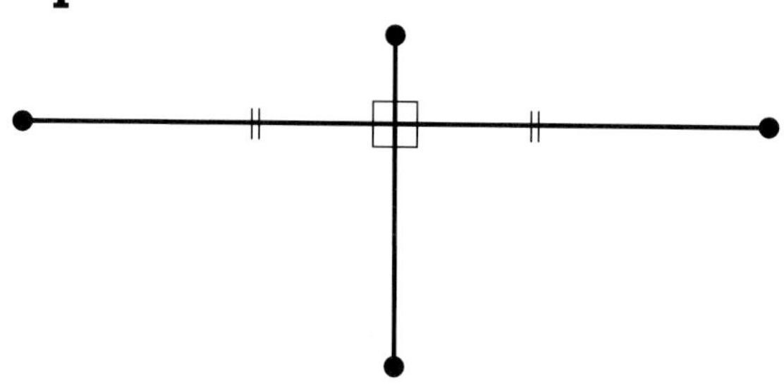

Name:

Each of these labels should be used.

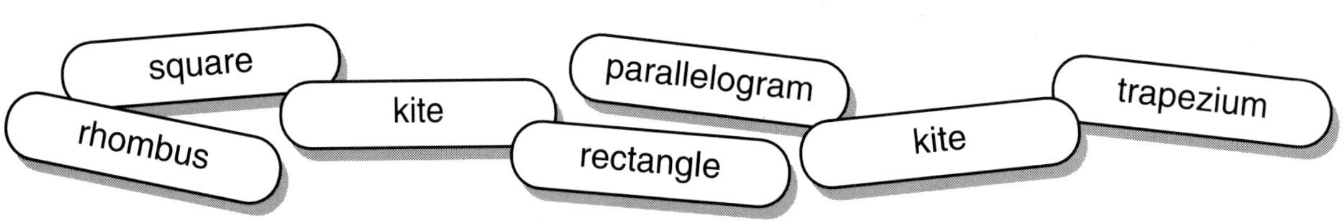

Jacob's Ladder

You must make:

(i) two identical rectangles from card
(ii) three thin rectangles from paper.
These must be longer than the card rectangles.

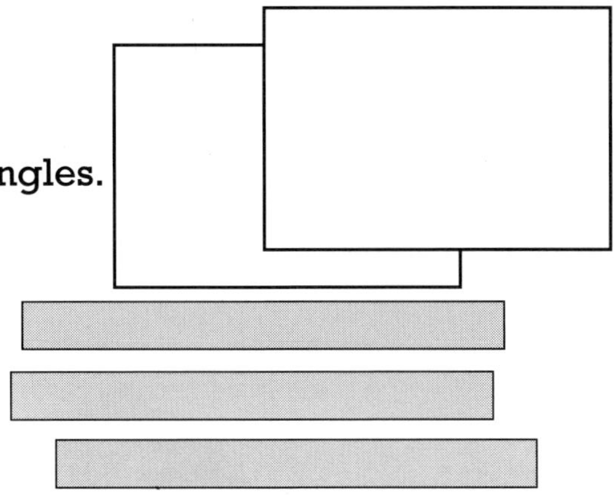

Glue the three strips to one card rectangle.

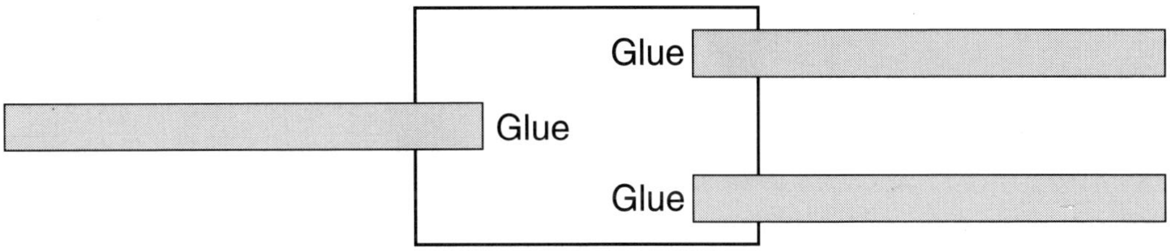

Flip it over.

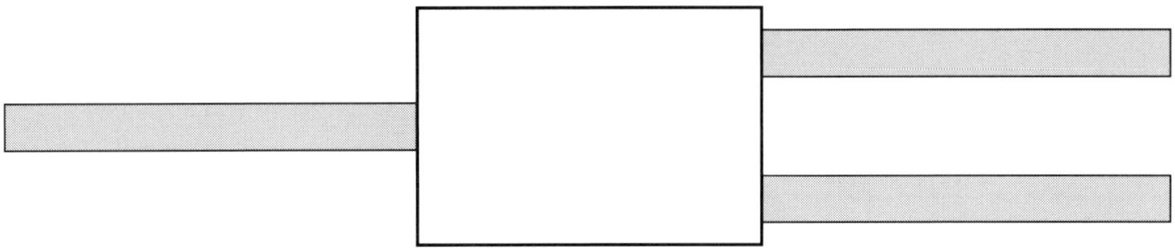

Fold the strips on top of the card.

Place the second card on top.

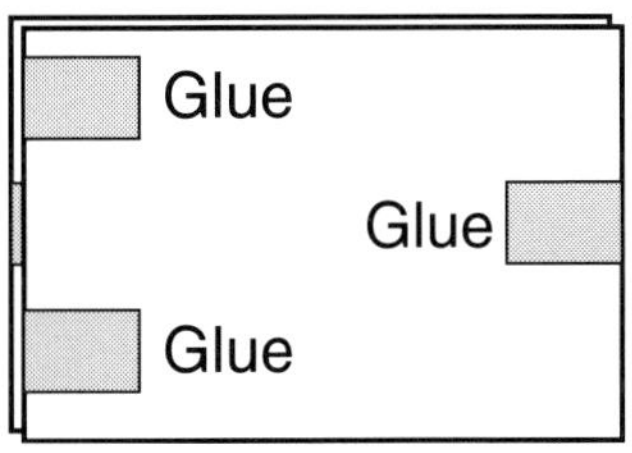

Fold the tabs which show on top of the card and glue them down.
This can be used for many things such as magic wallets or novelty greetings cards.

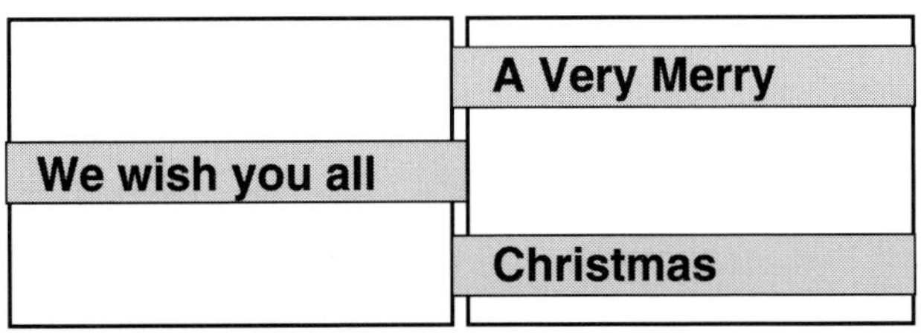

Open it one way and write a Christmas message.

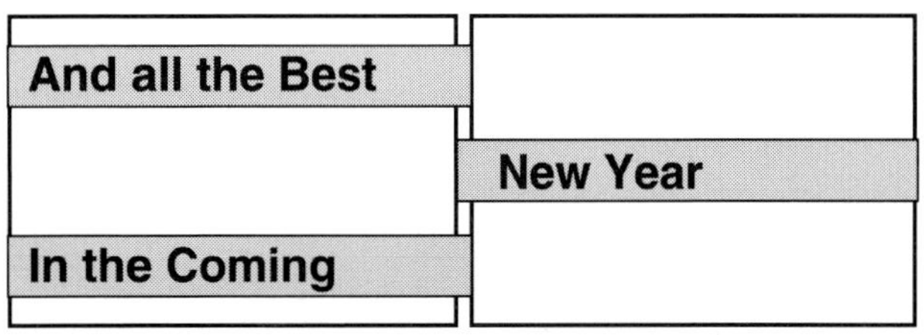

Open it the other way and give a New Year message.

Magic Squares

Play this card trick on your friends and show them your magical skills.

Cut out the 36 cards opposite.

S	Q	U	A	R	E
S	Q	U	A	R	E
S	Q	U	A	R	E
S	Q	U	A	R	E
S	Q	U	A	R	E
S	Q	U	A	R	E

Arrange them as above, but *face down*.

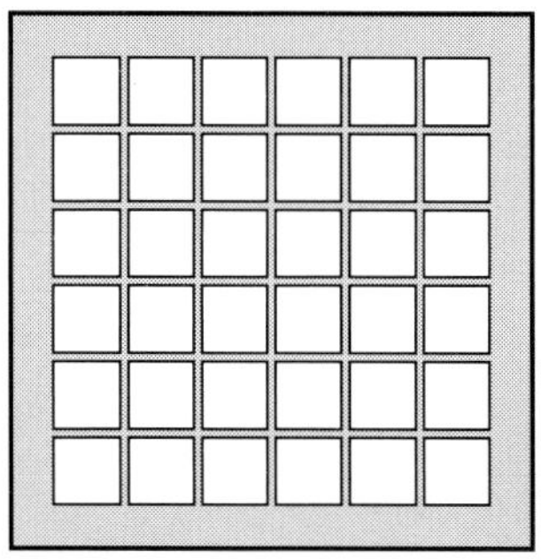

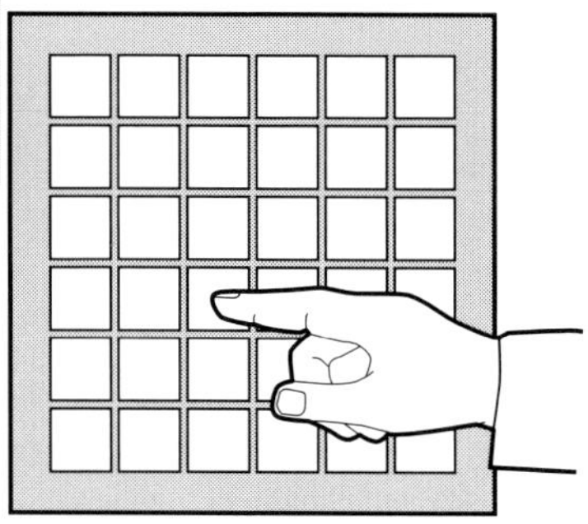

Ask someone to pick a card and lay it aside.

Remove all the other cards from that row and column.

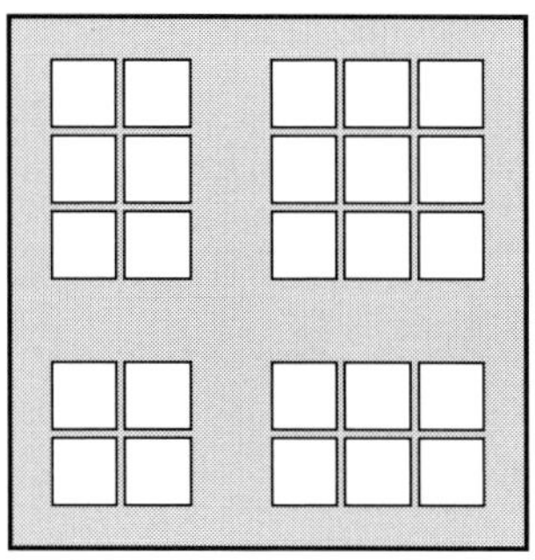

Repeat these steps another four times. (You now have five cards laid aside.)

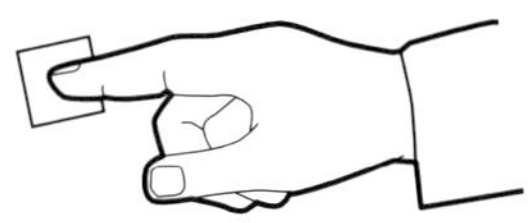

The last remaining card is also laid aside.

Turn over your six cards and you will be able to make the word SQUARE with them.

Puzzle Sheet

1

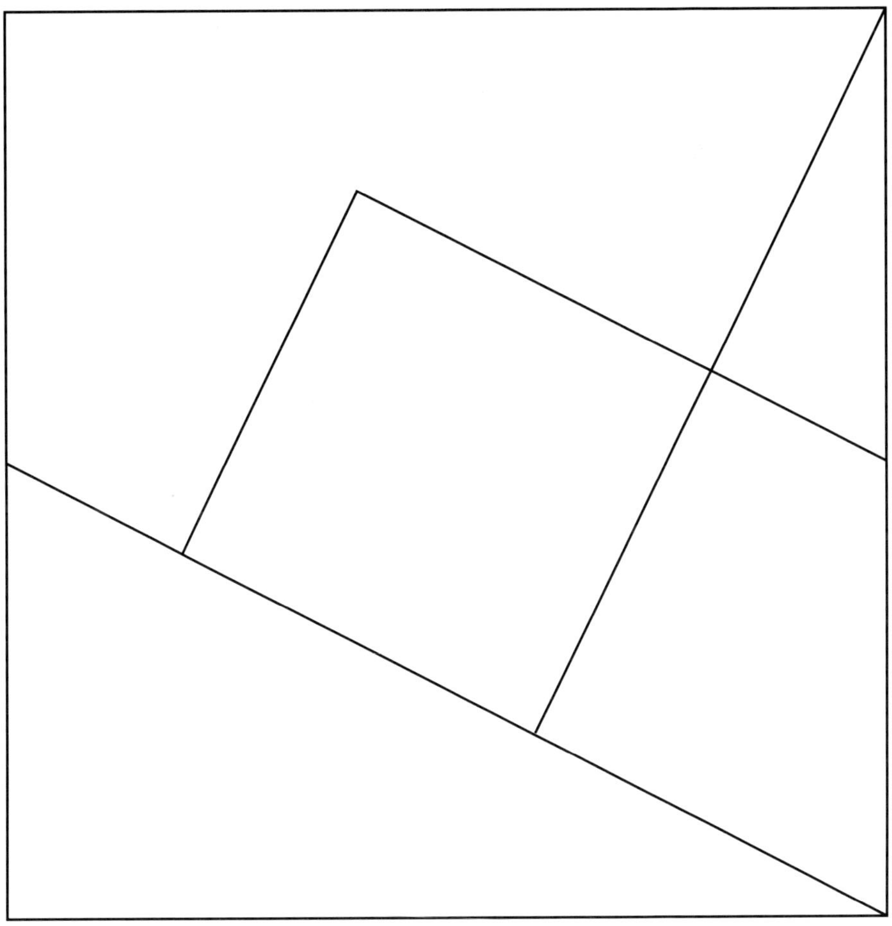

Cut the square up to make the five pieces.

Now rearrange the five pieces to make:

a a rectangle
b a right-angled triangle
c a cross
d the square again.

2 Cut this equilateral triangle into four pieces.

Use the pieces to make a square.

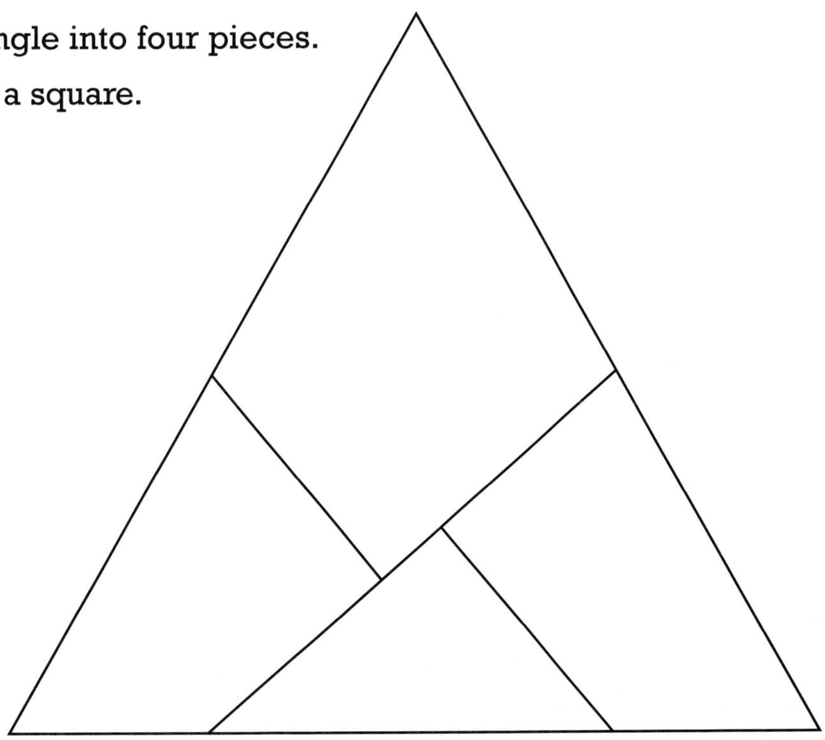

Pythagoras

You can always find the longest side of a right-angled triangle when the other two sides are given.

Example

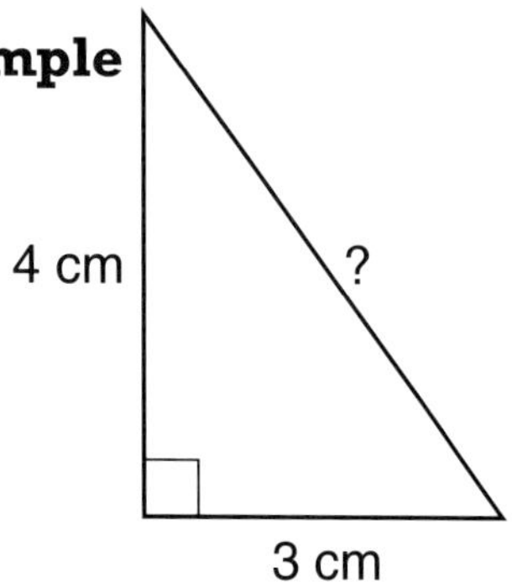

Step 1: Note the given numbers.	3 and 4
Step 2: Multiply each number by itself.	9 and 16
Step 3: Add your answers.	25
Step 4: Use the √ button on your calculator.	5

The missing side is 5 cm long.

1 Find the missing side in each triangle.

a

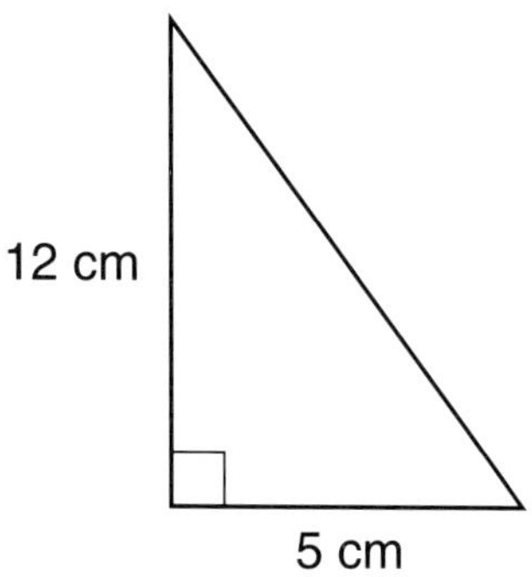

b

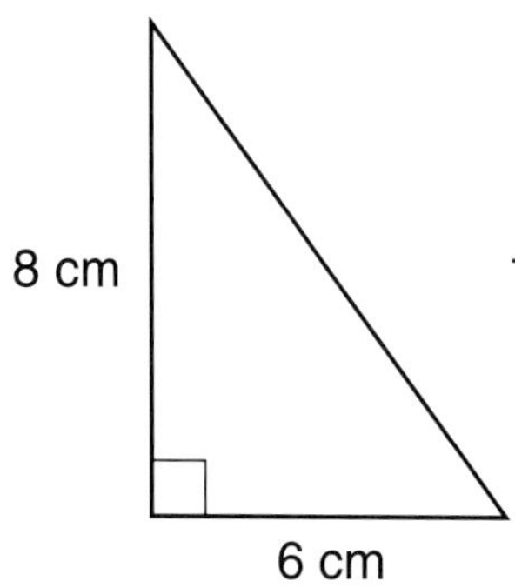

c

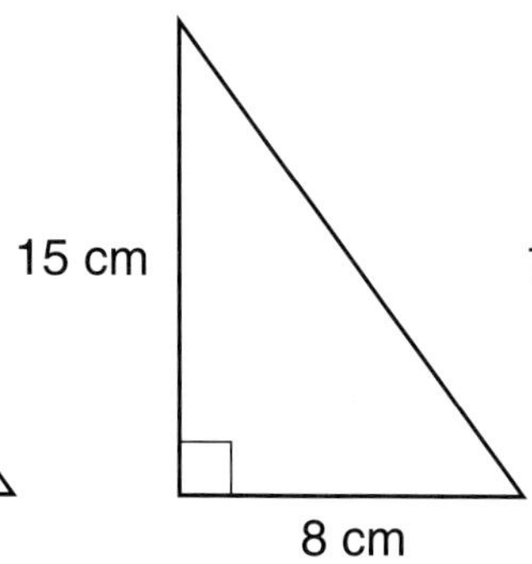

d

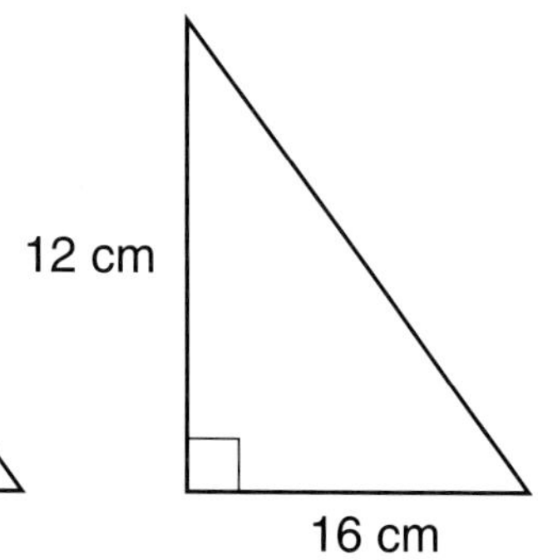

e

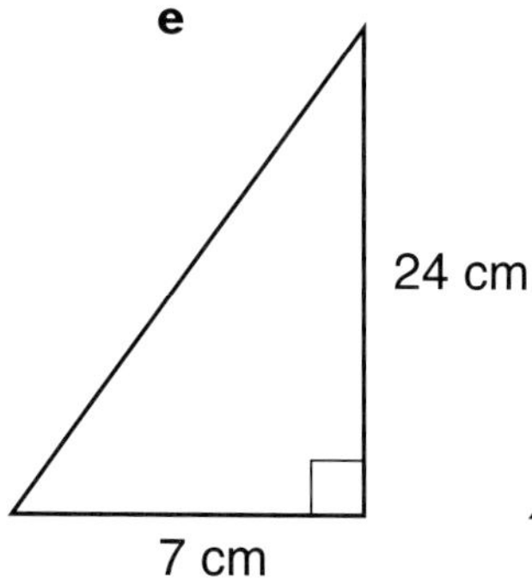

f

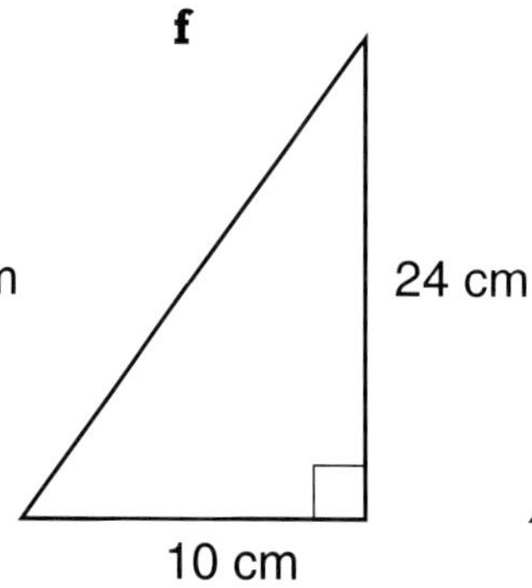

g

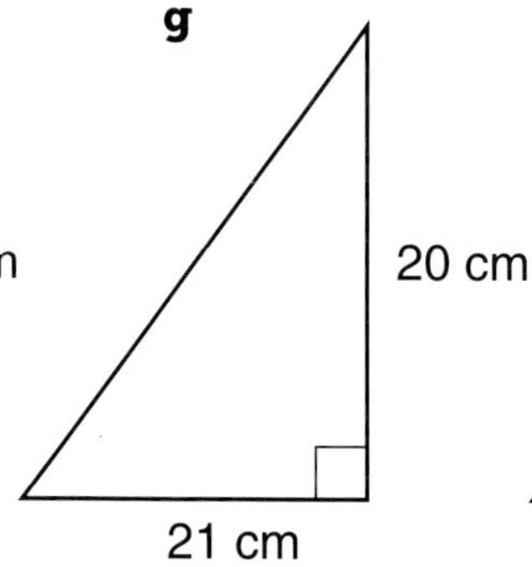

h

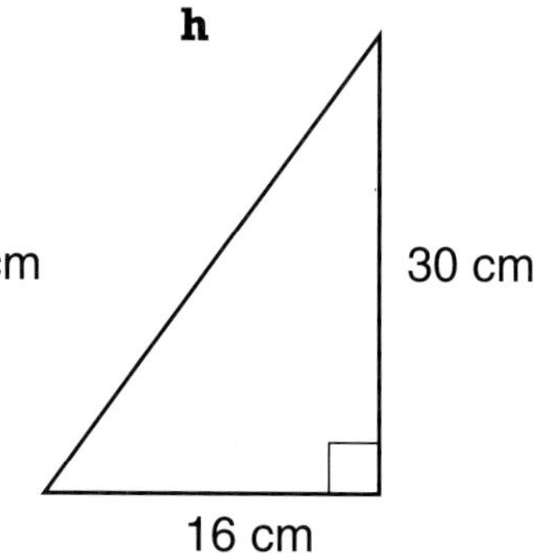

2

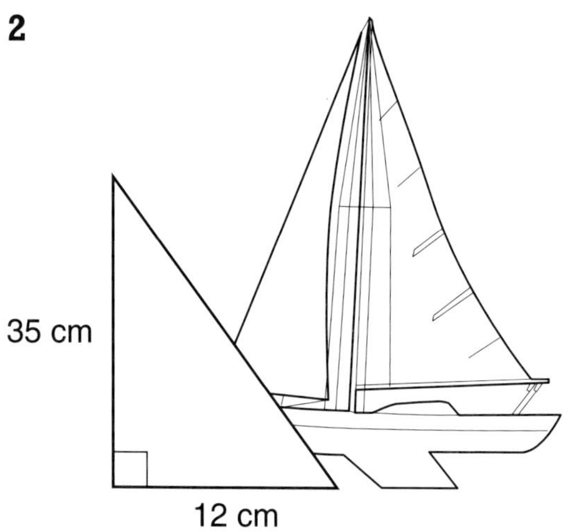

A model yacht has a sail with sides as shown.

How long is the third side of the sail?

12 MEASUREMENT

CURRICULUM COVERAGE

Standard Grade Guidelines
Foundation Level:
Estimate length.
Measure length to a reasonable degree of accuracy.
Understand the inter-relationship among the units (mm, cm, m, km).
Calculate the perimeter of rectilinear figures.
General Level:
Find the circumference of a circle.

National Curriculum
AT 3 Levels 3, 4 and 5.

NI Curriculum
AT Measures Levels 3, 4 and 5.

AIMS AND OBJECTIVES

To provide appropriate practice in estimating and measuring length.
To consolidate earlier work on length.
To introduce perimeter and to provide practice in calculating perimeters.
To provide bridging points to work at General Level.

NOTES

1 The worksheets provide larger size diagrams for students who are experiencing difficulty with measurement.
2 'The House that Jack Built' sheet can be enlarged since it carries its own scale with it.

TEACHER'S RESOURCES

Worksheet 1 provides extra work on measuring in millimetres.
Worksheet 2 contains work on changing units of measurement – kilometres, metres, centimetres and millimetres.
Worksheets 3 and 4 have work on calculating perimeters by adding the lengths of sides.
'The House that Jack Built' contains more perimeter measurement in context.
More Practice 1 asks students to estimate the circumference of circles (using diameter × 3).
More Practice 2 extends this to calculating the circumference using 3.14.

PROGRESS ROUTE

This chapter does not link directly with a chapter in *Book 3A*. It is, however, fundamental work and some students should now be prepared to tackle some of the Chapter 9 exercises on perimeter and area.

Worksheet 1

Measure the length and breadth of the rectangle in each stamp in millimetres. Complete the table.

a

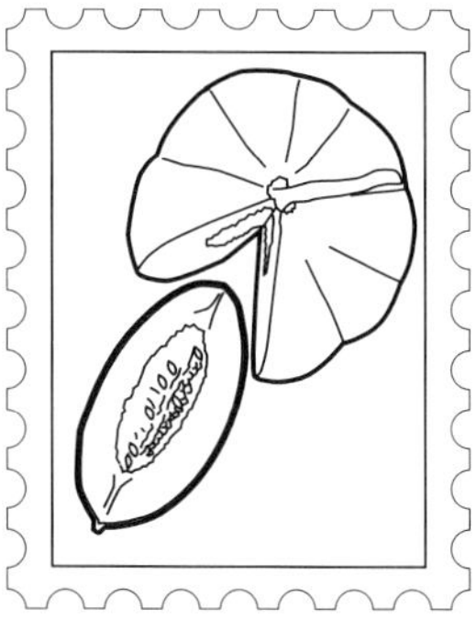

b

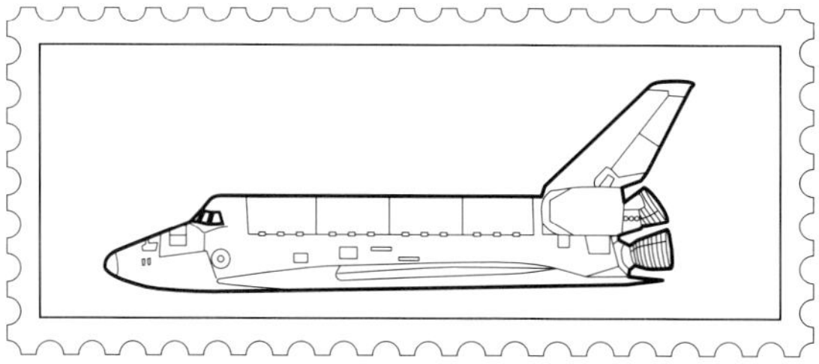

c

d

e

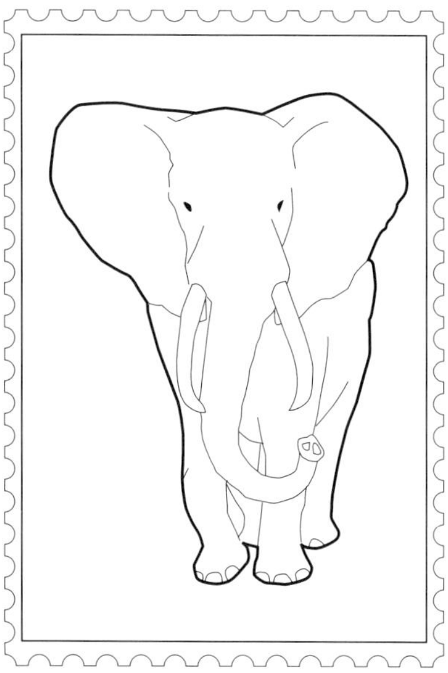

Stamp	Length (mm)	Breadth (mm)
a		
b		
c		
d		
e		
f		
g		
h		
i		
j		
k		

f

g

h

i

j

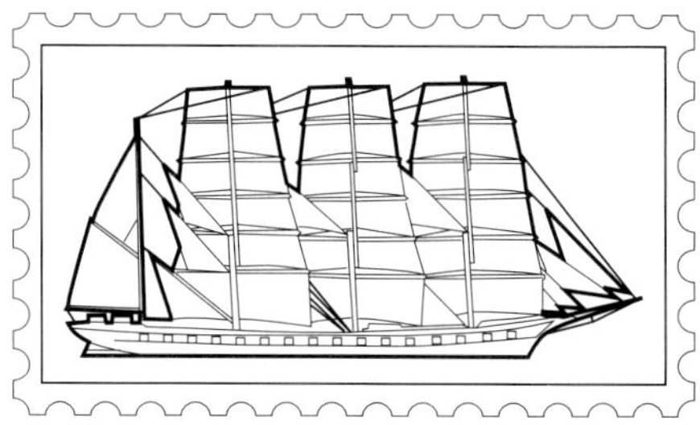

k

Worksheet 2

1 Find the matching lengths to complete the table.

0.23 m

0.39 m

0.98 m

1.43 m

1.48 m

2.34 m

39 cm | 98 cm | 390 mm | 230 mm | 2340 mm | 23 cm

234 cm | 1430 mm | 143 cm | 980 mm | 1480 mm | 148 cm

	Bottle	*Dog*	*Girl*	*Woman*	*Man*	*Elephant*
Metres	0.23 m	0.39 m				
Centimetres	23 cm					
Millimetres	mm					

2 Complete the table. The first column has been done.

Metres	0.55 m			3.27 m		
Centimetres	55 cm	142 cm			415 cm	
Millimetres	550 mm		720 mm			6410 mm

3 Complete the table.

Kilometres	3 km		0.6 km		1 km	
Metres	3000 m			100 m		
Centimetres	300 000 cm	50 000 cm				6000 cm

Worksheet 3

Maggie wants to make a patchwork placemat.
The time it will take her depends on the amount of stitching she will have to do.

1 Work out the perimeter of each patch.

2 Work out the total length of stitching needed.
(She will stitch round the outside too.)
All measurements are in centimetres.

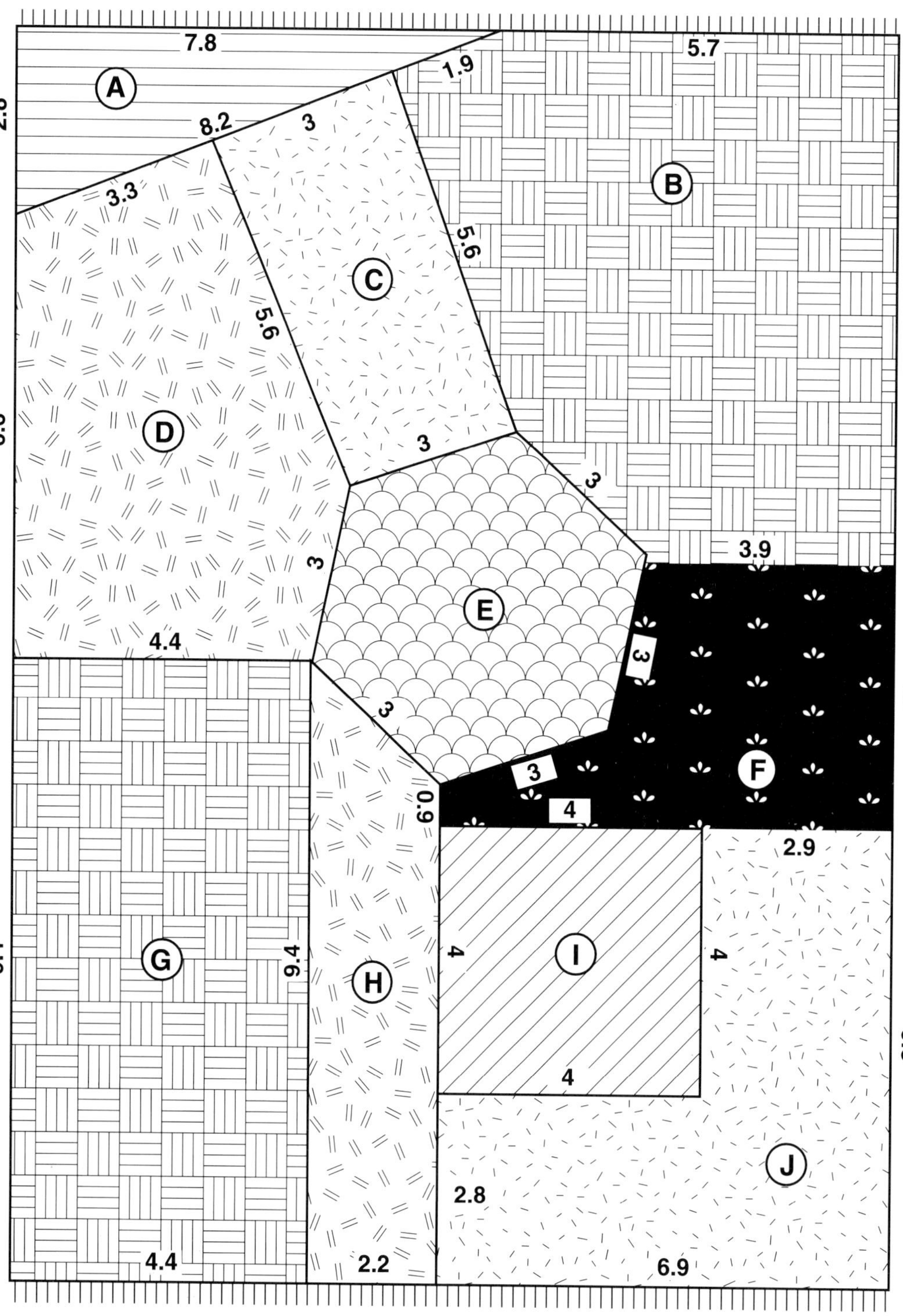

Worksheet 4

1 A square has a perimeter of 60 cm.

a How long is each side?
b Draw the square.

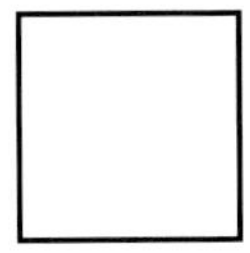

2 Work out the length of the missing side.

a

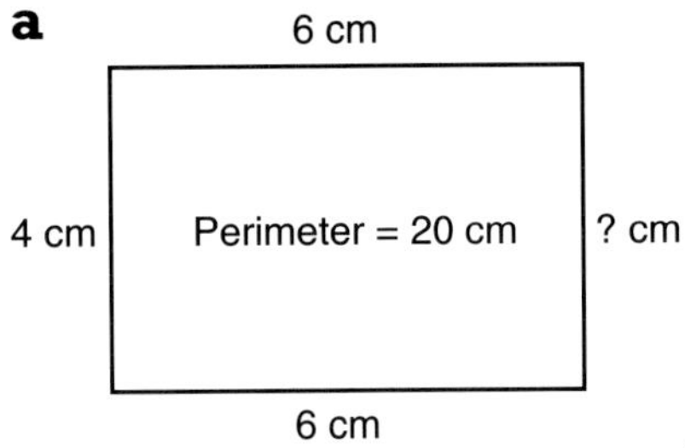

Don't measure

b

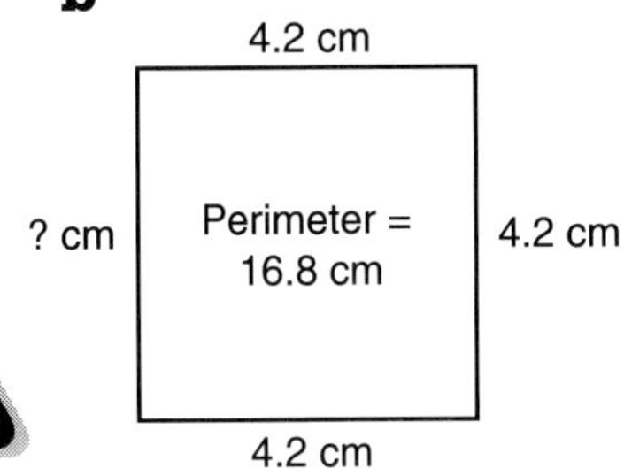

c

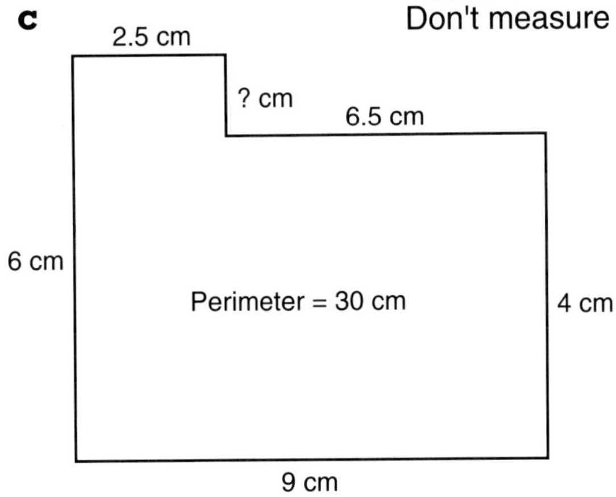

d

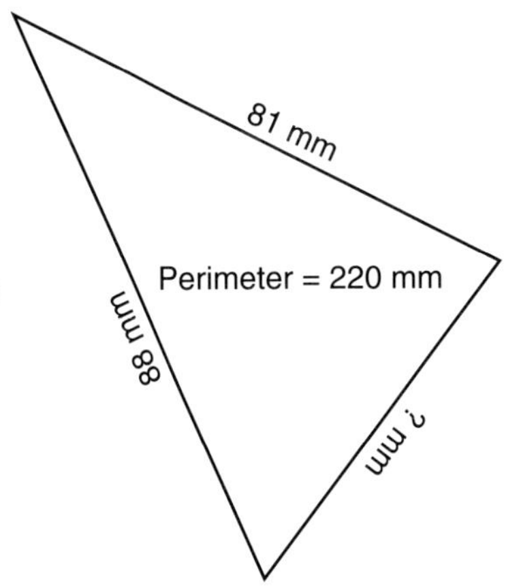

e

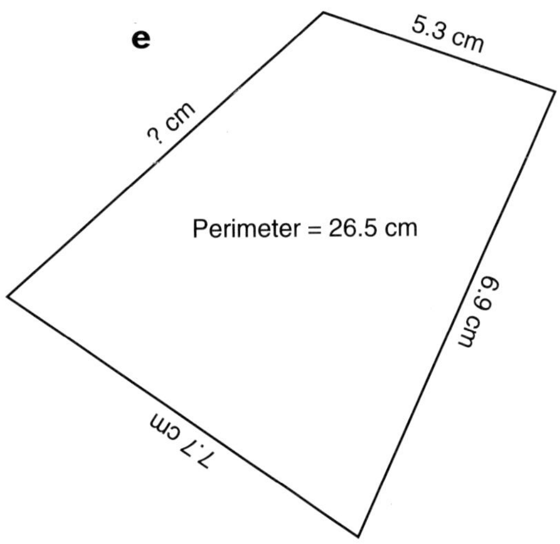

f

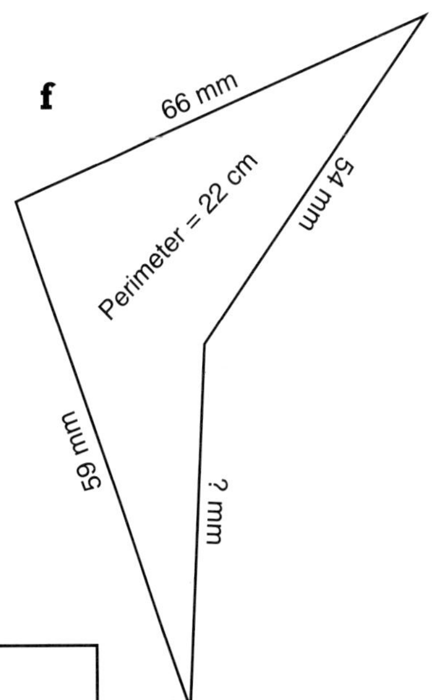

3 A rectangle has a perimeter of 60 cm.
Its length is 20 cm.

a What is its width?
b Draw the rectangle.

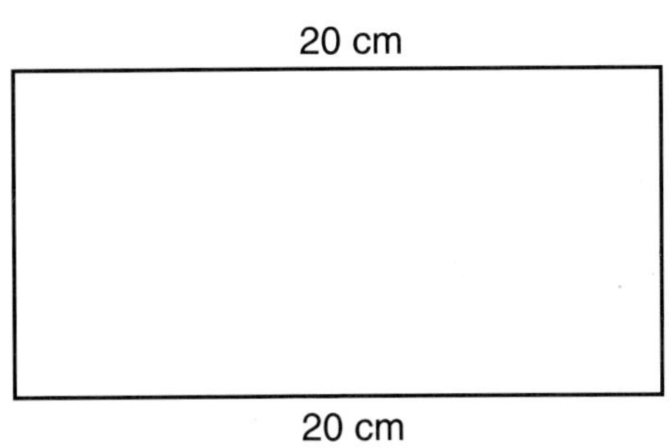

The House that Jack Built

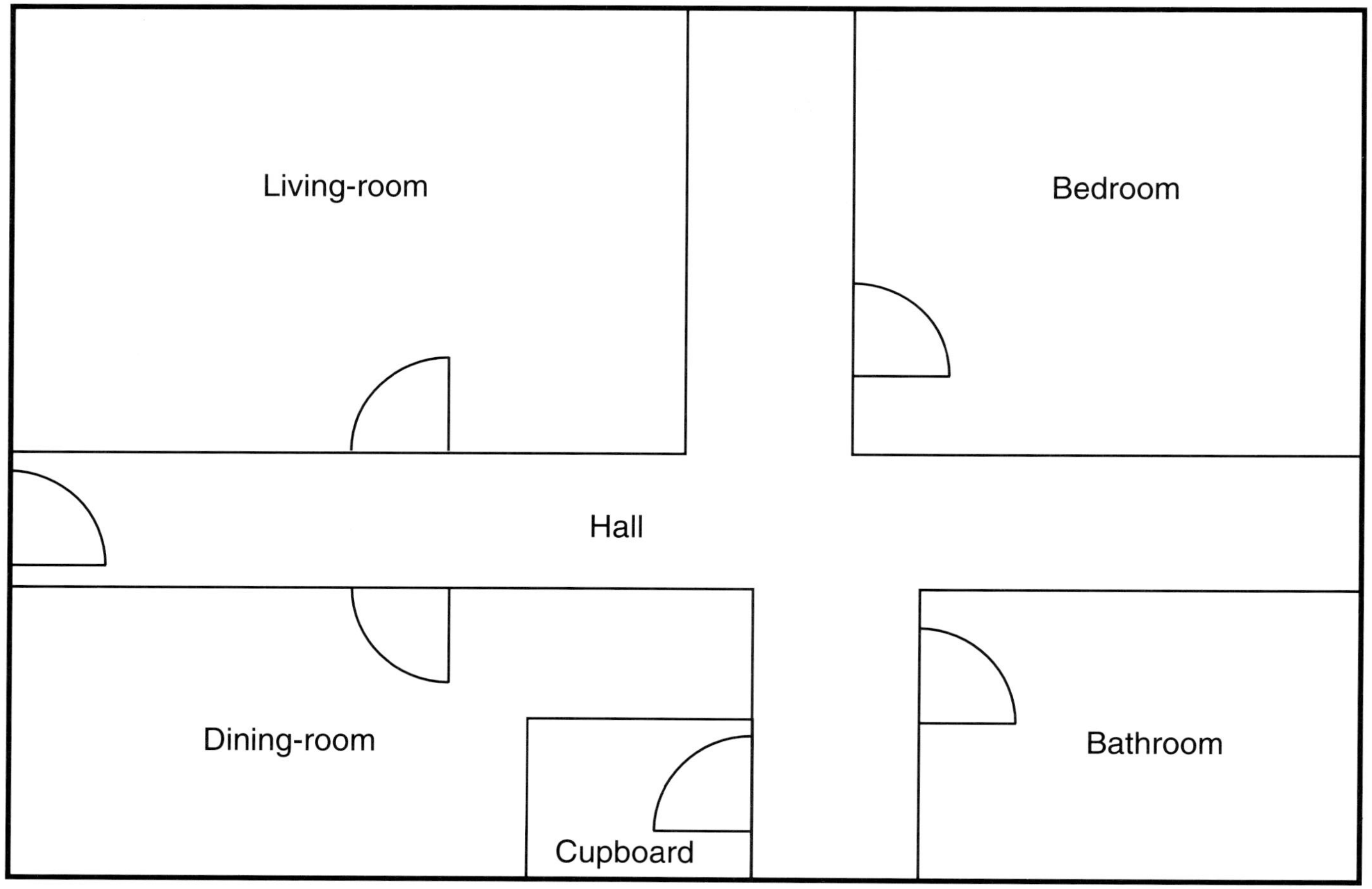

This is a plan of the house that Jack built.

The ruler below will allow you to measure the plan in metres.

The cost of papering a room depends on its perimeter.

1 **a** Measure each wall of the living-room.
b Work out its perimeter.

2 In a similar way, work out the perimeter of:

a the bedroom
b the dining-room
c the bathroom
d the cupboard.

3 The hall has 12 walls. Work out the perimeter of the hall.

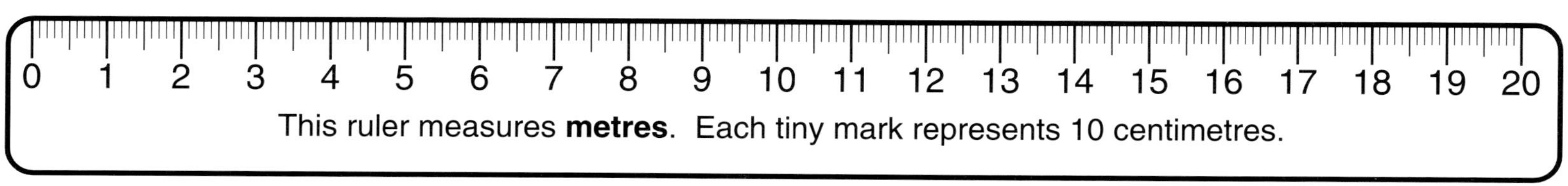

More Practice 1

(i) Measure the diameter of each circle.

Diameter —— ×3 —— Circumference

(ii) Estimate the circumference of each circle.

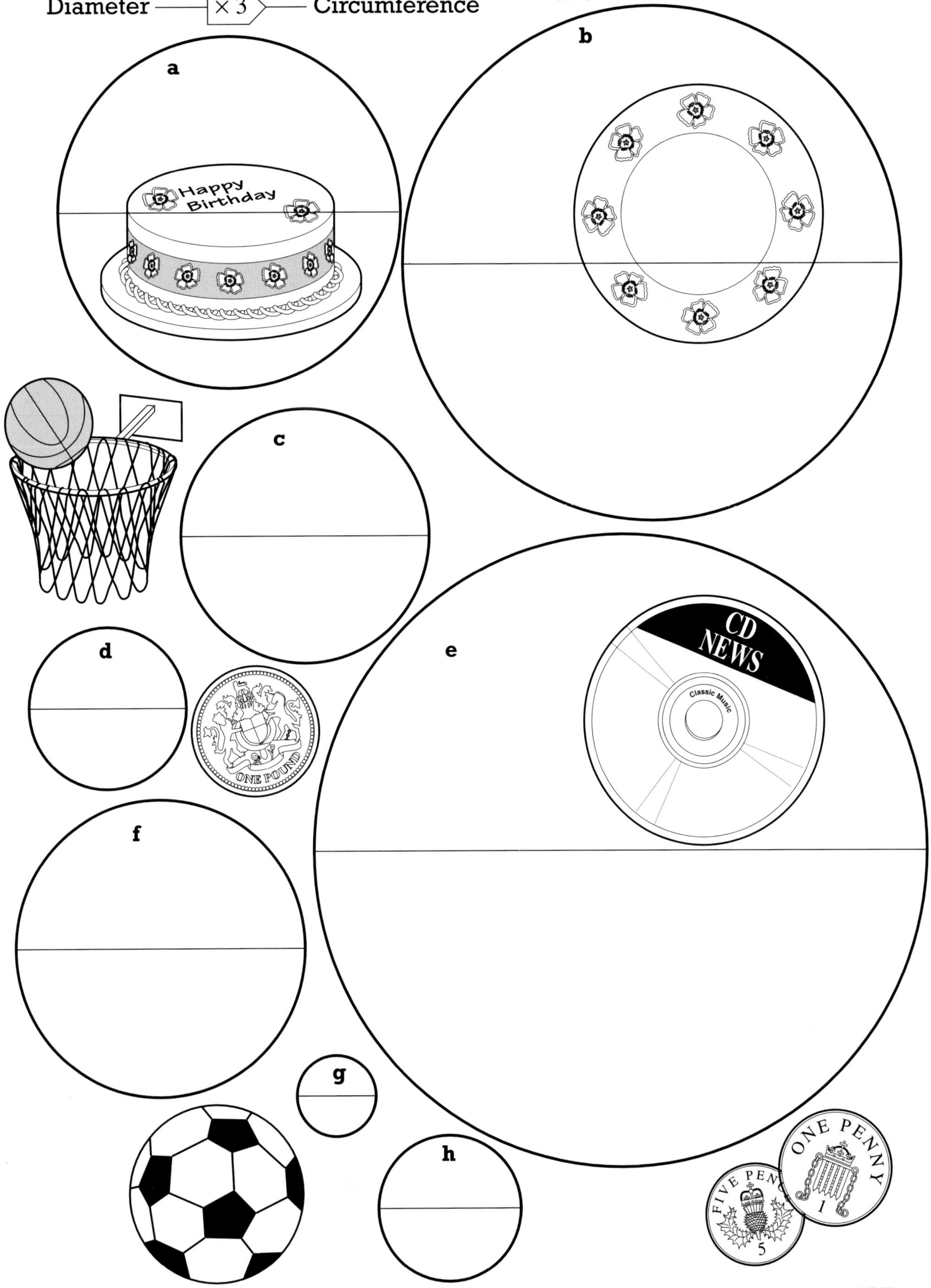

More Practice 2

To work out the circumference more accurately:

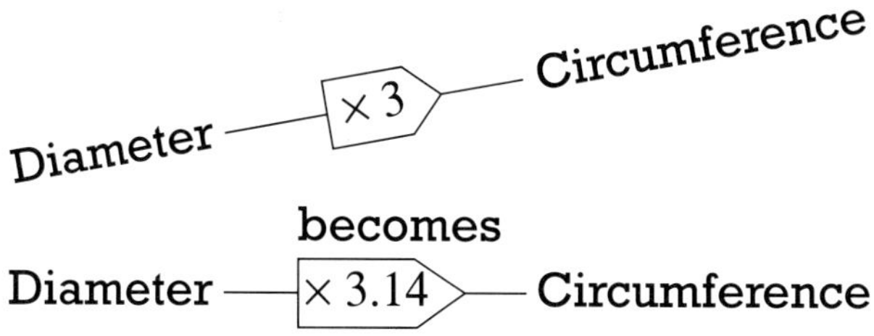

Example

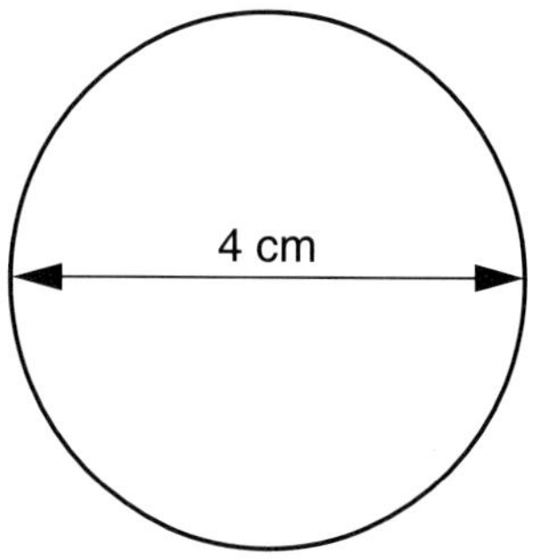

Circumference = Diameter × 3.14
= 4 × 3.14
= 12.56 cm

1 Use the number 3.14 to help you find the circumferences of these circles.

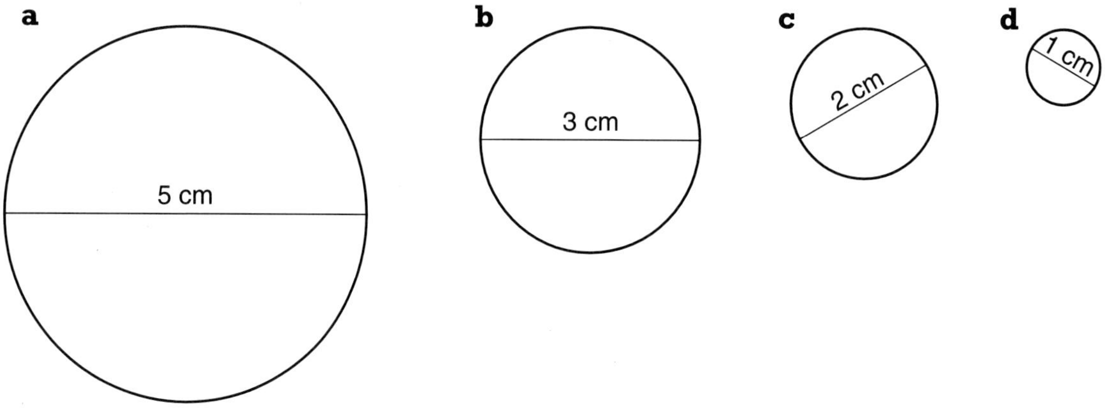

2 For each circle below, find:
(i) its diameter (ii) its circumference.

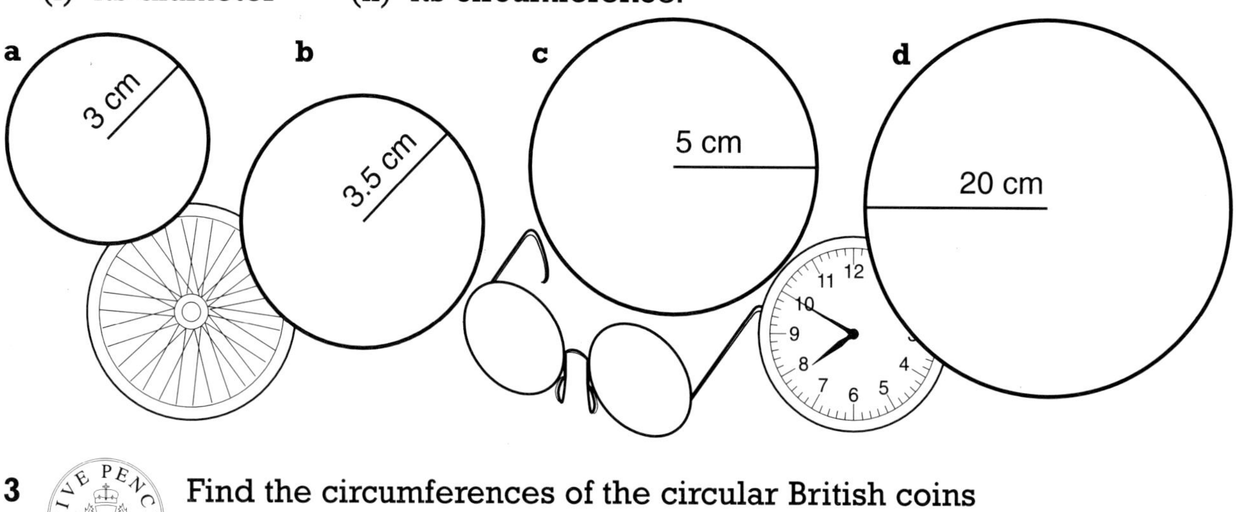

3 

Find the circumferences of the circular British coins using this method.

13 STATISTICS AND PROBABILITY

CURRICULUM COVERAGE

Standard Grade Guidelines
Foundation Level: See Notes below.

National Curriculum
AT 4 Levels 3, 4, 5 and 6.

NI Curriculum
At Handling Data Levels 3, 4, 5 and 6.

AIMS AND OBJECTIVES
To develop the student's skill of examining data with a view to drawing meaningful conclusions from it.
To introduce the student to the tools required for this task.
To produce contexts wherein the student can exercise his/her vocabulary of statistics and probability.

NOTES
The SEB Curriculum Guidelines only require that a Foundation candidate should be able to find the mean of ungrouped data. This requirement is covered by Chapter 10. It would not be lost time, however, to do some of this chapter with such candidates. The median and range are such simple concepts, yet they provide a useful tool for giving meaning to an exam mark otherwise divorced from its context. It will also add to students' investigative skills, and will exercise their ability to interpret information gleaned from familiar everyday contexts.

TEACHER'S RESOURCES
More Practice 1 is on calculating the mean.
More Practice 2 and 3 introduce the median and mode respectively.
More Practice 4 and 5 provide work on finding the median and range.
More Practice 6 covers probability.
Instructions for four dice games are included. These will strengthen the student's notion of the chances of an event happening. Each game has an element of its strategy tied up with an intuitive awareness of the odds. The games are:
1 Beetle Drive
2 Piggy
3 Snake Eyes
4 Cover Up.

PROGRESS ROUTE
With an introductory pointer that *P(n)* is the notation for 'the probability that *n* will happen', Chapter 12 of *Book 3A* should be accessible to a candidate who completes this chapter.

More Practice 1

1 Susan asked several people at the family get-together their ages.

Here is what she was told:
12, 6, 17, 27, 14, 26, 32, 18, 46, 50, 21, 65, 80, 10.

a How many people did she ask?
b What is the total of all the ages?
c What is the mean age?

2 A survey was carried out to find the number of hours pupils slept each night. Here are the results:

School next day	9, 10, 8, 9, 7, 8, 10, 11, 10, 11, 9, 8, 10, 11, 11, 10
No school next day	8, 7, 9, 10, 9, 9, 8, 8, 10, 9, 8, 7, 7, 9, 8, 10

a What was the mean number of hours a pupil slept when the next day was:
(i) a school day
(ii) not a school day?
b What was the difference between the two averages?
Can you suggest a reason?

3 Patrick likes astronomy.
He looks up a table which gives him how far each planet is from the sun.

a What is the mean distance from the sun?
b How many planets are more than the mean distance away?
The table also gives how long it takes each planet to go round the sun.
c What is the mean time?
d How many planets go round quicker than the mean?

	Distance	**Years**
Mercury	0.4	0.2
Venus	0.7	0.6
Earth	1	1
Mars	1.5	1.9
Jupiter	5.2	12
Saturn	9.5	29
Uranus	19.2	84
Neptune	30.1	165
Pluto	39.5	248

4

Harriet looked up the value of some works of art.
The prices were all in millions of pounds.

They were: 1, 23, 17, 2.6, 0.3, 10.5, 13.3, 8.7, 12, 1.8, 0.8.

a What was the total value of the works of art?
b What was the mean value?
c Another work of art worth £24 million was added to the list.
What is the mean value now?

More Practice 2: The Median

Seven boys were asked how much they got for pocket money.
Their replies were: £1, £2, £3, £1, £5, £4, £26.
The mean is (1 + 2 + 3 + 1 + 5 + 4 + 26) ÷ 7 = £6.
So six of the seven boys get less than average!

The mean doesn't give a very good idea of what the group gets for pocket money.
A better guide is the **median.**

Example 1
Step 1 Put the list in order: £1, £1, £2, £3, £4, £5, £26.
Step 2 Pick the middle one in the list: £3.
£3 is the median.
Three boys got less than it.
Three boys got more than it.

Example 2
Sophie listed her scores from the last eight tests:
2, 4, 6, 3, 7, 9, 4, 5.
What is the median score?
Step 1 Put the list in order: 2, 3, 4, 4, 5, 6, 7, 9.
Step 2 There are two middle scores: 4 and 5.
Step 3 Take their mean: (4 + 5) ÷ 2 = 4.5.
The median is 4.5.
Four scores are less than it.
Four scores are more than it.

1 When will there be one middle score and when will there be two?

2 

Ron plays nine holes of golf. He scores:

4, 5, 3, 6, 5, 6, 4, 7, 8.

a List the scores in order.
b Write down the middle score.
c How many scores are below the median score?

3 Mike and Sarah go sunbathing every day of their holidays.
Here is how long they spend each day:

35 minutes, 45 minutes, 23 minutes, 42 minutes, 55 minutes , 34 minutes.

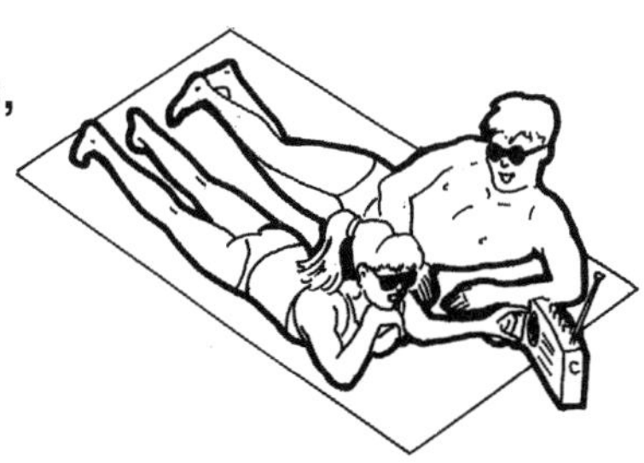

a List the times in order.
b List the two middle times.
c Work out the median time.
d How many were below the median?

More Practice 3: The Mode

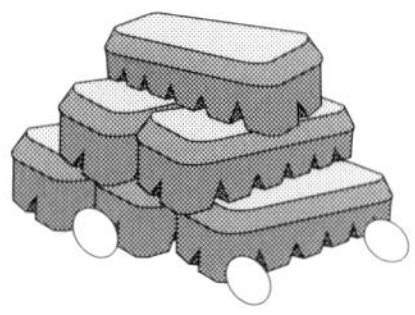

A shopkeeper sells size 2, size 3 and size 4 eggs.
He lists the sizes sold one morning in order:
2, 2, 2, 2, 2, 2, 2, 2, 2, 2, 3, 3, 3, 3, 4.

He is interested in which size is asked for the **most often**.
In this case it was size 2. This is called the **mode**.

1 A window cleaner surveys a housing scheme.
Before he sets his charges he wants to know the average number of windows per house.
This is what he finds:
6, 7, 8, 6, 9, 5, 7, 7, 8, 5, 6, 7, 7, 8, 7, 6, 7, 7, 7, 10.

a Calculate:
(i) the mean
(ii) the median number of windows.

b What is the mode?

c Which of these three averages will probably interest him most?

2

Jamila keeps this record of her use of the car phone:
3 minutes, 6 minutes, 4 minutes, 3 minutes, 3 minutes, 20 minutes, 5 minutes.

a Work out:
(i) the mean
(ii) the median
(iii) the mode length of a call.

b Suggest which one best shows her usage of the phone.

3 a At the end of play on a Saturday some football teams have had players sent off.
So some teams may finish with only 9 or 10 players while others finish with 11.
What is the mode for the size of team at the end of play?

b In the story *Treasure Island,* Long John Silver has only one leg, but what is the mode for the number of legs a pirate has?

c When researchers find out what is top of the music charts are they finding the mean, the median or the mode?

4 Is there a most common month to be born:

a in your class

b in the world?

More Practice 4: Making Sense of Marks

Good news:	I scored 90.
Bad news:	It was out of 200.
Good news:	The average was 80.
Bad news:	The highest pupil scored 190.

Just giving a score for a test can be misleading.
You want to know how everyone else did.
We often use the **median** and the **range** to help us.
The **range** is the difference between the highest and lowest mark.

Example 1 Look at these marks: 1, 1, 1, 2, 3, 4, 4, **4**, 5, 6, 7, 7, 7, 8, 8.
The median is 4.
The highest is 8. The lowest is 1. So the range is 8 – 1 = 7.

Example 2 I score 48. The median is 40. The range is 20.
Although I don't *know* the scores I can imagine this line:

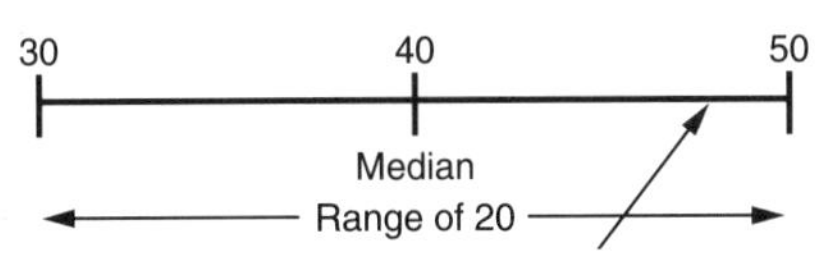

and this lets me see that 48 is quite a good mark.

1 Give the median and the range of each list.
a 1, 1, 1, 1, 2, 2, 2, 3, 3, 4, 4, 5, 6, 7, 8, 8, 9
b 12, 12, 13, 13, 13, 14, 14, 14, 15, 15, 16, 17
c 23, 24, 25, 25, 28, 35, 36, 48, 49
d 23, 36, 38, 45, 49, 56, 58, 67, 69, 72, 84, 96

2 Advani scores 61 in a test. The median is 50. The range is 80.
a What is half the range?
b Copy and complete this number line:
c Place the score of 61 on the line.
d Was 61 average, good or very good?

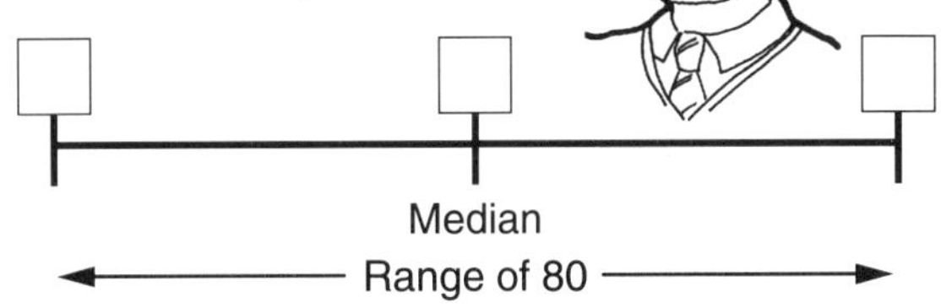

3 Draw similar lines to help you comment on:
a Tim's mark which was 34 (median 30, range 60)
b Mary's mark of 55 (median 50, range 10)
c Tracy's mark of 80 (median 90, range 20).

4 Jackie scored 65 in English. The median was 60. The range was 60.
She scored 64 in maths. The median was 50. The range was 30.
a Draw a number line for:
(i) the English exam
(ii) the maths exam.
b Show Jackie's mark on each.
c Which mark should Jackie be happier with?

More Practice 5

1 

Iain tests some dice to see if they are fair.

He throws one several times. He gets these results:
1, 3, 2, 5, 4, 3, 6, 5, 4, 2, 5, 1, 2, 6, 1, 6, 2, 3, 5, 4, 1.

a Put the list in order.
b What is the median?
c What is the range?
d Do you think the dice is fair?
e He tests a different dice and gets these results:
1, 3, 4, 2, 5, 1, 4, 3, 2, 5, 3, 3, 3, 1, 2, 1, 2, 4, 1, 2, 1.
Is this one fair? Give a reason for your answer.

2 A company claims to make bulbs which burn for 200 hours on average.

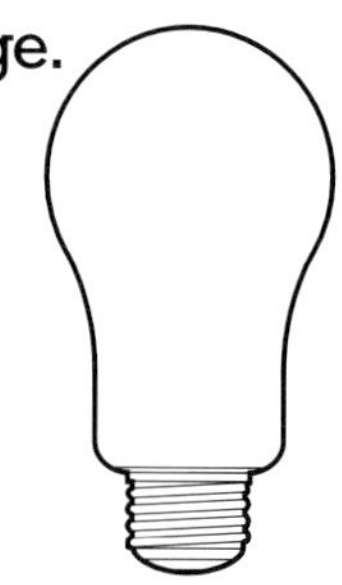

Some bulbs were tested. Here are the results:
180, 230, 219, 195, 194, 201, 213, 203, 189, 187, 199.

a Put the results in order.
b State the median life of a bulb.
c State the range.
d Comment on the company's claim.

3 

The manager of a cinema kept a note of how many people came to each viewing of a picture.

Mon 4 pm 347, 8 pm 541
Tue 4 pm 412, 8 pm 503
Wed 4 pm 351, 8 pm 352
Thu 4 pm 401, 8 pm 400
Fri 4 pm 368, 8 pm 487
Sat 4 pm 320, 8 pm 477

a What is the median for:
(i) the 4 pm showings (ii) the 8 pm showings?
b Calculate the median and range for all 12 showings.

4 Jamie's maths mark was 34. The median was 30. The range was 20.

Jamie used this information to draw a number line to see how good his mark was.

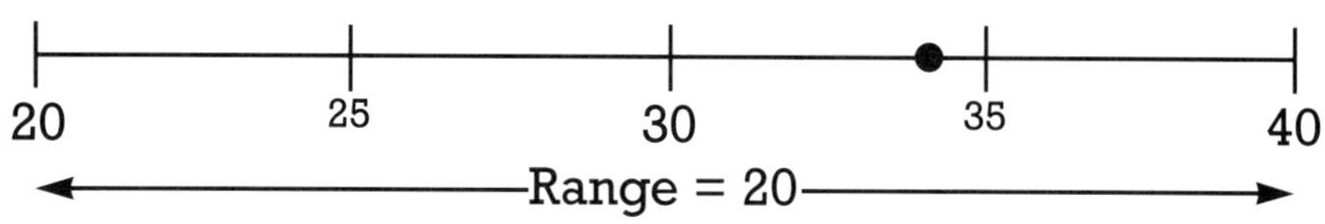

Make similar number lines for these:

a English mark 56. Median 50. Range 40.
b French mark 86. Median 70. Range 60.
c Physics mark 64. Median 65. Range 50.
d Biology mark 51. Median 45. Range 20.
e Music mark 45. Median 40. Range 80.

More Practice 6

1 Karen went for a walk in the country.
Her chances of seeing various animals are shown.

Butterfly	Fox	Kestrel	Horse	Rabbit
0.4	0.3	0.1	0.25	0.32

Arrange the animals in order with the most likely first.

2 Terence goes to an air show.
His chances of seeing different planes are shown.

Arrange the types in a list.
Put the most likely first.

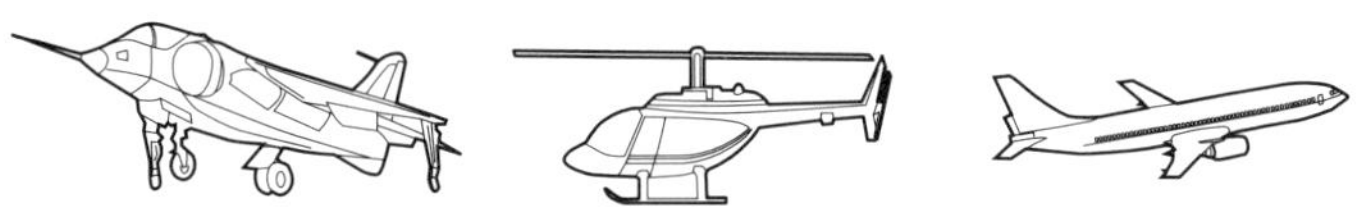

Harrier	Helicopter	Commercial jet
0.85	0.93	0.55

Dakota	Jaguar	Biplane
0.6	0.75	0.81

3 a

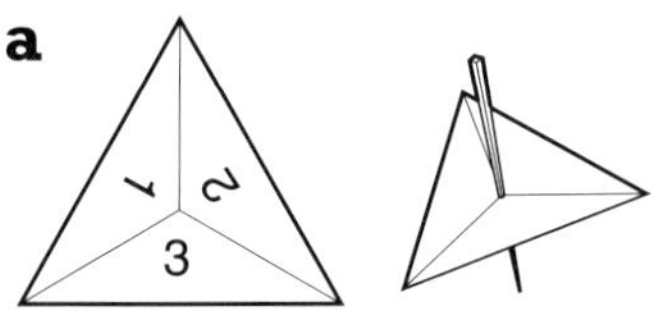

(i) How many odd numbers are on the spinner?
(ii) What is the probability of an even number?

b

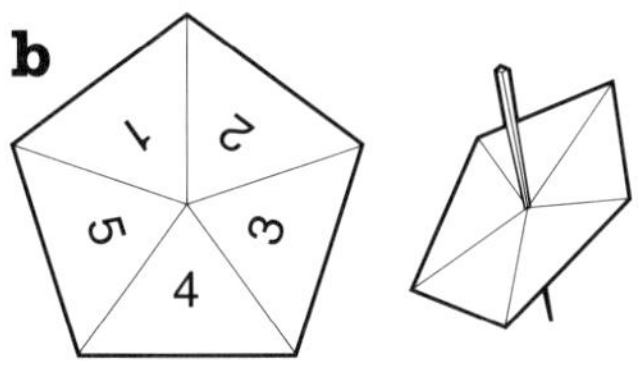

(i) How many odd numbers are on the spinner?
(ii) What is the probability of an even number?

c

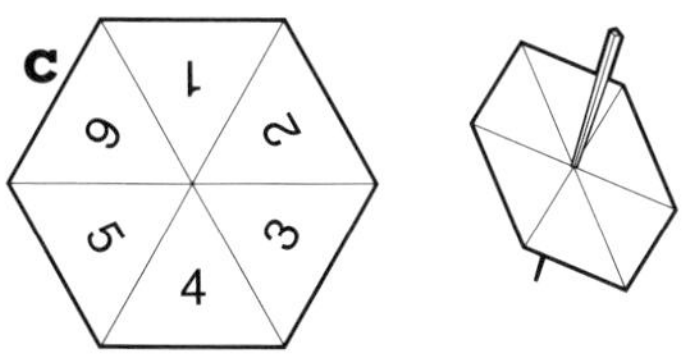

(i) How many odd numbers are on the spinner?
(ii) What is the probability of an even number?

d If you want a spinner to be fair when even numbers are winners, should you pick spinner **a**, **b** or **c**?

4 A school's filing system looks like this:

There are eight drawers.
Each drawer has 100 files.
People who have a name starting with 'M' take up a whole drawer.

a (i) How many files are there altogether?
(ii) How many people are there with a name starting with 'M'?

b 20 people are called Smith.
What is the probability that a person picked at random:
(i) has a name starting with 'M'
(ii) is called Smith?

INSTRUCTIONS FOR GAMES

Game 1: Beetle Drive

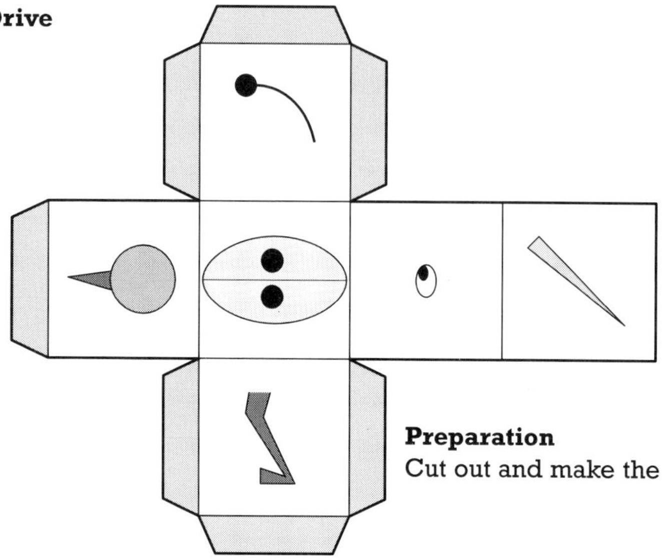

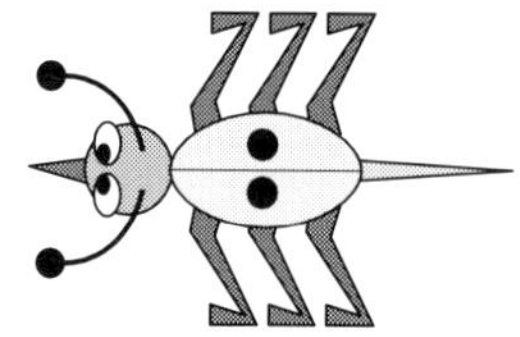

Preparation
Cut out and make the dice.

Rules
Each player throws the dice in turn.
This identifies a part of the beetle.

Before a player can do anything he/she must throw a body.
The player then draws the body on his/her card.

Thereafter if a player throws a sting, a leg or a head, he/she can draw them.

Before a player can draw the antennae or eyes he/she must have drawn a head.

Altogether, to complete a beetle, a player must throw one body, one head, six legs, one sting, two antennae and two eyes.

The first to finish wins.

Name...

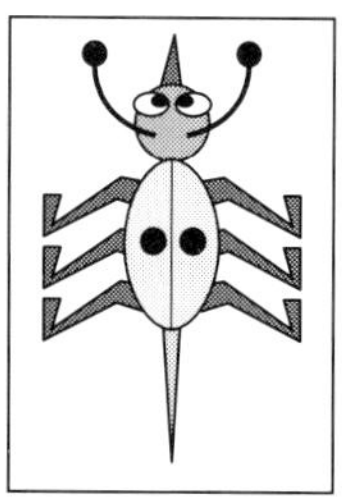	Game 1	Game 2
Game 3	Game 4	Game 5
Game 6	Game 7	Game 8

Name...

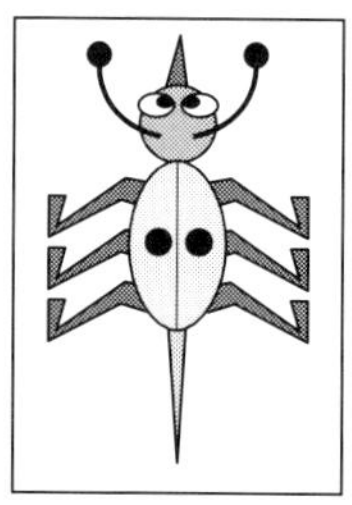	Game 1	Game 2
Game 3	Game 4	Game 5
Game 6	Game 7	Game 8

Game 2: Piggy

One dice is required.

A player on his/her turn can throw the dice as often as wished, totalling the score after each throw.
A turn finishes when a player:

- decides he/she has had enough, or
- throws a 1. If this happens the player's score for this round is reduced to zero!

The score so far is noted and the dice is passed on.
The first player to reach a score of 50 is the winner.

Game 3: Snake Eyes

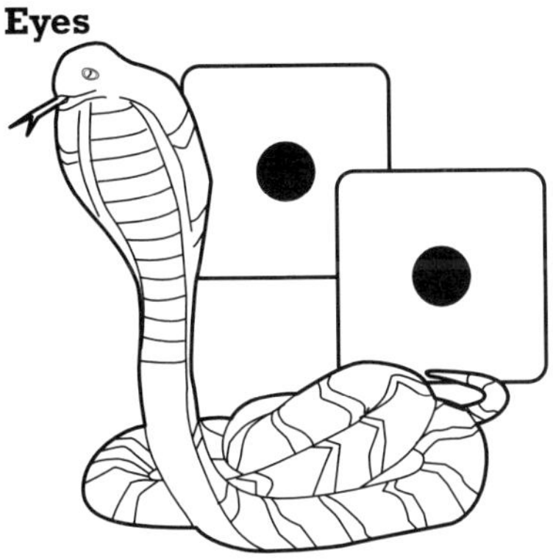

Two dice are required.

Each player takes a turn to throw the two dice.
Nothing happens unless a double is thrown.

A player scores 10 points for double 2, 3, 4 or 5, and 30 points for double 6.

Double 1 (Snake Eyes) reduces a player's score to zero.

The first player to reach a score of 50 is the winner.

Game 4: Cover Up

1	
2	
3	
4	
5	
6	
7	
8	
9	

1	
2	
3	
4	
5	
6	
7	
8	
9	

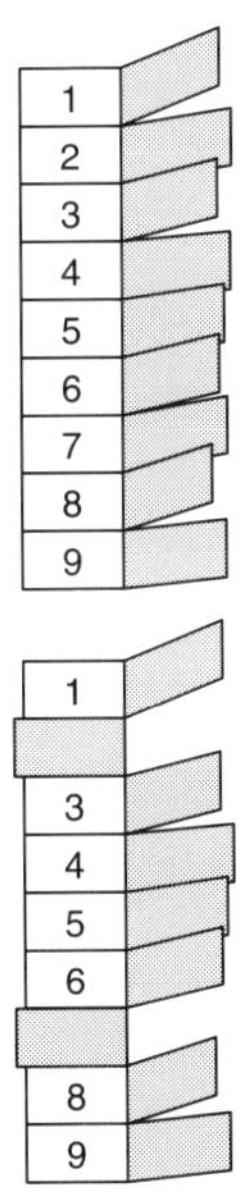

Example of a score of 9

Two dice are required.

Players take turns to play.

At first two dice are thrown.

The player totals the score.

The player must now cover up two numbers which add up to his/her score. For example, if the player scored 9, then he/she could cover up the 8 and 1, the 7 and 2, the 6 and 3, or the 5 and 4.

The numbers must not have been covered up already.

Once the numbers 7, 8 and 9 have been covered up a player only uses one dice.

A player's game finishes when he/she throws a score and can't cover up two numbers.

The numbers left uncovered count as points against the player.

The player with the lowest count is the winner.

14 ALGEBRA

CURRICULUM COVERAGE

Standard Grade Guidelines

Foundation Level:
Extending simple number patterns.
Evaluating formulae given in words.
With guidance, constructing formulae to describe a relationship between/among values in a table.
General Level:
Generalising simple number patterns.
Solving simple equations of the form $x + 3 = 5$, $2x = 3$, $3x - 5 = x + 11$.
Evaluating formulae expressed in symbols.
Multiplying expressions such as $2(x + 2y) = 2x + 4y$.
Simplifying simple algebraic expressions (use of shorthand).
Evaluating simple algebraic expressions (substitution).

National Curriculum

AT 2 Levels 4, 5 and 6.

NI Curriculum

AT Algebra Levels 4, 5 and 6.

AIMS AND OBJECTIVES

To consolidate earlier work on algebra.
To provide practice in manipulating and evaluating simple algebraic expressions.
To provide practice in solving simple equations and studying simple formulae.
To emphasise that using letters to stand for numbers is relevant for generalising real-life situations and for trying to solve real-life problems.

NOTES

1 A worksheet on evaluating formulae, which is required for the National Curriculum, is provided on pages 119–20. A worksheet on the equations required for the Foundation Tier of the National Curriculum is also provided, on page 118. The starred sections of this worksheet are required for the General Level of Standard Grade.
2 Much of the material in this chapter is not suitable for a candidate following a Foundation only course.
3 Advanced algebra techniques such as the distributive law (removing brackets and factorising) and equation solving using the distributive law are not covered here. See the Progress Route below.

TEACHER'S RESOURCES

More Practice 1 provides additional work on simplifying and evaluating algebraic expressions.
More Practice 2 has extra practice at solving equations of the type $x + 3 = 5$, $2y = 6$, $2y = 3$ and $2a + 1 = 9$.
More Practice 3 on evaluating formulae is provided to meet the requirements of the National Curriculum and students attempting Standard Grade at General Level.

PROGRESS ROUTE

Success at the check-up would allow students to use the More Practice sheets. If a student is successful at these then progress to *Book 3A* is possible. The review on Letters and Numbers is immediately accessible, while Chapter 6 on Brackets and Equations is now available to those requiring the distributive law. Chapter 11 on Formulae and Sequences also offers plenty of material if a student can cope with the More Practice sheets.

More Practice 1

1 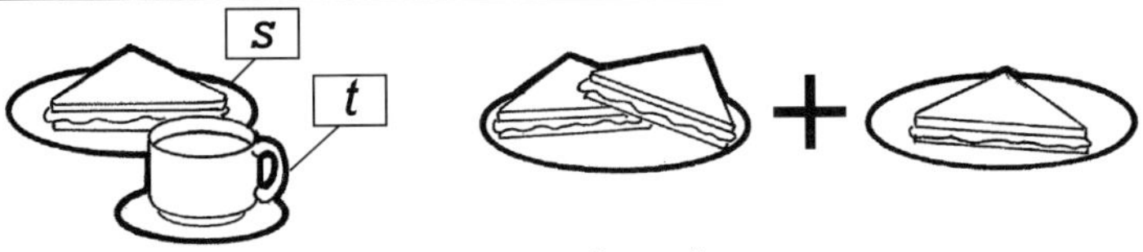

$2s + s = 3s$

Write similar statements for these.

a 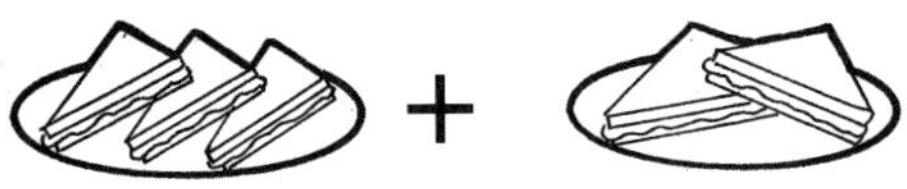

b 

2 Simplify the following.

a $2a + a$ **b** $3x - x$ **c** $y + 4y$ **d** $3m + 4m$
e $6t - 2t$ **f** $8w - 3w$ **g** $4h - 3h$ **h** $10n - n$
i $a + 3a + 6a$ **j** $7u + 4u - 6u$ **k** $3x + 5x - 6x$ **l** $y + 7y - 4y$
m $10m + m - 2m$ **n** $4c - 3c + 2c$ **o** $8t + t - 7t$ **p** $7a - a + 4a$

3 Write statements for these.

a 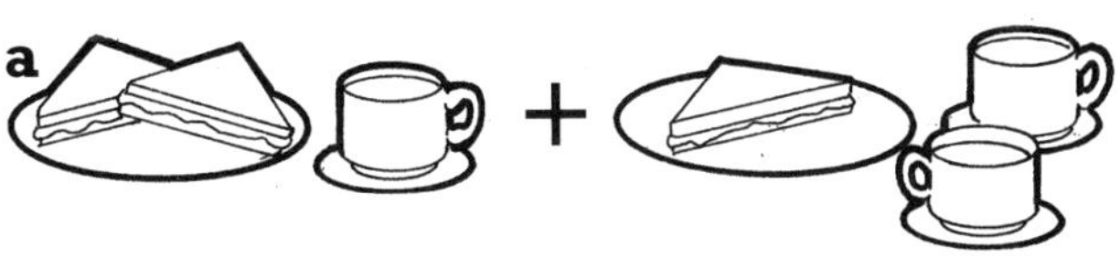

b 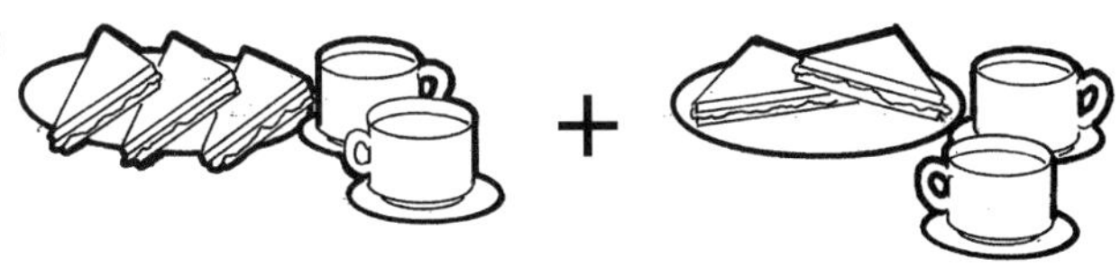

4 Tidy up the following.

a $3x + 2y + x + 4y$ **b** $5a + 3b + 4a + b$ **c** $6m + 3n + m + 2n$
d $5c + 3d + d + 2c$ **e** $4m + n + 7n + 4m$ **f** $4x + 3x + y + 7y$
g $6a - 5a + 4b - b$ **h** $10c - 9c + 3d - d$ **i** $4a + 5b - 2a + 3b$

5 Simplify the following.

a $4 \times a \times b$ **b** $3 \times d \times e$ **c** $h \times 5$ **d** $y \times 7$
e $6 \times b \times a$ **f** $c \times 4 \times d$ **g** $m \times 2 \times n$ **h** $b \times a \times 5$
i $c \times 2 \times b$ **j** $d \times 3 \times e \times 2$ **k** $3 \times c \times 2 \times d$ **l** $4 \times n \times 2 \times n \times 5$
m $m \times m$ **n** $n \times n \times n$ **o** $a \times a \times a \times a \times a$ **p** $h \times h \times 3 \times h \times 3$

6 If $a = 2$ and $b = 3$, calculate:

a $a + b$ **b** ab **c** b^2 **d** a^3 **e** $4ab$
f $2a - b$ **g** $b - a$ **h** $3b - 2a$ **i** $5a - 3b$ **j** b^3

7 

The plasterer charges £p an hour.
The decorator charges £d an hour.
If the plasterer works 4 hours and the decorator works 3 hours, the total will be: $4p + 3d$.

Work out the bill when:

a $p = 20$ and $d = 30$
b $p = 15$ and $d = 25$
c $p = 22$ and $d = 24$
d $p = 18$ and $d = 12$.

More Practice 2

1 What number is hidden by each finger?

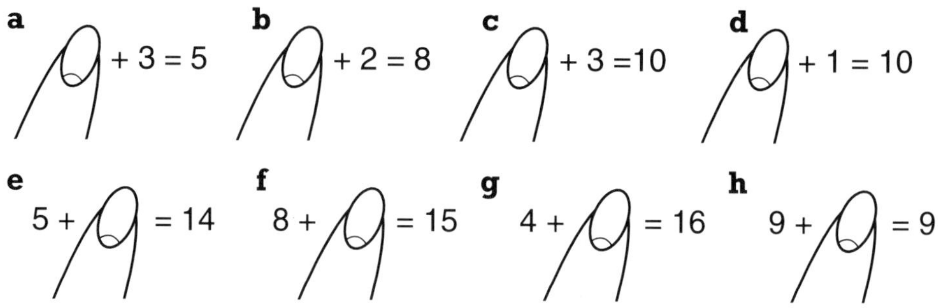

2 Find the unknown numbers in these equations.

a $5 + x = 25$ **b** $6 + x = 19$ **c** $4 + x = 31$ **d** $10 + x = 17$
e $x + 7 = 20$ **f** $x + 3 = 20$ **g** $x + 5 = 18$ **h** $x + 19 = 30$

3 What number is hidden by each finger?

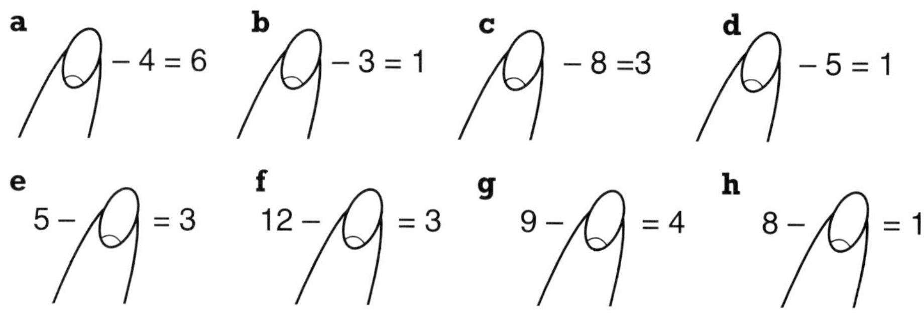

4 Find the unknown numbers in these equations.

a $7 - m = 7$ **b** $2 - d = 0$ **c** $a - 1 = 2$ **d** $x - 3 = 5$
e $a - 2 = 2$ **f** $t - 5 = 0$ **g** $y - 7 = 15$ **h** $x - 9 = 3$

5 What are the mystery numbers here?

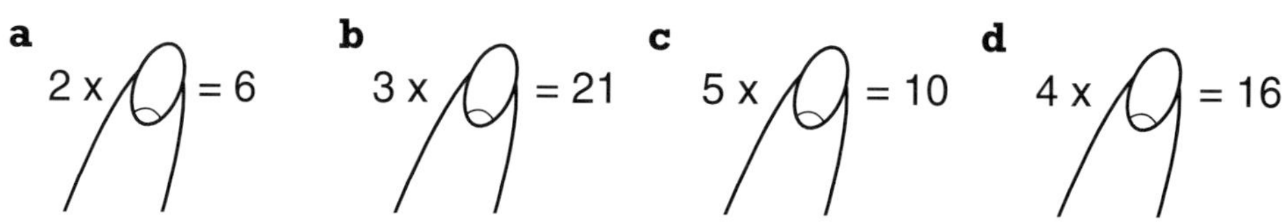

6 Find the unknown numbers in these equations.

a $3k = 3$ **b** $7t = 28$ **c** $6y = 42$ **d** $2a = 20$
e $9x = 27$ **f** $8m = 40$ **g** $4t = 28$ **h** $10t = 60$

7

Example

$2a + 1 = 9$

Cover up $2a$

+ 1 = 9

This tells us that $2a = 8$

... and so $a = 4$

Find the unknown numbers in these equations.

a $2a + 1 = 9$ **b** $2x + 3 = 11$ **c** $2y + 4 = 10$ **d** $2m + 2 = 12$
e $3y + 4 = 10$ **f** $5a + 3 = 18$ **g** $4t + 1 = 21$ **h** $6x + 5 = 17$
i $2y - 3 = 7$ **j** $2m - 6 = 14$ **k** $4a - 5 = 15$ **l** $4y - 3 = 5$

More Practice 3: Evaluating Formulae

The number of years **times 6 then add 30** gives the height.

Example The height of Sam's plant is given by the formula.

$$H = 6Y + 30$$

where H is its height and Y is its age.

Calculate the plant's height when it is 7 years old.

$H = 6Y + 30$
$H = 6 \times 7 + 30$
$= 42 + 30$
$= 72$ cm

1 $a = 4$, $b = 3$ and $c = 2$.

Find the values of W, F and T in these formulae.

a $W = a + b + c$ **b** $F = 2a + b - c$ **c** $T = ab - 3c$

2 **a** The diameter of a circle is double its radius.

$$d = 2r$$

Use the formula to find the diameter when the radius is:
(i) 5 cm (ii) 12 cm (iii) 20 cm (iv) 4.5 cm.

b The radius is half the diameter.

$$r = \frac{1}{2}d$$

Work out the radius of a circle with diameter:
(i) 14 cm (ii) 30 cm (iii) 100 cm (iv) 25 m.

3 The clock is 15 minutes fast.

$$A = T - 15$$

Find the actual time when the time on the clock is:

a 4 o'clock **b** 7 o'clock **c** 2.30 am
d 8.15 pm **e** 10.35 am.

4 Workers at a factory are paid according to the formula:

$$P = 8A + 10$$

where P is the wage in £ and A is the worker's age in years.

How much is paid to a worker whose age is:

a 16 **b** 18 **c** 20 **d** 40?

More Practice 3 (continued)

5 The area of a triangle can be found from the formula:

$$A = \frac{1}{2}bh$$

where A is the area,
b is the length of the base
and h is the height.

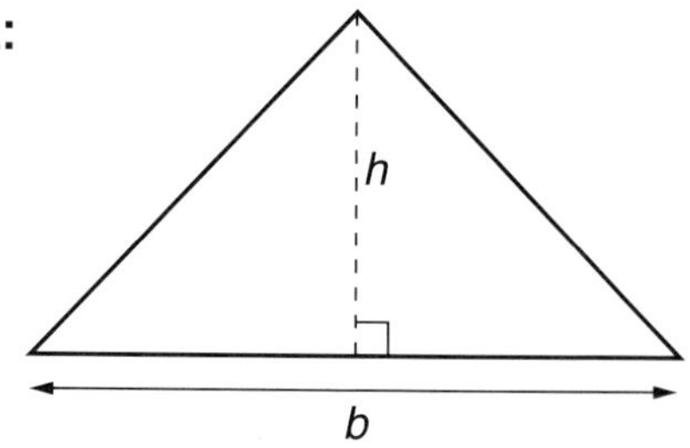

Find the areas of these triangles.
Measurements are in centimetres.

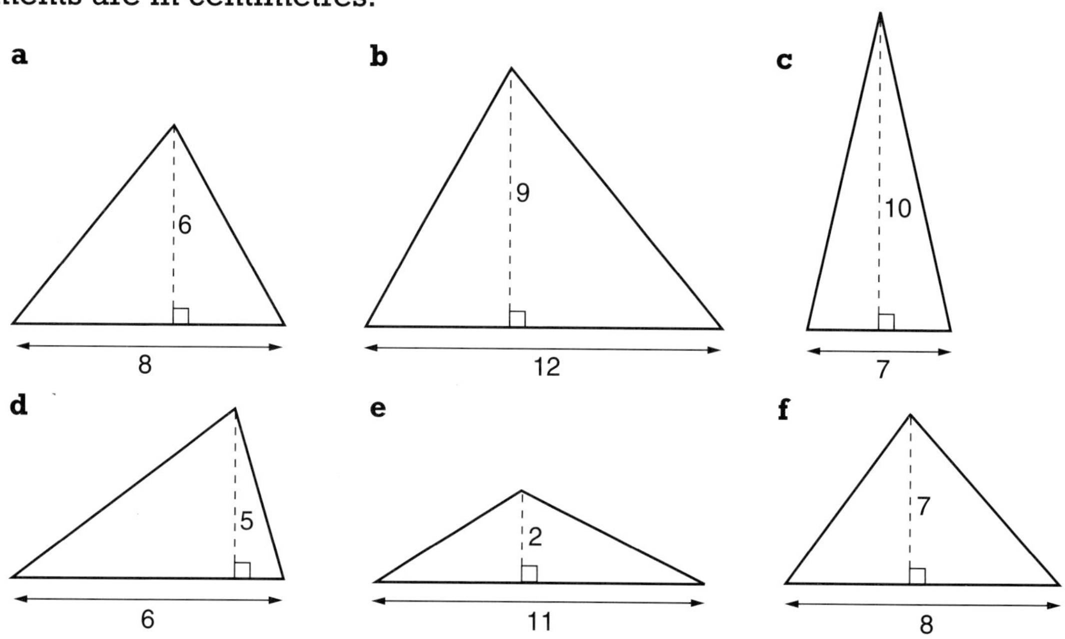

6 The daily cost of hiring a car from Rent-a-Car is worked out from the formula:

$$C = 0.08M + 12$$

where C is the cost in £
and M is the number of miles travelled.

How much does it cost to hire a car for one day if the number of miles travelled is:

a 100 **b** 200 **c** 350?

7 An object is dropped from a helicopter.
The distance it falls is given by the formula:

$$d = 5 \times t^2$$

where d is the distance in metres and t is the time it is falling in seconds.

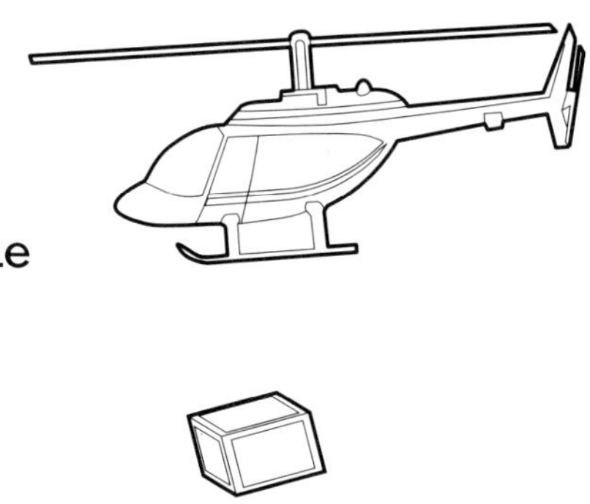

Use the formula to find the distance it falls in:

a 3 seconds **b** 5 seconds
c 8 seconds **d** 10 seconds.

ANSWERS

1 WHOLE NUMBERS AND DECIMALS

STUDENTS' BOOK

Page 1 Looking Back
1 a 59 **b** 48 **c** 56 **d** 8 **2 a** 40 **b** 400 **c** 320 **d** 3200 **3 a** 100 **b** 10 **c** 20 **d** 2
4 a 87.9 **b** 2.36 **5 a** 879 **b** 0.236 **6 a** 8754 **b** 4578 **c** eight thousand, seven hundred and fifty-four; four thousand, five hundred and seventy-eight **7 a** (i) hundreds (ii) T tens, U units, t tenths, h hundredths

b	H	T	U	.	t	h
	2	6	5	.	3	4
(i)	8	0	9	.	5	6
(ii)		2	8	.	3	2
(iii)	3	7	2	.	0	5
(iv)			9	.	8	
(v)			3	.	6	
(vi)	5	1	9	.		

8 a 31.9 **b** 325.75 **c** 52.2 **d** 6.9 **e** 12.8 **f** 6.3 **g** 2.82 **h** 1.61 **9 a** 20 **b** 50 **c** 90 **d** 90 **e** 80 **10 a** 370 **b** 570 **c** 190 **d** 950 **e** 790

Page 2 Exercise 1
1 a 19 **b** 13 **c** 6 **d** 0 **e** 10 **f** 13 **g** 20 **h** 11 **i** 7 **j** 5 **k** 3 **l** 2 **2** Across **1** 55 **2** 162 **4** 81 **5** 204 **7** 23 **8** 50 **9** 125 **11** 33 Down **1** 555 **2** 110 **3** 23 **4** 823 **6** 432 **8** 50 **10** 57

Page 3 Exercise 2
1 a 8, 6, 5, 4, 1 **b** 26, 12, 7, 4, 3 **c** 7.2, 3.5, 2.6, 1.4 **d** 29.4, 29.3, 16.4, 5.2 **2 a** 17, 19, 26, 32 **b** 7.9, 18.0, 18.4, 25.2 **c** 0.1, 1.0, 6.8, 14.9 **d** 14.3, 26.2, 40.0, 41.2 **3 b** The calculator shows 4.2 each time **4 a** 3.90, 3.06 **b** 17.50, 16.46 **c** 18.200, 18.165 **5 a** 3.09, 3.65, 3.80 **b** 6.66, 6.70, 6.71 **c** 12.42, 12.80, 12.90 **6** 10.68, 10.7, 10.8, 10.96, 11.19, 11.2

Page 4 Exercise 3
1 a 90 **b** 70 **c** 20 **d** 30 **e** 70 **f** 90 **g** 30 **h** 50 **i** 640 **j** 680 **k** 630 **l** 680 **m** 440 **n** 240 **o** 910 **p** 570 **2 a** 400 **b** 400 **c** 800 **d** 500 **e** 200 **f** 800 **g** 400 **h** 100 **i** 7500 **j** 3700 **k** 6900 **l** 1200 **m** 500 **n** 3400 **o** 9100 **p** 5600 **3 a** 3 **b** 3 **c** 4 **d** 7 **e** 6 **f** 7 **g** 2 **h** 2 **i** 1 **j** 25 **k** 169 **l** 579 **m** 809 **4 a** (i) 3.6 (ii) 6.2 (iii) 13.5 **b** (i) 4 (ii) 6 (iii) 14

Page 6 Exercise 4
1 4 trips **2** 4 journeys **3 a** £16.66 **b** 4 pence **4 a** 5 chocolates **b** 5 left over **5** £8.34 **6** 4 tins **7 a** 4 buses **b** 32 empty seats

Page 7 Exercise 5
1 a 0, 2, 4, 6, 8, 10, 12, 14, 16, 18 **b** 1, 3, 5, 7, 9, 11, 13, 15, 17, 19 **2 a** right **b** right **c** left **d** right **e** left **f** right **g** left **h** right **3** 11,13,17,19, 23, 29 **4 a** 31, 37, 59, 61 **b** 34 can be divided by 2 (or 17), 35 can be divided by 5 (or 7), 49 can be divided by 7, 51 can be divided by 3 (or 17) **5 a** 12-18-40- 66-104-150-178-314 **b** 7-11-19-43-59-29-31 **c** 7-11-19-25-49-57-31 **6 a** (i) 6 (ii) 12 (iii) 3 **b** Adam: 4, 3, 3, 16, 8, 2, 8; total is 44. Bill: 12, 1, 4, 3, 4, 12, 4; total is 40. Adam wins.

Page 8 Exercise 6
1 25, 36, 49, 64 **2 a** 100 **b** 225 **c** 625 **d** 1 000 000 **e** 900 **f** 2500 **g** 4096 **3** 441 = 21^2, 576 = 24^2 **4** a, b, e and g **5** 81, 144, 400, 169, 225, 289, 196, 121

Page 9 Exercise 7
1 a £3.64 **b** £1.36 **2** £140 **3** £3.45 **4 a** 154 miles **b** 178 miles **c** 24 miles **5** soups £7.25, haddock £9.70, pizzas £11.25, apple pies £11.40, ice-cream £2.15; total £41.75 **6 a** 847 000 **b** 846 700

7

Type	Number	Amount (p)
1p	18	18
2p	13	26
5p	23	115
10p	35	350
20p	27	540
50p	11	550
£1	7	700
Total	134	£22.99

8 a £1.08 **b** 8p **9 a** £7 946 775 **b** £4 556 775

Page 11 Check-up
1 a 27.09 **b** 7.94 **c** 54.4 **d** 93.6 **2 a** 23 **b** 3 **c** 35 **d** 4 **3 a** 30, 120, 148.6, 74 **b** 300, 1200, 1486, 740 **4 a** 500, 1760, 37.68, 28.1 **b** 50, 176, 3.768, 2.81 **5 a** 70 **b** 40 **c** 30 **d** 140 **6 a** 400 **b** 400 **c** 4700 **7 a** 32 000 **b** 31 700 **8** 35.6, 35.48, 35.01, 34.9, 34.84, 34.47 **9 a** three from 3, 81, 31, 49 **b** 2, 36, 90 **c** 2, 3, 31 **d** 36, 81, 49 **10 a** 15 is divisible by 3 and 5 **b** 100 = 10 × 10 **c** 3452 is divisible by 2

TEACHER'S BOOK

Page 2 Mental Test A
1 £1.98 **2** 61p **3** 20 **4** 121 **5** 807 310 **6** 21 **7** 362.3 **8** 19 **9** 11 **10** 30

Page 2 Mental Test B
1 50 **2** £7 **3** 14 **4** 121 **5** 28 000 **6** 3 metres **7** 5 coins **8** 27 **9** 3 scones **10** 6.9

Page 2 Mental Test C
1 £3.98 **2** 37p **3** 10 **4** 88 **5** 3 250 610 **6** 1.234 **7** 965.4 **8** 23 **9** 17 **10** 48

Page 2 Mental Test D
1 36 **2** £12 **3** 39 **4** 81 **5** 43 000 **6** 8 kilograms **7** 37 **8** 5 coins **9** 2 bars **10** 88

Page 4 More Practice 1: Paper Round
1 House number 1–314p, 2–270p, 5–355p, 6–290p, 8–373p, 10–417p, 11–116p, 14–264p, 15–522p, 16–625p, 20–534p, 24–409p, 29–228p, 30–578p **2** Total = £52.95 **3** 116 × 3p = £3.48

Page 5 More Practice 2: Milk Round
1 House number 1–£4.65, 3–£4.91, 4–£6.25, 5–£4.31, 7–£6.00, 10–£5.49, 11–£8.04, 12–£9.12, 15–£3.93, 16–£4.34, 24–£9.24, 30–£5.12
2 Total = £71.40

Page 6 More Practice 3
1 14p **2** £9.78 **3 a** £187.55 **b** £64.10 **c** £123.45 profit **4 a** Ahmed: 15.4, 15.36, 15.22; Bob: 15.86, 14.98, 14; Chris: 16, 15.72, 15.01; Dave: 15.16, 14.87, 14.39 **b** Chris wins **5 a** (i) £6 (ii) £5.40 (iii) £5 **b** £1 **6 a** 45 miles **b** (i) 50 miles (ii) 20 miles (iii) 55 miles (iv) 60 miles (v) 70 miles

Page 7 Rounding to 2 Decimal Places
1 a 3.24 **b** 12.24 **c** 23.52 **d** 34.25 **e** 294.11 **f** 4.36 **g** 5.33 **h** 1.51 **i** 14.67 **j** 40.38 **k** 19.56 **l** 24.74 **2 a** 4.24 **b** 7.32 **c** 6.46 **d** 8.08 **e** It is in the middle **f** 12.73 **3 a** 21.03 **b** 41.19 **c** 41.58 **d** 43.52 **e** 13.18 **f** 1.94 **4** 14.29 kg

Page 8 Rounding to 1 Decimal Place
1 a 8.5 **b** 3.6 **c** 12.8 **d** 19.1 **e** 80.3 **f** 15.4 **g** 26.1 **h** 85.6 **i** 52.3 **j** 51.0 **2 a** 8.7 **b** 1.7 **c** 36.4 **d** It is in the middle **e** 96.1 **f** 3.7 **g** 11.7 **h** 36.8 **i** 47.1 **j** 26.0 **3 a** 16.1 **b** 50.0 **c** 24.1 **d** 12.0 **e** 56.3 **f** 3.0 **g** 0.8 **h** 14.5 **4** 13.6 metres (plus the spaces between the vehicles)

2 SYMMETRY

STUDENTS' BOOK

Page 12 Looking Back
1 a, b and e
2 a b c

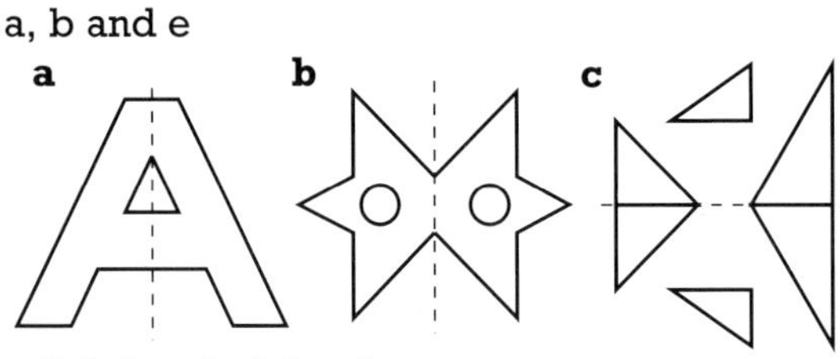

3 a 2 **b** 1 **c** 3 **d** 2 **e** 1

Page 14 Exercise 1
1 a b c

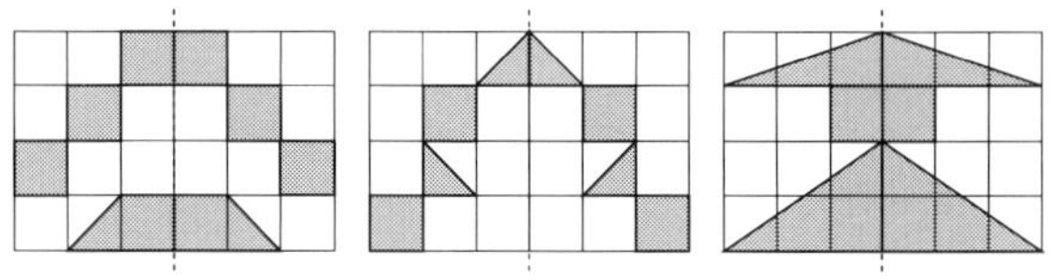

2 a b c

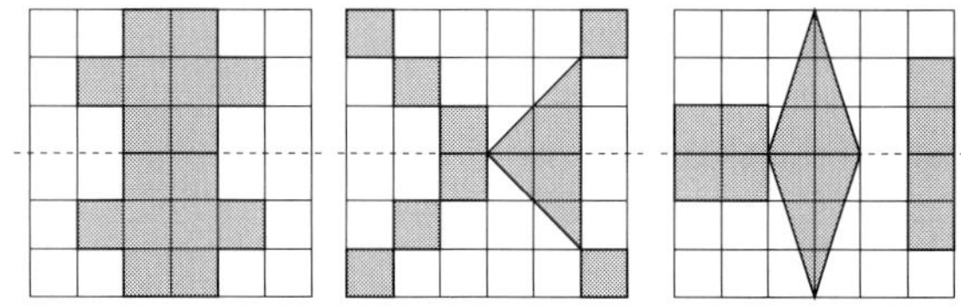

3 a b c

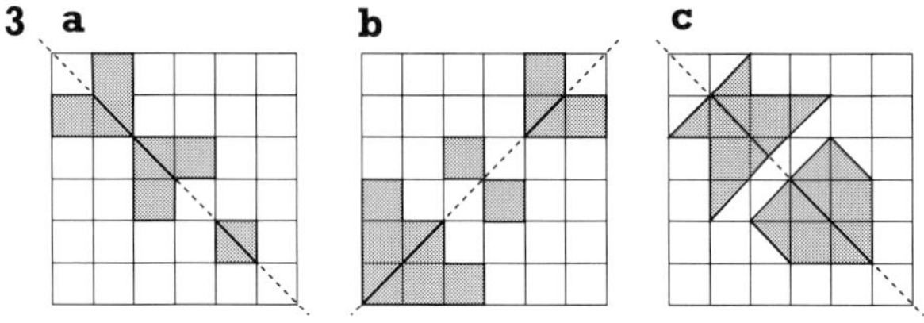

Page 15 Exercise 2
1 HAVE YOU THE TIME **2** MEET ME AT THE ABBEY **3** COME TO MY HOME AT TWO **4** THE BOOK MAY BE OUT

Page 16 Exercise 3
1 a $a = 90$ **b** $b = 40$ **c** $c = 50$ **2 a** $e = 35$ **b** $f = 62$ **c** $g = 83$ **3 a** $a = 90$ **b** $b = 72$ **c** $c = 18$
4 a a rectangle **b** (i) 90 (ii) 90 **5 a** (i) CB (ii) AD **b** (i) CBD (ii) BAD **6 a** (i) BM (ii) DP **b** (i) BCP (ii) MAD **7 a** (i) EF, GH, GF (ii) AE, CG, DG **b** (i) BEF, DGH, CGF (ii) FEG, HGE, FGE

Page 17 Exercise 4
1 b and c **2 a** 2 cm **b** 4 cm **c** 3 cm **d** 2.5 cm
3
a
b
c

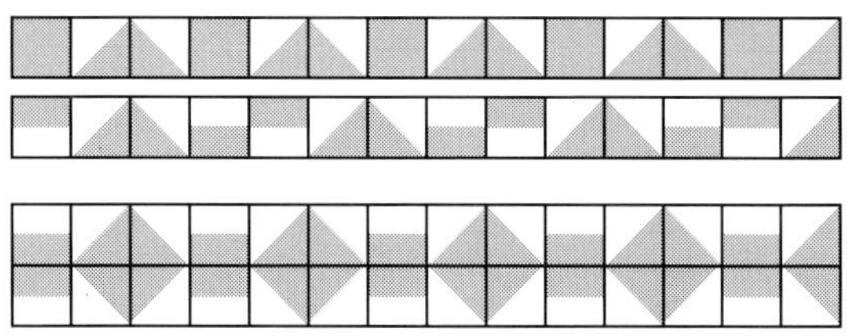

4

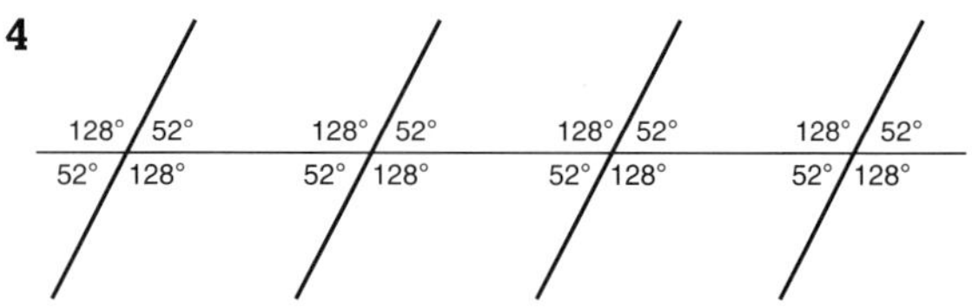

Page 19 Exercise 5

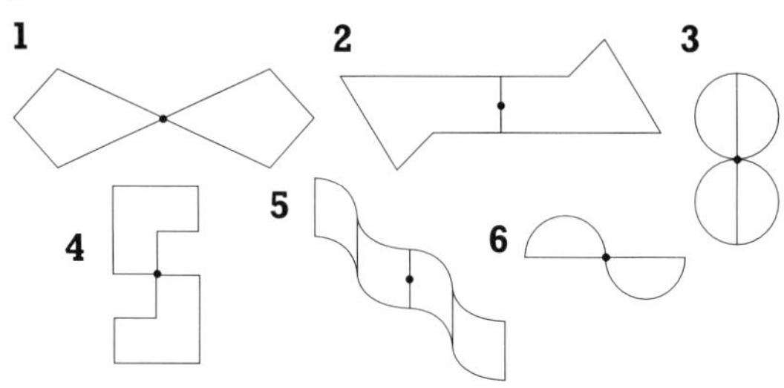

Page 20 Exercise 6

1 a 8 **b** 4 **c** 3 **d** 5 **e** 6 **f** 2 **g** 7 **2 a** 2, 3, 6 **b** 1, 4, 5

Page 21 Exercise 6B

1 a

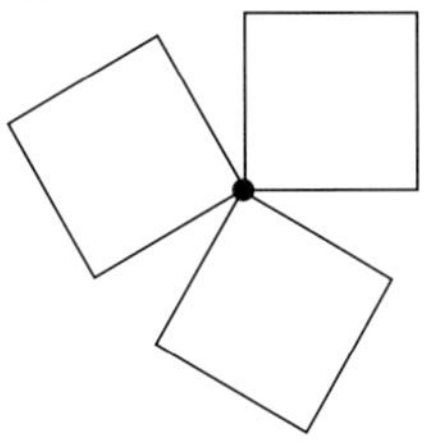

b

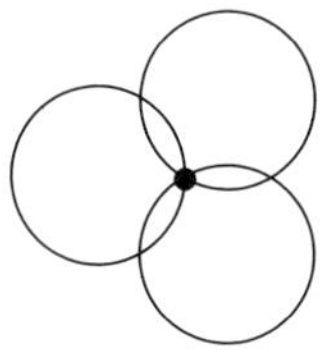

c

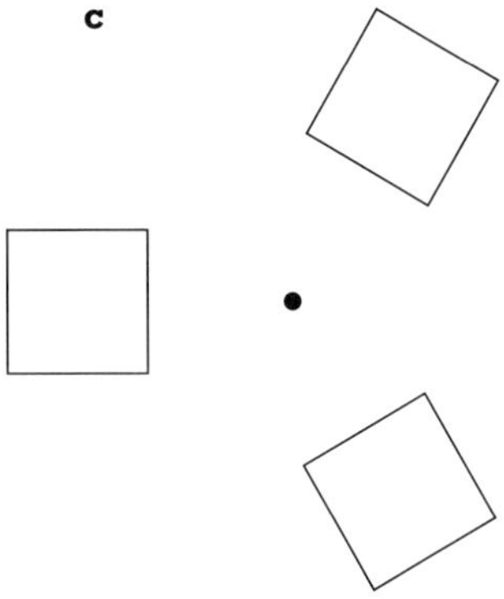

2

a

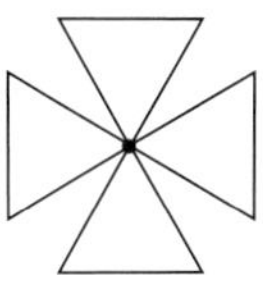

b

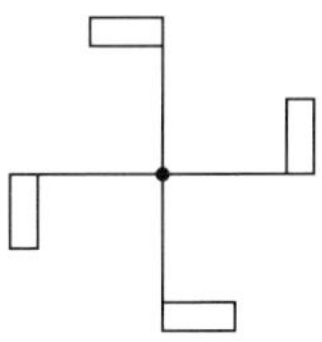

c

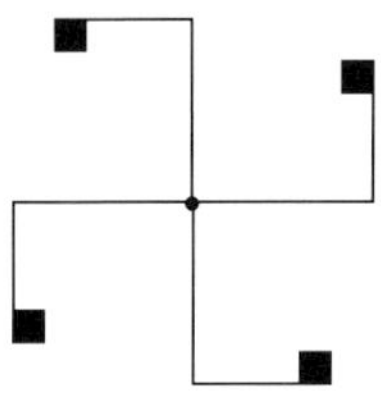

3

b

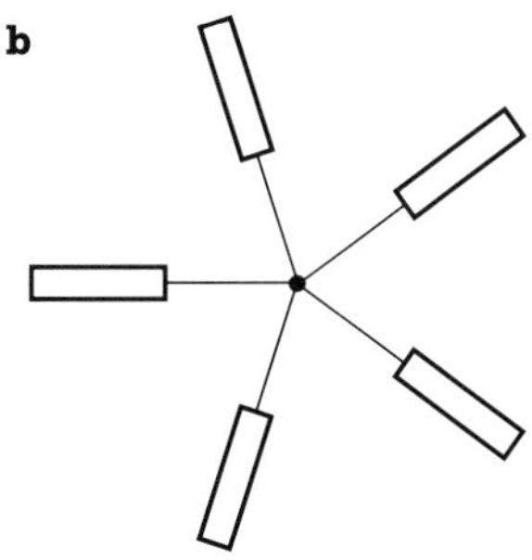

c

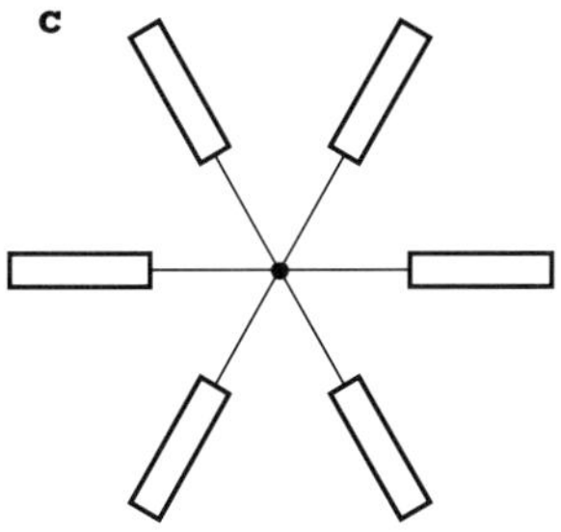

Page 22 Check-up

1

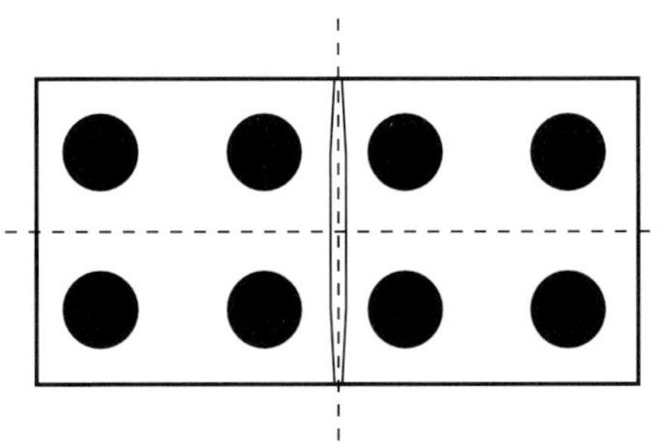

2

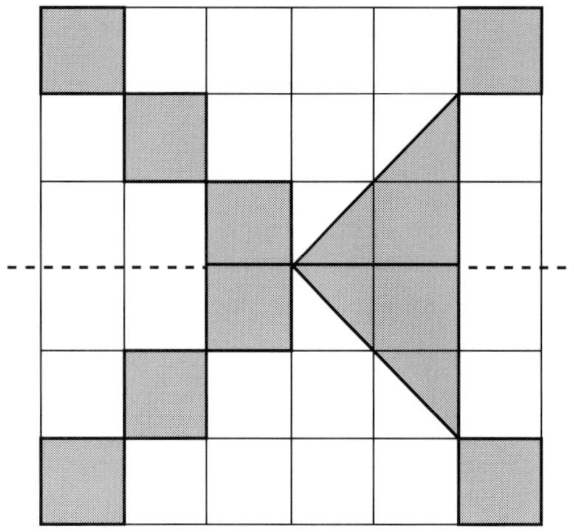

3 a LP **b** MN **c** (i) 90 (ii) 58

5

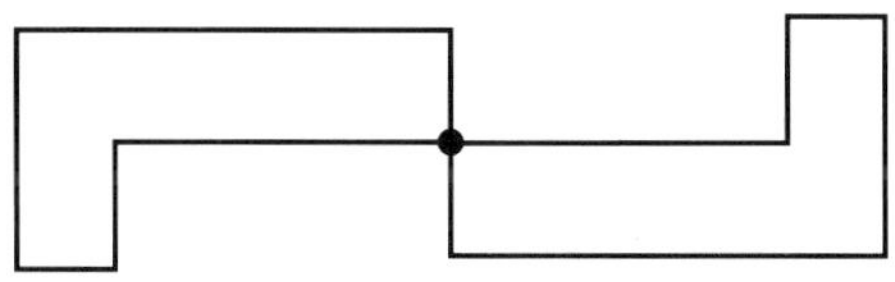

6 3

TEACHER'S BOOK

Page 14 Worksheet 1

1 1 **2** 3 **3** 1 **4** 1 **5** none **6** 5 **7** 1 **8** none **9** 1 **10** none **11** none **12** 4 **13** 1 **14** none **15** 2

Page 15 Worksheet 2

1

a

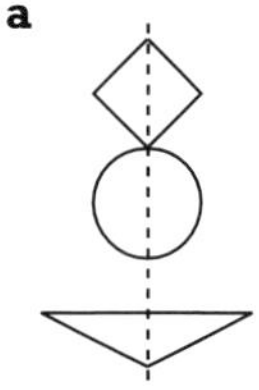

b

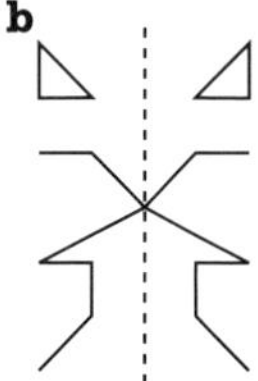

c

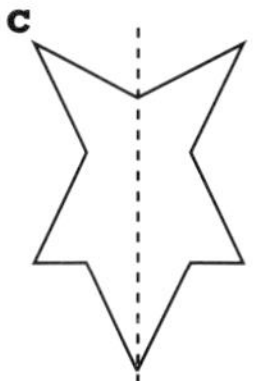

d

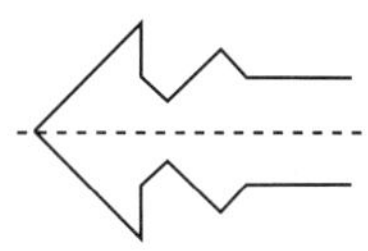

e

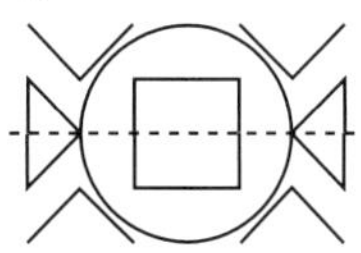

f

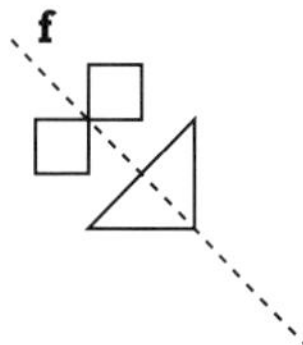

g

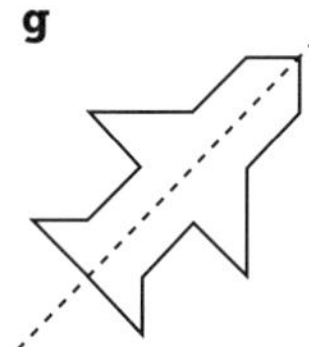

2

a

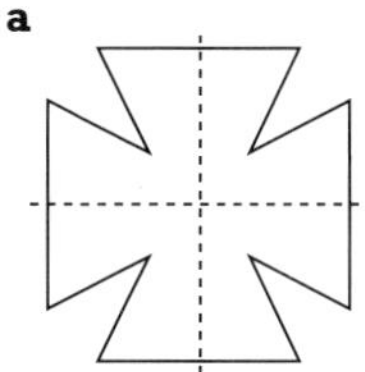

b

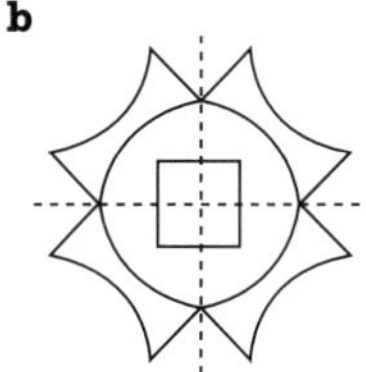

c

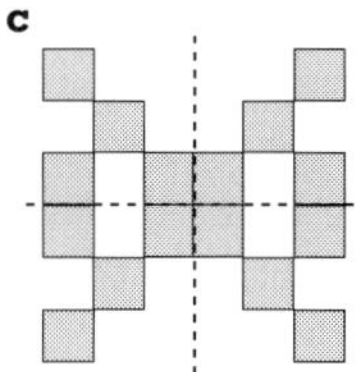

3

a **b**

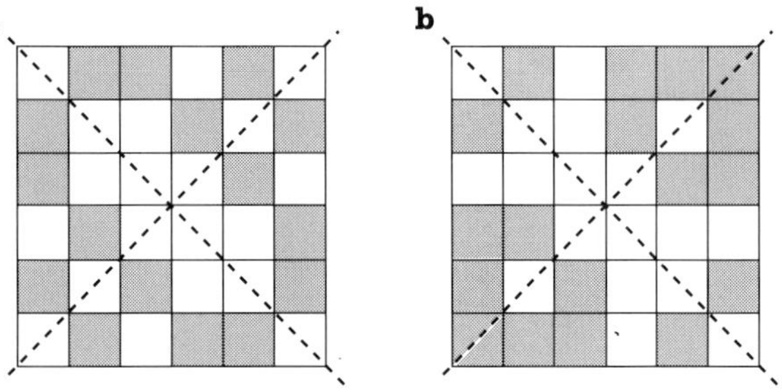

Page 16 Worksheet 3

2

Shape	Axes of symmetry
Square	4
Rectangle	2
Kite	1
Rhombus	2
Parallelogram	0
Trapezium 1	1
Trapezium 2	none
Equilateral triangle	3
Regular hexagon	6

Page 19 More Practice 1

2

a **b** **c** **d** **e** **f**

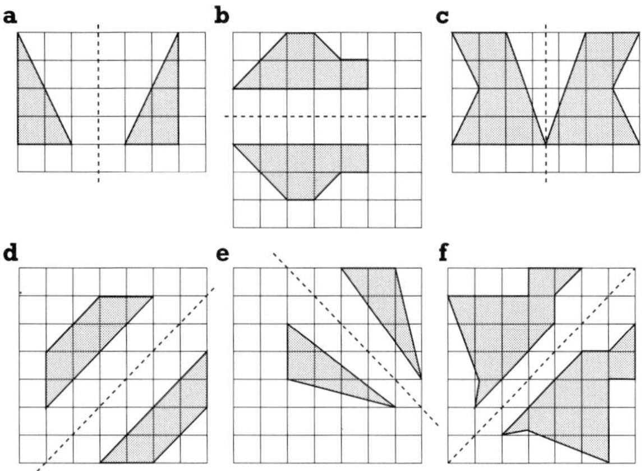

3 STRUCTURED DIAGRAMS

STUDENTS' BOOK

Page 23 Looking Back

1 a 4 **b** 9 **c** 5 **d** 11 **2 a** 4 **b** 2 **c** 18 **d** 20p **3 a** 15 **b** 2 **4 a** 100p **b** 200p **c** 350p **5** left, forward 5, left, forward 2, right, forward 2, left, forward 1, right, forward 1

Page 24 Exercise 1

1 no milk, sugar; no milk, no sugar **2** Laura; no one **3** stop, go, stop; stop, go, go; go, stop, stop; go, stop, go; go, go, stop; go, go, go **4 b** 12, 13, 21, 23, 31, 32 **c** 123, 132, 213, 231, 312, 321 **5 a** (1,1), (1,2), (1,3), (2,1), (2,2), (2,3), (3,1), (3,2), (3,3) **b** (1,1), (1,2), (1,3), (2,2), (2,3), (3,3)

Page 27 Exercise 2

1 a 3 **b** 3 **c** 5 **d** 10 **2 a** 7 **b** 12 **c** 3 **d** 17 **3 a** 3 **b** 0 **c** 12 **d** 8 **4 a** 7 **b** 6 **c** 8 **d** 21 **5 a** 7 **b** 15 **c** 17 **d** 30 **6 a** (i) 10 (ii) 12 (iii) 7 (iv) 9 **b** 24 **7 a** (i) 16 (ii) 14 (iii) 6 (iv) 3 **b** 23

Page 29 Exercise 3

1 a 1 **b** 5 **2** 4 **3** 5 **4** 4 **5** 12

Page 30 Exercise 4

1 a 4 **b** 6 **c** 16 **2 a** 15 cm **b** 12 cm **c** 9 cm **3 a** 20 kg **b** 2 kg **c** 33 is 1 kg above average **4 a** £0.35 **b** £2.10 **c** £1.40 **5 a** (i) 86 °F (ii) 113 °F (iii) 212 °F **b** (i) 10 °C (ii) 5 °C (iii) 50 °C **6 a** £6 **b** £15 **c** £8 **7 a** 120 min **b** 130 min **8 a** £235 **b** £246.75 **c** £493.50

Page 33 Check-up

1 8 possible faces **2 a** 11 **b** 8 **c** 1 **3** 2 **4 a** £11 **b** £26.10 **c** (i) £5.80 (ii) £5.50

TEACHER'S BOOK

Page 24 Worksheet 2

1a PTA, PAT, TPA, TAP, APT, ATP **b** PAT, TAP, APT **2** 27 pictures are possible **3** 24 ways

Page 26 Worksheet 4

1 1 **2** 1 **3** 1 **4** 8 + 5 + 5 = 18, too many

Page 27 More Practice on Tree Diagrams

1 Indians, Vikings, Greeks; Greeks, Indians, Vikings; Greeks, Vikings, Indians; Vikings, Indians, Greeks; Vikings, Greeks, Indians
2 cake, pear, banana; cake, banana, pear; pear, banana, cake; pear, cake, banana; banana, cake, pear; banana, pear, cake; **3** 27 numbers
4 11 soups **5** 64 possible patterns

4 A PROBLEM SOLVING TOOLKIT

STUDENTS' BOOK

Page 34 Exercise 1

1 3, 7 **2** 3, 4 **3** 4, 9 **4** 6, 11

5

a **b** **c** **d**

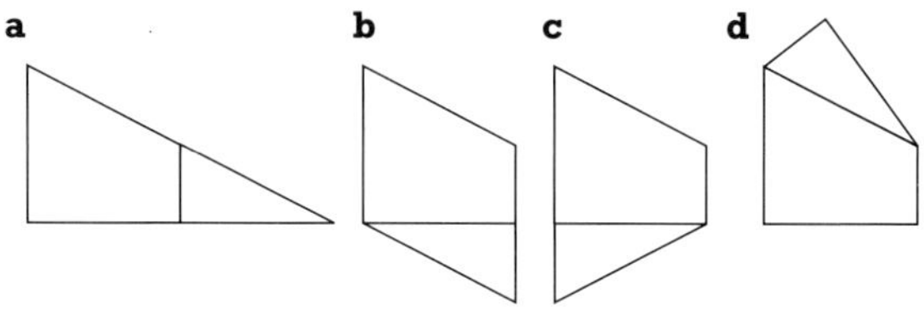

6

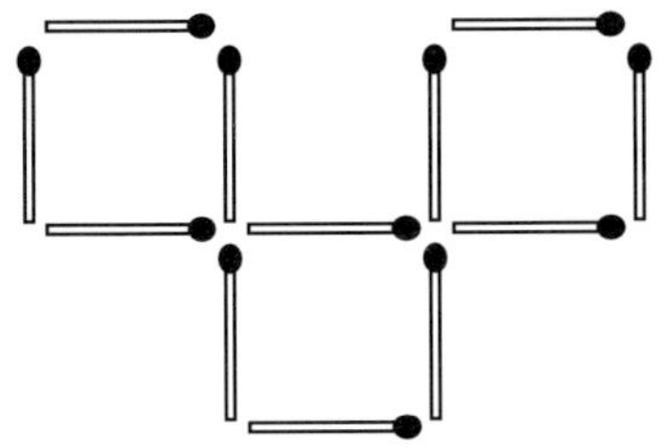

7 a(i) **(ii)** **(iii)** **(iv)** **(v)** **(vi)**

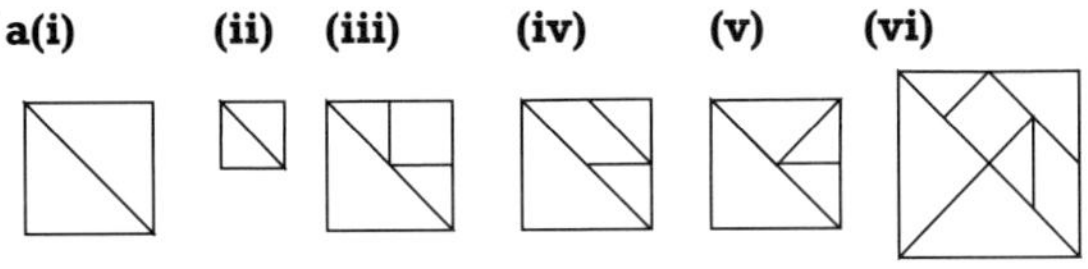

b(i) **(ii)** **(iii)**

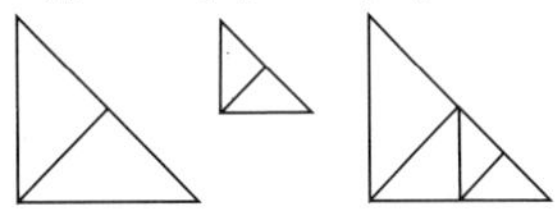

c(i) **(ii)** **(iii)** **(iv)** **(v)**

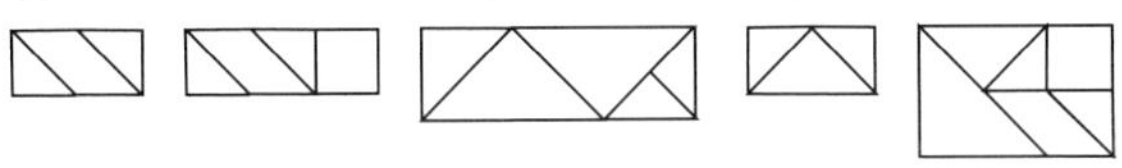

8 a **b** **c**

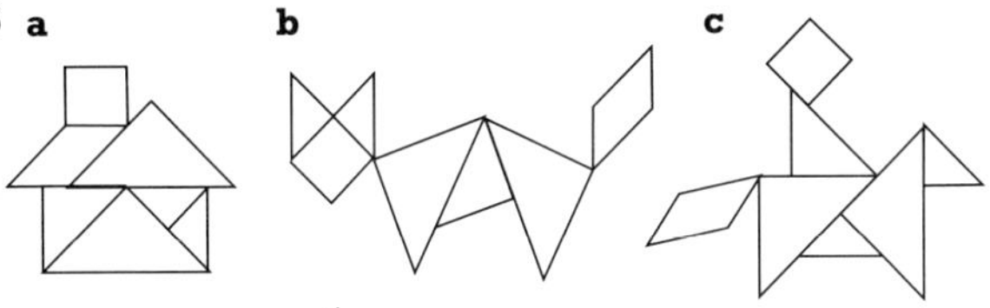

d **e**

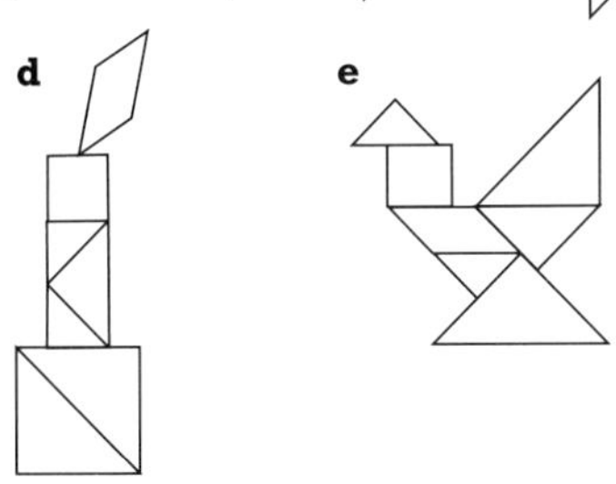

Page 36 Exercise 2
1 6 moves **2** 15 moves **3** 13 moves **4** Meg, Kim, Lee, Will, Fred **5** 8
6

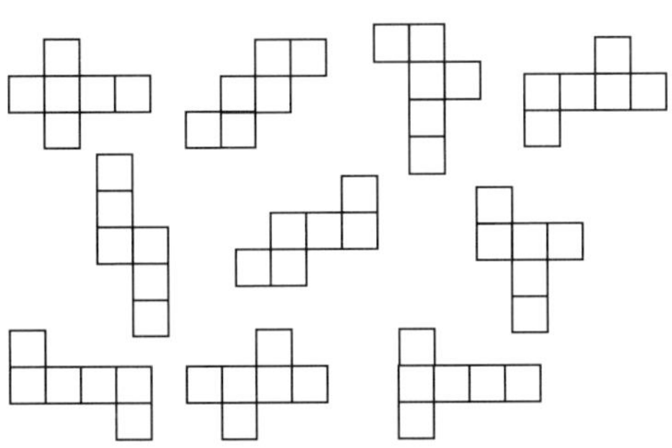

Page 38 Exercise 3
1 6 **2** 24 **3** 36 **4** Frank, Fang, goldfish; Ellie, Bronx, dog; Ito, Rambo, snake; Sally, Killer, cat
5 Bakula, witch, 1st; Colin, monster, 2nd; Adam, mummy, 3rd; Dave, skeleton, 4th

6 a

Away team (columns), Home team (rows)

	A	B	C
A		B	A
B	B		B
C	C	C	

b

Name	Won	Drawn	Lost	Points
Alder	1	0	3	2
Baxter	3	0	1	6
Crown	2	0	2	4

c Baxter

Page 40 Exercise 4
1 a (i) 2 (ii) add 1 (iii) 21 **b** (i) 4 (ii) add 2 (iii) 42 **c** (i) 3 (ii) subtract 2 (iii) 28 **d** (i) 6 (ii) subtract 1 (iii) 59 **e** (i) 5 (ii) subtract 3 (iii) 47 **f** (i) 2 (ii) add 14 (iii) 34 **g** (i) 3 (ii) add 2 (iii) 32 **h** (i) 10 (ii) subtract 1 (iii) 99 **2 a** 61 **b** 102 **c** 118 **3 a** 10 **b** times 2 add 2 **c** 42

Page 41 Exercise 5
1 799 **2** 50 **3 a** 140 **b** 48 **4** 28 **5** 5050
6 500 500

Page 43 Check-up
1 15 **2** take rabbit across, return, take cabbage, return with rabbit, take tiger, return, take rabbit **3** 13 triangles **4 a** Paris **b** bus **5 a** (i) times 5 subtract 3 (ii) 47 **b** (i) times 7 add 16 (ii) 86 **c** (i) times 6 add 3 (ii) 63 **6 a** 705 **b** 304

TEACHER'S BOOK

Page 35 Worksheet 2

1

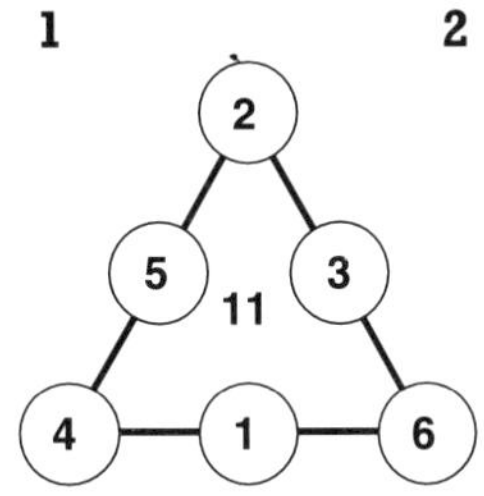

2

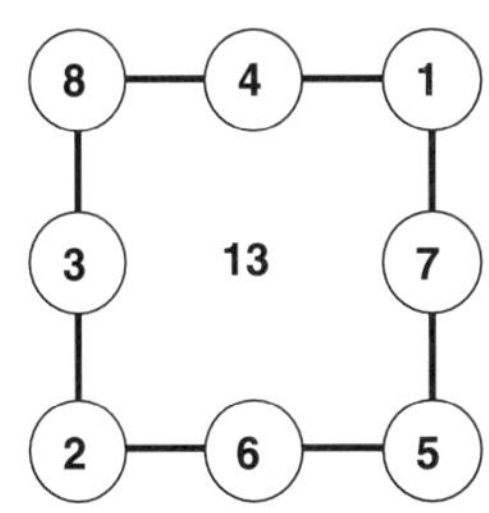

3

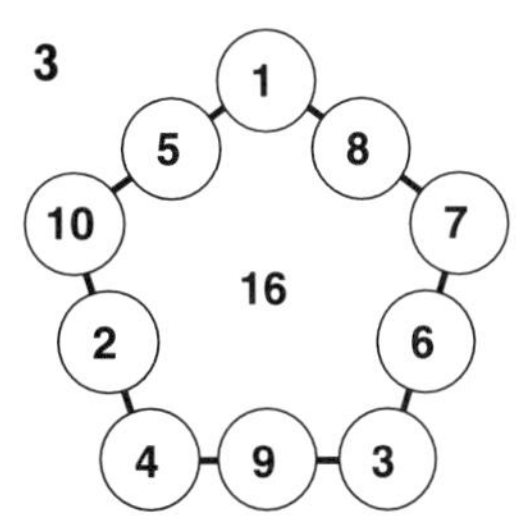

4

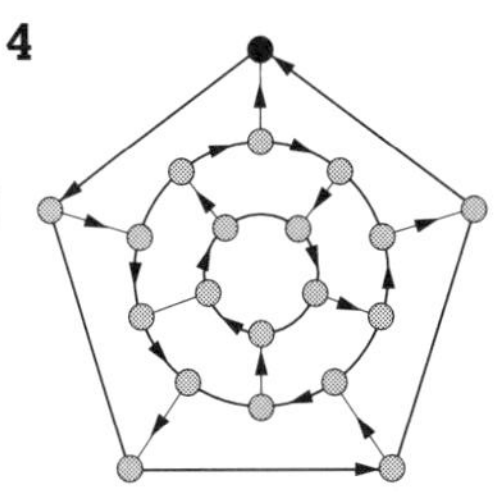

Page 38 Worksheet 5
Nets 1, 2, 4, 5, 6, 7, 10 and 12

Page 40 Worksheet 7
1 a (i) add 2 (ii) 22 **b** (i) times 3 add 2 (ii) 62 **c** (i) times 4 add 2 (ii) 82 **d** (i) times 6 add 2 (ii) 122 **2 a** 14 **b** 57 **3** 100

5 SCALES

STUDENTS' BOOK

Page 45 Looking Back

1 a Jon 15, Alan 27, Sam 39 **b** Sam **2a** and **b** Lerwick 7 °C, Aberdeen 11 °C, Glasgow 16 °C, Oban 19 °C **3** Oak 47 feet, Elm 34 feet, Ash 18 feet

Page 46 Exercise 1

1 Sandy £4, Aaron £13, Richard £18, Matthew £22 **2 a** Sandy £26, Aaron £44, Richard £52, Matthew £37 **b** Richard's

3

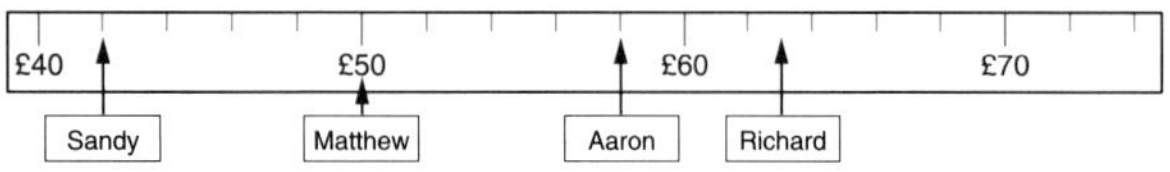

Page 47 Exercise 2

1 Kathleen 70, Morven 100, Lorna 180, Karen 225, Jo 310 **2 a** 300 miles **b** 100 miles **c** 250 miles **d** 125 miles **e** 175 miles **f** 350 miles
3 a £80 **b** £140 **c** £60 **d** £350 **e** £150 **f** June, as most money was collected then **g** school holidays **4a** 100 **b** 1500 **c** Wednesday, low attendance figures

d

Mon	Tue	Wed	Thu	Fri	Sat
1500	2000	600	2250	2900	3200

Page 49 Exercise 3

1 a Common daisy 1.8 cm **b** Buttercup 2.2 cm **c** Pansy 3.3 cm **d** Thistle 2.9 cm
2 a 1.5 litres **b** 0.6 litre **c** 1.1 litres **3 a** 2.4 kg **b** 0.6 kg **c** 3.3 kg **d** 1.8 kg **4 a** 2.3 kg **b** 1.7 kg
5 a 36.2 °C **b** 35.6 °C **c** 36.8 °C **d** 38.2 °C **e** 37.5 °C

Page 51 Exercise 4

1 a 1.55 **b** 1.63 **c** 1.68 **d** 1.77 **e** 1.81 **f** 6.82 **g** 6.93 **h** 6.99 **p** 0.93 **q** 1.01 **r** 1.07 **t** 4.37 **u** 4.25 **v** 4.19 **x** 15.36 **y** 15.28 **z** 15.21

2

Bird	Buzzard	Kite	Osprey	Gannet	Eagle
Wingspan (metres)	1.14	1.4	1.45	1.75	2.01

Page 52 Exercise 5

1 a Luxor 40 °C, Cairo 34 °C, Algiers 31 °C, London 28 °C, San Francisco 24 °C, Auckland 13 °C **b** Athens 91 °F, Montreal 84 °F, Moscow 77 °F, Dublin 72 °F, Perth 63 °F
2 Tara 37.5 °C, Jim 38.4 °C, Lesley 38.1 °C, Laura 36.9 °C **3 a** 200 °C **b** 150 °C **c** 225 °C

Page 53 Exercise 6

1 a –5 °C **b** –1 °C **c** 7 °C **d** –3 °C **2 a** –1 °C **b** –3 °C **c** 2 °C **d** –2 °C **e** –1 °C **f** –2 °C
3 a Eskdalemuir, Aviemore, Stornoway **b** –3 °C **c** 4 °C **d** Glasgow **e** 5 °C

Page 54 Exercise 7

1 a 7 metres **b** –1 metre **c** scuba divers **d** –3.5 metres **e** 5.5 metres **f** swimmers **g** 2.5 metres **h** 1.5 metres **i** 1.5 metres
2 a (i) £15 profit (ii) £16 profit (iii) £11.50 profit **b** May, June, September **c** September **d** £11 loss **e** £7 **f** £13

Page 55 Exercise 8

1 a (i) 0 ml (ii) about 300 ml (iii) about 860 ml **b** about 1 and $\frac{3}{4}$ pints **2 a** 38 mph **b** about 110 km/hour **c** about 51 mph **d** about 16 km/hour **e** about 47 km/hour

Page 56 Check-up

1 a £140 **b** £380 **c** £240 **d** £120 **2** 1.8 kg **3** 1.3 litres **4** 1.97 metres **5 a** Tunis 29 °C, Edinburgh 14 °C, Dunedin –1 °C, McMurdo Sound –18 °C **b** 15 °C **c** 23 °C **d** –9 °C
6 about 104 km per hour

TEACHER'S BOOK

Page 42 Worksheet 1

1 a 1903 **b** 1910 **c** 1919 **d** 1923 **e** 1928 **f** 1930

2

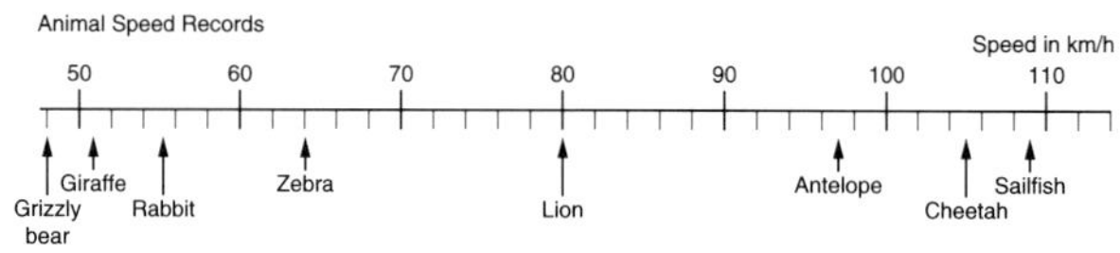

Page 43 Worksheet 2

a 300 **b** 375 **c** 450 **d** 125 **e** 145 **f** 940 **g** 1020 **h** 1080 **i** 3750 **j** 4500 **k** 5250 **l** 750 **m** 690 **n** 640 **v** 19 500 **w** 20 500 **x** 1225 **y** 1125 **z** 1050

Page 44 Worksheet 3

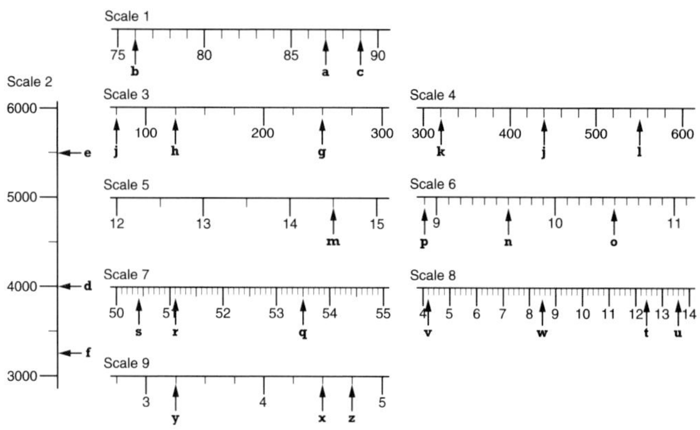

Page 45 Worksheet 4
1 Chay 1.74 m, Oliver 1.84 m, Alastair 1.80 m, Julie 1.82 m, Euan 1.91 m, Louise 1.76 m, Steven 1.88 m, Sue 1.71 m
2

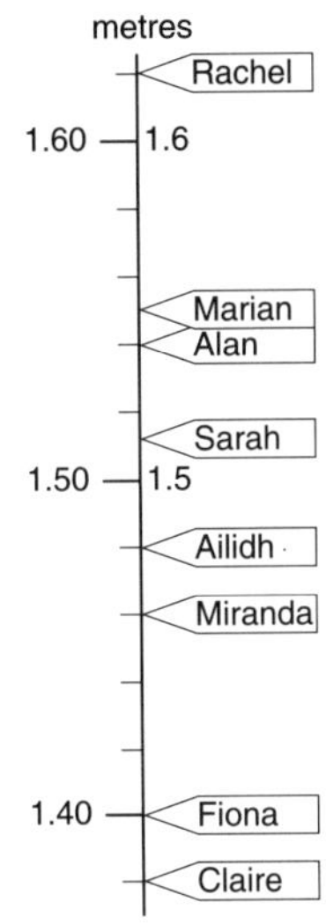

Page 46 More Practice 1: Temperatures Below Zero
1 a –5 °C **b** –4 °C **c** 16 °C **d** –8 °C **e** 7 am and 10 pm **2 a** –2 °C **b** –1 °C **c** –5 °C, –3 °C, –1 °C, 0 °C, 3 °C, 5 °C **d** –1 °C **e** –1 °C **f** –4 °C **g** 1 °C, –2 °C, 3 °C, –3 °C, –10 °C

Page 47 More Practice 2: Special Agent 003
1 14 metres **2** 2 metres **3** 6 metres **4** E **5** –8 metres **6** –7 metres **7** –3 metres **8** F **9** –4 metres **10** E or I **11** 22 metres **12** 14 metres

Page 48 More Practice 3: Comparing Scales
1 a 1.8 kg **b** 2 lb 4 oz **c** about 2 lb 8 oz **d** 0.1 kg **2 a** 27 °C **b** 61 °F **c** 82 °C **d** 24 °C and 32 °C

6 FRACTIONS AND PERCENTAGES

STUDENTS' BOOK

Page 58 Looking Back
1 a half **b** third **c** sixth **d** quarter **e** fifth **2 a** 10 **b** 2 **c** 3 **3 a** 12 **b** 11 **c** 4 **4** 6 **5** Amy 150 g, Ben 100 g, Colin 50 g **6** £44

Page 59 Exercise 1
1 a (i) 0.5 (ii) 0.25 (iii) 0.2 (iv) 0.125 (v) 0.1 **b** (i) 0.3333333 (ii) 0.1666666 (iii) 0.1111111 **2 a** 13 **b** 14 **c** 9 **d** 12 **e** 8 **f** 6 **g** 9 **h** 6 **i** 9 **j** 2 **k** 2 **l** 3 **3 a** 8 **b** 16 **4** 400 m **5 a** 30 **b** 15 **c** 20 **6 a** 50 **b** 25 **c** 20

Page 60 Exercise 2
1 a (i) 0.6 (ii) 0.75 (iii) 0.8 (iv) 0.375 (v) 0.7 **b** (i) 0.2222222 (ii) 0.5555555 (iii) 0.1111111 **2 a** 14 **b** 30 **c** 30 **d** 40 **e** 16 **f** 6 **g** 15 **h** 35 **i** 15 **j** 14 **k** 12 **l** 85 **3 a** 600 g **b** 300 g **4 a** 24 **b** 6 **5 a** 54 **b** one tenth **c** 6 **6 a** 0.03 **b** 0.09 **c** 0.17 **d** 0.29 **e** 0.87 **7 a** 145 **b** 160 **c** 35 **d** 465

Page 61 Exercise 3
1 a $\frac{6}{100}$ **b** $\frac{12}{100}$ **c** $\frac{36}{100}$ **d** $\frac{79}{100}$ **e** $\frac{99}{100}$ **2 a** 0.16 **b** 0.28 **c** 0.03 **d** 0.07 **e** 0.69 **3 a** (i) 0.5 (ii) 0.25 (iii) 0.1 (iv) 0.2 **b** (i) 0.25 (ii) 0.5 (iii) 0.2 (iv) 0.1 **c** (i) quarter (ii) half (iii) fifth (iv) tenth **4 a** 24 **b** 27 **c** 10 **d** 8 **e** 9 **f** 2 **g** 45 **h** 6 **5 a** £2.40 **b** £4 **c** £5.60 **d** £1.60 **6 a** £7.20 **b** £5.40 **c** £6.60 **7 a** 10 g **b** 30 g **c** 100 g

Page 63 Exercise 4
1 a (i) £17.28 (ii) £198.72 **b** (i) £4 (ii) £46 **c** (i) £26 (ii) £299 **2 a** (i) £2 (ii) £18 **b** (i) £9 (ii) £36 **c** (i) £18 (ii) £18 **3 a** £30 **b** £2.40 **c** £0.24 **4 a** (i) £40 (ii) £38 **b** (i) £80 (ii) £72 **5 a** (i) £36 (ii) £636 **b** (i) £150 (ii) £2650 **c** (i) £7.20 (ii) £127.20 **6 a** £36.75 **b** £210 **c** £120.75 **d** £84

Page 64 Exercise 5
1 a 10p **b** 16p **c** 8p **d** 13p **e** 7p **f** 11p **2 a** 3p **b** 4p **c** 0p **d** 8p **e** 1p **f** 5p **3 a** 22p **b** 55p **c** 33p **d** 44p **4 a** £8.80 **b** £12.96 **c** £10.08 **d** £20.70

Page 65 Exercise 6
1 a £2.10 **b** £4.55 **c** £9.80 **d** £0.35 **e** £21.70 **f** £17.15 **g** £1750 **2 a** £143.35 **b** £373.65 **c** £84.60 **d** £4.70 **e** £220.90 **f** £70.50 **g** £2350 **3 a** £5.41 **b** (i) **4** Pagesetter £117.50, Fast Draw £211.50, Merlin's Way £58.75, Card Games £70.50, Adventure Hill £141, Maze Trails £94, Mist £82.25, Battle Zone £70.50

Page 66 Check-up
1 a 0.125 **b** 0.0625 **2 a** 6 **b** 11 **3 a** 0.625 **b** 0.6 **4 a** 20 **b** 21 **5 a** 9 **b** 12 **6 a** 13/100 **b** 37/100 **7 a** 0.43 **b** 0.71 **8 a** 9 **b** 45 **9 a** 33 **b** 27 **10 a** £0.37 **b** £1.11 **11 a** £0.30 **b** £5.30 **12** £0.63 **13 a** 9p **b** 99p **14 a** £3.85 **b** £25.85

TEACHER'S BOOK

Page 50 More Practice 1
1 a 32 **b** 31 **c** 13 **d** 17 **e** 17 **f** 13 **g** 12 **h** 13 **i** 32 **j** 12 **k** 13 **l** 10 **2 a** 57 **b** 19 **c** 38 **d** total 114 **3 a** 30 **b** 4 **c** 6 **d** 20 **e** total 60 **4 a** 30 **b** 120 **c** 300 **d** 100 **e** 50 **f** total 600

Page 51 More Practice 2
1 a (i) £0.40 (ii) £0.30 (iii) £0.24 (iv) £0.20 b £0.06 c £1.20 2 a 30/100 b 3/100 c 27/100 d 61/100 e 36/100 f 70/100 g 83/100 h 4/100 i 8/100 j 50/100 k 72/100 l 96/100 3 a 0.05 b 0.07 c 0.09 d 0.11 e 0.38 f 0.45 g 0.74 h 0.64 i 0.88 j 0.41 k 0.01 l 0.86 4 a 4.5 b 27 c 96 d 110 e 56 f 300 g 12.8 h 462 i 4 j 13 k 5 l 4 5 a 10 b 25 c 3 6 8 size 3, 5 size 2, 3 size 1, 4 size 4 7 27, 57, 39, 27

Page 52 More Practice 3
1 £2.00, £0.50, £1.50; £0.60, £0.15, £0.45; £1.20, £0.30, £0.90; £0.80, £0.20, £0.60 2 125p, 5p, 130p; 275p, 11p, 286p; 50p, 2p, 52p; 75p, 3p, 78p 3 a £2500 b £500 c £300 d £200 e £1000 4 a £87.50 b £3.85 c £15.05 d £21.70 5 a £10, £1.75, £11.75 b £400, £70, £470

Page 53 Fractions on the Calculator
1 a $\frac{1}{11}$ b $\frac{1}{10}$ c $\frac{1}{9}$ d $\frac{1}{6}$ e $\frac{1}{8}$ f $\frac{3}{4}$ g $\frac{3}{5}$ h $\frac{3}{10}$ i $\frac{1}{4}$ j $\frac{1}{5}$
2 a $\frac{1}{5}$ b $\frac{1}{8}$ c $\frac{1}{9}$ d $\frac{1}{12}$ e $\frac{2}{3}$ f $\frac{2}{5}$ g $\frac{5}{6}$ h $\frac{17}{12}$ 3 half
4 a $\frac{1}{3}$ b $\frac{1}{4}$ c $\frac{1}{6}$ d $\frac{1}{9}$ e $\frac{2}{9}$ f $\frac{2}{7}$ g $\frac{5}{8}$ h $\frac{2}{15}$ 5 $\frac{5}{12}$ h

Page 54 Extension Work
1 40% 2 33.333% 3 75% 4 70% 5 a 20% b 40% 6 a 70% b (i) 75% (ii) better 7 a 25% b 80% c 62.5% d 43%

7 ANGLE

STUDENTS' BOOK

Page 67 Looking Back
1 a 4 b 1 c 1 d 2 e 10 2 acute a, e, k; right d, g; obtuse c, h, i; straight b, f, j 3 a 30° b 80° c 113° 4 b 5.8 cm c ∠YXZ = 89°, ∠XZY = 51°

Page 69 Exercise 1
1 d, f, i 2 acute 34°, 85°; right 90°; obtuse 126°, 173°, 94°, 133°; straight 180°; reflex 204°, 300°, 253°, 340°,187° 3 acute b, d; right e; obtuse g; straight a, h; reflex c, f 4 f, d acute; a, g right; c obtuse; e, b reflex 5 a obtuse b right c obtuse d reflex e acute f reflex g obtuse h acute i acute j acute k obtuse l reflex m acute

Page 72 Exercise 2
1 a 90° b 35° c 108° d 67° e 94° f 43° 2 a ∠ABD =117° b ∠YZP =142° 3 50° 4 a 45° b 30° c 54° d 15° e 9° f 11° g 58° h 55° 5 a ∠DCB = 32° b ∠RST = 51°

Page 74 Exercise 3
1 90° 2 8 3 22.5° 4 a 12 b 4 c 2 d 9 e 36 5 a 230° b 170° c 60° 6 a 90° b 135° c 90° d 180° e 135° f 90° g 120° h 90° 7 a 73° b 123° 8a 55° b 90° c 80° d 25° 9 a 90° b 36° c 60° d 30° e 120°

Page 76 Exercise 4
2 20° 3 a 50° b 125° c 40° d 52° 5 a 70° b 34° c 60° 6 ∠ABC = 44°, ∠YZX = 42°, ∠MNL = 48°

Page 79 Check-up
1 a 180° straight b 35° acute c 90° right d 245° reflex e 150° obtuse 2 356°, 200° and 300° 3 a 35° b 60° c 27° d 121° 4 a 4 b 6 c 2 5 a 45° b 135° c 120° 6 a 48° b 32° c 74°

TEACHER'S BOOK

Page 58 More Practice 1
1 $a = 80°$, $b = 135°$, $c = 40°$, $d = 20°$, $e = 90°$, $f = 100°$ 2 $p = 50°$, $q = 150°$, $r = 60°$, $s = 100°$, $t = 35°$

Page 59 More Practice 2
1 $a = 325°$, $b = 350°$, $c = 255°$, $d = 234°$, $e = 283°$, $f = 220°$ 2 $a = 240°$, $b = 60°$, $c = 230°$, $d = 90°$, $e = 280°$, $f = 220°$

Page 60 More Practice 3
1 $a = 100°$, $b = 95°$ 2 $a = 80°$, $b = 170°$ 3 $a = 22°$, $b = 31°$, $c = 43°$ 4 54° 5 $x = 56°$, $y = 124°$

Page 61 More Practice 4
1 a 120° b 90° c 72° d 60° e 45° 2 51° 3 a 45° b 147° c 30° d 30° e 141° 4 110° 5 139° 6 a 45° b (i) 90° (ii) 135° (iii) 225° (iv) 315°

Page 62 Vertically Opposites

1 a
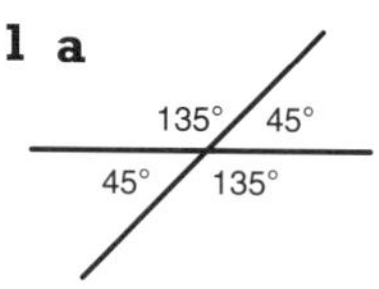

b
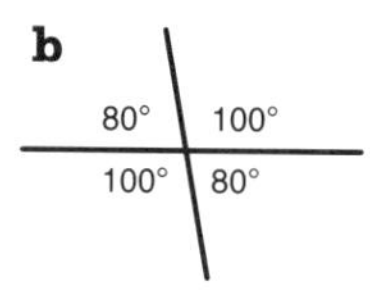

c
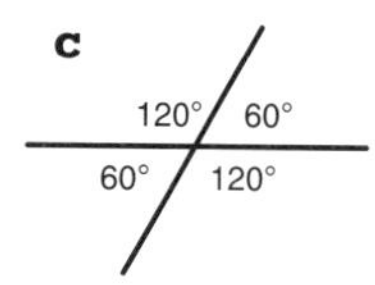

2 a
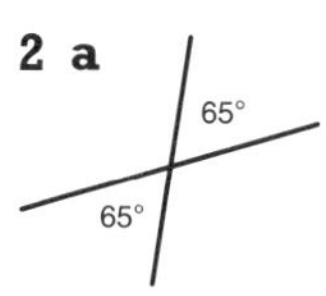

b
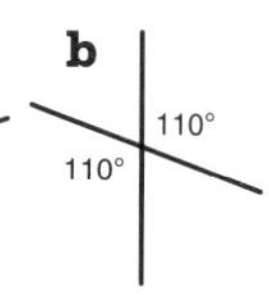

c
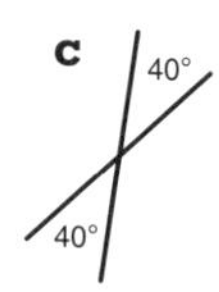

d
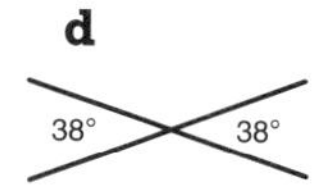

3 $a = 105°$, $b = 75°$, $p = 112°$, $q = 68°$, $t = 54°$, $v = 126°$

Page 63 Angles and Parallels

1 a 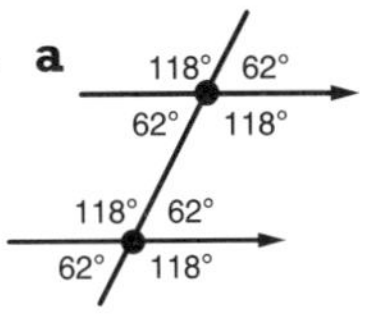

b 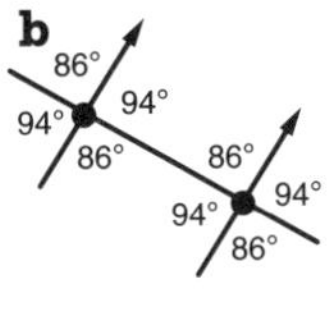

c 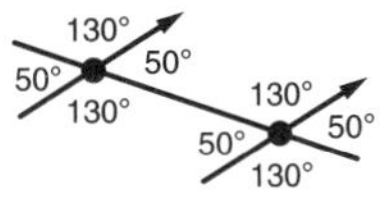

2 a 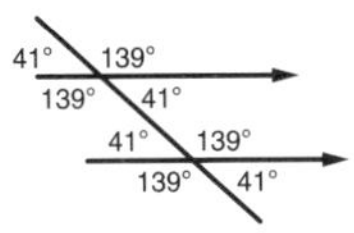

b 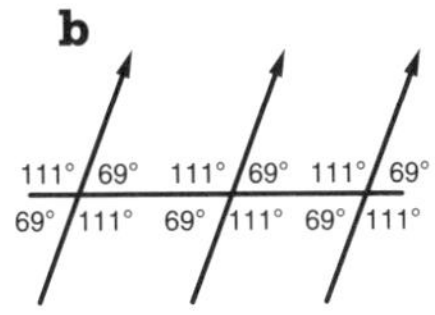

c 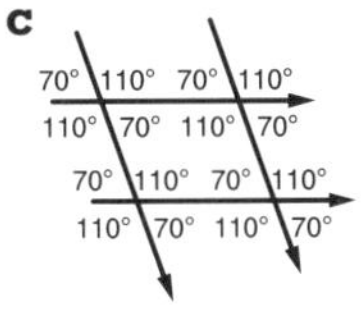

3 $x = 80°$, $y = 100°$

4 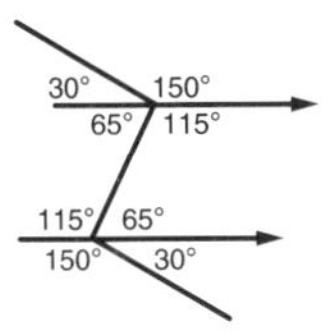

8 TIME

STUDENTS' BOOK

Page 80 Looking Back

1 a 18.03.95 **b** 03.10.98 **c** 20.08.90 **2 a** 26th September 1998 **b** 13th May 1999 **c** 30th November 1997 **3 a** Five (minutes) past seven **b** Twenty-five (minutes) past nine in the morning **c** Ten (minutes) to nine **d** Twenty-five (minutes) to twelve at night **4 a** 6.30 am **b** 2 pm **c** 3.30 pm **d** 6.50 pm **5 a** Half-past six in the morning **b** Two o'clock in the afternoon **c** Half-past three in the afternoon **d** Ten minutes to seven in the evening **6 a** 04 30 **b** 13 00 **c** 19 40 **d** 06 45 **7** 10 hours, 45 minutes **8** 9 hours, 10 minutes **9 a** 8 minutes **b** 1 hour, 19 minutes **c** 42 minutes **d** 50 minutes

Page 81 Exercise 1

1 a (i) 13th July 1994 (ii) 22nd October 1993 (iii) 26th March 1994 **b** (i) 31st March 1992 (ii) 11th November 1991 (iii) 22nd February 1992 (iv) 30th March 1990 **c** (i) 09 08 91 (ii) 23 04 96 (iii) 12 12 92

2 a

JUNE

S	M	T	W	T	F	S
				1	2	3
4	5	6	7	8	9	10
11	12	13	14	15	16	17
18	19	20	21	22	23	24
25	26	27	28	29	30	

JULY

S	M	T	W	T	F	S
						1
2	3	4	5	6	7	8
9	10	11	12	13	14	15
16	17	18	19	20	21	22
23	24	25	26	27	28	29
30	31					

b (i) Saturday (ii) Friday (iii) Monday (iv) Monday (v) Thursday **3 a** Friday **b** 4, 4 **c** 14 **d** 9

Page 83 Exercise 1B

1 a 44 days **b** 36 days **c** 47 days **d** 47 days **2 a** 22 days **b** 17 days **c** 51 days **d** 83 days

Page 84 Exercise 2

1 a 120 **b** 300 **c** 600 **d** 30 **e** 90 **2 a** 120 **b** 240 **c** 30 **d** 90 **e** 3 **f** $2\frac{1}{2}$ **3 a** 48 **b** 168 **c** 12 **d** 6 **e** $1\frac{1}{2}$ **f** 3 **4 a** (i) 125 minutes (ii) 2 hours, 5 minutes **b** 1 hour, 35 minutes **c** 2.05 pm or five past two in the afternoon

5

Bus 1	Bus 2	Bus 3	Bus 4
06 00	06 20	06 40	07 00
06 35	06 55	07 15	07 35

6 a 29 minutes and 26 seconds **b** 4 minutes and 52 seconds **7** 15 minutes

Page 85 Exercise 3

1 a 20 minutes **b** 1 hour 5 minutes
2 a 15 minutes **b** 2 hours 20 minutes
3 25 minutes **4** 8 hours 45 minutes
5 a 5 minutes slow **b** 5 minutes fast
c 19 minutes fast **d** 20 minutes fast

Page 87 Exercise 4

1 b, c and f **2 a** 366 **b** 366 **c** 365 **d** 365 **e** 365 **f** 366 **3 a** 60 **b** 59 **c** 59 **4** 1972 and 1976 **5 a** (i) and (iii) **c** 2012 **6 a** (i) and (iii) **c** 2014

Page 88 Exercise 5

1 a 15 minutes **b** 45 minutes **c** (i) 9.00 am (ii) 3.30 pm (iii) $6\frac{1}{2}$ hours **d** 3 hours 15 minutes **3 a** No. Period 1 (Assembly) lasts for 15 minutes each morning; Periods 2, 3 and 4 last for 55 minutes each morning; Periods 5 and 6 last for an hour each afternoon. **b** 11.05 am, 15 minutes **c** Science 3 periods, Music 1 period, Maths 3 periods, Home Economics 2 periods, PE 2 periods, Technical 2 periods, Social Subjects 3 periods, French 3 periods, Guidance 1 period, Computing 1 period, Art 1 period **d** English 2 hours 45 minutes, Science 2 hours 50 minutes, Music 55 minutes, Maths 2 hours 50 minutes, Home Economics 1 hour 55 minutes, PE 1 hour 55 minutes, Technical 1 hour 55 minutes, Social Subjects 2 hours 55 minutes, French 2 hours 50 minutes, Guidance 55 minutes, Computing 1 hour, Art 1 hour

Page 89 Exercise 6
1 a Every half hour between 06 30 and 09 00 **b** 53 minutes **c** 32 minutes **d** 07 42 **2 a** 08 30 to 17 30, 9 hours (including lunch and other breaks) **b** 2 **c** Monday 9 hours 7 minutes, Tuesday 9 hours 3 minutes, Wednesday 9 hours 11 minutes, Thursday 9 hours 8 minutes, Friday 8 hours 55 minutes, Weekly total 45 hours 24 minutes **3 a** pm **b** Channel 4 **c** $1\frac{1}{2}$ hours **d** 5 minutes **e** 6.20 pm

Page 90 Check-up
1 a

S	M	T	W	T	F	S
				1	2	3
4	5	6	7	8	9	10
11	12	13	14	15	16	17
18	19	20	21	22	23	24
25	26	27	28	29	30	

b (i) 4 (ii) 4 **c** (i) Wednesday (ii) Sunday **2 a** Tom 9th October 1983, Tracy 29th February 1984 **b** It was a leap year **c** (i) Tom (ii) almost 5 months **3** 36 days **4 a** 7 hours 5 minutes **b** 15 minutes **5** 480 **6** 09 45 **7** b; 96 divides by 4, 94 doesn't **8 a** (i) 2.30 am (ii) 02 30 **b** (i) 3 pm (ii) 15 00 **c** (i) 11.20 am (ii) 11 20 **d** (i) 6.45 pm (ii) 18 45 **9** The Screamers 15 minutes, The Ravers 25 minutes, Shoe Shine Boys 1 hour 20 minutes **10 a** 15 minutes **b** 11 minutes **c** 48 minutes **d** 4 hours 38 minutes

TEACHER'S BOOK

Page 66 Mental Test A
1 61 **3** 4 months **4** 9 weeks **5** 45 minutes **6** 3 hours **7** 1 hour 10 minutes **8** 4.30 pm **9** 11.50 am **10** 6.30 am

Page 66 Mental Test B
1 07 00 **2** 8.15 am **3** Twenty minutes past eight **4** Twenty-five past eleven **5** 1.20 pm **6** 14 00 **7** One and a half hours **8** 8.45 pm **9** 1 hour 45 minutes **10** 3 hours 40 minutes

Page 67 Time for Cross-number Puzzles
1 Across **1** 31 **2** 365 **4** 26 **5** 301 **9** 24 **10** 300 **11** 15 Down **1** 366 **2** 360 **3** 52 **4** 2.30 **6** 120 **7** 14 **8** 100
2 Across **1** 1100 **3** 2230 **6** 1912 **7** 1400 **8** 1315 **10** 2300 **11** 0515 **12** 0000 **14** 1352 **16** 2355 **17** 2000 **18** 0015 Down **1** 1012 **2** 0100 **3** 2110 **4** 2235 **5** 0655 **9** 1135 **12** 0220 **13** 0050 **14** 1925 **15** 2400

Page 68 More Practice: Television Programmes
1 a/b Pop Video 30 minutes, Pop Hits 35 minutes **c** 65 minutes **2 a** 2 **b** 3 hours 10 minutes **3 a** 4 **b** 3 hours 35 minutes (3 hours 45 minutes if Weather and Programme News is included) **4 a** 3, Moby Dick, The Great Escape, Mercy **b** 6 hours 15 minutes **5** 19 hours 10 minutes

Page 69 Intervals over Midnight
1 a 1 hour **b** 2 hours **c** 4 hours **d** 6 hours **e** 10 hours **f** 12 hours **g** 14 hours **h** 17 hours
2 a 1 hour 30 minutes **b** 2 hours 30 minutes **c** 5 hours 30 minutes **d** 7 hours 30 minutes **e** 1 hour 20 minutes **f** 3 hours 10 minutes **g** 9 hours 40 minutes **h** 8 hours 50 minutes
3 a 3 hours **b** 6 hours **c** 11 hours **d** 14 hours **e** 5 hours 30 minutes **f** 8 hours 20 minutes **g** 7 hours 45 minutes **h** 4 hours 5 minutes
4 22 00 is 2 hours before midnight, 06 00 is 6 hours after midnight. The total time is 8 hours
5 20 20 is 3 hours 40 minutes before midnight, 10 15 is 10 hours 15 minutes after midnight. The total time is 13 hours 55 minutes **6 a** 12 hours **b** 11 hours 30 minutes **c** 16 hours **d** 16 hours 45 minutes **e** 9 hours 30 minutes **f** 13 hours 15 minutes

Page 70 Intervals over Midnight and Noon
1 a 3 **b** 5 **c** 9 **d** 6 **e** 12 **2 a** 2 hours 30 minutes **b** 5 hours 30 minutes **c** 7 hours 30 minutes **d** 1 hour 15 minutes **e** 3 hours 20 minutes **f** 2 hours 45 minutes **g** 9 hours 10 minutes **h** 4 hours 40 minutes **3 a** 5 hours **b** 9 hours **c** 6 hours 30 minutes **d** 1 hour 15 minutes **e** 5 hours 20 minutes **f** 7 hours 5 minutes **g** 3 hours 45 minutes **h** 5 hours 40 minutes
4 5 hours 45 minutes **5** 9 hours 10 minutes
6 14 hours 15 minutes **7** 3 hours 50 minutes
8 a 8 hours 25 minutes **b** 9 hours 45 minutes

Page 71 Time Intervals
1 Time Worked
Monday 5 hours 30 minutes
Tuesday 5 hours 20 minutes
Wednesday 6 hours 15 minutes
Thursday 4 hours 30 minutes
Friday 4 hours 55 minutes
Total time 26 hours 30 minutes
2 Time worked
Monday 10 hours
Tuesday 9 hours 45 minutes
Wednesday 10 hours 30 minutes
Thursday 9 hours 40 minutes
Friday 9 hours 40 minutes
Total time 49 hours 35 minutes
3 a 1 hour 58 minutes **b** 5 hours 23 minutes **c** 03 20
4 New arrival time: 00 20, 01 15, 01 05, 01 00, 00 26

9 CHARTS AND TABLES

STUDENTS' BOOK

Page 92 Exercise 1
1 a 15 inches **b** 7 pounds **c** (i) Dot (ii) 17 inches **d** (i) Dot (ii) 9 pounds **e** Patch and Rover **f** 28 pounds **2 a** 0.1 cm **b** Aviemore **c** Aviemore **d** 2.4 hours **3 a** 19 °C **b** (i) Aberdeen (ii) 7°C **c** 12 °C **d** (i) Oban (ii) 21 °C **e** 7 °C

Page 94 Exercise 2
1 a £55 **b** £560 **c** £260 **d** 2 nights **e** 2 children **2 a** £192 **b** £325 **c** (i) P and Q Ferries (ii) £280 **d** (i) P and Q Ferries (ii) August **e** £32.50 **3 a** £65 **b** £180 **c** £41 **d** £55 **e** £20

Page 96 Exercise 3
1 a (i) 45p (ii) £4.50 **b** (i) 42p (ii) £12.60 **c** (i) £18.90 (ii) £7.65 **2 a** £60 **b** £28.80 **c** (i) £19.20 (ii) £112.50 (iii) £69.60 **3 a** (i) £25.50 (ii) £76.50 **b** £459.80 **c** £1331 **4a** (i) 9p (ii) £1.35 **b** £2.80 **c** 8 copies at 10p each = 80p, 12 copies at 9p each = £1.08, total = £1.88 **d** 23 copies **5 a** 80p **b** £1.35 **c** £1.76

Page 98 Exercise 5
1 a 52p **b** 91p **c** £3.90 **2 a** £1.69 **b** £5.85 **c** £4.81 **3 a** £7.80 **b** £11.05 **c** £16.25 **4 a** 6 **b** 12 **c** 64 rolls
5

Number of rolls	Cost
1	15p
2	30p
3	45p
4	60p
5	75p
6	90p
7	£1.05
8	£1.20
9	£1.35
10	£1.50
20	£3.00
30	£4.50
40	£6.00
50	£7.50

Page 99 Check-up
1 a 242 calories **b** 109 + 72 = 181 calories **2 a** £23.10 **b** £36.90 **3 a** 88 km **b** 27 + 46 + 58 = 131 km **4 a** 3.18 kg **b** 6.81 kg **c** 31.75 kg **d** 61.28 kg

TEACHER'S BOOK

Page 73 Worksheet 1
1 a 86 miles **b** 145 miles **c** Aberdeen to Stranraer **d** Edinburgh and Glasgow **e** Edinburgh to Stranraer **f** 256 miles

2

Arvale			
6	Beldale		
13	7	Canville	
11	8	9	Denton

Page 74 Worksheet 2
1 a £4.50 **b** £7.60 **c** £2.55 **2 a** £13.60 **b** £19.95 **3** 6 pounds **4 a** £8.80 **b** £15.65 **c** £86.80

Page 75 Worksheet 3
1 a 400 pesetas **b** 140 pesetas **c** 2600 pesetas **d** 1460 pesetas **2** £6 **3** £15 **4 a** £4.50 **b** £23 **c** £17.60 **5** 730 pesetas **6** £6.99 in Britain, £7.10 in Tenerife; 11 pence cheaper in Britain **7** 5000 pesetas

Page 76 Worksheet 4
1

Length in metres	Cost
1	£2.45
2	£4.90
3	£7.35
4	£9.80
5	£12.25
6	£14.70
7	£17.15
8	£19.60
9	£22.05
10	£24.50
20	£49.00
30	£73.50
40	£98.00
50	£122.50

a £12.25 **b** £19.60 **c** 3 metres **d** (i) £29.40 (ii) £63.70 **e** £245
2

Litres	Gallons
1	0.22
2	0.44
3	0.66
4	0.88
5	1.10
6	1.32
7	1.54
8	1.76
9	1.98
10	2.20
20	4.40
30	6.60
40	8.80
50	11.00

a (i) 0.88 gallon (ii) 1.98 gallons (iii) 6.6 gallons **b** (i) 3.74 gallons (ii) 4.84 gallons (iii) 15.4 gallons **c** 5.5 gallons **d** 110 gallons

Page 77 More Practice 1
1 a 14 litres **b** Wednesday morning **c** 8.5 litres **d** (i) Beatrice (ii) 5.5 litres (iii) Tuesday afternoon **e** 20.5 litres **f** 95.5 litres **2 a** £295 **b** £310 **c** (i) Anglo-French (ii) day

Page 78 More Practice 2
1 a 25p **b** 52p **c** outside Europe **d** 38p **e** 88p **f** 36p **2 a** 69 °F **b** 12 hours **c** July and August **d** June **e** 16 °F **f** 7 hours

Page 79 More Practice 3
1 a £31.50 **b** £43.20 **c** (i) £78.75 (ii) £78 (iii) Student Services are cheaper by 75p **d** £1.05 **2 a** (i) £34 (ii) £52 (iii) £41.65 **b** 48 cost £40.80, 50 cost £40; so it is cheaper by 80p to buy 50

10 GRAPHS

STUDENTS' BOOK

Page 100 Looking Back
1 a Think or Swim **b** 135 **c** 65 **d** Think or Swim and Best Of **2 a** Medium roast **b** 8 **c** 174 **d** no **3 a** 5 **b** (i)150 (ii) 200 **c** 5 and 6 **d** 250
4 B stands for Swiss Soft Centre, C stands for Alpine White, D stands for Mixed Continental

Page 102 Exercise 1
1 a red **b** both least popular **c** 20 **d** red, blue, green, white, beige, yellow, black **e** no spaces **2 a** 9 **b** 11 **c** Red Admiral **d** Red Admiral, Tortoiseshell, Purple Emperor, Peacock, Cabbage White, Comma, Painted Lady **e** no **3 a** Athens **b** Athens, Barbados, Cardiff, Edinburgh and London **c** 21° **d** 2° **e** 14° **f** 5° **g** Auckland and Iceland **h** yes **4 a** Purple Emperor **b** Purple Emperor **c** Common Blue **d** Marbled White and Small Copper **e** Painted Lady and White Admiral **f** 4 **g** White Admiral **h** Purple Emperor, Painted Lady/White Admiral, Marbled White, Common Blue, Small Copper **i** Purple Emperor, White Admiral, Painted Lady, Marbled White, Small Copper, Common Blue

Page 104 Exercise 2
1 a 20 kg **b** 8 kg **c** 56 kg **d** he lost 4 kg **e** 4 and 5 **f** weeks 7 and 8 **g** 72 kg **h** 52 kg **2 a** In general the graph is rising **b** In general the graph is falling **c** The graph rises then falls sharply **3 a** 9.30 am **b** half an hour **c** 22 miles **d** 30 miles **e** 1 hour **f** 16 miles **g** 14 miles **4 a** (i) 3 (ii) 9 **b** 1.5 **c** 4 **5 a** (i) 9 (ii) 23 (iii) 36 **b** (i) 7 (ii) 9 (iii) 2 **6 a** (i) 12 (ii) 18 (iii) 30 **b** (i) 25 (ii) 34 (iii) 44 **7 a** (i) 38 (ii) 27 (iii) 15 **b** (i) 110 (ii) 50 (iii) 40

Page 107 Exercise 3
1 a Chinese **b** a quarter **c** a half **d** 20 **e** Chinese, British/Indian, Italian **2 a** (i) guitar (ii) drum (iii) piano **b** (i) a quarter (ii) a third **c** a half

Page 108 Exercise 4
1 £2.56 **2** 63% **3** 53.5 kg **4** £90.35 **5** 108 kg **6** 74 °F

Page 109 Check-up
1 a Harry **b** Bill **c** Fiona and Iain **d** Iain **2 a** 70 km **b** half an hour **c** 11 am **d** 2 hours **e** 2 pm **3 a** There is a steady rise in the rainfall throughout March **b** The temperature drops quickly then tails off **c** The number of pupils stays roughly the same **4 a** (i) 0.4 (ii) 2.2 (iii) 4.4 **b** (i) 4 (ii) 7 (iii) 9 **5 a** a quarter **b** 9 **c** (i) bike (ii) bus **6** 22 °C

TEACHER'S BOOK

Page 81 Worksheet 1

1

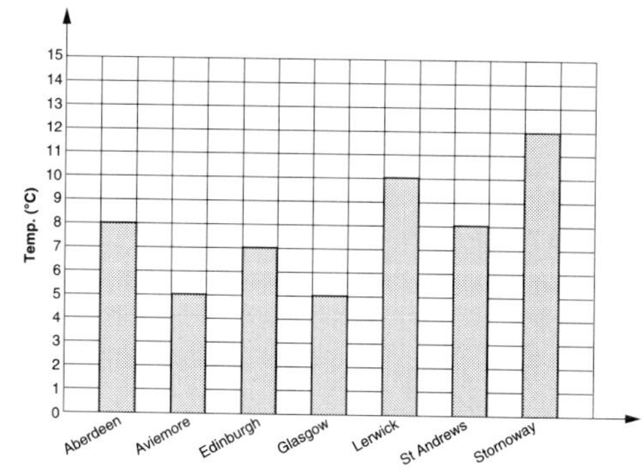

2

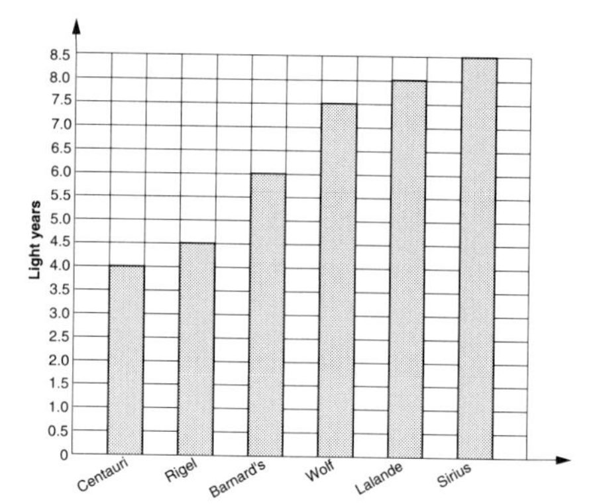

a 8 light years **b** Sirius **c** 2.5 light years

3

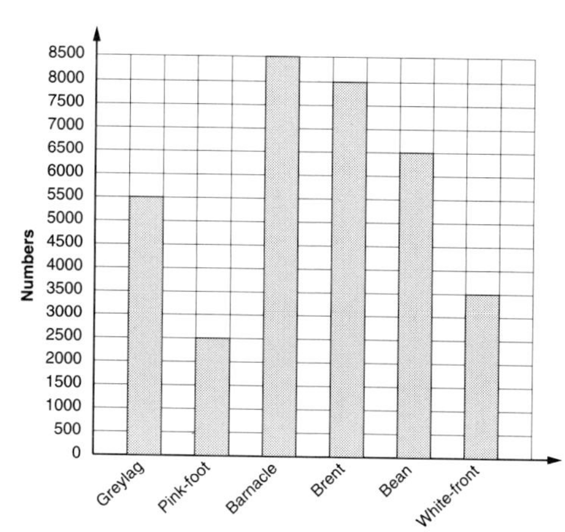

a Barnacle, Brent, Bean, Greylag, White-fronted, Pink-footed **b** 34 500 **c** Barnacle, Brent

Page 83 Worksheet 2

1 a

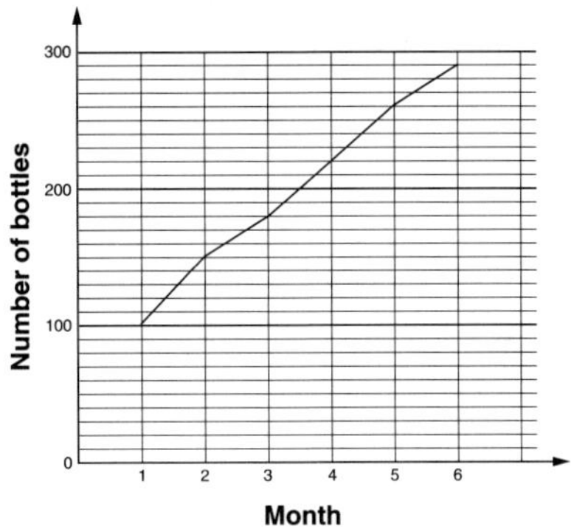

b The sales increase over the 6-month period

2 a

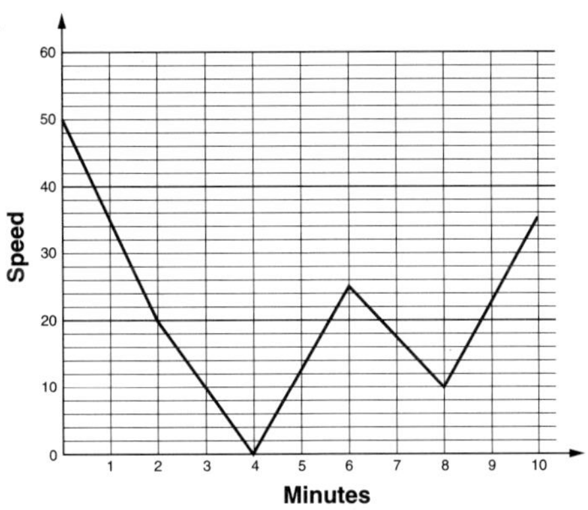

b The bike gradually slows down and stops after 4 minutes, speeds up again, slows down and finally increases speed

3 a

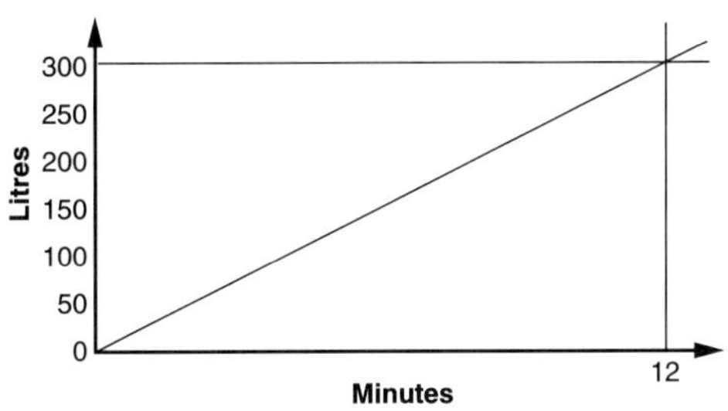

b The straight line graph shows the tank filling up at a constant rate

Page 84 More Practice 1

1 a 20 miles **b** quarter of an hour **c** 8 pm **d** 40 mph **e** 8.30 pm **f** 25 miles **g** 2 and a quarter hours **h** 10.45 pm **i** half an hour
2 a 15 miles **b** 1 and a quarter hours **c** half an hour **d** 11 pm

Page 85 More Practice 2

1

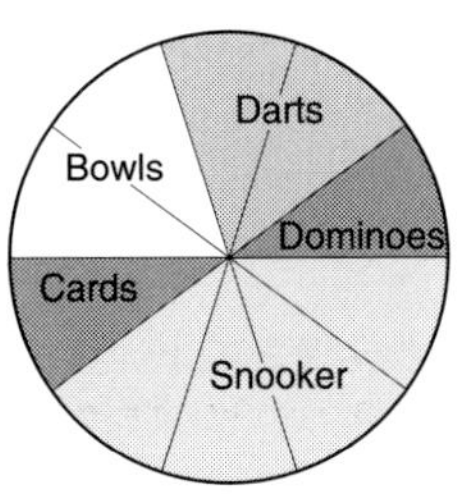

2

	News	*Herald*	*Post*	*Mail*
Number	60	45	30	15
Parts	4	3	2	1

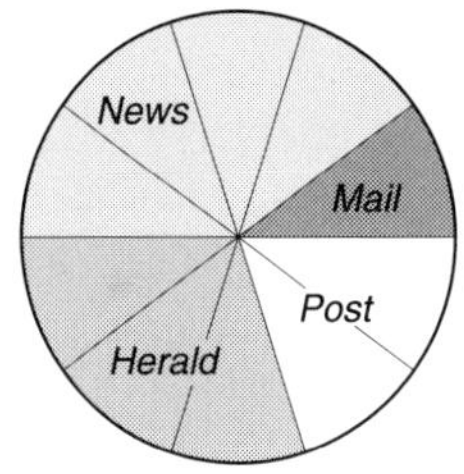

3

	String	Brass	Woodwind	Piano	Drums
Number	24	12	36	36	12
Parts	2	1	3	3	1

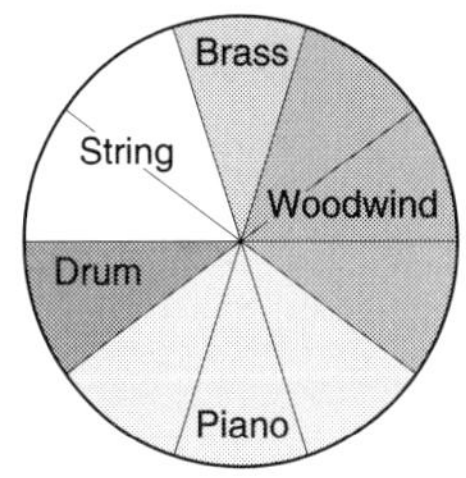

4

	Chips	Chow mein	Curry	Burger	Pizza
Number	25%	20%	15%	30%	10%
Parts	5	4	3	6	2

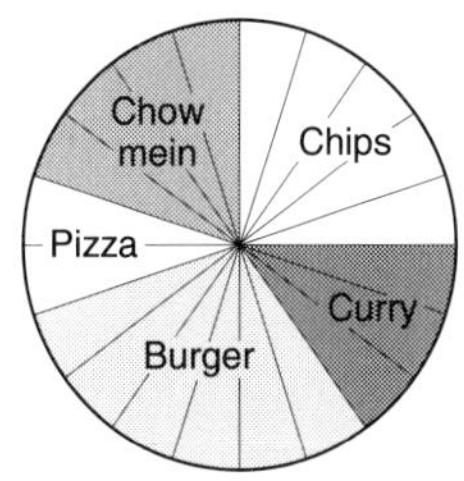

Page 86 More Practice 3

1

City	Votes	Parts
Edinburgh	75	5
Vienna	45	3
Paris	60	4
New York	30	2
London	15	1
Rome	75	5

a 15 votes **b**

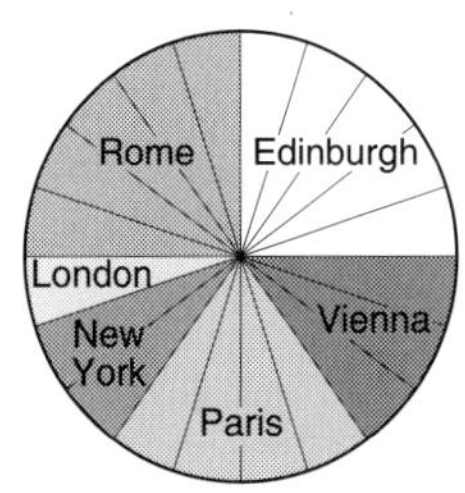

2 a 6 **b** 11/50 **c** 66 **d** 11/50 **e** 168 **3a** 50 **b** 10 **c** 40 **d** 40 **e** 60

11 2-D SHAPES

STUDENTS' BOOK

Page 111 Looking Back

1 a-c

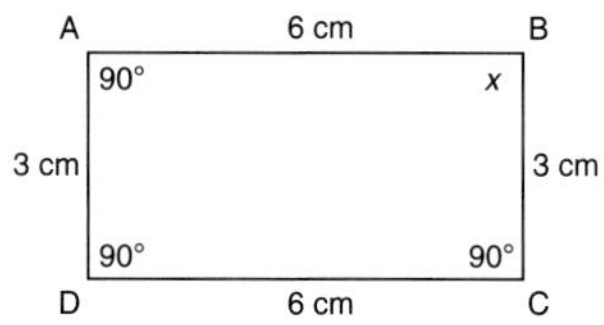

d

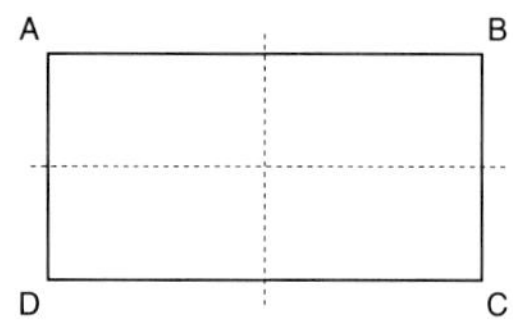

2 **a-c**

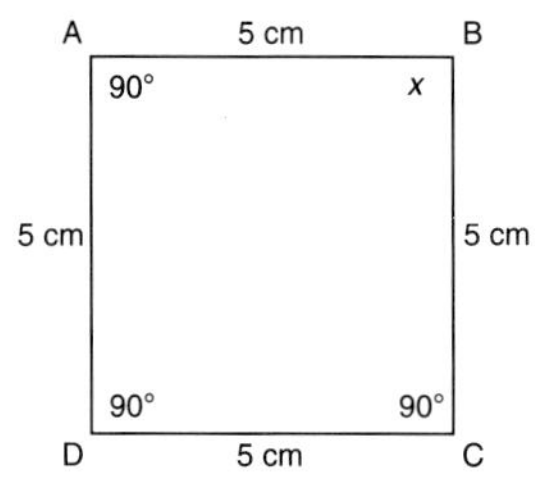

d

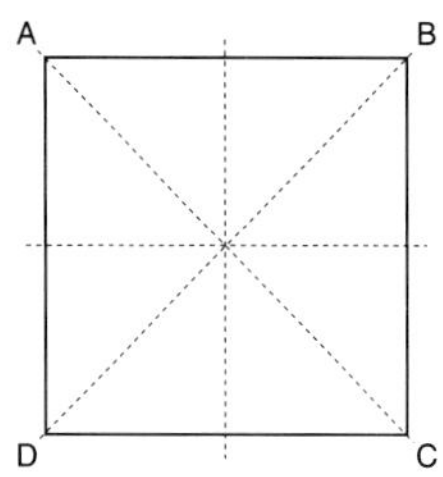

3 a circumference **b** diameter **c** radius **d** centre **4 a** 70° **b** 144° **c** 125°

Page 112 Exercise 1

1 a *a* = 95° **b** *b* = 77° **c** *c* = 38°, *d* = 90°, *e* = 62° **d** *f* = 60°, *g* = 40° **2 a** (i) 53° (ii) 37° (iii) 93° **b** 45° **3 a** 30° **b** (i) 100° (ii) 100° **c** *c* = 5°, *d* = 20°, *e* = 5° **4 a** 101° **b** 30° **5 a** 74° **b** 23° **6a** 51° **b** 48° **c** 55° **7 a** 42° **b** 30° **c** 55° **d** 40°

Page 114 Exercise 2

3 32° **4** (i) 30° (ii) 30° (iii) 60° **5** *e* = 35°, *f* = 110° **6** 60° **7 a** 2 **b** 2 **c** (i) 60° (ii) 60° (iii) 120° (iv) 30°

Page 116 Exercise 3

1 a

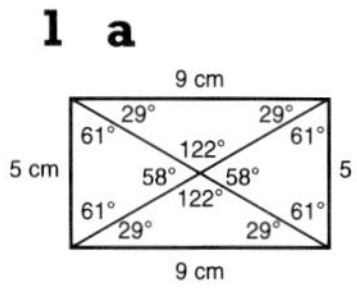

b

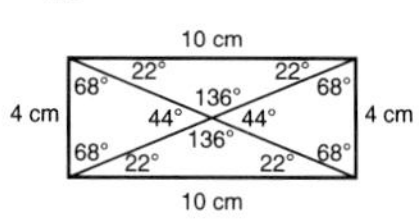

c

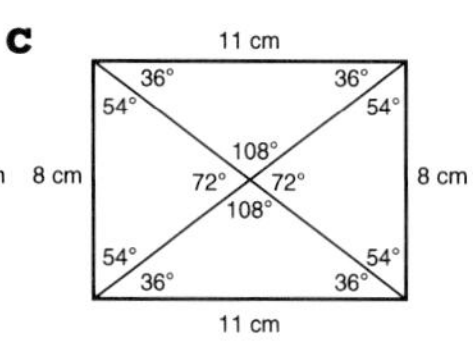

2 a (i) 12 (ii) 12 (iii) 12 **b** 24 cm **3** 2 m **4** 8 m **5 a** (i) 40 m (ii) 30 m **b** 50 m **6 a** 13 m **b** 13 m **c** 5 m **7** 13 m

8

a

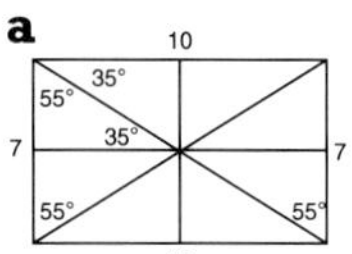

b

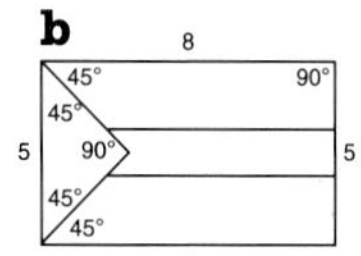

c

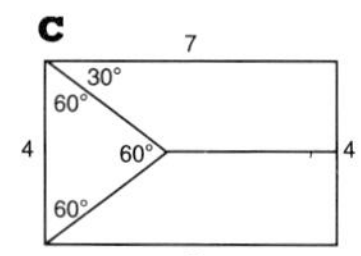

d

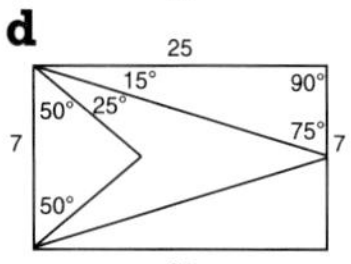

e

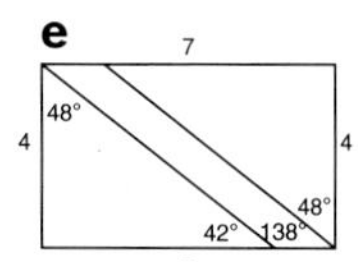

f

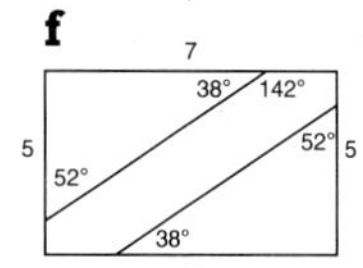

Page 119 Exercise 4

1 8 **2 a** (i) 45° (ii) 135° **b** 6 cm **3 a** 160 cm **b** 120 cm **c** 20 **4 a** 48 cm **b** (i) 36 cm (ii) 60 cm (iii) 84 cm (iv) 108 cm **c** (i) 2 (ii) 6 (iii) 8 **5 a** 20 **b** 10 **c** 200

Page 121 Exercise 5

1 a 24 mm **b** 36 mm **c** 30 mm **d** 44 mm **2 a** 10 mm **b** 8.5 mm **c** 13 mm **d** 12 mm **e** 11 mm **3 a** 36 cm **b** 12 cm **4 a** 6 cm **b** 24 cm **c** 6 cm **5 a** 21 cm **b** 14 cm **6**12 cm

Page 122 Check-up

1 a 50° **b** 83° **2 a** (i) 90° (ii) 48° **b** (i) 42° (ii) 42°

3

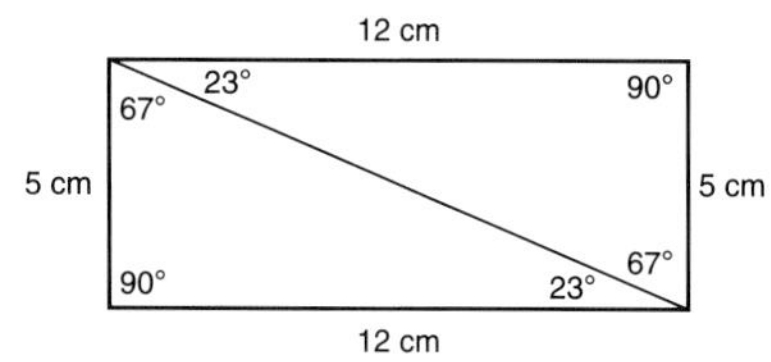

4 a 16 cm **b** 90° **5 a** 3 cm **b** 8 cm **6 a** 22 mm **b** 22 mm **c** 110 cm

TEACHER'S BOOK

Page 90 Worksheet 1

1 a *a* = 60°, *b* = 40° **b** *c* = 55°, *d* = 43°, *e* = 98° **c** *f* = 50°, *g* = 75°, *h* = 105° **d** *j* = 40°, *k* = 45° **e** *m* = 60°, *n* = 72°, *p* = 40°

2

a

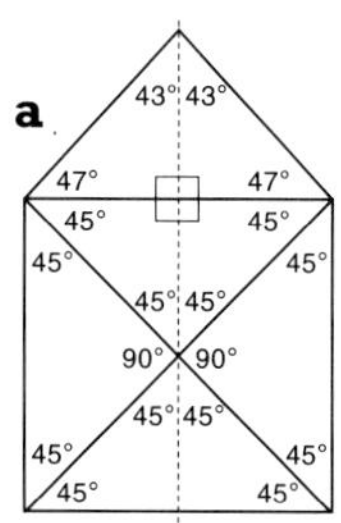

b

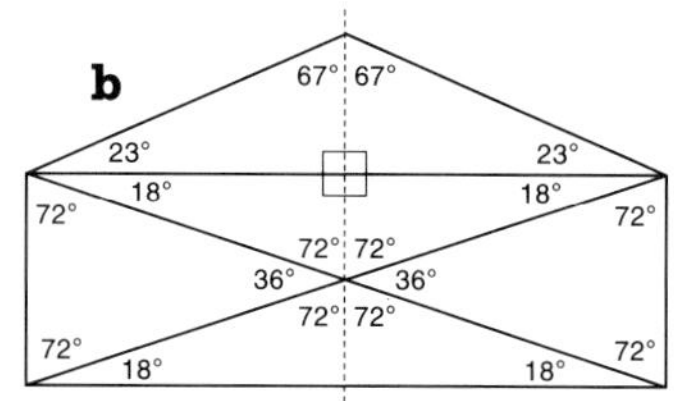

c

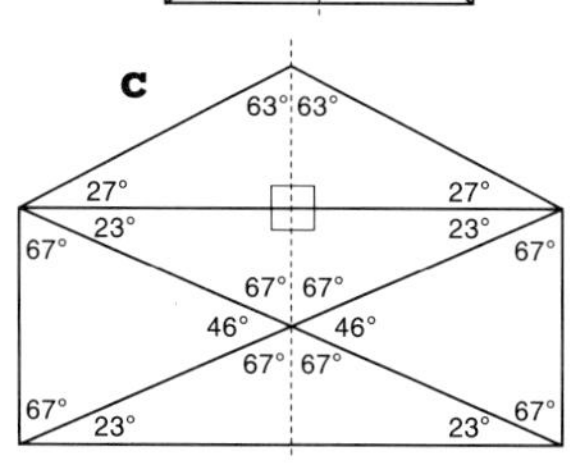

d

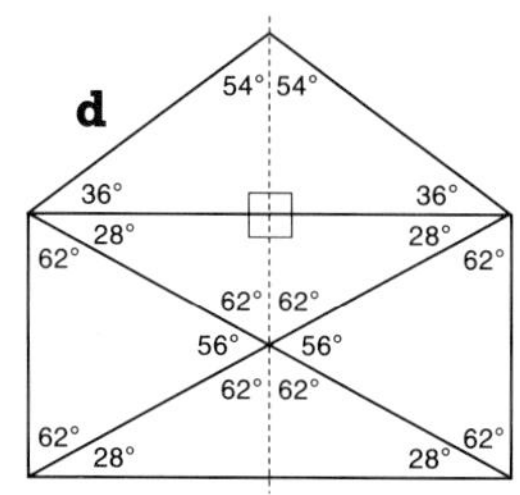

Page 92 Worksheet 3

1 a 12 cm **b** 12 cm **c** 18 cm **2** 60 m **3** 1 cm **4** 30 **5** 24

Page 98 Pythagoras

1 a 13 cm **b** 10 cm **c** 17 cm **d** 20 cm **e** 25 cm **f** 26 cm **g** 29 cm **h** 34 cm **2** 37 cm

12 MEASUREMENT

STUDENTS' BOOK

Page 124 Looking Back
1 a km **b** m **c** mm **d** mm **e** m **f** km **g** cm
2 b (i) 11 cm (ii) 15 cm (iii) 6 cm **4 a** 1.23 m
b 2.56 m **c** 1.82 m **5 a** 152 cm **b** 463 cm
c 208 cm **6** David, Beth, Adam, Carol, Fraser, Grant, Emma

Page 125 Exercise 1
1 a 64 mm **b** 37 mm **c** 78 mm **d** 53 mm
2 a 47 mm **b** 20 mm **c** 63 mm **d** 32 mm
3 a 46 mm **b** 62 mm **c** 44 mm **d** 91 mm
e 98 mm **4 a** (i) 114 mm (ii) 80 mm (iii) 85 mm
(iv) 66 mm (v) 46 mm **c** (i), (iii), (ii), (iv), (v)
5 b (i) 22 mm, 22 mm (ii) 24 mm, 30 mm
(iii) 20 mm, 40mm (iv) 25 mm, 40 mm
(v) 25 mm, 50 mm

Page 128 Exercise 2
1 a 20 mm **b** 53 mm **c** 19 mm **d** 133 mm
e 116 mm **2 a** 3800 cm **b** 400 cm **c** 260 cm
d 1800 cm **e** 120 cm **3 a** 2000 m **b** 3500 m
c 12 000 m **d** 1750 m **e** 600 m **4 a** 1300 m, 1020 m, 1250 m **b** Danielle, Bryan, Alan, Ellen, Colin **5 a** = **b** > **c** > **d** > **e** = **f** >

Page 129 Exercise 2B
1 a 1.2 km **b** 23 km **c** 0.56 km **d** 0.3 km
e 75.1 km **2 a** 1.2 m **b** 13 m **c** 7.4 m **d** 0.8 m
e 150 m **3 a** 13 cm **b** 2 cm **c** 62 cm **d** 8 cm
e 119 cm **4 a** 12.3 cm, 10.9 cm, 11.1 cm, 13.8 cm, 12.5 cm **b** Fuzzy, Edna, Iggy, Chops, Grin, Amy, Huggy, Dimple, Bounce **5 a** 7.27 m,7.19 m, 7.26 m, 7.09 m **b** No. 2, No. 4, No. 1, No. 3, No. 5, No. 6 **6 a** Manchester 64 km, Birmingham 128 km, Kendal 115 km, Lincoln 136 km, Nottingham 104 km, Preston 90 km
b Manchester, Preston, Nottingham, Kendal, Birmingham, Lincoln

Page 130 Exercise 3
1 a 20 cm **b** 18 cm **c** 24 cm **d** 21 cm **e** 36 cm
f 16 cm **2 a** 192 m **b** 72 m **c** 180 m **3 a** 180 mm
b 160 mm **c** 120 mm **d** 182 mm **e** 243 mm
f 380 mm **4 a** 18 cm **b** 16 cm **c** 12 cm
d 18.2 cm **e** 24.3 cm **f** 38 cm **5 a** 186 mm
b 280 mm **c** 294 mm **d** 280 mm

Page 132 Exercise 4
1 a (i) 5 m (ii) 60 m **b** (i) 4 m (ii) 52 m **c** (i) 4 m (ii) 46 m **d** (i) 7.5 m and 15 m (ii) 95 m **e** (i) 18 m (ii) 72 m **2 a** (i) p = 12 m, q = 8 m, r = 8 m, s = 20 m, t = 10 m, u = 55 m (ii) 80 m, 126 m, 138 m
b Science Block **c** Games Hall **d** 344 m

Page 134 Exercise 5
1 a 15 cm **b** 12 cm **c** 18 cm **d** 255 mm
e 126 mm **f** 105 mm **2 a** 6 cm **b** 5.1 cm
c 66 mm **d** 78 mm **3 a** 120 m **b** 150 m **c** 60 m
d 240 m

Page 135 Check-up
1 a (i) 30 mm (ii) 3 cm **b** (i) 56 mm (ii) 5.6 cm
c (i) 77 mm (ii) 7.7 cm **d** (i) 62 mm (ii) 6.2 cm
3 a 130 mm **b** 23 mm **c** 500 cm **d** 420 cm
e 5000 m **f** 2300 m **g** 4 mm **h** 50 cm **i** 500 m
4 a 3 cm **b** 2.5 cm **c** 6 m **d** 5.6 m **e** 7 km
f 3.4 km **g** 0.6 cm **h** 0.4 m **i** 0.2 km
5 a 115 mm, 109 mm, 66 mm, 103 mm, 85 mm
b 56 mm, 66 mm, 82 mm, 85 mm, 102 mm, 103 mm, 107 mm, 109 mm, 115 mm, 116 mm
6 a 60 cm **b** 74 cm **c** 140 mm **7 a** 45 m **b** 320 m

TEACHER'S BOOK

Page 100 Worksheet 1
a 37 mm, 28 mm **b** 67 mm, 24 mm **c** 46 mm, 46 mm **d** 22 mm, 102 mm **e** 70 mm, 48 mm
f 28 mm, 25 mm **g** 25 mm, 17 mm **h** 61 mm, 28 mm **i** 52 mm, 56 mm **j** 27 mm, 52 mm
k 16 mm, 34 mm

Page 101 Worksheet 2

1

0.23 m	0.39 m	0.98 m	1.43 m	1.48 m	2.34 m
23 cm	39 cm	98 cm	143 cm	148 cm	234 cm
230 mm	390 mm	980 mm	1430 mm	1480 mm	2340 mm

2

0.55 m	1.42 m	0.72 m	3.27 m	4.15 m	6.41 m
55 cm	142 cm	72 cm	327 cm	415 cm	641 cm
550 mm	1420 mm	720 mm	3270 mm	4150 mm	6410 mm

3

3 km	0.5 km	0.6 km	0.1 km	1 km	0.06 km
3000 m	500 m	600 m	100 m	1000 m	60 m
300 000 cm	50 000 cm	60 000 cm	10 000 cm	100 000 cm	6000 mm

Page 102 Worksheet 3
1 A 18.8 cm, B 28 cm, C 17.2 cm, D 22.9 cm, E 18 cm, F 21.8 cm, G 27.6 cm, H 22.3 cm, I 16 cm, J 27.4 cm **2** 142.3 cm

Page 103 Worksheet 4
1 a 15 cm **2 a** 4 cm **b** 4.2 cm **c** 2 cm **d** 51 mm
e 6.6 cm **f** 41 mm **3 a** 10 cm

Page 104 The House that Jack Built
1 a 9 m, 6.2 m **b** 30.4 m **2 a** 26.0 m **b** 27.4 m
c 19.4 m **d** 10.4 m **3** 59.6 m

Page 105 More Practice 1
a (i) 6.5 cm (ii) 19.5 cm **b** (i) 9.4 cm (ii) 28.2 cm
c (i) 4.7 cm (ii) 14.1 cm **d** (i) 3 cm (ii) 9 cm
e (i) 11.6 cm (ii) 34.8 cm **f** (i) 5.5cm (ii) 16.5 cm
g (i) 1.5 cm (ii) 4.5 cm **h** (i) 2.7 cm (ii) 8.1 cm

Page 106 More Practice 2
1 a 15.7 cm **b** 9.42 cm **c** 6.28 cm **d** 3.14 cm
2 a (i) 6 cm (ii) 18.84 cm **b** (i) 7 cm (ii) 21.98 cm
c (i)10 cm (ii) 31.4 cm **d** (i) 40 cm (ii) 125.6 cm
3 1p 6.28 cm, 2p 7.85 cm, 5p 5.338 cm, 10p 7.536 cm, £1 6.908 cm

13 STATISTICS AND PROBABILITY

STUDENTS' BOOK

Page 136 Looking Back
1 6, 6.85, 6.9, 7, 7.09, 7.9, 8 **2** £31 **3 a** 50 cm
b (i) 90 cm (ii) 100 cm **c** 10 cm **d** 70 cm
4 a certain **b** evens **c** very likely **d** less than evens **e** impossible

Page 137 Exercise 1
1 a 2 **b** 3 **2 a** no **b** yes, 3.2 litres weigh 3.2 kg
c no **d** yes **3** b, d, e, h, j and l

Page 138 Exercise 2
1 a (i) petrol used increases as you travel (ii) sensible **b** (i) number of pairs increases with time (ii) not sensible **c** (i) height increases with time (ii) sensible **d** (i) number of strokes decreasing as the game progresses (ii) not sensible **e** (i) feet get longer the older he is (ii) sensible **f** (i) coffee cools down with time (ii) sensible

Page 139 Exercise 3
1 a 6 **b** 210 minutes **c** 35 minutes **2 a** 5
b 317 km **c** 63.4 km **3 a** 7 **b** 15 **c** older **4 a** 5
b first Wednesday

Page 140 Exercise 4
1 a ladder **b** fir **c** yacht **d** horse **2 a** (i) 1, 2
(ii) 3, 4, 5, 6 **b** 1, 2, 3, 4, 5, 6 **c** Ted **3 a** (i) 2
(ii) 3 **b** lose **4 a** (i) 1 (ii) 1 **b** even

Page 141 Exercise 5
1 a 2 **b** 5 **c** 0.4 **2 a** 0.25 **b** 0.25 **c** 0.125 **d** 0.5
3 a 0.25 **b** 0.67 **c** 0.33 **d** 0.083 **4 a** 9 **b** 3
c (i) 0.33 (ii) 0.11 **5 a** 0.5 **b** 0.33 **c** 0.167
6 a 0.33 **b** 0.25 **c** 0.83 **7 a** 0.23 **b** 0.08 **c** 0.15

Page 143 Check-up
1 a (i) no (ii) no (iii) yes (iv) yes **b** (iii) 5, 6, 7 (iv) 2.5 g (v) 1.5 minutes **2** 16 cm **3 a** 0.5 **b** 0.7 **c** 0

TEACHER'S BOOK

Page 108 More Practice 1
1 a 14 **b** 424 **c** 30.3 **2 a** (i) 9.5 (ii) 8.5 **b** 1 hour
3 a 11.9 **b** 3 **c** 60.2 years **d** 6 **4 a** £91 million
b £8.3 million **c** £9.6 million

Page 109 More Practice 2: The Median
1 An odd number of scores gives one middle score; an even number gives two **2 a** 3, 4, 4, 5, 5, 6, 6, 7, 8 **b** 5 **c** 3 **3 a** 23, 34, 35, 42, 45, 55
b 35, 42 **c** 38.5 **d** 3

Page 110 More Practice 3: The Mode
1 a (i) 7 (ii) 7 **b** 7 **c** He will be interested in the most common number of windows per house
2 a (i) 6.3 (ii) 4 (iii) 3 **b** the mean **3 a** 11 **b** 2
c mode

Page 111 More Practice 4: Making Sense of Marks
1 a 3, 8 **b** 14, 5 **c** 28, 26 **d** 57, 73 **2 a** 40
b/c

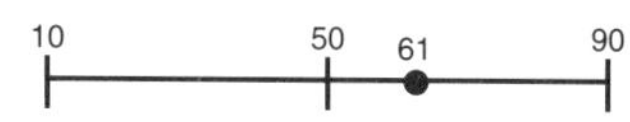

d good

3

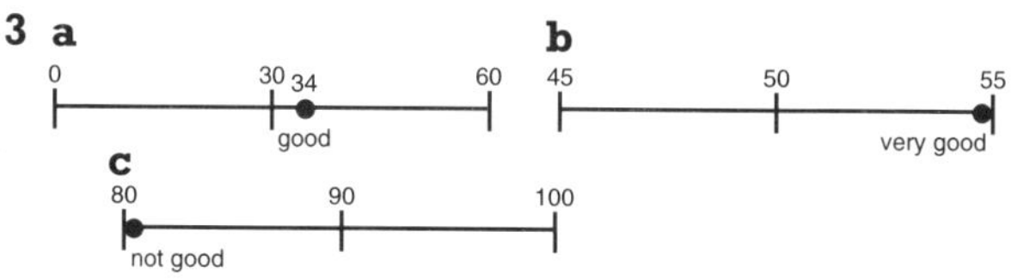

4 a/b

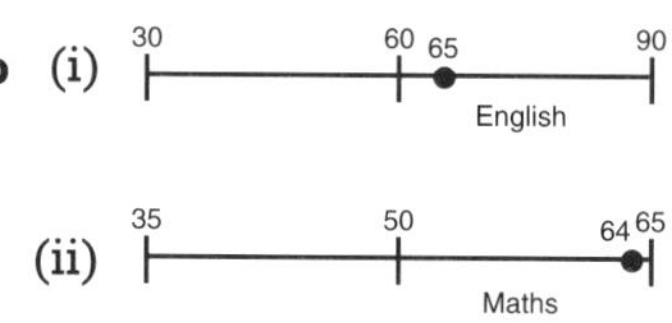

c maths

Page 112 More Practice 5
1 a 1, 1, 1, 1, 2, 2, 2, 2, 3, 3, 3, 4, 4, 4, 5, 5, 5, 5, 6, 6, 6 **b** 3 **c** 5 **d** yes **e** no, no sixes **2 a** 180, 187, 189, 194, 195, 199, 201, 203, 213, 219, 230
b 199 **c** 50 **d** claim is fair **3 a** (i) 359.5 (ii) 482
b 400.5, 221

4

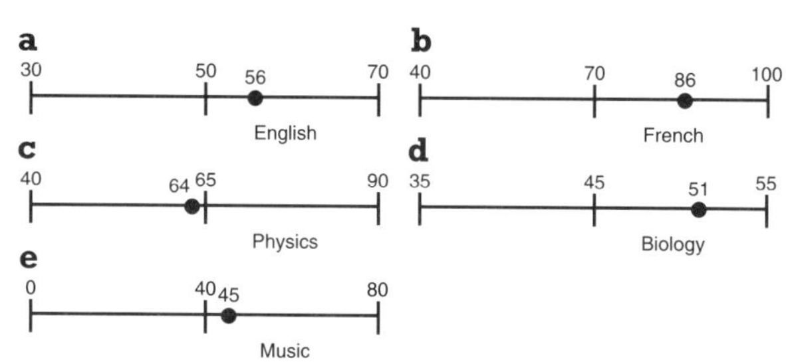

Page 113 More Practice 6
1 butterfly, rabbit, fox, horse, kestrel
2 helicopter, harrier, biplane, jaguar, dakota, commercial jet **3 a** (i) 2 (ii) 0.333 **b** (i) 3 (ii) 0.4
c (i) 3 (ii) 0.5 **d** c **4 a** (i) 800 (ii) 100 **b** (i) 0.125 (ii) 0.025

14 ALGEBRA

STUDENTS' BOOK

Page 144 Looking Back

1 a 7 **b** 16 **c** 4 **d** 6 **2 a** 4 **b** 5 **c** 2, 3 **3 a** 10, 12 **b** 9, 11 **c** 16, 20 **d** 25, 30 **4 a** 4 **b** 7 **c** 2 **d** 7 **e** 20 **f** 6

Page 145 Exercise 1

1 a 16, 19 **b** 52, 62 **c** 25, 31 **d** 18, 21 **e** 30, 36 **f** 54, 65 **2 a** 1/6, 1/7 **b** 10, 1 **c** 76, 70 **d** $4 \times 5 = 20$, $5 \times 6 = 30$ **e** 9×4, 11×5 **f** 90, 85 **3** 15, 21 **4** 25, 36

Page 146 Exercise 2

1 a 8 **b** 12 **c** 6 **d** 5 **2 a** $x + 3$ **b** $2x + 7$ **c** $3x + 2$ **3 a** $4 \times 7 = 28$ matches **b** $4 \times 9 = 36$ matches **c** $4 \times x = 4x$ **4 a** 24 metres **b** $4x$ metres **c** $5y$ metres **d** $6z$ metres **5 a** $x - 3$ km **b** $y - 14$ km **c** $z - 22$ km **d** $2 - x$ km **e** $12 - y$ km **f** $9 - z$ km

Page 148 Exercise 3

1 a $2a$ **b** $3x$ **c** $4t$ **d** $6y$ **e** $9a$ **f** x **g** $11d$ **h** $7b$ **i** $6c$ **j** $8a$ **k** $7h$ **l** $16y$ **m** $6a$ **n** $2t$ **o** $2m$ **p** 0 **2 a** $6a + 5b$ **b** $4m + 3n$ **c** $5x + 5y$ **d** $2d + 2e$ **e** $2v + w$ **f** $5a + 2b$ **g** $2x + 2y$ **h** $4a + 2b$ **i** $5m + 5n$ **j** $3b + 3c$ **k** $3x + 2y$ **l** $2a + b$ **3 a** $3y$ **b** $5b$ **c** $4a$ **d** $7d$ **e** cd **f** xy **g** ab **h** cd **i** bcd **j** abc **k** $5ab$ **l** $7mn$ **m** $6bc$ **n** $3pq$ **o** $5ab$ **p** $3cde$ **q** hmt **r** dmy **s** $4abc$ **t** b^2 **u** n^2 **v** m^3 **w** y^5 **x** a^2b^2

Page 149 Exercise 4

1 a £12 **b** £5 **c** £8 **d** £22 **e** £22 **2 a** 8 **b** 2 **c** 15 **d** 10 **e** 18 **f** 30 **3 a** 11 **b** 3 **c** 28 **d** 8 **e** 21 **f** 16 **4 a** 7 **b** 12 **c** 11 **d** 20 **5 a** 11 **b** 4 **c** 24 **d** 6 **e** 24 **f** 3 **g** 2 **h** 8 **i** 3 **j** 30 **k** 11 **l** 18 **m** 11 **n** 10 **o** 0 **p** 18 **q** 1 **r** 64

Page 150 Exercise 5

1 a 7 **b** 4 **c** 10 **d** 15 **e** 10 **f** 2 **g** 7 **h** 5 **2 a** 4 **b** 4 **c** 5 **d** 3 **e** 4 **f** 5 **g** 1 **h** 2 **i** 6 **j** 3 **k** 5 **l** 10 **m** 18 **n** 0 **o** 5 **p** 19 **3 a** 4 **b** 4 **c** 5 **d** 2 **e** 5 **f** 4 **g** 7 **h** 2 **4 a** 3 **b** 4 **c** 2 **d** 3 **e** 5 **f** 4 **g** 5 **h** 2 **i** 10 **j** 0 **k** 0 **l** 1 **m** 25 **n** 6 **o** 8 **p** 9

Page 151 Exercise 6

1 a 12 **b** 20 **c** 24 **d** 40 **2 a** 20 **b** 40 **c** 80 **3 a** 96 **b** 120 **c** 144 **4 a** 27 **b** 72 **c** 108 **5 a** 4 **b** 10 **c** 15 **d** 9 **6 a** £25 **b** £55 **c** £85 **7 a** £20 **b** £110 **c** £85 **d** £74.30

8 a

Charge (£)	1 day	2 days	3 days	4 days	5 days	6 days
Rent-a-Car	18	26	34	42	50	58
De-Luxe Hire	21	30	39	48	57	66

b Rent-a-Car is cheaper

Page 153 Exercise 7

1 a

Age in weeks	1	2	3	4	5	6
Height in cm	5	6	7	8	9	10

b Age in weeks add 4 gives the height in cm **c** 14 cm **2 a/b** Number of pearls: 4, 5, 6, 7, 8, 9 **c** Size number add 3 gives the number of pearls **d** 13 pearls **3 b** Number of leaves: 2, 4, 6, 8, 10, 12, 20 **c** Number of weeks times 2 gives the number of leaves **4 b** Number of bulbs needed: 3, 5, 7, 9, 11, 13, 21 **c** Size of letter times 2 add 1 gives the number of bulbs needed **5 b** Number of bulbs needed: 4, 7, 10, 13, 16, 19, 31 **c** Size of letter times 3 add 1 gives the number of bulbs needed **6** Size number times 5 add 1 gives the number of bulbs

Page 156 Check-up

1 a 26, 32 **b** 37, 33 **2** $4 + d$ **3 a** $12y$ **b** $4x$ **c** $3a + 2b$ **d** $2mn$ **e** a^4 **f** $6y^2$ **4 a** 12 **b** 12 **c** 20 **d** 1 **5 a** 5 **b** 3 **c** 10 **d** 6 **e** 0 **f** 3 **g** 1 **h** 3 **6 a** £3 is possibly the charge for post and packing **b** (i) £53 (ii) £78 (iii) £128 **7 b** Number of pearls: 3, 4, 5, 6, 7, 8 **c** Size number add 2 gives the number of pearls **d** 12 pearls

TEACHER'S BOOK

Page 117 More Practice 1

1 a $3s + 2s = 5s$ **b** $3t + 4t = 7t$ **2 a** $3a$ **b** $2x$ **c** $5y$ **d** $7m$ **e** $4t$ **f** $5w$ **g** h **h** $9n$ **i** $10a$ **j** $5u$ **k** $2x$ **l** $4y$ **m** $9m$ **n** $3c$ **o** $2t$ **p** $10a$ **3 a** $2s + t + s + 2t = 3s + 3t$ **b** $3s + 2t + 2s + 2t = 5s + 4t$ **4 a** $4x + 6y$ **b** $9a + 4b$ **c** $7m + 5n$ **d** $7c + 4d$ **e** $8m + 8n$ **f** $7x + 8y$ **g** $a + 3b$ **h** $c + 2d$ **i** $2a + 8b$ **5 a** $4ab$ **b** $3de$ **c** $5h$ **d** $7y$ **e** $6ab$ **f** $4cd$ **g** $2mn$ **h** $5ab$ **i** $2bc$ **j** $6de$ **k** $6cd$ **l** $40n^2$ **m** m^2 **n** n^3 **o** a^5 **p** $9h^3$ **6 a** 5 **b** 6 **c** 9 **d** 8 **e** 24 **f** 1 **g** 1 **h** 5 **i** 1 **j** 27 **7 a** £170 **b** £135 **c** £160 **d** £108

Page 118 More Practice 2

1 a 2 **b** 6 **c** 7 **d** 9 **e** 9 **f** 7 **g** 12 **h** 0 **2 a** 20 **b** 13 **c** 27 **d** 7 **e** 13 **f** 17 **g** 13 **h** 11 **3 a** 10 **b** 4 **c** 11 **d** 6 **e** 2 **f** 9 **g** 5 **h** 7 **4 a** 0 **b** 2 **c** 3 **d** 8 **e** 4 **f** 5 **g** 22 **h** 12 **5 a** 3 **b** 7 **c** 2 **d** 4 **6 a** 1 **b** 4 **c** 7 **d** 10 **e** 3 **f** 5 **g** 7 **h** 6 **7 a** 4 **b** 4 **c** 3 **d** 5 **e** 2 **f** 3 **g** 5 **h** 2 **i** 5 **j** 10 **k** 5 **l** 2

Page 119 More Practice 3

1 a 9 **b** 9 **c** 6 **2 a** (i) 10 cm (ii) 24 cm (iii) 40 cm (iv) 9 cm **b** (i) 7 cm (ii) 15 cm (iii) 50 cm (iv) 12.5 m **3 a** 3.45 **b** 6.45 **c** 2.15 am **d** 8 pm **e** 10.20 am **4 a** £138 **b** £154 **c** £170 **d** £330 **5 a** 24 cm^2 **b** 54 cm^2 **c** 35 cm^2 **d** 15 cm^2 **e** 11 cm^2 **f** 28 cm^2 **6 a** £20 **b** £28 **c** £40 **7 a** 45 m **b** 125 m **c** 320 m **d** 500 m